I0875095

CIVIL CODE

OF THE

REPUBLIC

UZBEKISTAN

Russian, Eurasian, and East European Codes of Law

Butler, W. E., *Civil Code of the Republic Kazakhstan.* (Clark, New Jersey, Talbot Publishing, 2021) ISBN 978-1-616196493

Butler, W. E., *Civil Code of the Russian Federation.* (Clark, New Jersey, Talbot Publishing, 2021). 2 vols.. ISBN 978-1-61619-654-7

Butler, W. E. *Criminal Code of the Russian Federation.* (Clark, New Jersey, Talbot Publishing, 2022) ISBN 978-1-61619-664-8

Butler, W. E. *Civil Code of the Republic Uzbekistan.* (Clark, New Jersey, Talbot Publishing, 2023) ISBN 978-1-61619-683-7

The Vinogradoff Institute • Penn State Dickinson Law

CIVIL CODE OF THE REPUBLIC UZBEKISTAN

TRANSLATED AND EDITED BY

WILLIAM E. BUTLER

John Edward Fowler Distinguished Professor of Law,
Penn State Dickinson Law
Emeritus Professor of Comparative Law,
University College London
Foreign Member, National Academy of Sciences of Ukraine,
and National Academy of Legal Sciences of Ukraine

TALBOT PUBLISHING
Clark, New Jersey

Copyright © 2023 by William Elliott Butler (1939-)

ISBN: 978-1-61619-683-7

All rights reserved. No part of this publication may be reproduced, stored in a retrieval system, or transmitted, in any form or by any means, electronic, mechanical, photocopying, recording, or otherwise, without the prior written permission of the publisher or the copyright holder or holders, except in the case of brief quotations embodied in critical reviews and certain other noncommercial uses permitted by copyright law.

TALBOT PUBLISHING

AN IMPRINT OF

The Lawbook Exchange, Ltd., 33 Terminal Ave, Clark, New Jersey 07066-1323

Please seee our website for a selection of our other publications and fine facsimile reprints of classic works of legal history www.lawbookexchange.com

Library of Congress Cataloging-in-Publication Data

Names: Uzbekistan, enacting jurisdiction. | Butler, William Elliott, 1939- editor, translator. | Vinogradoff Institute (Dickinson School of Law).

Title: Civil ode of the Republic of Uzbekistan / translated and edited by William E. Butler, John Edward Fowler Distinguished Professor of Law, Penn State Dickinson Law Emeritus Professor of Comparative Law, University College London Foreign Member, National Academy of Sciences of Ukraine, and National Academy of Legal Sciences of Ukraine.

Other titles: Ŭzbekiston Respublikasining Fuqarolik kodeksi (1995). English (Butler)

Description: Clark, New Jersey : Talbot Publishing, an imprint of the Lawbook Exchange, Ltd., [2023] | Series: Russian, Eurasian, and East European codes of law | At head of title: The Vinogradoff Institute, Penn State Dickinson Law. | Includes bibliographical references. | Summary: "A translation of the civil code of the Republic Uzbekistan with an introduction by William E. Butler"-- Provided by publisher.

Identifiers: LCCN 2023011197 | ISBN 9781616196837 (hardcover)

Subjects: LCSH: Civil law--Uzbekistan. | LCGFT: Statutes and codes.

Classification: LCC KLW49.A291995 B88 2023 | DDC 346.587--dc23/eng/20230525

LC record available at https://lccn.loc.gov/2023011197

Printed in the United States of America on acid-free paper

THE CIVIL CODE OF UZBEKISTAN

W. E. BUTLER

Just as the other Independent States, the Republic Uzbekistan had in place when the former Soviet Union disappeared its own Civil Code of the Uzbek SSR confirmed on 23 March 1963. The 1963 Civil Code of the Uzbek SSR in all material respects reproduced the 1961 Fundamental Principles of Civil Legislation of the USSR and Union Republics. However, Uzbekistan did not emulate Kazakhstan and the Russian Federation by introducing the 1991 Fundamental Principles of Civil Legislation of the USSR and Republics into force in Uzbekistan. Rather, the 1963 Civil Code was partially replaced and augmented by a series of individual laws on Land (20 June 1990, as amended), ownership (31 October 1990, as amended), entrepreneurship (15 February 1991, as amended), enterprises (15 February 1991, as amended), foreign economic activity (13 June 1991, as amended), lease (19 November 1991, as amended), pledge (9 December 1992, as amended), insurance (6 May 1993, as amended), trademarks and service marks (7 May 1993), foreign investments (5 May 1994, as amended), bankruptcy (5 May 1994, as amended), the protection of electronic computer and data base programs (6 May 1994), inventions, utility models, and industrial designs (6 May 1994), and the law on joint-stock societies (26 April 1996), among the most salient.[1]

The Republic Uzbekistan was the first member of the Commonwealth of Independent States to enact a full Civil Code. It has relied in considerable measure upon the Model Civil Code developed within the Inter-Parliamentary Assembly of the CIS, but in a number of respects has departed from that Model. In particular, the number of articles devoted to juridical persons is considerably less because in Uzbekistan detailed regulation is to be left to individual laws.[2] Family law is being retained intact as the object of a separate Code in Uzbekistan, but international private law has been incorporated into the Civil Code.

It should be noted that the entire Code entered into force simultaneously, from 1 March 1997, even though it was enacted in two parts over a period of nearly nine months.

Status juris: 1 January 2023

1 For a list of the laws of Uzbekistan since independence, see W. E. Butler, *Uzbekistan Legislation* (Tashkent, Adolat, 1999).

2 These are collected and translated in W. E. Butler (ed. & transl.), *Uzbekistan Legal Texts* (London and The Hague, Kluwer Law International/Simmonds & Hill, 1999).

TABLE OF CONTENTS

Civil Code of Uzbekistan Detailed Contents

Part One

Section I. General Provisions

Subsection 1. Basic Provisions

Chapter 1. Civil Legislation

Chapter 2. Origin of Civil Rights and Duties. Effectuation and Defense of Civil Rights

Subsection 2. Persons

Chapter 3. Citizens (Natural Persons)

Subsection 5. Periods. Limitations

Chapter 11. Calculation of Periods

Chapter 12. Limitations

Section II. Right of Ownership and Other Rights to Thing

Chapter 13. General Provisions

Chapter 14. Right of Economic Jurisdiction. Right of Operative Management

Chapter 15. Acquisition and Termination of Right of Ownership

Subsection 2. General Provisions on Contract

Chapter 26. Concept and Conditions of Contract

Chapter 27. Conclusion of Contract

Chapter 40. Transport Expediting

Chapter 41. Loan and Credit

§ 1. Loan

§ 2. Credit

Chapter 42. Financing Under Assignment of Monetary Demand

Chapter 43. Bank Deposit

Chapter 51. Keeping

§ 1. General Provisions on Keeping

§ 2. Individual Types of Keeping

Chapter 57. Obligations as Consequence of Causing Harm

§ 1. General Provisions

CIVIL CODE OF THE REPUBLIC UZBEKISTAN

[Confirmed by Law of the Republic Uzbekistan, No. 163-I,

21 December 1995, as amended by Laws of 27 December 1996; 30 August 1997; 1 May 1998; 25 December 1998;

20 August 1999 (Section XV); 15 December 2000

(Section I, point 13); 30 August 2001 (Section V); 7

December 2001 (Section VIII); 30 August 2002 (Section VII);

13 December 2002 (Section XIII); 25 April 2003 (Section XIII); 13 December 2003 (Section IX); 30 April 2004

(Section IX); 27 August 2004 (Section IX); 4 April 2006; 18 September 2006; 27 September 2006; 8 January 2007; 16 January 2007; 5 April 2007; 13 April 2007; 14 December 2007; 31

December 2008; 22 September 2009; 17 September 2010;

22 September 2010; 14 May 2010; 14 May 2014; 11 December 2014; 20 August 2015; 25 April 2016; 18 April 2017;

14 September 2017; 30 December 2017; 9 January 2018;

18 April 2018; 26 July 2018; 11 October 2018; 4 March 2019; 20 March 2019; 23 May 2019; 22 October 2019; 3 December 2019; 11 December 2019; 14 January 2020; 5 October 2020; 20 August 2021; 12 October 2021; 9 February 2022; 29 March 2022; 20 April 2022; 17 May 2022; 6 June 2022; 29 June 2022; 3 November 2022; and 7 November 2022.

entered into force: 1 March 1997]

PART ONE

Section I. General Provisions

Subsection 1. Basic Provisions

Chapter 1. Civil Legislation

Article 1. Basic Principles of Civil Legislation

Civil legislation shall be based on recognition of the equality of the participants of the relations regulated by it, the inviolability of ownership, the freedom of contract, the inadmissibility of arbitrary interference by anyone in private matters, and the necessity for the unobstructed effectuation of civil rights, ensuring the restoration of rights violated, and the judicial defense thereof.

Citizens (natural persons) and juridical persons shall acquire and effectuate their civil rights by their own will and in their own interest. They shall be free in establishing their rights and duties on the basis of contract and in determining any conditions of a contract which are not contrary to legislation.

Goods, services, and financial assets shall move freely throughout the entire territory of the Republic Uzbekistan.

Limitations on the free movement of goods and services may be introduced in accordance with legislation if this is necessary in order to ensure safety, defense of human life and health, and the protection of nature and objects of cultural heritage [as amended by Law of 18 April 2018, No. ЗРУ-476].

Article 2. Relations Regulated by Civil Legislation

Civil legislation shall determine the legal status of the participants of civil turnover, the grounds for the origin and the procedure for the effectuation of the right of ownership and other rights to a thing and rights to the results of intellectual activity, shall regulate contractual and other obligations, and also other property and related personal nonproperty relations.

Citizens, juridical persons, and the State shall be the participants of relations regulated by civil legislation.

The rules established by civil legislation shall apply to relations with the participation of foreign citizens, stateless persons, and foreign juridical persons unless provided otherwise by a law.

Personal nonproperty relations and personal relations not connected with property [relations] shall be regulated by civil legislation insofar as not provided otherwise by legislative acts or does not arise from the essence of these relations.

Civil legislation shall apply to family and labor relations and relations relating to the use of natural resources and protection of the environment which meet the indicia specified in paragraph one of the present Article in those instances when these relations are not regulated by special legislative acts.

Civil legislation shall not apply to property relations based on administrative subordination of one party to another, including to tax, financial, and other administrative relations, except for instances provided by legislation.

Article 3. Acts of Civil Legislation

Civil legislation shall consist of the present Code, other laws and other acts of legislation regulating relations specified in paragraphs one, four, and five of Article 2 of the present Code.

Norms of civil legislation contained in other laws and other acts of legislation must correspond to the present Code.

Ministries, departments, and other State agencies may issue acts which regulate civil relations in the instances and within the limits provided for by the present Code, other laws, and other acts of legislation.

Article 4. Operation of Civil Legislation in Time

Acts of civil legislation shall not have retroactive force and shall apply to relations which arose after the introduction thereof into operation.

The operation of a law shall extend to relations which arose before the introduction thereof into operation only in instances when this is expressly provided for by a law.

With regard to relations which arose before the introduction into operation of an act of civil legislation, it shall apply to the rights and duties which arose after the introduction thereof into operation.

If after the conclusion of a contract a law establishing rules obligatory for the parties which are different from those which operated when concluding the contract, the conditions of the concluded contract shall retain force, except for instances when it is established in the law that its operation extends to relations which arose from contracts previously concluded.

Article 5. Application of Civil Legislation by Analogy

In instances when relations provided for by Article 2, paragraphs one, four, and five of the present Code have not been expressly regulated by legislation or by agreement of the parties, a norm of civil legislation regulating similar relations (analogy of lex) shall apply.

When it is impossible to use analogy of lex in the said instances, the rights and duties of the parties shall be determined by proceeding from the general principles and sense of civil legislation (analogy of jus) and the requirements of good faith, reasonableness, and justness.

The application by analogy of norms which limit civil rights and establish responsibility shall not be permitted.

Article 6. Customs of Business Turnover. Local Customs and Traditions

A custom of business turnover shall be deemed to be a rule of behavior which has been formed and extensively applied in any domain of entrepreneurial activity and is not provided for by legislation irrespective of whether it has been fixed in any document.

Local customs and traditions shall apply to relations regulated by civil legislation in the absence of respective norms therein.

Customs of business turnover and local customs and traditions which are contrary to norms of legislation or a contract binding upon the participants of the respective relation shall not be applied.

Article 7. Civil Legislation and International Treaties and Agreements

If other rules have been established by an international treaty or agreement than those which have been provided for by civil legislation, the rules of the international treaty or agreement shall apply.

Chapter 2. Origin of Civil Rights and Duties. Effectuation and Defense of Civil Rights

Article 8. Grounds for Civil Rights and Duties to Arise

Civil rights and duties shall arise from the grounds provided for by legislation, and also from the actions of citizens and juridical persons, which although not provided for by them but by virtue of the general principles and sense of civil legislation give rise to civil rights and duties.

Civil rights and duties shall arise:

(1) from contracts and other transactions provided for by a law, and also from contracts and other transactions which, although not provided for by a law, are not contrary thereto;

(2) from acts of State agencies and agencies of self-government of citizens which have been provided for by a law as a ground for civil rights and duties to arise;

(3) from a judicial decision which has established civil rights and duties;

(4) as a result of the acquisition of property on the grounds permitted by a law;

(5) as a result of the creation of works of science, literature, art, inventions, and other results of intellectual activity;

(6) as a consequence of the causing of harm to another person;

(7) as a consequence of unjust enrichment;

(8) as a consequence of other actions of citizens and juridical persons;

(9) as a consequence of events with which legislation connects the ensuing of civil-law consequences.

The rights to property subject to State registration shall arise from the moment of registration of the respective rights thereto, unless established otherwise by a law.

Article 9. Effectuation of Civil Rights

Citizens and juridical persons shall dispose of the civil rights belonging to them at their discretion, including the right to the defense thereof.

The refusal of citizens and juridical persons to effectuate rights belonging to them shall not entail the termination of those rights except for instances provided for by a law.

The effectuation of civil rights must not violate the rights and the interests protected by a law of other persons. The good faith, reasonableness, and justness of the actions of the participants of civil-law relations shall be presupposed.

When effectuating their rights, citizens and juridical persons must respect the moral principles and moral norms of society, and entrepreneurs must also comply with the rules of business ethics.

The actions of citizens and juridical persons directed towards causing harm to another person, toward the abuse of right in other forms, and also to the effectuation of a right contrary to its purpose, shall not be permitted.

In the event of the failure to comply with the requirements provided for by paragraphs three, four, and five of the present Article, a court may refuse a person the defense of the right belonging to him.

Article 10. Judicial Defense of Civil Rights

The defense of civil rights shall be effectuated in accordance with the systemic jurisdiction of cases established by procedural legislation, or by contract, by a court, by an economic court, or by an arbitration court (hereinafter: court) [as amended by Law of 14 September 2017, No. ЗРУ-446. СЗ РУ (2017), no. 37, item 978].

The defense of civil rights in an administrative procedure shall be effectuated only in the instances provided for by a law. A decision adopted in an administrative procedure may be appealed to a court.

Article 11. Means of Defense of Civil Rights

The defense of civil rights shall be effectuated by means of:

recognition of the right;

restoration of the situation which existed before the violation of the right and suppressing actions violating a right or creating a threat to violate it;

recognition of a transaction to be invalid and the application of the consequences of the invalidity thereof;

recognition of an act of a State agency or agency of self-government of citizens to be invalid;

self-defense of right;

awarding performance of a duty in kind;

compensation of losses;

recovery of a penalty;

contributory compensation for moral harm;

termination or change of legal relation;

failure by a court to apply an act of a State agency or agency of self-government of citizens which is contrary to a law.

The defense of civil rights also may be effectuated by other means provided for by a law.

Article 12. Deeming Act of State Agency or Agency of Self-Government of Citizens to be Invalid

An act of a State agency or agency of self-government of citizens not corresponding to legislation and violating civil rights and interests of a citizen or juridical person protected by a law may be deemed by a court to be invalid.

In the event that an act is deemed by a court to be invalid, the violated right shall be subject to defense by the means provided for by Article 11 of the present Code.

Article 13. Self-Defense of Civil Rights

The self-defense of civil rights shall be permitted.

Means of self-defense must be commensurate to the violation and not exceed the limits of actions necessary to suppress it.

Article 14. Compensation of Losses

A person whose right has been violated may demand full compensation of losses caused to him unless compensation of losses in a lesser amount has been provided for by a law or contract.

By losses is understood expenses which the person whose right has been violated made or must make in order to restore the violated right, loss or damage of his property (real damage), and also revenues not received which this person would have received under ordinary conditions of civil turnover if his right had not been violated (lost advantage).

If the person who has violated a right has received revenues as a consequence thereof, the person whose right was violated shall have the right to demand compensation together with the other losses, for lost advantage in an amount of not less than such revenues.

Article 15. Compensation of Losses Caused by State Agencies and Agencies of Self-Government of Citizens

Losses caused to a citizen or juridical person as a result of the illegal actions (or failure to act) of State agencies, agencies of self-government of citizens, or officials of these agencies, including the publication of the act of a State agency or agency of self-government of citizens which does not correspond to legislation, shall be subject to compensation by the State or agency of self-government of citizens. By decision of a court compensation of losses may be placed on officials of State agencies and agencies of self-government of citizens through whose fault the losses were caused [as amended by Law of 15 December 2000, No. 175-II. Ведомости Олий Мажлиса (2001), no. 1-2, item 23].

Subsection 2. Persons

Chapter 3. Citizens (Natural Persons)

Article 16. Concept of Citizen (Natural Person)

By citizen (natural person) is understood citizens of the Republic Uzbekistan, citizens of other States, and also stateless persons.

The provisions of the present Code shall apply to all citizens unless established otherwise by a law.

Article 17. Legal Capacity of Citizens

The capacity to have civil rights and duties (legal capacity) shall be recognized in equal measure for all citizens.

The legal capacity of a citizen shall arise at the moment of his birth and terminate with his death.

Article 18. Content of Legal Capacity of Citizens

Citizens may:

have property by right of ownership, inherit and bequeath property, have savings in a bank; engage in entrepreneurial, dekhkan (farmer) economy, and other activity not prohibited by a law; use hired labor; create juridical persons; conclude transactions and participate in obligations; demand compensation for harm; select type of occupation and place of residence; have the right of author to works of science, literature and art, inventions and other results of intellectual activity protected by a law.

Citizens also may have other property and personal nonproperty rights.

Article 19. Name of Citizen

A citizen shall acquire and effectuate rights and duties under his own name, including surname and own forename, and also patronymic unless it arises otherwise from a law or national custom.

A citizen may use a pseudonym (fictitious name) in the instances and in the procedure provided for by a law.

A citizen shall have the right to change his name in the procedure established by a law. The change of name by a citizen shall not be grounds for the termination or change of his rights and duties acquired under the previous name.

A citizen shall be obliged to take necessary measures to inform his debtors and creditors about the change of his name and shall bear the risk of the consequences caused by these persons lacking information about the change of his name.

A citizen who has changed name shall have the right to demand the making, at his expense, of respective changes in documents formalized in his previous name.

A name received by a citizen at birth, and also a change of name, shall be subject to registration in the procedure established for the registration of acts of civil status.

The acquisition of rights and duties under the name of another person shall not be permitted.

Article 20. Defense of Name

The person who contests the right to the bearing of his name or whose interests are violated in connection with the unempowered use of his name may demand from the offender termination of the violation and a retraction. If the violation was made intentionally, the person who suffered may additionally demand contributory compensation for damage. Revenue received by the offender may be demanded as contributory compensation. In the event of an intentional violation, the person who suffered also shall have the right to compensation of moral harm.

The demands specified in paragraph one of the present Article relating to the termination of actions or retraction may also be put forward by a person who is not the bearer of the name or personal honor but has by reason of family position an interest worthy of defense in termination of the actions or retraction. This person also may seek the fulfillment of the demands relating to the defense of name and honor of another person after his death. Demands for contributory compensation of damage with regard to violations of name and honor after death shall not be recognized.

Article 21. Place of Residence of Citizen

The place where a citizen permanently or primarily resides shall be deemed to be the place of residence.

The place of residence of minors who have not attained fourteen years of age or citizens under trusteeship shall be deemed to be the place of residence of their legal representatives – parents, adoptive parents, or trustees.

Article 22. Dispositive Legal Capacity of Citizen

The capacity of a citizen by his own actions to acquire and effectuate civil rights, to create civil duties for himself, and to perform them (dispositive legal capacity) shall arise in full with the ensuing of majority, that is, upon attaining eighteen years of age.

A citizen who on legal grounds has entered into marriage before attaining majority shall acquire dispositive legal capacity in full from the time of entering into marriage.

Dispositive legal capacity acquired as a result of concluding a marriage shall be retained in full also in the event of dissolution of the marriage before attaining eighteen years of age.

When deeming a marriage to be invalid a court may adopt a decision concerning the loss by the minor spouse of full dispositive legal capacity from the moment determined by the court.

Article 23. Inadmissibility of Limitation of Legal Capacity and Dispositive Legal Capacity of Citizen

No one may be limited in legal capacity and dispositive legal capacity other than in the instances and in the procedure established by a law.

The failure to comply with the conditions and procedure established by a law for the limitation of dispositive legal capacity of a citizen shall entail the invalidity of the act of the State agency establishing the respective limitation.

The full or partial renunciation by a citizen of legal capacity or dispositive legal capacity and other transactions directed towards a limitation of legal capacity or dispositive legal capacity shall be void except for instances when such transactions are permitted by a law.

Article 24. Entrepreneurial Activity of Citizen

A citizen shall have the right to engage in entrepreneurial activity from the moment of State registration as an individual entrepreneur.

The rules of the present Code shall apply to the entrepreneurial activity of citizens effectuated without the formation of a juridical person unless it arises otherwise from legislation or the essence of the legal relation.

A citizen effectuating entrepreneurial activity without the formation of a juridical person in violation of the requirements of paragraph one of the present Article shall not have the right to refer with respect to transactions concluded by him to the fact that he is not an entrepreneur. A court may apply to such transactions the rules of the present Code concerning obligations connected with the effectuation of entrepreneurial activity.

Article 25. Property Responsibility of Citizen

A citizen shall be liable for his obligations with all of the property belonging to him except for property against which execution may not be levied in accordance with a law.

Article 26. Bankruptcy of Individual Entrepreneur and Natural Person Who Has Lost Status of Individual Entrepreneur [as amended by Law of 30 December 2017, No. ЗРУ-455. Национальная база данных законодательства (30 December 2017), No. 03/18/455/0492]

An individual entrepreneur who is not in a state to satisfy the demands of creditors connected with the effectuation by him of entrepreneurial activity may be deemed to be bankrupt in the established procedure [as amended by Law of 30 December 2017, No. ЗРУ-455. Национальная база данных законодательства (30 December 2017), No. 03/18/455/0492].

A natural person who has lost the status of an individual entrepreneur and who is not in a state to satisfy the demands of creditors, if the respective demands arise from his previous entrepreneurial activity, may be deemed to be bankrupt in the established procedure [added by Law of 30 December 2017, No. ЗРУ-455. Национальная база данных законодательства (30 December 2017), No. 03/18/455/0492].

When effectuating the procedure for deeming a person specified in paragraphs one or two of the present Article to be bankrupt, the creditors thereof with regard to obligations not connected with the effectuation of entrepreneurial activity by him also shall have the right to present their demands. The demands of the said creditors not declared by them in this procedure shall retain force after the completion of the bankruptcy proceeding [as amended by Law of 30 December 2017, No. ЗРУ-455. Национальная база данных законодательства (30 December 2017), No. 03/18/455/0492].

The demands of creditors of the person specified in paragraphs one or two of the present Article, in the event of him being deemed bankrupt, shall be satisfied in the procedure provided for by Article 56 of the present Code [as amended by Law of 30 December 2017, No. ЗРУ-455. Национальная база данных законодательства (30 December 2017), No. 03/18/455/0492].

The grounds and procedure for a court to deem a person to be bankrupt or the declaration by him of his own bankruptcy shall be established by legislation [as amended by Law of 30 December 2017, No. ЗРУ-455. Национальная база данных законодательства (30 December 2017), No. 03/18/455/0492].

Article 27. Dispositive Legal Capacity of Minors from Fourteen to Eighteen Years of Age

Minors in age from fourteen to eighteen years shall conclude transactions, except those named in paragraph three of the present Article, with the written consent of their parents, adoptive parents, or guardians. A transaction concluded by such a minor shall be valid also in the event of the subsequent written approval thereof by his parents, adoptive parents, or guardians.

Minors in age from fourteen to eighteen years shall have the right autonomously, without the consent of the parents, adoptive parents, and guardians, to:

(1) dispose of their earnings, stipends, and other revenues;

(2) effectuate the rights of an author of a work of science, literature or art, invention, or other result of his intellectual activity protected by a law;

(3) make deposits, in accordance with a law, in credit institutions and dispose of them;

(4) conclude petty domestic transactions and other transactions provided for by Article 29, paragraph two, of the present Code.

Minors in age from fourteen to eighteen years shall autonomously bear property responsibility for transactions concluded by them in accordance with paragraphs one and two of the present Article. For the harm caused by them such minors shall bear responsibility in accordance with the present Code.

When there are sufficient grounds a court may, upon the petition of parents, adoptive parents, or guardians or the agency of trusteeship and guardianship, limit or deprive a minor from fourteen to eighteen years of age of the right to autonomously dispose of his earnings, stipend, or other revenues, except for instances when this minor acquired dispositive legal capacity in full in accordance with Article 22, paragraph two, or with Article 28 of the present Code.

Article 28. Emancipation

A minor who has attained sixteen years of age may be declared to have full dispositive legal capacity if he works under a labor contract or, with the consent of parents, adoptive parents, or guardian, engages in entrepreneurial activity.

A minor shall be declared to have full dispositive legal capacity (emancipation) by decision of an agency of trusteeship and guardianship — with the consent of both parents, adoptive parents, or the guardian, or in the absence of such consent — by decision of a court.

Parents, adoptive parents, and guardians shall not bear responsibility for obligations of an emancipated minor, in particular, obligations which arose as a consequence of harm caused by him.

Article 29. Dispositive Legal Capacity of Minors Who Have Not Attained Fourteen Years of Age

Transactions, except those specified in paragraph two of the present Article, may be concluded for minors who have not attained fourteen years of age (youth) only in their names by the parents, adoptive parents, or trustees.

Youth in age from six to fourteen years shall have the right autonomously to conclude:

(1) petty domestic transactions;

(2) transactions directed towards receiving advantages without compensation which do not require notarial certification or State registration;

(3) transactions relating to the disposition of assets granted by a legal representative or with the consent of the last by a third person for a specified purpose or for free disposition.

The parents, adoptive parents, or trustees shall bear property responsibility for transactions of a youth, including transactions concluded by him autonomously, unless it is proved that the obligation was violated not through their fault. These persons in accordance with a law also shall be liable for harm caused by a youth.

Article 30. Deeming of Citizen to Lack Dispositive Legal Capacity

A citizen who as a consequence of mental disturbance (mental illness or feeble-mindedness) can not understand the significance of his actions or direct them may be deemed by a court to lack dispositive legal capacity in the procedure established by legislation, and a trusteeship shall be established over him.

Transactions in the name of a citizen deemed to lack dispositive legal capacity shall be concluded by his trustee.

If the grounds by virtue of which a citizen was deemed to lack dispositive legal capacity have disappeared, the court shall deem him to have dispositive legal capacity and shall vacate the trusteeship established over him.

Article 31. Limitation of Dispositive Legal Capacity of Citizen

A citizen who as a consequence of abusing alcoholic beverages or narcotic means places his family in a grave material position may be limited in dispositive legal capacity by a court in the procedure established by civil procedure legislation. A guardianship shall be established over him. He shall have the right autonomously to conclude petty domestic transactions. He may conclude other transactions, and also receive earnings, pension, and other revenues and dispose of them only with the consent of the guardian. However, such citizen shall autonomously bear property responsibility for transactions concluded by him and for harm caused by him.

If the grounds by virtue of which a citizen was limited in dispositive legal capacity have disappeared, a court shall vacate the limitation of his dispositive legal capacity. The guardianship established over the citizen shall be vacated on the basis of the decision of a court.

Article 32. Trusteeship and Guardianship

Trusteeship and guardianship shall be established in order to defend the rights and interests of persons who lack dispositive legal capacity or who are not citizens with full dispositive legal capacity. Trusteeship and guardianship over minors also shall be established for the purpose of nurturing them. The rights and duties of trustees and guardians corresponding thereto shall be determined by legislation.

Trustees and guardians shall act in defense of the rights and interests of their wards in relations with any persons, including in courts, without a special power.

A trusteeship and guardianship over minors shall be established when they have no parents or adoptive parents, the deprivation of parents by a court of parental rights, and also in instances when such citizens for other reasons are left without parental care, in particular, when the parents evade nurturing them or defending their rights and interests.

Article 33. Deeming of Citizen to be Missing

A citizen may, upon the application of interested persons, be deemed by a court to be missing if within a year there is no information at his place of residence concerning his whereabouts.

When it is impossible to establish the date of receipt of the last information concerning the absent person, the commencement of calculation of the period for deeming a person to be missing shall be considered to be the first date of the month following that in which the last information was received concerning the missing person, and when it is impossible to establish this month, the first of January of the following year.

Article 34. Consequences of Deeming Citizen to be Missing

The property of a citizen deemed to be missing shall, when permanent management is necessary, on the basis of the decision of a court be transferred to the person who is determined by the agency of trusteeship and guardianship and shall operate on the basis of a contract on trust management concluded with this agency.

From this property maintenance shall be issued to citizens whom the missing person is obliged to maintain according to a law, and indebtedness shall be repaid with regard to taxes and other obligations of the missing person.

An agency of trusteeship and guardianship may also before the expiry of one year from the date of receiving information about the whereabouts of the missing citizen determine the person to protect his property.

The consequences of deeming a person to be missing which are not provided for by the present Article shall be determined by a law.

Article 35. Vacating Decision on Deeming Citizen to be Missing

In the event of the appearance or discovery of the whereabouts of a citizen deemed to be missing a court shall vacate the decision deeming him to be missing. The management of the property of this citizen shall be vacated on the basis of the decision of the court.

Article 36. Declaration of Citizen to be Deceased

A citizen may be declared by a court to be deceased upon the application of interested persons if there is no information at his place of residence concerning his whereabouts in the course of three years, and if he was missing under circumstances threatening death or giving grounds to suppose he perished from a specific accident, within six months.

A military serviceman or other citizen who is missing in connection with military actions may be declared by a court to be deceased not earlier than upon the expiry of two years from the date the military actions end.

The date of death of a citizen declared to be deceased shall be considered to be the date of entry into legal force of the decision of the court declaring him to be deceased. In the event a citizen is declared to be deceased who is missing under circumstances threatening death or giving grounds to suppose he perished in a specific accident, the court may deem the date of death of this citizen to be the date of the presupposed perishing.

The declaration of a citizen to be deceased shall entail with respect to the rights and duties of such citizen those consequences which his death would have entailed.

Article 37. Consequences of Appearance of Citizen Declared to be Deceased

In the event of the appearance or discovery of the whereabouts of a citizen declared to be deceased, the decision declaring him to be deceased shall be vacated by the court.

After the vacating of the decision concerning the declaration of a citizen to be deceased, he shall have the right within three years to demand and obtain in a judicial proceeding from any person the return of property preserved which passed to this person without compensation, except for instances provided for by Article 229, paragraphs two and four, of the present Code.

If the property of a citizen declared to be deceased was alienated by his legal successors to third persons who at the moment of the appearance of the citizen had not paid the purchase price in full, the right of demand of the unpaid amount shall pass to the citizen who has appeared.

Persons to whom property of a citizen declared to be deceased has passed according to transactions for compensation shall be obliged to return this property to him if it is proved that, in acquiring the property, they knew that the citizen declared to be deceased is alive. If it is impossible to return such property in kind, the value thereof shall be compensated.

If the property of a person declared to be deceased has passed by right of inheritance to the State and was realized, then after the vacating of the decision concerning the declaration of the citizen to be deceased, the amount received from the realization of the property shall be returned to him.

Article 38. Registration of Acts of Civil Status

The following acts of civil status shall be subject to State registration:

(1) birth;

(2) death;

(3) conclusion of marriage;

(4) dissolution of marriage [as amended by Law of 25 December 1998, No. 729-I. Ведомости Олий Мажлиса (1999), no. 1, item 20].

Acts of civil status shall be registered by agencies for the registry of acts of civil status by means of making respective entries in the book for the registration of acts of civil status (documentary books) and the issuance to citizens of certificates on the basis of these entries.

Events and facts – adoption, establishment of paternity, change of surname, forename, patronymic, and change of sex shall find their reflection in acts of civil status provided for by paragraph one of the present Article by means of making respective changes therein [added by Law of 25 December 1998, No. 729-I. Ведомости Олий Мажлиса (1999), no. 1, item 20].

The correction and the changing of entries of acts of civil status shall be done by the agency for the registry of acts of civil status when there are sufficient grounds and there is the absence of a dispute between interested persons.

When there is a dispute between interested persons, or the refusal of an agency for the registry of acts of civil status to correct or change an entry, the dispute shall be settled by a court.

The annulment and restoration of entries of acts of civil status shall be done by the agency for the registry of acts of civil status, and when there is a dispute between interested persons or material divergences in entries of acts of civil status -- on the basis of the decision of a court [added by Law of 25 December 1998, No. 729-I. Ведомости Олий Мажлиса (1999), no. 1, item 20].

Agencies effectuating the registration of acts of civil status and determining the procedure for the registration of these acts, the procedure for the change, restoration, and annulment of entries of acts of civil status, the forms of the documentary books and certificates, and also the procedure and periods for keeping the documentary books, shall be determined by legislation.

Chapter 4. Juridical Persons

§ 1. General Provisions

Article 39. Concept of Juridical Person

A juridical person shall be deemed to be an organization which has solitary property in ownership, economic jurisdiction, or operative management and is liable for its obligations with such property and may in its own name acquire and effectuate property and personal nonproperty rights, bear duties, and be a plaintiff or defendant in court.

Juridical persons must have an autonomous balance sheet or estimate.

Article 40. Types of Juridical Persons

An organization pursuing the deriving of profit as the basic purpose of its activity (commercial organization) or not having the deriving of profit as such purpose (noncommercial organization) may be a juridical person.

A juridical person which is a commercial organization may be created in the form of an economic partnership and society, production cooperative, unitary enterprise, and in other form provided for by legislative acts.

A juridical person which is a noncommercial organization may be created in the form of a social association, social fund to be financed by the owner of the institution, and also in other form provided for by legislative acts.

A noncommercial organization may engage in entrepreneurial activity within the limits corresponding to its charter purposes.

Juridical persons may combine in associations (or unions) and other associations in accordance with a law [as amended by Law of 15 December 2000, No. 175-II. Ведомости Олий Мажлиса (2001), no. 1-2, item 23].

A juridical person shall operate on the basis of the present Code, other acts of legislation, and also a charter and other constitutive documents.

Article 41. Legal Capacity of Juridical Person

A juridical person shall possess civil legal capacity in accordance with the purposes of its activity provided for in its constitutive documents.

The legal capacity of a juridical person shall arise at the moment of its creation (Article 44, paragraph four, of the present Code) and shall terminate at the moment of the completion of its liquidation (Article 55, paragraph ten, of the present Code).

The special legal capacity of a juridical person shall be determined by its charter, statute, or by legislation.

A juridical person may engage in individual types of activity, a list of which shall be determined by a legislative act, only on the basis of a special authorization (or license).

A juridical person may be limited in rights only in the instances and in the procedure provided for by a law. A decision concerning the limitation of the rights of a juridical person may be appealed to a court.

Article 42. Arising of Juridical Persons

Juridical persons shall be created by the owner or person empowered by it or on the basis of a regulation of an empowered agency, and also in the procedure provided for by legislation.

The owners of property, subjects of the right of economic jurisdiction or operative management, or persons empowered by them shall be deemed to be the founders of juridical persons.

Article 43. Constitutive Documents of Juridical Person

A juridical person shall operate on the basis of a charter, or a constitutive contract and a charter, or only a constitutive contract. In the instances provided for by a law, a juridical person which is not a commercial organization may operate on the basis of a statute on organizations of the particular type.

The constitutive contract of a juridical person shall be concluded, and the charter confirmed, by its founders.

A juridical person created in accordance with the present Code by one founder shall operate on the basis of a charter confirmed by that founder.

The name of the juridical person, its location (or postal address), the procedure for the management of the activity of the juridical person must be determined in the charter and other constitutive documents of the juridical person, and also they shall contain other information provided for by the law on juridical persons of the respective type. The subject and purpose of activity of the juridical person must be determined in the constitutive documents of noncommercial organizations and unitary enterprises, and in the instances provided for by a law, also other commercial organizations [as amended by Laws of 20 August 1999, No. 832-I, and of 20 August 2021, No. ЗРУ-709].

In a constitutive contract the parties (or founders) shall be obliged to create a juridical person and determine the procedure for joint activity relating to its creation and the conditions for the transfer of their property to it and participation in its activity. The conditions and procedure for distribution among the participants of profit and losses, the management of the activity of the juridical person, and the withdrawal of founders (or participants) from the composition thereof shall also be determined by the contract. Other conditions also may be included in the constitutive documents by consent of the founders.

Changes of constitutive documents shall receive force for third persons from the moment of their State registration, and in the instances established by a law, from the moment of informing the agency effectuating State registration of such changes. Juridical persons and their founders shall not have the right to refer to the lack of registration of such changes in relations with third persons who have acted by taking these changes into account.

Article 44. State Registration of Juridical Persons

A juridical person shall be subject to State registration in the procedure determined by legislation. The data of State registration shall be included in the unified State register of juridical persons open for general familiarization.

A violation of the procedure established by a law for the formation of a juridical person or the failure of its constitutive documents to conform to law shall entail refusal of the State registration of the juridical person. A refusal of registration of juridical persons for which a notification procedure of State registration shall be effectuated in accordance with legislation. A refusal of registration for reasons of inadvisability of the creation of the juridical person shall not be permitted [as amended by Law of 13 April 2007, No. ЗРУ-91. СЗ РУ (2007), no. 15, item 154].

The refusal of State registration, and also a violation of the periods for registration, may be appealed to a court.

A juridical person shall be considered to be created from the moment of the State registration thereof.

A juridical person shall be subject to re-registration only in the instances established by a law.

Article 45. Organs of Juridical Person

A juridical person shall acquire civil rights and assume civil duties through its organs operating in accordance with legislation and the constitutive documents. The procedure for the appointment or election of the organs of a juridical person shall be determined by legislation and the constitutive documents.

In the instances provided for by a law a juridical person may acquire civil rights and assume civil duties through its participants.

A person who by virtue of a law or constitutive documents of a juridical person acts in its name must operate in the interests of the juridical person represented by him in good faith and reasonably. He shall be obliged at the demand of the founders (or participants, members) of the juridical person, insofar as not provided otherwise by a law or contract, to compensate losses caused by him to the juridical person.

Article 46. Name and Location of Juridical Person

A juridical person shall have its own name containing an indication of its organizational-legal form. The names of noncommercial organizations and unitary enterprises, and in the instances provided for by a law, other commercial organizations, must contain an indication of the character of activity of the juridical person.

The inclusion in the name of a juridical person of indications to an official full or abbreviated name (or name of the State) and the inclusion of such name or elements of State symbols in the requisites of documents of advertising materials of a juridical person shall be permitted in the procedure determined by the Government of the Republic Uzbekistan.

The location of a juridical person shall be determined by the place of its State registration, unless established otherwise in accordance with a law in the constitutive documents of the juridical person.

A juridical person must have a postal address at which communication is effectuated with it and shall be obliged to inform the empowered State agencies about a change of its postal address [added by Law of 20 August 1999, No. 832-I, and of 20 August 2021, No. 3PY-709].

The name and location (or postal address) of a juridical person shall be specified in its constitutive documents [as amended by Laws of 20 August 1999, No. 832-I, and of 20 August 2021, No. 3PY-709].

A juridical person which is a commercial organization must have a firm name.

A juridical person shall have the exclusive right to the use its firm name.

A person who unlawfully uses another's firm name shall be obliged, at the demand of the possessor of the right to the firm name, to terminate the use thereof and compensate the losses caused.

Article 47. Representations and Branches

A solitary subdivision of a juridical person situated outside the location thereof which represents the interests of the juridical person and effectuates the defense thereof shall be a representation.

A solitary subdivision of a juridical person situated outside the location thereof and effectuating all or part of its functions, including the function of representation, shall be a branch.

Representations and branches shall not be juridical persons unless provided otherwise by a law. They shall be endowed with property by the juridical person which created them and shall operate on the basis of Statutes confirmed by them. The directors of representations and branches shall be appointed by the juridical person and operate on the basis of the power of attorney thereof.

Article 48. Responsibility of Juridical Person

A juridical person shall be liable for its obligations with all of the property belonging to them.

A State enterprise and an institution being financed by the owner shall be liable for its obligations in the procedure and on the conditions established by Article 72, paragraph five, and Article 76, paragraph three, of the present Code.

The founder (or participant) of a juridical person or the owner of its property shall not be liable for obligations of the juridical person, and the juridical person shall not be liable for the obligations of the founder (or participant) or owner, except for the instances provided for by the present Code or by the constitutive documents of the juridical person.

If the insolvency (or bankruptcy) of a juridical person has been caused by the unlawful actions of the person acting as the founder (or participant) or by the owner of property of the juridical person who has the right to give instructions which are binding upon this juridical person, subsidiary responsibility for its obligations may be placed upon such persons in the event the property of the juridical person is insufficient [as amended by Law of 27 December 1996, No. 357-I. Ведомости Олий Мажлиса (1997), no. 2, item 56].

The founder (or participant) or owner of the property of a juridical person shall have the right to give instructions which are binding only in the event when this right is provided for in the constitutive documents of this juridical person [added by Law of 27 December 1996, No. 357-I. Ведомости Олий Мажлиса (1997), no. 2, item 56].

The insolvency (or bankruptcy) of a juridical person shall be considered to be caused by the founder (or participant) or by the owner who has the right to give instructions which are binding on this juridical person only if he has used the said right for the purpose of the performance of actions by the juridical person knowingly knowing that as a consequence thereof the insolvency (or bankruptcy) of this juridical person shall ensue [added by Law of 27 December 1996, No. 357-I. Ведомости Олий Мажлиса (1997), no. 2, item 56].

Article 49. Reorganization of Juridical Person

The reorganization of a juridical person (merger, accession, division, separation, transformation) may be effectuated by decision of its founders (or participants) or the organ of the juridical person empowered therefor by the constitutive documents.

In the instances established by a law the reorganization of a juridical person in the form of its division or the separation from its composition of one or several juridical persons therefrom shall be effectuated by decision of empowered State agencies or by decision of a court.

If the founders (or participants) of a juridical person, organ empowered by them, or organ of the juridical person empowered to reorganize it by its constitutive documents does not effectuate the reorganization of the juridical person within the period specified in the decision of the empowered State agency, the court upon the suit of the said State agency shall appoint an administrator of the juridical person and charge him with effectuating the reorganization of this juridical person. From the moment of appointment of the administrator to him shall pass the powers relating to managing the affairs of the juridical person. The administrator shall act in the name of the juridical person in court, draw up the separation balance sheet and transfer it for consideration of the court together with the constitutive documents of the juridical persons arising as a result of the reorganization. The confirmation by the court of the said documents shall be the grounds for State registration of the newly arisen juridical persons.

In the instances established by a law the reorganization of juridical persons in the form of merger, accession, or transformation may be effectuated only with the consent of empowered State agencies.

The juridical person shall be considered to be reorganized, except for instances of reorganization in the form of accession, from the moment of State registration of the juridical persons which have arisen anew.

In the event of the reorganization of a juridical person in the form of accession thereto of another juridical person, the first of them shall be considered to be reorganized from the moment of making an entry in the unified State register of juridical persons concerning the termination of the activity of the juridical person which has acceded.

Article 50. Legal Succession In Event of Reorganization of Juridical Persons

In the event of the merger of juridical persons the rights and duties of each of them shall pass to the juridical person which newly arises in accordance with the act of transfer.

In the event of the accession of a juridical person to another juridical person, to the last shall pass the rights and duties of the acceding juridical person in accordance with the act of transfer.

In the event of the division of a juridical person its rights and duties shall pass to the juridical persons which newly arose in accordance with the division balance sheet.

In the event of separation from a juridical person of one or several juridical persons, to each of them shall pass the rights and duties of the reorganized juridical person in accordance with the separation balance sheet.

In the event of the transformation of a juridical person of one type into a juridical person of another type (change of organizational-legal form), to the juridical person which arises anew shall pass the rights and duties of the reorganized juridical person in accordance with the act of transfer.

Article 51. Act of Transfer and Division Balance Sheet

The act of transfer and division balance sheet must contain provisions concerning legal succession regarding all obligations of the reorganized juridical person with respect to all creditors and debtors thereof, including obligations being contested by the parties.

The act of transfer and division balance sheet shall be confirmed by the founders (or participants) of the juridical person or by the agency which adopted the decision concerning reorganization of the juridical persons and shall be submitted together with the constitutive documents for the

State registration of the juridical persons which newly arose or the making of changes in the constitutive documents of existing juridical persons.

The failure to submit together with the constitutive documents the act of transfer or division balance sheet respectively, and also the absence therein of provisions concerning legal succession with regard to the obligations of the reorganized juridical person, shall entail a refusal of State registration of the juridical persons which newly arose.

Article 52. Guarantees of Rights of Creditors of Juridical Person in Event of its Reorganization

The founders (or participants) of the juridical person or agency which adopted the decision concerning the reorganization of a juridical person shall be obliged in writing to inform the creditors of the juridical person being reorganized thereof.

The creditor of the juridical person being reorganized shall have the right to demand the termination or the performance before time of the obligation, the debtor with regard to which this juridical person is, and compensation of losses.

If the division balance sheet does not make it possible to determine the legal successor of the reorganized juridical person, the juridical persons which newly arose shall bear joint and several responsibility for the obligations of the reorganized juridical person to its creditors.

Article 53. Liquidation of Juridical Person

The liquidation of a juridical person shall entail the termination thereof without the transfer of rights and duties by way of legal succession to other persons.

A juridical person may be liquidated by:

decision of its founders (or participants) or the organ of the juridical person empowered by the constitutive documents, including in connection with the expiry of the period for which the juridical person was created, achievement of the purpose for which it was created, or the deeming by a court of the registration of the juridical person to be invalid in connection with violations of legislation permitted during its creation if such violations are of an ineradicable character;

decision of a court in the event of the effectuation of activity without a license activity (or actions) without authorization or without notification of an empowered agency, or activity prohibited by a law, unless provided otherwise by legislation, and also in other instances provided for by the present Code [as amended by Laws of 1 May 1998, No. 621-I, of 20 August 1999, No. 832-I, of 11 December 2014, No. 3PY-381, of 20 August 2021, No. 3PY-709, and of 12 October 2021, No. 3PY-721];

by decision of the registering agency in the event of the failure to restore activity within three years from the moment of transfer in the established procedure of a non-active regime in connection with the failure to effectuate financial-economic activity, except for non-State commercial organizations [paragraph added by Law of 11 December 2019, No. 3PY-592].

Duties relating to the effectuation of the liquidation of a juridical person may be entrusted by decision of a court concerning the liquidation of a juridical person to its founders (or participants), or organ empowered to liquidate the juridical person by its constitutive documents.

Article 54. Duties of Person Which Adopted Decision Concerning Liquidation of Juridical Person

The founders (or participants) of a juridical person or agency which adopted the decision concerning liquidation of the juridical person shall be obliged immediately in writing to inform the agency thereof which effectuates the State registration of juridical persons, which shall place in the unified State register of juridical persons information concerning the fact that the juridical person is in the process of liquidation.

The founders (or participants) of a juridical person or agency which has adopted the decision concerning the liquidation of a juridical person shall appoint a liquidator – liquidation commission or natural person and establish in accordance with the present Code the procedure and periods of liquidation. In the event of the adoption of a decision concerning the liquidation of a juridical person by a court, the liquidator shall be appointed by agreement with the agency effectuating the State registration of juridical persons [as amended by Laws of 4 April 2006, No. 3PY-28, and of 14 December 2007, No. 3PY-127. C3 PY (2007), no. 50-51, item 506].

From the moment of the appointment of the liquidator, the powers relating to the management of the affairs of the juridical person shall pass thereto. The liquidator shall appear in court in the name of the juridical person being liquidated [as amended by Law of 14 December 2007, No. 3PY-127. C3 PY (2007), no. 50-51, item 506].

Article 55. Procedure for Liquidation of Juridical Person

The liquidator shall publish in the mass media an announcement concerning the liquidation of a juridical person. An announcement concerning the voluntary liquidation of a juridical person-subject ot entrepreneurship shall be placed by the registering agency on its official website [as amended by Laws of 14 December 2007, No. 3РУ-127, and of 11 December 2019, No. 3РУ-592].

In the announcement concerning the liquidation of a juridical person shall be specified the procedure and period for the declaration of demands of its creditors. This period may not be less than two months from the moment of the publication on liquidation [paragraph added by Law of 11 December 2019, No. 3РУ-592].

The liquidator shall take measures to elicit creditors and receive debtor indebtedness, and also inform creditors in writing concerning the liquidation of a juridical person [as amended by Law of 14 December 2007, No. 3РУ-127. С3 РУ (2007), no. 50-51, item 506].

After the period ends for the presentation of demands by creditors, the liquidator shall draw up the interim liquidation balance sheet, which shall contain information concerning the composition of the property of the juridical person being liquidated, a list of demands presented by creditors, and also the results of their consideration [as amended by Law of 14 December 2007, No. 3РУ-127].

The interim liquidation balance sheet shall be confirmed by the founders (or participants) of a juridical person or agency which adopted the decision concerning the liquidation of the juridical person. In the event of the adoption of a decision concerning the liquidation of a juridical person by a court, the interim liquidation balance sheet shall be confirmed by agreement with the agency effectuating the State registration of juridical persons [as amended by Law of 4 April 2006, No. 3РУ-28].

If a juridical person being liquidated (except institutions) has monetary means which are insufficient to satisfy the demands of creditors, the liquidator shall effectuate the sale of the property of the juridical person at a public sale in the procedure established for the execution of judicial decisions [as amended by Law of 14 December 2007, No. 3РУ-127].

The payment of monetary amounts to creditors of a juridical person being liquidated shall be by the liquidator in the order of priority established by Article 56 of the present Code and in accordance with the interim liquidation balance sheet, commencing from the date of its confirmation [as amended by Law of 14 December 2007, No. 3РУ-127. С3 РУ (2007), no. 50-51, item 506].

After the completion of the settlement of accounts with creditors, the liquidator shall draw up the liquidation balance sheet, which shall be confirmed by the founders (or participants) of the juridical person or by the agency which adopted the decision concerning the liquidation of the juridical person. In the event of the adoption of a decision concerning the liquidation of a juridical person by a court, the liquidation balance sheet shall be confirmed by agreement with the agency effectuating the State registration of juridical persons [as amended by Laws of 4 April 2006, No. ЗРУ-28, and of 14 December 2007, No. ЗРУ-127].

In the event that the property of a State enterprise being liquidated is insufficient, and the institution being liquidated has monetary means to satisfy the demands of creditors, the last shall have the right to bring suit in a court to satisfy the remaining part of the demands at the expense of the owner of the property of this enterprise or institution.

The procedure and peculiarities of the liquidation oof enterprises not effectuating financial-economic activity from the moment of State registration, and also the founders of which are absent, shall be regulated by legislation [added by Law of 20 August 2021, No. ЗРУ-709].

The property of a juridical person remaining after the satisfaction of the demands of creditors shall be transferred to its founders (or participants) having rights to a thing in this property or rights of obligations with respect to this juridical person, unless provided otherwise by legislation.

The procedure and peculiarities of the liquidation of enterprises not effectuating financial and economic activity from the moment of State registration, and also whose founders are absent, shall be regulated by legislation [added by Law of 20 August 1999, No. 832-I].

The liquidation of a juridical person shall be considered to be completed and the juridical person to have terminated existence after the making of entries thereof in the unified State register of juridical persons.

Article 56. Satisfaction of Demands of Creditors

When liquidating a juridical person in first priority shall be satisfied the demands of citizens arising from labor law relations, relating to the recovery of alimony and the payment of remuneration under authors' contracts, and also the demands of citizens to whom the juridical person being liquidated bears responsibility for the causing of harm to human life and health by means of capitalization of the respective time payments.

The demands of the other creditors shall be satisfied in the procedure and on the conditions provided for by legislation.

Article 57. Insolvency (or Bankruptcy) of Juridical Person

A juridical person which is a commercial organization, except for a State enterprise, and also a juridical person operating in the form of a consumer cooperative or social foundation, may, by decision of a court, be deemed to be insolvent (or bankrupt) if it is not in a state to satisfy the demands of creditors.

Deeming a juridical person to be bankrupt shall entail its liquidation.

A juridical person which is a commercial organization, and also a juridical person operating in the form of a consumer cooperative or social foundation, when the indicia of bankruptcy are present, shall apply to a court with an application to deem it bankrupt [as amended by Law of 25 April 2003, No. 482-II. Ведомости Олий Мажлиса (2003), no. 5, item 67].

The grounds for deeming a juridical person to be bankrupt, and also the procedure for the liquidation of such juridical person, shall be established by a law [as amended by Law of 25 April 2003, No. 482-II. Ведомости Олий Мажлиса (2003), no. 5, item 67].

§ 2. Commercial Organizations

Article 58. Basic Provisions on Economic Partnerships and Societies

Commercial organizations with a charter fund (or charter capital) divided into participatory shares (or contributions) or into the stocks of the founders (or participants) shall be deemed to be economic partnerships and societies. The property created at the expense of contributions of the founders (or participants), and also produced and acquired by the economic partnership or society in the process of its activity, shall belong to it by right of ownership.

Economic partnerships and societies may be created in the form of a full partnership, kommandit partnership, society with limited or additional responsibility, and joint-stock society.

Individual entrepreneurs and(or) commercial organizations may be participants of full partnerships and full partners in kommandit partnerships.

Citizens and juridical persons may be participants of economic societies and contributors to kommandit partnerships.

Agencies of State power shall not have the right to act as participants of economic societies and contributors to kommandit partnerships unless established otherwise by a law.

Institutions financed by owners may be participants of economic societies and contributors to kommandit partnerships with the authorization of the owner unless provided otherwise by a law.

The participation of individual categories of citizens in economic partnerships and societies, except for joint-stock societies, may be prohibited or limited by a law [as amended by Law of 14 May 2014, No. ЗРУ-372. СЗ РУ (2014), no. 20, item 222].

Economic partnerships and societies may be the founders (or participants) of other economic partnerships and societies except for instances provided for by the present Code and by other laws.

Money, securities, other things or property rights, or other alienable rights having monetary value may be a contribution to the property of an economic partnership or society.

The monetary valuation of the contribution of a participant of an economic society shall be made by agreement between the founders (or participants) of the society and in the instances provided for by a law shall be subject to valuation by an appraisal organization [as amended by Law of 17 September 2010, No. ЗРУ-257. СЗ РУ (2010), no. 37, item 315].

Economic partnerships, and societies (except joint-stock societies) shall not have the right to issue stocks.

Article 59. Rights and Duties of Participants of Economic Partnership or Society

The participants of an economic partnership or society shall have the right to:

participate in the management of the affairs of the partnership or society, except for instances provided for other laws;

receive information concerning the activity of the partnership or society and familiarize themselves with its bookkeeping records and other documentation in the procedure established by the constitutive documents;

take part in the distribution of profit;

receive in the event of the liquidation of the partnership or society the part of the property remaining after the settlement of accounts with creditors or the value thereof.

The participants of an economic partnership or society also may have other rights provided for by the present Code, other legislation, or constitutive documents of a partnership or society.

The participants of an economic partnership or society shall be obliged to:

make contributions in the procedure, amounts, means, and periods provided for by the constitutive documents;

not divulge confidential information concerning the activity of the partnership or society.

The participants of an economic partnership or society may also bear other duties provided for by its constitutive documents.

Article 60. Full Partnership

A partnership whose participants in accordance with a contract concluded between them engage in entrepreneurial activity in the name of the partnership and bear responsibility for its obligations with all of the property belonging to them, shall be deemed to be a full [partnership].

A person may be a participant only of one full partnership.

The firm name of a full partnership must contain either the names of all its participants, and the words "full partnership", or the name of one or several participants with the addition of the words "and company," and also the words "full partnership".

Article 61. Kommandit Partnership

A kommandit partnership shall be deemed to be a partnership in which together with participants effectuating entrepreneurial activity in the name of the partnership and liable for the obligations of the partnership with all of their property (full partners) there are one or several participants (contributors, kommanditists) who shall bear the risk of losses connected with the activity of the partnership within the limits of the amounts of the contributions made by them and shall not take part in the effectuation by the partnership of entrepreneurial activity.

The rights of full partners participating in a kommandit partnership and their responsibility for the obligations of the partnership shall be determined by the rules of the present Code.

A person may be a full partner only in one kommandit partnership.

A participant of a full partnership may not be a full partner in a kommandit partnership.

A full partner in a kommandit partnership may not be contributor in the partnership and a participant of another full partnership.

The firm name of a kommandit partnership must contain the name(s) of all of the full partners and also the words "komandit partnership", or the name of not less than one full partner with the addition of the words "and company" and also the words "kommandit partnership".

If the name of a contributor is included in the firm name of a kommandit partnership, such contributor shall become a full partner.

The rules on the full partnership shall apply to a kommandit partnership insofar as this is not contrary to the provisions of the present Code.

Article 62. Limited Responsibility Society

A limited responsibility society shall be deemed to be a society founded by one or several persons, the charter fund (or charter capital) of which is divided into participatory shares of amounts specified by the constitutive documents. The participants of a limited responsibility society shall not be liable for its obligations and shall bear the risk of losses connected with the activity of the society within the limits of the value of the contributions made by them.

The participants of a society who have not made contributions in full shall bear joint and several responsibility for its obligations within the limits of the value of the unpaid portion of the contribution of each of the participants.

The firm name of a limited responsibility society must contain the name of the society, and also the words "limited responsibility".

The legal status of a limited responsibility society and the rights and duties of its participants shall be determined by the present Code and by other legislative acts.

Article 63. Additional Responsibility Society

An additional responsibility society shall be deemed to be a society founded by one or several persons, whose charter capital has been divided into participatory shares of the amounts specified by the constitutive documents. The participants of such a society shall jointly and severally bear subsidiary responsibility for its obligations with their property in a multiple identical for all of the value of their contributions determined by the constitutive documents of the society. In the event of the insolvency (bankruptcy) of one of the participants, his responsibility for the obligations of the society shall be distributed among the remaining participants in proportion to their contributions unless another procedure for the distribution of responsibility has been provided for by the constitutive documents of the society.

The firm name of an additional responsibility society must contain the name of the society and also the words "additional responsibility".

The rules of the present Code on the limited responsibility society shall apply to the additional responsibility society insofar as the present Article does not provide otherwise.

Article 64. Joint-Stock Society

A joint-stock society shall be deemed to be a society whose charter fund has been divided into a determined number of stocks. The participants of a joint-stock society (stockholders) shall not be liable for its obligations and shall bear the risk of losses connected with the activity of the society within the limits of the value of the stocks belonging to them.

Stockholders who have not fully paid up stocks shall bear joint and several responsibility for the obligations of the joint-stock society within the limits of the unpaid portion of the value of the stocks belonging to them.

The firm name of a joint-stock society must contain its name and an indication that the society is a joint-stock [society].

The legal status of a joint-stock society and the rights and duties of the stockholders shall be determined by the present Code and other legislative acts.

Article 65. Open Joint-Stock Society [lost force by Law of 14 May 2014, No. ЗРУ-372. СЗ РУ (2014), item 20, no. 222]

Article 66. Closed Joint-Stock Society [lost force by Law of 14 May 2014, No. ЗРУ-372. СЗ РУ (2014), item 20, no. 222]

Article 67. Subsidiary Economic Society

An economic society shall be deemed to be a subsidiary if another (principal) economic society or partnership by virtue of predominant participation in its charter capital, or in accordance with a contract concluded between them, or otherwise has the possibility to determine the decisions adopted by that society.

A subsidiary economic society shall be a juridical person.

A subsidiary economic society shall not have the right to have in ownership a participatory share in the charter fund (or charter capital) of its principal society (or partnership). A subsidiary economic society which has acquired a participatory share in the charter fund (or charter capital) of its principal society (or partnership) before the entry into force of the prohibition established by the present paragraph shall not have the right to vote at the general meeting of participants or stockholders of its principal society (or partnership) [paragraph added by Law of 9 January 2018, No. ЗРУ-459].

A subsidiary economic society shall not be liable for the debts of its principal society (or partnership).

In the event of the insolvency (or bankruptcy) of the subsidiary economic society through the fault of the principal society (or partnership) the last shall bear subsidiary responsibility for its debts.

The participants (or stockholders) of a subsidiary society shall have the right to demand compensation by the principal society (or partnership) for losses caused through its fault to the subsidiary society unless established otherwise by a law.

Article 68. Dependent Economic Society

An economic society shall be deemed to be dependent if another participating society has more than 20% of its voting stocks (or participatory shares) [as amended by Law of 14 May 2014, No. ЗРУ-372. СЗ РУ (2014), item 20, no. 222].

A dependent economic society shall be a juridical person.

A dependent economic society shall not have the right to have in ownership a participatory share in the charter fund (or charter capital) of another participating society. A dependent economic society which has acquired a participatory share in the charter fund (or charter capital) of another participating society before the entry into force of the prohibition established in the present paragraph shall not have the right to vote at the general meeting of participants or stockholders of another participating society [paragraph added by Law of 9 January 2018, No. ЗРУ-459].

A participating society shall be obliged to publish in the procedure provided for by a law information immediately about the respective part of the charter fund acquired by it of a dependent society.

The limits of mutual participation of economic societies in the charter funds of one another and the number of votes which one of such societies may use at the general meeting of participants or stockholders of the other society shall be determined by a law.

Article 69. Production Cooperatives

A production cooperative shall be deemed to be a voluntary association of citizens on the basis of membership for the purpose of joint production or other economic activity based on their personal participation and the combining of property share contributions by the members (or participants) thereof. The participation of juridical persons also in its activity may be provided for by a law and by the constitutive documents of the production cooperative.

Members of a production cooperative shall bear subsidiary responsibility for the obligations of the cooperative within the amounts and in the procedure provided for by a law and by the charter of the cooperative.

The firm name of a cooperative must contain its name and also the words "production cooperative".

The legal status of production cooperatives and the rights and duties of their members shall be determined by the present Code and by other legislative acts.

Article 70. Unitary Enterprise

A commercial organization not endowed with the right of ownership to property consolidated to it by the owner shall be deemed to be a unitary enterprise.

The property of a unitary enterprise shall be indivisible and may not be distributed according to contributions (or participatory shares, shares), including among the workers of the enterprise.

The charter of a unitary enterprise must contain, besides the information specified in Article 43, paragraphs four and five, of the present Code, information concerning the amount of the charter fund of the enterprise and the procedure and sources for forming it.

The property of the unitary enterprise shall belong to it by right of economic jurisdiction or operative management.

The firm name of a unitary enterprise must contain an indication of the owner of its property.

The management organ of a unitary enterprise shall be the director, and also the supervisory council, if this is provided by the charter of the unitary enterprise. The director and supervisory council of a unitary enterprise shall be appointed by the owner of the property or by an agency empowered by the owner and accountable to it [as amended by Law of 29 March 2022, No. 3PY-760].

A unitary enterprise shall be liable for its obligations with all of the property belonging to it.

A unitary enterprise shall not bear responsibility for the obligations of the owner of its property.

A unitary enterprise shall not have the right to have in ownership a participatory share in the charter fund (or charter capital) of its owner. A unitary enterprise which has acquired a participatory share in the charter fund (or charter capital) of its owner before the entry into force of the prohibition established in the present paragraph shall not have the right to vote at the general meeting of participants of the economic society (or partnership) [paragraph added by Law of 9 January 2018, No. 3PY-459].

The legal status of unitary enterprises shall be determined by the present Code and by other legislation.

The owner of the property of a unitary enterprise shall not be liable for the obligations of the enterprise, except for instances provided for by Article 48, paragraphs three and four, of the present Codei. This rule also shall apply to the responsibility of a unitary enterprise which has founded a subsidiary enterprise for the obligations of the last.

Article 71. Unitary Enterprise Based on Right of Economic Jurisdiction

A unitary enterprise based on the right of economic jurisdiction shall be created by decision of the owner or agency empowered by it.

The constitutive document of an enterprise based on the right of economic jurisdiction shall be its charter, confirmed in the established procedure.

A unitary enterprise based on the right of economic jurisdiction may create as a juridical person another unitary enterprise by means of transferring to it in the established procedure part of its property in economic jurisdiction (subsidiary enterprise).

The founder shall confirm the charter of the subsidiary enterprise and appoint the director thereof.

Article 72. State Unitary Enterprise Based on Right of Operative Management

In the instances provided for by legislation, by decision of the Government of the Republic Uzbekistan a State unitary enterprise based on the right of operative management (State enterprise) may be formed on the base of property in State ownership [as amended by Law of 20 August 2015, No. ЗРУ-391. СЗ РУ (2015), item 33, no. 439].

The constitutive document of a State enterprise shall be its charter.

The firm name of a State enterprise based on the right of operative management must contain an indication that this enterprise is a State [enterprise].

The rights of a State enterprise to the property consolidated to it shall be determined in accordance with Articles 178 and 179 of the present Code.

The State shall bear subsidiary responsibility for the obligations of the State enterprise if its property is insufficient.

A State enterprise may be reorganized or liquidated by decision of which it was founded.

§ 3. Noncommercial Organizations

Article 73. Consumer Cooperative

A voluntary association of citizens on the basis of membership for the purpose of satisfying material (or property) requirements of participants effectuated by means of combining the property (share) contributions of the members thereof shall be deemed to be a consumer cooperative.

The charter of a consumer cooperative must contain, besides that specified in Article 43, paragraphs four and five, of the present Code, the following information: data concerning the amount of share contributions of the members of the cooperative; the composition and procedure for the making of share contributions by members of the cooperative and their responsibility for a violation of the obligation relating to the making of the contributions; the composition and competence of the management organs of the cooperative and the procedure for the adoption of decisions by them, including on questions, the decisions regarding which are adopted unanimously or by a qualified majority of votes; and the procedure for the covering by members of the cooperative of losses incurred by it.

The name of the consumer cooperative must contain an indication of the principal purpose of its activity, and also either the word "cooperative" or the words "consumer cooperative" or "consumer society".

The members of the consumer cooperative shall be obliged within three months after confirmation of the annual balance sheet to cover losses which have formed by means of additional contributions. In the event of the failure to fulfill this duty, the cooperative may be liquidated in a judicial proceeding at the demand of the creditors.

The members of a consumer cooperative shall bear subsidiary responsibility for its obligations within the limits of the uncontributed portion of the additional contribution of each member of the cooperative. In this event the members of the cooperative shall be liable jointly and severally.

The rules of the present Code on commercial organizations shall apply to the commercial activity of a consumer cooperative.

The legal status of consumer cooperatives, and also the rights and duties of their members, shall be determined in accordance with the present Code and other legislative acts.

Article 74. Social Associations

Social associations shall be deemed to be voluntary associations of citizens who have combined in the procedure established by law on the basis of a community of their interests in order to satisfy spiritual or other nonmaterial requirements.

Social and religious organizations shall have the right to effectuate production and other entrepreneurial activity provided for by their charters.

The participants (or members) of social associations shall not retain rights to property transferred in ownership by them to such organizations, including membership dues. They shall not be liable for the obligations of social associations in which they participate as members, and the said associations shall not be liable for the obligations of their members.

The peculiarities of the legal status of social associations shall be determined by a law.

Article 75. Social Foundations

A social foundation shall be deemed to be a non-State, noncommercial organization not having membership, created by citizens and/or juridical persons on the basis of voluntary property contributions, and pursuing philanthropic, social, cultural, educational, and other socially-useful purposes [as amended by Law of 30 April 2004, No. 621-II. C3 PY (2004), no. 25, item 287].

The property transferred to the social foundation by its founder(s) or testator shall be the ownership of the foundation. The founder(s) of the foundation or the executor of a will in the event a foundation is created according to a will shall not be liable for the obligations of the foundation, and the foundation shall not be liable for the obligations of its founder(s) or executor of the will [as amended by Law of 30 April 2004, No. 621-II. C3 PY (2004), no. 25, item 287].

The property of a social foundation shall be used for the fulfillment of charter purposes and tasks of the foundation and to cover administrative expenses. The foundation may in accordance with legislation engage in entrepreneurial activity within the limits corresponding to its charter purposes. The participation of the foundation in the charter fund (or charter capital) of commercial organizations shall be effectuated in the procedure established by legislation [as amended by Law of 30 April 2004, No. 621-II. C3 PY (2004), no. 25, item 287].

A social foundation shall be obliged annually to publish a report on its activity [as amended by Law of 30 April 2004, No. 621-II. C3 PY (2004), no. 25, item 287].

The procedure for the management of the social foundation and the procedure for forming its organs shall be determined by its charter.

The charter of a social foundation must, besides that specified in Article 43, paragraph four, of the present Code, contain the following information: the structure, powers, and procedure for forming the organs of the foundation, the procedure for the appointment (or election) and relieving of officials of organs of the foundation; sources of forming the property of the foundation; the rights and duties of the foundation; its representations and branches for the management of property; the procedure for opening representations and the creation of branches of the foundation; the procedure for the reorganization and liquidation of the foundation; the procedure for use of the property of the foundation in the event of its liquidation; and the procedure for making changes in and additions to the charter of the foundation [as amended by Law of 30 April 2004, No. 621-II. C3 PY (2004), no. 25, item 287].

The charter of the social foundation may contain a description of the symbols of the foundation which must be registered in the established procedure, and also other provisions not contrary to legislation [added by Law of 30 April 2004, No. 621-II. СЗ РУ (2004), no. 25, item 287].

The peculiarities of the legal status of social foundations shall be determined by legislation [added by Law of 30 April 2004, No. 621-II. СЗ РУ (2004), no. 25, item 287].

Article 76. Institutions

An institution shall be deemed to be an organization created by the owner in order to effectuate management, socio-cultural, or other functions of a noncommercial character and financed by it wholly or partially.

The rights of an institution to property consolidated to it and to property acquired by it shall be determined in accordance with Articles 178 and 180 of the present Code.

The institution shall be liable for its obligations with the monetary means at its disposition. The owner of the respective property shall bear subsidiary responsibility for its obligations in the event of their insufficiency.

The peculiarities of the legal status of individual types of State and other institutions shall be determined by legislation.

Article 77. Associations of Juridical Persons [as amended by Law of 15 December 2000 No. 175-II. Ведомости Олий Мажлиса (2001), no. 1-2, item 23]

Commercial organizations may for the purposes of coordinating their entrepreneurial activity, and also of representing and defending common property interests, combine into associations (or unions) and other associations which are noncommercial organizations. If by decision of the participants to an association (or union) and other association is entrusted the conducting of entrepreneurial activity, such associations (or unions) and other association shall be subject to transformation into an economic society or partnership in the procedure provided by the present Code, or may create economic societies or participate in them for the effectuation of entrepreneurial activity [as amended by Law of 15 December 2000 No. 175-II. Ведомости Олий Мажлиса (2001), no. 1-2, item 23].

Noncommercial organizations may for the purpose of coordinating their activity, and also representation and defense of common interests, create associations in the form of associations [*ассоциации*] or unions [as amended by Law of 15 December 2000 No. 175-II. Ведомости Олий Мажлиса (2001), no. 1-2, item 23].

An association (or union) or other association shall be a juridical person [as amended by Law of 15 December 2000 No. 175-II. Ведомости Олий Мажлиса (2001), no. 1-2, item 23].

Members of an association (or union) and other association shall retain their autonomy and the rights of a juridical person [as amended by Law of 15 December 2000 No. 175-II. Ведомости Олий Мажлиса (2001), no. 1-2, item 23].

An association (or union) and other association shall not be liable for the obligations of its members [as amended by Law of 15 December 2000 No. 175-II. Ведомости Олий Мажлиса (2001), no. 1-2, item 23].

Members of an association (or union) and other association shall bear subsidiary responsibility for its obligations in the amount and in the procedure provided for by the constitutive documents of the association (or union) and other association [as amended by Law of 15 December 2000 No. 175-II. Ведомости Олий Мажлиса (2001), no. 1-2, item 23].

The name of an association (or union) and other association must contain an indication of the principal subject of the activity thereof with inclusion of the word "association" or "union" or words specifying the type of association. The peculiarities of the legal status of associations of juridical persons may be established by legislation [as amended by Law of 15 December 2000 No. 175-II. Ведомости Олий Мажлиса (2001), no. 1-2, item 23].

Article 78. Agencies of Self-Government of Citizens

Agencies of self-government of citizens as juridical persons shall be participants of civil-law relations.

The property created or acquired by agencies of self-government of citizens shall be their ownership.

The legal status of agencies of self-government of citizens shall be determined by legislation.

Chapter 5. The State as Participant of Civil-Law Relations

Article 79. Participation of the State in Civil-Law Relations

The State shall participate in relations regulated by civil legislation on equal grounds with other participants of these relations.

Agencies of State power and administration and other agencies specially empowered by them shall participate in the name of the State in relations regulated by civil legislation.

The State shall be liable for its civil-law obligations with the assets in its ownership.

Article 80. Delimitation of Responsibility of State and Juridical Persons

A juridical person created by the State shall not be liable for its obligations. The State shall not be liable for the obligations of juridical persons created by it except for instances provided for by a law.

The rules of the present Article shall not extend to instances when the State on the basis of a contract concluded by it as assumed a suretyship (or guarantee) for obligations of the juridical person or the said juridical person assumed a suretyship (or guarantee) for obligations of the State.

Subsection 3. Objects

Chapter 6. General Provisions

Article 81. Types of Objects of Civil Rights

To objects of civil rights shall be relegated things, including money and securities, other articles, property, including property rights; work and services, inventions; industrial designs; works of science, literature, art, and other results of intellectual activity, and also personal nonproperty rights and other material and nonmaterial benefits.

Article 82. Circulability of Objects of Civil Rights

Objects of civil rights may be freely alienated or be transferred from one person to another by way of universal legal succession (inheritance, reorganization of juridical person) or by other means unless they have been withdrawn from turnover or are limited in turnover.

Types of objects of civil rights whose being in turnover is not permitted (objects withdrawn from turnover) must be expressly specified in a law.

Types of objects of civil rights which may belong only to specified participants of turnover or whose being in turnover is permitted by a special authorization (objects of limited circulability) shall be determined in the procedure established by a law.

Chapter 7. Material Benefits

Article 83. Types of Property

Property as an object of civil rights shall be subdivided into immoveable and moveable.

To immoveable property shall be relegated: plots of land and subsoil, buildings, installations, perennial plantings, and other property stably connected with land; that is, objects whose movement without commensurate damage to the designation thereof is impossible [as amended by Law of 5 April 2007, No. 3PУ-83. C3 PУ (2007), no. 14, item 132].

Other property also may be relegated by a law to immoveable.

The peculiarities of the acquisition and termination of rights to immoveable property shall be established by a law [as amended by Law of 7 November 2022, No. 3PУ-801].

Property not relegated to immoveable shall be deemed to be moveable property. The registration of rights to moveable property shall not be required except for instances specified in a law.

Article 84. State Registration of Immoveable

The right of ownership and other rights to a thing in an immovable, the origin thereof, transfer, limitation, and termination of these rights shall be subject to State registration.

The agency effectuating State registration of rights to an immovable and transactions with it shall be obliged upon the petition of the rightholder to certify the registration made by means of the issuance of a document concerning the registered right or transaction or by making inscriptions on the document submitted for registration.

The agency effectuating State registration of rights to an immovable and transactions with it shall be obliged to provide information concerning the registration made and the rights registered to any person.

The information shall be provided in any agency effectuating the registration of an immovable irrespective of the place of performing the registration.

A refusal of State registration of the right to an immovable or transaction with it or a violation of the periods of registration may be appealed to a court.

The procedure of State registration and the grounds for refusal of registration shall be established by legislation.

Article 85. Enterprise

An enterprise as a whole shall as a property complex be deemed to be an immoveable.

An enterprise as a whole or part thereof may be the object of a purchase-sale, pledge, lease, and other transactions connected with the establishment, change, and termination of rights to a thing.

Within an enterprise as a property complex shall be all types of property designated for its activity, including land plots, buildings, installations, equipment, tools, raw material, products, right of demand, debts, and also rights to designation which individualize the enterprise, its products, work, and services (firm name, trademarks, service marks), and other exclusive rights, unless provided otherwise by a law or contract.

Article 86. Classification of Things

Things as an object of civil rights shall be subdivided into:

individually-determined and determined by generic indicia;

divisible and indivisible;

consumable and nonconsumable;

principal things and appurtenances;

complex things.

Article 87. Individually-Determined Things and Things Determined by Generic Characteristics

A thing endowed with special indicia inherent only to it which separate it from the mass of homogeneous things and thereby individualize this thing shall be deemed to be individually-determined. To individually-determined things shall be relegated unique, that is, things single in their nature, and also things solitary by a determined means (seal, placement of special marks, conferment of number, figure, and the like).

Individually-determined things shall be nonreplaceable.

Things determined by generic indicia shall be deemed to be things possessing indicia inherent to all things of that nature and determined by number, weight, measure, and the like.

Things determined by generic characteristics shall be replaceable.

Article 88. Divisible and Indivisible Things

A thing as a result of the separation of which each part thereof retains the property of the whole and does not lose in so doing its economic (or special-purpose) designation shall be deemed to be divisible.

A thing, as a result of the separation of which part thereof loses the properties of the initial thing and changes its economic (or special-purpose) designation, shall be deemed to be indivisible.

Article 89. Things Consumable and Nonconsumable

Things which as a result of one-time use are destroyed or cease to exist in initial form (raw material, fuel, products of nourishment, and so forth) shall be deemed to be consumable.

Things intended for repeated use, retaining in so doing their initial form for an extended time and wearing out gradually (buildings, equipment, means of transport, and the like), shall be deemed to be nonconsumable.

Article 90. Principal Thing and Appurtenance

An autonomous thing connected with another thing (appurtenance) by the essence of relations arising during the use thereof shall be deemed to be the principal thing.

A thing called upon to serve a principal thing and connected therewith by a common purpose shall be deemed to be an appurtenance.

An appurtenance shall follow the fate of the principal thing unless established otherwise by legislative acts or a contract.

Article 91. Complex Things

If various kinds of thing form a single whole presupposing the use thereof for a purpose determined by the essence of the combination, they shall be considered to be one thing (complex thing).

The operation of a transaction concluded with regard to a complex thing shall extend to all of its constituent parts unless provided otherwise by a contract.

Article 92. Right to Fruits and Revenues

Fruits and revenues brought by a thing shall belong to the owner of the thing unless provided otherwise by a law or by the contract.

Article 93. Fauna

To fauna shall apply the general rules on property insofar as not established otherwise by legislation.

When effectuating rights the cruel treatment of fauna shall not be permitted.

Article 94. Money (Currency)

The som shall be monetary unit of the Republic Uzbekistan.

The som shall be the legal means of payment obligatory for acceptance at face value.

Payments shall be effectuated in the form of cash and noncash settlement accounts.

The instances, procedure, and conditions for the settlement of accounts in foreign currency shall be determined by legislation.

Article 95. Currency Valuables

The types of property deemed to be currency valuables and the procedure for concluding transactions with them shall be determined by a law.

The right of ownership in currency valuables shall be defended on the general grounds.

Article 96. Securities

Securities shall be documents certifying, in compliance with the established form and obligatory requisites, property rights whose effectuation or transfer shall be possible only in the event of the presentation thereof.

With the transfer of the securities shall pass all rights in aggregate which are certified by them.

There shall be relegated to securities: bond, bill of exchange, cheque, deposit and savings certificates, bill of lading, stock, and other documents which have been relegated to securities by legislation [as amended by Law of 22 September 2009, No. ЗРУ-223. СЗ РУ (2009), no. 39, item 423].

Chapter 8. Nonmaterial Benefits

Article 97. Results of Intellectual Activity

In the instances and in the procedure established by the present Code and other laws the exclusive right of a citizen or juridical person shall be recognized to objectively expressed results of intellectual activity and means of individualization of a juridical person equated thereto, products of a natural or juridical person, work or services fulfilled by them (firm name, trademark, service mark, and others).

The use of the results of intellectual activity and the means of individualization which are the object of exclusive rights may be effectuated by third persons only with the authorization of the possessor of the right [as amended by Law of 16 January 2007, No. ЗРУ-79. СЗ РУ (2007), no. 3, item 21].

Article 98. Employment and Commercial Secrecy

Information constituting an employment and commercial secret, when the information has actual or potential commercial value by virtue of its being unknown to third persons for whom there is no free access on legal grounds and the possessor of the information takes measures to protect the confidentiality thereof, shall be defended by civil legislation.

Article 99. Personal Property Rights and Other Nonmaterial Benefits

Life and health, the honor and dignity of the person, personal inviolability, business reputation, inviolability of private life, private and family secrecy, the right to name, the right of authorship, other personal nonproperty rights and other nonmaterial benefits which belong to a citizen from birth or by virtue of a law shall be inalienable and not transferable by other means. In the instance and in the procedure provided for by a law, personal property rights and other nonmaterial benefits which belonged to a deceased person may be effectuated and defended by other persons, including heirs of the possessor of the right.

Article 100. Defense of Honor, Dignity, and Business Reputation

A citizen shall have the right to demand through a court the refutation of information defaming his honor, dignity, or business reputation, unless the disseminator of such information proves that it corresponds to reality.

Upon the demand of interested persons the defense of the honor and dignity of a citizen shall also be permitted after his death.

If information defaming the honor, dignity, or business reputation of the citizen has been disseminated in the mass media, it must be refuted in the same mass media.

If the said information is contained in a document emanating from an organization, the document shall be subject to replacement or recall.

The procedure for refutation in other instances shall be established by a court.

A citizen with respect to whom the mass media have published information impinging upon his rights or interests protected by a law shall have the right to publish in his defense in the same mass media.

If the decision of a court has not been fulfilled, the court shall have the right to impose a fine on the violator to be recovered in the amount and in the procedure provided for by legislation. The payment of the fine shall not relieve the violator from the duty to fulfill the action provided for by the court decision.

A citizen with respect to whom information has been disseminated which defames his honor, dignity or business reputation shall have the right, together with the refutation of such information, to demand compensation of losses and moral harm caused by the dissemination thereof.

The rules of the present Article concerning the defense of business reputation of a citizen respectively shall apply to the defense of the business reputation of a juridical person.

Subsection 4. Transactions and Representation

Chapter 9. Transactions

§ 1. Concept, Types, and Form of Transactions

Article 101. Concept of Transactions

The actions of citizens and juridical persons directed towards the establishment, change, or termination of civil rights and duties shall be deemed to be transactions.

Article 102. Types of Transactions

Transactions may be unilateral, bilateral, or multilateral (contracts).

A transaction for the conclusion of which in accordance with legislation or by agreement of the parties the expression of the will of one party is necessary and sufficient shall be considered to be unilateral.

The expression of the concordant will of two parties (bilateral transaction), or three or more parties (multilateral transaction) shall be necessary for the conclusion of a contract.

Article 103. Legal Regulation of Unilateral Transactions

A unilateral transaction shall create duties for the person who concluded the transaction. It may create duties for other persons only in the instances established by legislative acts or by agreement with these persons.

The general provisions on obligations and on contracts (Section III of the present Code) shall apply to unilateral transactions respectively insofar as this is not contrary to legislation or to the nature and essence of the transaction.

Article 104. Transactions Concluded Under a Condition

A transaction shall be considered to be concluded under a condition subsequent if the parties have made the arising of rights and duties dependent upon a circumstance relative to which it is unknown as to whether this will ensue or not.

A transaction shall be considered to be concluded under a condition precedent if the parties have made the termination of rights and duties dependent upon a circumstance relative to which it is unknown whether this will ensue or not.

If the ensuing of the condition is obstructed by a party not in good faith for whom the ensuing of the condition is disadvantageous, the condition shall be deemed to have ensued.

If the ensuing of the condition is facilitated by a party not in good faith for whom the ensuing of the condition is advantageous, the condition shall be deemed not to have ensued.

Article 105. Form of Transactions

Transactions shall be concluded orally or in writing (simple or notarial).

Silence shall be deemed to be an expression of will to conclude a transaction in the instances provided for by legislation or by agreement of the parties.

Article 106. Oral Form of Transaction

A transaction for which the written form has not been established by legislation or by agreement of the parties may be concluded orally, including those to be performed when concluding it. Such transaction shall be considered to be concluded also when from the behavior of the person his will to conclude the transaction is manifest.

A transaction confirmed by the issuance of a token, ticket, or other ordinarily accepted mark of confirmation shall be deemed to be concluded orally unless established otherwise by legislation.

Transactions in performance of a contract concluded in writing may, by agreement of the parties, be concluded orally unless this is contrary to legislation or a contract.

Article 107. Written Form of Transaction

A transaction concluded in written form must be signed by the parties or their representatives unless it arises otherwise from the customs of business turnover.

The use of means of facsimile copying of a signature, if this is not contrary to legislation or the requirement of one of the participants, shall be permitted when concluding a transaction.

Bilateral transactions may be concluded by means of the exchange of documents, each of which is signed by the party from which it emanates.

To the concluding of a transaction in written form shall be equated, unless established otherwise by legislation or agreement of the parties, the exchange of letters, telegrams, phonograms, teletypes, faxes, or other documents which determine the subjects and the content of their expression of will.

Additional requirements which must correspond to the form of the transaction (conclusion on a letterhead of a determined form, affixing a seal (when there is a seal), and others) and providing for the consequences of the failure to comply with these requirements may be established by legislation and by agreement of the parties [as amended by Law of 20 August 2015, No. 3PY-391. C3 PY (2015), no. 33, item 439].

If a citizen as a consequence of physical defect, illness, or illiteracy can not sign in his own hand, then at his request another citizen may sign the transaction. The signature of the last must be certified by a notary or by another official having the right to perform such a notarial action, specifying the reasons by virtue of which the person concluding the transaction could not sign it in his own hand.

The party who has performed a transaction concluded in written form shall have the right to demand a document from the other party confirming performance. The party who has performed an oral entrepreneurial transaction, except for transactions to be performed when concluding them, shall have the same right.

Article 108. Simple Written Form of Transaction

There shall be concluded in simple written form, except for transactions requiring notarial certification:

(1) transactions of juridical persons between themselves and with citizens;

(2) transactions of citizens between themselves for an amount exceeding not less than ten times the amount of established minimum base calculation amounts, and in the instances provided for by a law, irrespective of the amount of the transaction [as amended by Law of 3 December 2019, No. ЗРУ-586].

Compliance with the simple written form shall not be required for transactions which in accordance with Article 106 of the present Code may be concluded orally.

Article 109. Consequences of Failure to Comply with Simple Written Form of Transaction

The failure to comply with the simple written form of a transaction shall not entail the invalidity thereof, but shall deprive the party of the right, in the event of a dispute, to confirm the conclusion, content, or performance thereof by witness testimony.

The parties shall have the right to confirm the conclusion, content, or performance of a transaction by written or other evidence.

In the instances expressly specified in a law or in the agreement of the parties the failure to comply with the simple written form of a transaction shall entail its invalidity.

Article 110. Notarial Certification of Transaction

The notarial certification of a transaction shall be effectuated by means of the performing on the document of an endorsement of certification corresponding to the requirements of Article 107 of the present Code by a notary or other official having the right to perform such a notarial action.

Notarial certification of transactions shall be obligatory:

(1) in the instances specified in a law;

(2) at the request of any of the parties.

Article 111. State Registration of Transactions

Transactions with land plots and other immovable property (alienation, mortgage, long-term lease, acceptance of inheritance, and others) shall be subject to State registration.

The procedure for the registration of transactions with an immoveable and conducting the respective registers shall be determined by legislation.

State registration of transactions with movable property of determined types may be established by legislation.

Article 112. Consequences of Failure to Comply with Notarial Form of Transaction and Requirements for Registration Thereof

The failure to comply with the notarial form or the requirements concerning State registration of a transaction shall entail its invalidity. Such a transaction shall be considered to be null.

If one of the parties wholly or partially has performed a transaction requiring notarial certification, and the other party has evaded notarial formalization of the transaction, the court shall have the right at the demand of the party who performed the transaction to deem the transaction to be valid. In this event subsequent notarial formalization of the transaction shall not be required.

If a transaction requiring State registration has been concluded in the proper form but one of the parties evades the registration thereof, a court shall have the right at the demand of the other party to render a decision concerning registration of the transaction. In this event the transaction shall be registered in accordance with the decision of the court.

In the instances provided for by paragraphs two and three of the present Article the party who unjustifiably evades notarial certification or State registration of a transaction must compensate the other party for losses caused by the delay in concluding the transaction.

§ 2. Invalidity of Transactions

Article 113. Contested and Null Transactions

A transaction shall be invalid on the grounds established by the present Code by virtue of being deemed such by a court (contested transaction) or irrespective of such deeming (null transaction).

A demand to deem a contested transaction to be invalid may be brought by the persons specified in the present Code.

A demand concerning the application of the consequences of the invalidity of a null transaction may be presented by any interested person. The court shall have the right to apply such consequences at its own initiative.

Article 114. General Provisions on Consequences of Invalidity of Transaction

An invalid transaction shall not entail legal consequences, except for those which are connected with its invalidity, and shall be invalid from the moment of its conclusion.

In the event of the invalidity of a transaction, each of the parties shall be obliged to return to the other everything received according to the transaction, and if it is impossible to return that received in kind (including when that received is expressed in the use of property, work fulfilled, or service provided), to compensate its value in money, unless other consequences of the invalidity of the transaction have been provided for by a law.

Article 115. Failure to Comply with Form of Transaction Required by a Law

The failure to comply with the form required by a law shall entail the invalidity of the transaction only when such consequence is expressly specified in a law.

Article 116. Invalidity of Transaction Not Conforming to Requirements of Legislation

A transaction whose content does not correspond to the requirements of legislation, and also concluded for a purpose knowingly contrary to the foundations of the legal order or morality, shall be null. The rules provided for by Article 114, paragraph two, of the present Code shall apply to such transaction.

Article 117. Invalidity of Transaction Concluded by Person Who Has Not Attained Fourteen Years of Age

A transaction concluded by a person who has not attained fourteen years of age shall be null, except for transactions provided for by Article 29, paragraph two, of the present Code.

Each of the parties with regard to such transaction shall be obliged to return to the other party everything received with regard to the transaction, and if it is impossible to return that received in kind — to compensate the value thereof in money. The party which has dispositive legal capacity shall be obliged, in addition, to compensate the other party for real damage incurred by it if it knew or should have known about the lack of dispositive legal capacity of the other party.

Article 118. Invalidity of Transaction Concluded by Minor from Fourteen to Eighteen Years of Age

A transaction concluded by a minor from fourteen to eighteen years of age without the consent of his parents, adoptive parents, or guardian in the instances when such consent is required in accordance with Article 27 of the present Code may be deemed by a court to be invalid upon the suit of the parents, adoptive parents, or guardian. If such transaction is deemed to be invalid, the rules provided for by Article 117, paragraph two, of the present Code shall apply.

The rules of the present Article shall not extend to transactions of minors who have come to have full dispositive legal capacity in the instances provided for by Article 22, paragraph two, and Article 28 of the present Code.

Article 119. Invalidity of Transaction Concluded by Citizen Deemed to Lack Dispositive Legal Capacity

A transaction concluded by a citizen deemed to lack dispositive legal capacity as a consequence of mental disturbance (or mental illness or feeble-mindedness) shall be null. The rules provided for by Article 117, paragraph two, of the present Code shall apply to such transaction.

Article 120. Invalidity of Transaction Concluded by Citizen Limited in Dispositive Legal Capacity

A transaction concluded without the consent of the guardian by a citizen limited in dispositive legal capacity as a consequence of the abuse of alcoholic beverages or narcotic means may be deemed by a court to be invalid. If such transaction is deemed to be invalid, the rules provided for by Article 117, paragraph two, of the present Code shall apply.

The rules of the present Article shall not extend to petty domestic transactions to be performed when concluding them in accordance with Article 29, paragraph two, of the present Code.

Article 121. Invalidity of Transaction Concluded by Citizen Not Capable of Understanding the Significance of His Actions or Guiding Them

A transaction concluded by a citizen, although having dispositive legal capacity but at the moment of concluding it was in such a state that he was not capable of understanding the significance of his actions or guiding them, may be deemed by a court to be invalid upon the suit of this citizen or other persons whose rights or interests protected by law have been violated as a result of the conclusion thereof.

A transaction concluded by a citizen who is subsequently deemed to lack dispositive legal capacity may be deemed by a court to be invalid upon the suit of his trustee if it is proved that at the moment of concluding the transaction the citizen was not capable of understanding the significance of his actions or guiding them.

If a transaction is deemed to be invalid on the grounds of the present Article, the rules provided for by Article 117, paragraph two, of the present Code shall apply.

The other party must compensate expenses incurred, loss, or damage of property to the party which at the moment of concluding the transaction could not understand the significance of his actions or guide them if he knew or should have known about the state of the citizen who concluded the contract with it.

Article 122. Invalidity of Transaction Concluded Under Influence of Delusion

A transaction concluded under the influence of delusion having material significance may be deemed to be invalid by a court upon the suit of the party who acted under the influence of delusion.

Delusion relative to the nature of the transaction, the identity or qualities of its subject which significantly reduce the possibility of using it for its purpose shall have material significance. Delusion relative to the motives for the transaction shall not have material significance.

If the transaction is deemed to be invalid as concluded under the influence of delusion, the rules provided for by Article 114, paragraph two, of the present Code shall apply.

In addition, the party at whose suit the transaction was deemed to be invalid shall have the right to demand from the other party compensation for real damage caused to it if it is proved that the delusion arose through the fault of the other party. If this is not proved, the party at whose suit the transaction was deemed to be invalid shall be obliged to compensate the other party at its demand for real damage caused to it even if the delusion arose through circumstances not dependent upon the deluded party.

Article 123. Invalidity of Transaction Concluded Under Influence of Fraud, Coercion, Threat, or Ill-Intentioned Agreement of Representative of One Party with Other Party or Confluence of Grave Circumstances

A transaction concluded under the influence of fraud, coercion, threat, or ill-intentioned agreement of a representative of one party with the other party, and also a transaction which a citizen was forced to conclude as a consequence of the confluence of grave circumstances on conditions extremely disadvantageous for himself which the other party took advantage of (cabalistic transaction), may be deemed by a court to be invalid upon the suit of the victim.

If the transaction was deemed invalid on one of the grounds specified, then the other party shall return to the victim everything performed by it under the transaction, and if it is impossible to return everything received in kind, the value thereof shall be compensated in money. Property received under a transaction by the victim from the other party, and also that due it in compensation for that transferred to the other party, shall go to the revenue of the State. If it is impossible to transfer the property to the revenue of the State in kind the value thereof in money shall be recovered. In addition, the victim shall be compensated by the other party for expenses incurred by it, and the loss of or damage to its property.

Article 124. Invalidity of Fictitious and Sham Transactions

A transaction concluded only for form, without the intention to create legal consequences, shall be null (fictitious transaction).

If a transaction is concluded for the purpose of concealing another transaction (sham transaction), then the rules relating to such transaction which the parties actually had in view shall apply.

Article 125. Invalidity of Transaction Exceeding the Limits of Its Legal Capacity of Juridical Person

A transaction concluded by a juridical person which is contrary to the charter tasks or does not have a license to engage in the respective activity may be deemed by a court to be invalid upon the suit of its founder (or participant), or empowered State agency.

Article 126. Consequences of Limitation of Powers to Conclude Transaction

If the powers of a person to conclude a transaction have been limited by a contract or the powers of the organ of a juridical person, by its constitutive documents, in comparison with those they have been determined in a power of attorney or in a law, or which may be considered to be obvious from the situation in which the transaction was concluded, and when concluding it such person or organ exceeded the limits of these limitations, the transaction may be deemed by a court to be invalid upon the suit of the person in whose interests the limitations were established only in instances when it is proved that the other party to the transaction knew or knowingly should have known about the said limitations.

Article 127. Moment from Which Transaction is Considered to be Invalid

A transaction deemed to be invalid shall be considered to be invalid from the moment of its conclusion. If it arises from the content of the transaction that it may only be terminated in future, the operation of the transaction deemed to be invalid shall terminate in future.

Article 128. Consequences of Invalidity of Part of Trans-action

The invalidity of part of the transaction shall not entail the invalidity of its other parts if it is possible to suppose that the transaction would have been concluded also without including the invalid part thereof.

Chapter 10. Representation and Power of Attorney

Article 129. Representation

A transaction concluded by one person (representative) in the name of another person (person represented) by virtue of a power based on a power of attorney, law, decision of a court, or act of an empowered State agency shall directly create, change, and terminate civil rights and duties of the person represented.

The conclusion through a representative of a transaction which by its character may be concluded only personally, and also other transactions in instances provided for by legislative acts, shall not be permitted.

A representative may not conclude transactions in the name of the person represented either with respect to himself personally or with respect to another person whose representative he is simultaneously, except for instances of commercial representation.

Article 130. Representation of Person With Dispositive Legal Capacity

Persons with dispositive legal capacity may conclude transactions through representatives chosen by them except for instances when the transaction by its character may be concluded only personally, and also instances specified in a law.

Article 131. Representation of Person Who Lacks Dispositive Legal Capacity

The parents, adoptive parents, and trustees shall conclude transactions in the name of citizens who lack dispositive legal capacity.

Article 132. Representation Without Power

A transaction concluded in the name of another person which is not empowered or exceeding the power shall create, change, and terminate rights and duties for the person represented only in the event of subsequent approval of this transaction by the person represented. Such transaction shall be deemed to be approved also if the person represented performed actions testifying to his acceptance of the performance.

Subsequent approval of the transaction by the person represented shall make it valid from the moment of conclusion.

Article 133. Commercial Representation

A person who permanently and autonomously is representing in the name of entrepreneurs when they conclude contracts (commercial representative) shall operate on the basis of a written contract containing an indication of the power of the representative, and in the absence of such indications, also a power of attorney.

A commercial representative may simultaneously represent the interests of various parties to a contract concluded with the participation thereof only with the consent of these parties also in other instances provided for by legislation.

A commercial representative shall have the right to demand the payment of stipulated remuneration and costs incurred by him when performing the commission from the parties to the contract in equal participatory shares unless provided otherwise by agreement between them.

A commercial representative shall be obliged to preserve the secrecy of the information which became known to him concerning trade transactions also after the performance of the commission given to him.

The peculiarities of commercial representation in individual spheres of entrepreneurial activity shall be established by legislation.

Article 134. Power of Attorney

A power of attorney shall be deemed to be a written power issued by one person (principal) to another person (attorney) for representation to third persons. The attorney shall operate within the limits of the powers presented to him under the power of attorney.

A power of attorney in the name of a juridical person, and also to a juridical person, may be issued only for the conclusion of transactions which are not contrary to the purposes of the activity of the juridical person specified in the charter (or statute).

Article 135. Form of Power of Attorney

A power of attorney shall be formalized in simple written form or notarial.

A power of attorney for the conclusion of transactions requiring a notarial form or actions with respect to juridical persons must be notarially certified, except for instances provided for by Articles 136, 137, and 138 of the present Code and other instances when another form of power of attorney is established by legislation.

Article 136. Powers of Attorney Equated to Notarially Certified

There shall be equated to notarially certified powers of attorney:

powers of attorney of military servicemen and other persons being treated in military hospitals, sanatoriums, and other military treatment institutions certified by the heads, their deputies for medical affairs, and the senior or duty doctors of these institutions, except powers of attorney for the driving and disposition of means of motor vehicle transport [as amended by Law of 27 September 2006, No. 3PY-56. C3 PY (2006), no. 39, item 385];

powers of attorney of military servicemen, and in centers for the stationing of military units, formations, institutions, and military training institutions where there are no notarial offices and other agencies which perform notarial actions, also the powers of attorney of workers and employees, members of their families and members of the families of military servicemen certified by the commanders (or heads) of these units, formations, institutions, or educational institutions, except powers of attorney for the driving and disposition of means of motor vehicle transport [as amended by Law of 27 September 2006, No. ЗРУ-56. СЗ РУ (2006), no. 39, item 385];

powers of attorney of persons in places of deprivation of freedom or confined under guard certified by the heads of the respective institutions, except powers of attorney for the driving and disposition of means of motor vehicle transport [as amended by Law of 27 September 2006, No. ЗРУ-56. СЗ РУ (2006), no. 39, item 385].

Article 137. Other Forms of Power of Attorney

A power of attorney to receive correspondence, including monetary and parcel, to receive earnings and other payments connected with labor relations, to receive the remuneration of authors and inventors, pensions, benefits, and stipends, and also amounts from institutions of banks may be certified also by the organization in which the principal works or studies, housing-operations organization servicing the house in which he resides, agencies of self-government of citizens at his place of residence or the administration of a treatment institution in which a citizen is situated for treatment.

Article 138. Power of Attorney of Juridical Person

A power of attorney in the name of a juridical person shall be issued over the signature of the director, with the seal of this juridical person (when there is a seal) affixed [as amended by Law of 20 August 2015, No. ЗРУ-391. СЗ РУ (2015), no. 33, item 439].

A power of attorney in the name of a juridical person based on State ownership for the receipt or issuance of money and other property valuables must be signed also by the chief (or senior) bookkeeper of this juridical person. The procedure for the issuance and form of power of attorney for the performance of operations in a bank shall be determined by legislation.

Article 139. Period of Power of Attorney

A power of attorney may be issued for a period of not more than three years. If the period has not been specified in the power of attorney, it shall retain force for one year from the date of the issuance thereof.

A power of attorney in which the date of its issuance has not been specified shall be invalid.

A power of attorney certified by a notary and intended for the performance of actions beyond the limits of the Republic Uzbekistan and not containing an indication of the period of its operation shall retain force until the revocation thereof by the person who has issued the power of attorney.

Article 140. Transfer of Powers Under Power of Attorney to Another Person (Transfer of Power of Attorney)

A person to whom the power of attorney was issued must personally perform those actions for which he is empowered. He may transfer the power of attorney to perform them to another person if empowered to do so by the power of attorney or forced by virtue of circumstances in order to protect the interests of the person who issued the power of attorney.

A power of attorney under which powers are transferred to another person issued must be notarially certified, except for instances provided for by Articles 136, 137, and 138 of the present Code.

The period of operation of a power of attorney issued under a transfer of power of attorney may not exceed the period of operation of the basic power of attorney on the basis of which it was issued.

The person who transferred the power of attorney to another person must notify the person who issued the power of attorney thereof and communicate to him necessary information about this person and his place of residence. The failure to fulfill the said duties shall place on the person who transferred the power responsibility for the actions of the person to whom he transferred the power as they were his own.

Article 141. Termination of Power of Attorney

The operation of a power of attorney shall terminate as a consequence of:

(1) expiry of the period of the power of attorney;

(2) revocation of the power of attorney by the person who issued it;

(3) renunciation by the person to whom the power of attorney was issued;

(4) termination of the activity of the juridical person in whose name the power of attorney was issued;

(5) termination of the activity of the juridical person to whom the power of attorney was issued;

(6) deeming of a citizen to whom the power of attorney was issued to lack dispositive legal capacity, to be of limited dispositive legal capacity, to be missing, or to be dead;

(7) deeming of the citizen to whom the power of attorney was issued to lack dispositive legal capacity, to be of limited dispositive legal capacity, to be missing or to be dead.

A person who issued the power of attorney may at any time revoke the power of attorney, and the person to whom the power of attorney was issued, to renounce it. An agreement concerning the waiver of this right shall be invalid.

The transfer of a power of attorney shall lose force with the termination of the power of attorney.

Article 142. Notification of Persons Concerning Termination of Power of Attorney

A person who has issued a power of attorney shall be obliged to notify the person to whom the power of attorney was issued about the revocation thereof, as well as third persons known to him with respect to whom the power of attorney was issued for representation. The same duty shall be placed on the legal successors of the person who issued a power of attorney in instances of the termination thereof on the grounds provided for in Article 141, paragraph one, subpoints (4)-(7), of the present Code.

Article 143. Actions Performed by Person To Whom Power of Attorney Was Issued After Termination of Power of Attorney

The actions performed by the person to whom a power of attorney was issued before this person knew or should have known about its termination shall retain force for the person who issued the power of attorney or his legal successors with respect to third persons.

The actions performed by the person to whom the power of attorney was issued after this person knew or should have known about the termination of the power of attorney shall not give rise to rights and duties for the person who issued the power of attorney.

The rule of this Article shall not apply if the third person knew or should have known that the operation of the power of attorney had terminated.

Article 144. Duty to Return Power of Attorney

Upon the termination of the operation of a power of attorney the person to whom it was issued or his heirs (or legal successors) must immediately return the power of attorney.

Subsection 5. Periods. Limitations

Chapter 11. Calculation of Periods

Article 145. Determination of Period

A period established by legislation or a transaction, and also designated by a court, shall be determined by a calendar date or by the expiry of a period of time which shall be calculated by years, months, weeks, days, or hours.

A period may also be determined by specifying an event which must inevitably ensue.

Article 146. Commencement of Period Determined by Period of Time

The running of a period determined by a period of time shall commence on the following day after the calendar date or ensuing of the event by which its commencement is determined.

Article 147. Ending of Period Determined by Period of Time

A period calculated by years shall expire in the corresponding month and date of the last year of the period.

The rules for periods calculated by months shall apply to a period calculated by a half-year.

To a period calculated by quarters of a year shall apply the rules for periods calculated by months. The quarter shall be considered to be equal to three months, and the quarters shall be calculated from the beginning of the year.

A period calculated by months shall expire on the corresponding date of the last month of the period.

A period determined as a half-month shall be considered as a period calculated by days and shall be considered to be equal to fifteen days.

If the ending of a period calculated by months comes in a month in which there is no corresponding date, the period shall expire on the last day of that month.

A period calculated by weeks shall expire on the corresponding day of the last week of the period.

Article 148. Procedure for Performing Actions on Last Day of Period

If a period has been designated for performing any action whatever, it may be fulfilled up to 24:00 hours of the last day of the period.

If this action had to be performed in an organization, the period shall expire at the hour when in this organization the respective operations terminate according to the established rules.

All written applications and notifications and money transfers handed in to a communications organization or transferred by other means of communication before 24:00 hours of the last day of the period shall be considered to be made within the period.

Chapter 12. Limitations

Article 149. Concept of Limitations

A limitation is the period within the limits of which a person may defend his violated right by means of bringing a suit.

Article 150. General Period of Limitations

The general period of limitations shall be three years.

Article 151. Special Periods of Limitations

Special periods of limitations may be established for individual types of demands by legislation which are reduced or are longer in comparison with the general period [as amended by Law of 20 March 2019, No. ЗРУ-531].

The rules of Articles 152-162 of the present Code shall extend to special periods of limitation unless established otherwise by a law.

Article 152. Invalidity of Agreement to Change Periods of Limitations

Periods of limitations and the procedure for calculating them may not be changed by agreement of the parties.

The grounds for the suspension and interruption of the running of periods of limitations shall be established by the present Code.

Article 153. Application of Limitations

A demand concerning the defense of a violated right shall be accepted for consideration by a court irrespective of the expiry of the period of limitations.

Limitations shall be applied by a court only upon the application of the party to the dispute which was made before the rendering of the decision by the court.

The expiry of the period of limitations concerning the application of which a party to the dispute has applied for shall be grounds for the court to render a decision to reject the suit.

Article 154. Commencement of Running of Period of Limitations

The running of the period of limitations shall commence from the day when the person knew or should have known about the violation of his right. Exceptions from this rule shall be established by the present Code and by other laws.

With regard to obligations with a determined period of performance, the running of the limitations shall commence upon the end of the period for performance.

With regard to obligations the period for the performance of which has not been determined or has been determined as the moment of demand, the running of limitations shall commence from the moment when the right arises with the creditor to submit a demand concerning the performance of the obligation, and if the debtor is granted an exemption period for performance of such demand, the calculation of limitations shall commence upon the ending of the said period.

With regard to regressive obligations the running of the limitations shall commence from the moment of performance of the principal obligation.

Article 155. Period of Limitations in Event of Change of Persons in Obligation

The change of persons in an obligation shall not entail a change of the period of limitations and the procedure for calculating it.

Article 156. Suspension of Running of Period of Limitations

The running of the period of limitations shall be suspended:

(1) if the bringing of suit has been hindered by an extraordinary and unavoidable event under the particular conditions (insuperable force);

(2) by virtue of a deferral for the performance of an obligation established by the Government of the Republic Uzbekistan (moratorium);

(3) if the plaintiff or defendant is in the Armed Forces, border guard, or internal forces which are transferred to a military situation;

(4) if the legal representatives of a person who lacks dispositive legal capacity are absent;

(5) by virtue of the suspension of the operation of an act of legislation regulating the respective relation;

(6) in the event of the conclusion of an agreement on conducting the procedure of mediation [added by Law of 20 March 2019, No. 3PY-531]

The running of the period of limitations shall be suspended if the circumstances specified in the present Article arose or have continued to exist during the last six months of the period of limitations, and if this period is less than six months, the running of the period of limitations.

The running of the period shall continue from the date of termination of the circumstances serving as the grounds for suspension of the limitation, the remaining part of the period being lengthened up to six months, and if the period of limitations is less than six months, up to the period of limitations.

Article 157. Interruption of Running of Period of Limitations

The running of the period of limitations shall be interrupted by bringing suit in the established procedure, and also by the performance of actions by the obliged person which testify to recognition of the debt.

After the interruption, the running of the period of limitations shall commence anew, and the time which elapsed before interruption shall not be calculated in the new period.

Article 158. Running of Period of Limitations in Event of Leaving Suit Without Consideration

If a suit has been left without consideration by a court, then the running of the period of limitations which commenced before bringing suit shall continue in the general procedure.

If a suit brought in a criminal case has been left by a court without consideration, then the running of the period of limitations which commenced before bringing suit shall be suspended until the entry into legal force of the judgment by which the suit was left without consideration, and the time during which the limitation was suspended shall not be calculated in the period of limitations. In so doing if the remaining portion of the period is less than six months, it shall be lengthened up to six months.

Article 159. Restoration of Period of Limitations

If the court deems the reason for the lapsing of the period of limitations to be justifiable, the right violated shall be subject to defense. The reasons for the lapse of a period of limitations may be deemed to be justifiable if they occurred in the last six months of the period of limitations, and if this period is equal to six months or to less than six months, the running of the period of limitations.

Article 160. Suspension, Interruption and Restoration of Special Period of Limitations

The rules concerning the suspension, interruption, and restoration of the period of limitations (Articles 156, 157, and 159 of the present Code) also shall apply to a special period of limitations unless established otherwise by a law.

Article 161. Performance of Duty Upon Expiry of Period of Limitations

A person who has performed a duty upon the expiry of the period of limitations shall not have the right to demand back that which has been performed, irrespective of the fact that at the moment of performance he knew or did not know about the expiry of the limitations.

Article 162. Application of Period of Limitations to Additional Demands

The period of limitations regarding additional demands (penalty, pledge, suretyship, and the like) shall expire with the expiry of the period of limitations regarding the principal demand.

Article 163. Demands to Which Limitations Do Not Extend

Limitations shall not extend to:

demands concerning the defense of personal nonproperty rights and other nonmaterial benefits, except for instances provided for by legislation;

demands of depositors against a bank concerning the issuance of deposits;

demands concerning compensation of harm caused to the life or health of a citizen. Demands presented upon the expiry of the period of limitations shall be satisfied for not more than three years preceding the bringing of suit;

demands concerning compensation of damage caused by a crime;

demands of the owner or other possessor concerning the elimination of any violations of his right, although these violations were not connected with a deprivation of possession (Article 231 of the present Code) [as amended by Law of 20 March 2019, No. 3PY-531];

demands concerning the return of property which represents historical, cultural, and scientific-artistic value and other valuable objects exported beyond the limits of the country before the proclamation of its independence;

other demands in the instances established by a law.

Section II. Right of Ownership and Other Rights to Thing

Chapter 13. General Provisions

Article 164. Concept of Right of Ownership

The right of ownership is the right of a person to possess, use, and dispose of property belonging to him at his discretion and in his interests, and also to demand the elimination of any violations of his right of ownership from whosoever they emanate. The right of ownership is without limit of time.

Article 165. Content of Rights to Thing of Persons Who Are Not Owners

The rights to a thing, together with the right of ownership, shall be in particular:

the right of economic jurisdiction and the right of operative management;

the right of inheritable possession for life of a land plot;

the right of permanent possession and use of a land plot;

servitudes.

The transfer of the right of ownership to property to another person shall not be grounds for the termination of other rights to a thing to this property unless provided otherwise by legislation.

The rights of a thing of a person who is not the owner shall be defended against the violation thereof in the procedure provided for by Article 232 of the present Code.

Article 166. Inviolability of Ownership

Ownership shall be inviolable and protected by a law.

The inviolability of ownership shall consist of refraining from a violation of the rights of ownership by all subjects juxtaposed to the owner.

The seizure of property from the owner, and also the limitation of his powers, shall be permitted only in the instances provided for by a law [as amended by Law of 7 November 2022, No. ЗРУ-801].

Article 167. Forms of Ownership

Ownership in the Republic Uzbekistan shall be in the form of private and public.

Article 168. Subjects of Right of Ownership

Citizens, juridical persons, and the State shall be subjects of the right of ownership.

Property may belong by right of ownership to one person or to two or more persons.

The peculiarities of the acquisition and termination of the right of ownership to property, the possession, use, and disposition of it depending upon whether the property is in the ownership of a citizen, juridical person, or the State, shall be established by legislation.

Article 169. Objects of Right of Ownership

Land, the subsoil, waters, airspace, flora and fauna, and other natural resources, enterprises, things, including buildings, apartments, installations, equipment, raw material and products, money, securities, and other property, and also objects of intellectual property, may be in ownership.

Article 170. Right of Ownership and Other Rights to Thing in Land and Other Natural Resources

The right of ownership and other rights to a thing in land and other natural resources shall be regulated by the present Code and other laws.

Article 171. Peculiarities of Effectuation of Right of Ownership and Other Rights to Thing in Dwelling Premise

The peculiarities of the effectuation of the right of ownership and other rights to a thing in a dwelling premise shall be regulated by legislation.

Article 172. Conditions of Effectuation of Right of Ownership

The effectuation by the owner of his powers must not violate the rights and the interests protected by law of other persons.

In the instances, on the conditions, and within the limits provided for by legislative acts the owners shall be obliged to permit the limited use of his property by other persons.

An owner shall not have the right to abuse his dominant position and to perform other actions impinging upon the rights and interests protected by law of other persons.

When effectuating his right, an owner shall be obliged to take measures preventing the infliction of damage by him on the health of citizens and the environment.

Article 173. Right of Limited Use of Another's Land Plot (Servitude)

The owner of immoveable property (land plot, other immoveable) shall have the right to demand from the owner of the neighboring land plot and, when necessary, also from the owner of another land plot the granting of the right of limited use of another's land plot (servitude).

A servitude may be established in order to ensure the passage across another's land plot, the laying and operation of electric transmission lines, communications, and pipelines, ensuring water supply, and also other needs of the owner of immoveable property which cannot be ensured without the establishment of a servitude.

The encumberment of a land plot by a servitude shall not deprive the owner of the plot of the rights of possession, use, and disposition of this plot.

A servitude shall be established by agreement between the person demanding the establishment of the servitude and the owner of another's land plot and shall be subject to registration in the procedure established for the registration of the rights to immoveable property. In the event of the failure to reach agreement concerning the establishment of or the conditions of the servitude, the dispute shall be settled by a court upon the suit of the person requiring the establishment of the servitude.

A servitude may be established also in the interests of and at the demand of a person to whom the plot was granted by right of inheritable possession for life or the right of permanent possession and use on the conditions and in the procedure provided for by paragraphs one, two, three, and four of the present Article.

The owner of a plot encumbered by a servitude shall have the right, unless provided otherwise by a law, to demand from the person in whose interests the servitude was established a commensurate payment for the use of the plot.

Article 174. Burden of Maintenance of Property

The owner shall bear the burden of maintenance of the property belonging to him unless provided otherwise by legislation or by contract.

Article 175. Risk of Accidental Perishing or Spoilage of Property

The risk of accidental perishing or spoilage of property shall be borne by the owner of the property unless provided otherwise by legislation or by contract.

Chapter 14. Right of Economic Jurisdiction. Right of Operative Management

Article 176. Right of Economic Jurisdiction

A unitary enterprise to which property belongs by right of economic jurisdiction shall possess, use, and dispose of this property within the limits determined by the present Code.

Article 177. Rights of Owner With Respect to Property in Economic Jurisdiction

The owner of property in economic jurisdiction shall in accordance with a law decide the question of the creation of an enterprise, determination of the subject and purposes of its activity, its reorganization and liquidation, appoint the director (or head) of the enterprise, effectuate control over the use of the property belonging to the enterprise according to its designation and preservation.

The owner shall have the right to receive part of the profit from the use of the property in economic jurisdiction of the enterprise.

A unitary enterprise shall not have the right to sell immoveable property belonging to it by right of economic jurisdiction, lease it out, pledge it, or contribute it to the charter fund of economic partnerships and societies or by other means dispose of this property without the consent of the owner.

The remainder of the property belonging to the enterprise it shall dispose of autonomously.

Article 178. Right of Operative Management

A State enterprise, and also institution with respect to property consolidated to it, shall effectuate within the limits established by a law and in accordance with the purpose of its activity, the planning tasks of the owner, and designation of the property the rights of possession, use, and disposition thereof.

The owner of property consolidated to a State enterprise or institution shall have the right to remove the property which is surplus, not being used, or being used not for its purpose and to dispose of it at its discretion.

Article 179. Disposition of Property of State Enterprise

A State enterprise shall have the right to alienate or by other means dispose of property consolidated to it only with the consent of the owner of this property.

A State enterprise autonomously shall realize the products produced by it unless established otherwise by legislation.

The procedure for the distribution of revenues of a State enterprise shall be determined by the owner of its property.

Article 180. Disposition of Property of Institution

An institution shall not have the right to alienate or by other means to dispose of property consolidated to it and the property acquired at the expense of means allotted to it according to the estimate.

If in accordance with the constitutive documents the right has been granted to an institution to effectuate activities which bring revenues, the revenues received from such activity and the property acquired at the expense of these revenues shall be at the autonomous disposition of the institution and shall be taken into account on a separate balance sheet.

Article 181. Acquisition and Termination of Right of Economic Jurisdiction and Right of Operative Management

The right of economic jurisdiction or right of operative management of property with respect to which a decision has been adopted by the owner concerning consolidation to a unitary enterprise or to an institution shall arise in that enterprise or institution from the moment of the transfer of the property unless established otherwise by legislation or by decision of the owner.

The fruits, products, and revenues from the use of property in economic jurisdiction or operative management, and also property acquired by a unitary enterprise or institution under a contract or on other grounds, shall be in the economic jurisdiction or operative management of the enterprise or institution in the procedure established by the present Code and by other legislation for the acquisition of the right of ownership.

The right of economic jurisdiction and the right of operative management of property shall terminate by decision of the owner and on other grounds provided for by legislation.

Chapter 15. Acquisition and Termination of Right of Ownership

Article 182. Grounds for Acquisition of Right of Ownership

The grounds for the acquisition of the right of ownership shall be: labor activity, entrepreneurial and other economic activity relating to the use of property, including the creation, increment, and acquisition of property under transactions; the privatization of State property; inheritance; acquisitive prescription; and other grounds not contrary to legislation.

Article 183. Creation and Increment of Property

The right of ownership may arise as a result of the creation of new or the increment of property which the owner has.

The results of economic and other use of property, including products, fruits, and other revenues, shall belong to the owner of property unless provided otherwise by legislation or a contract.

Article 184. Acquisition of Property Under Transaction

Property may be acquired in ownership on the grounds of contracts of purchase-sale, barter, gift, and other transactions not prohibited by a law.

In the event of the transfer of property to a new owner, to it by way of universal legal succession shall pass the rights and duties of the former owner unless stipulated otherwise by legislative acts.

Article 185. Moment of Arising of Right of Ownership in Acquirer of Property Under Contract

The right of ownership in the acquirer of a thing by contract shall arise from the moment of the transfer of the thing unless provided otherwise by legislation or by a contract.

If the contract on the alienation of property is subject to State registration or notarial certification, the right of ownership in the acquirer shall arise from the moment of registration or certification of the contract, and when both notarial certification and State registration are necessary, from the moment of registration thereof.

Article 186. Transfer of Thing

The handing over of a thing to the acquirer shall be deemed to be the transfer, and likewise the handing over to a transport organization or communications organization for despatch to the acquirer of the thing alienated without the obligation of delivery.

A thing shall be considered to be handed over to the acquirer from the moment of its actual receipt in the possession of the acquirer or person specified by him.

If at the moment of concluding a contract on the alienation of a thing it is already in the possession of the acquirer, the thing shall be deemed to be transferred to him from this moment.

The transfer of a bill of lading or other goods-disposition document therefor shall be equated to the transfer of a thing.

Article 187. Acquisitive Prescription

A person who is not the owner of property but in good faith, openly, and uninterruptedly possesses as his own immovable property for fifteen years or other property for five years shall acquire the right of ownership in such property (acquisitive prescription).

The right of ownership in immovable and other property subject to State registration shall arise in the person who acquired this property by virtue of acquisitive prescription from the moment of such registration.

Until the acquisition of the right of ownership in property by virtue of acquisitive prescription, the person possessing the property as his own shall have the right to defend his possession against third persons who are not the owners of the property, and also who do not have the rights to possession thereof by virtue of another ground provided for by a law or contract.

A person referring to the prescription of possession may combine to the time of his possession all of the time during which this property was possessed by he whom this person is the legal successor of.

The running of the period of acquisitive prescription with respect to things situated with a person from whose possession they may be demanded and obtained in accordance with Articles 228, 229, 230, and 232 of the present Code shall commence not earlier than the expiry of the period of limitations with respect to the corresponding demands.

Article 188. Right of Ownership to Land Plots

The right of ownership of citizens and juridical persons to land plots shall arise in the instances, in the procedure, and on the conditions provided for by legislation.

Article 189. Conversion into Ownership of Things Generally Accessible for Gathering

The procedure and conditions for conversion into the ownership of citizens by means of gathering or other permissible means of wild fruits, nuts, mushrooms, berries, and other generally-accessible objects of flora and fauna and inanimate nature may be determined by legislation.

Article 190. Improvident Maintenance of Objects of Material Cultural Legacy [as amended by Law of 18 April 2018, No. ЗРУ-476]

If the owner improvidently treats an object of material cultural legacy belonging to him and does not ensure the preservation thereof, the respective agencies effectuating State administration in the domain of the protection and use of objects of cultural legacy shall give a warning to the owner concerning the termination of the improvident treatment of the object of material cultural legacy.

If the owner does not fulfill this demand, then by suit of the respective agencies a court may render a decision concerning the seizure of the object of material cultural legacy, which shall pass to the ownership of the State. The cost of the seized object of material cultural legacy shall be compensated to the owner in the amount established by agreement, and in the event of a dispute, by a court [as amended by Law of 18 April 2018, No. ЗРУ-476].

In the event of urgency the suit concerning seizure of the object of material cultural legacy may be filed without prior warning [as amended by Law of 18 April 2018, No. ЗРУ-476].

Article 191. Masterless Thing

A thing which has no owner or whose owner is unknown shall be masterless.

Unless this is excluded by the rules on find, on neglected animals and treasure, the right of ownership in masterless movable things may be acquired by virtue of acquisitive prescription.

Masterless immovable things shall be accepted for recording by the agency effectuating State registration of immovable property upon the application of the respective State agency or agency of self-government of citizens.

Upon the expiry of one year from the day of the masterless immovable thing being put for recording, the agency empowered to manage State property or agency of self-government of citizens may apply to a court with a demand to deem the right of this thing as having entered State ownership [as amended by Law of 25 April 2016, No. ЗРУ-405. СЗ РУ (2016), no. 17, item 173].

A masterless immovable thing not deemed by decision of a court to have entered into State ownership may be accepted anew into the possession, use, and disposition of the owner who left it, or acquired in ownership by virtue of acquisitive prescription.

The procedure for eliciting and recording masterless things shall be determined by the Government of the Republic Uzbekistan.

Article 192. Find

The finder of a lost thing shall be obliged immediately to inform the person who lost it thereof or the owner of the thing or some other persons known to him as having the right to receive it and shall return the found thing to this person.

If a thing has been found in a premise or on transport it shall be subject to being handed over to a person representing the possessor of this premise or means of transport. The person to whom the find has been handed over shall acquire the rights and bear the duties of the person who found the thing.

If the person having the right to demand the return of a found thing is unknown or his whereabouts are unknown, the finder of the thing shall be obliged to declare the find to the internal affairs agency or agency of self-government of citizens [as amended by Law of 23 May 2019, No. ЗРУ-542].

The finder of a thing shall have the right to keep it or to hand it over for keeping to the internal affairs agency, respective State agency, or agency of self-government or to a person specified by them [as amended by Law of 23 May 2019, No. ЗРУ-542].

Article 193. Acquisition of Right of Ownership in Find

If in the course of six months from the moment of declaring the find to the internal affairs agency or respective State agency, the person empowered to receive the found thing has not been established or does not himself declare his right to the thing to the person who found it, or to the internal affairs agency or respective State agency or agency of self-government of citizens, the finder of the thing shall acquire the right of ownership to it [as amended by Law of 23 May 2019, No. ЗРУ-542].

If the finder of a thing refuses to acquire the found thing in ownership, it shall enter State ownership.

Article 194. Compensation for Expenses Connected with Find and Remuneration to Finder of Thing

The finder and returner of a thing to the person empowered to receive it shall have the right to receive from this person, and in instances of the thing passing into State ownership, or the ownership of an agency of self-government of citizens — from the respective State agency or agency of self-government of citizens, compensation of expenses connected with keeping, handing over, or realization of the thing, and also expenditures for discovering the person empowered to receive the thing.

The finder of a thing shall have the right to demand from the person empowered to receive the thing remuneration for the find in the amount of up to 20% of the value of the thing.

If found documents or other things are of value only to the person empowered to receive them, the amount of remuneration shall be determined by agreement with this person, and in the event of failure to reach agreement, by a court. When the person empowered to demand the return of a found thing publicly promised remuneration for the find, the remuneration shall be paid on the conditions of the public promise of a reward.

The right to remuneration shall arise unless the finder of the thing has not declared the find or has attempted to conceal it.

Article 195. Neglected Animals

A person who has detained neglected or stray livestock or other neglected domestic or tame animals shall be obliged to return them to their owner, and if the owner of the animals or his whereabouts is unknown, not later than within three days from the moment of detention to declare the discovered animals to the internal affairs agency, respective State agency, or agency of self-government of citizens, which shall take measures to seek the owner [as amended by Law of 23 May 2019, No. 3PY-542].

During the search for the owner of the animals they may be left by the person who detained them with himself for maintenance and for use, or handed over for maintenance and use to another person having the necessary conditions for this. At the request of the person who detained neglected animals, the seeking of a person who has the necessary conditions for their maintenance and the transfer of the animals thereto shall be effectuated by the sections for the capture of stray livestock attached to district and city public amenity administrations, respective State agency, or agency of self-government of citizens [as amended by Law of 23 May 2019, No. 3PY-542].

The person who has detained neglected animals and the person to whom they have been transferred for maintenance and use shall be obliged to maintain them properly and in the event of fault shall be liable for the perishing and spoilage to the animals within the limits of the value thereof.

Article 196. Treasure

Treasure, that is, money and valuable objects buried in the earth or concealed by other means whose owner can not be established or by virtue of a law has lost the right to them shall enter into the ownership of the person to whom the property belongs (land plot, structure, etc.) where the treasure was concealed, and the person who discovered the treasure, in equal participatory shares, unless established otherwise by an agreement between them.

When a treasure is discovered by a person who has made diggings or searches for the valuables without the consent of the owner of the land plot or other property where the treasure was concealed, the treasure shall be subject to transfer to the owner of the land plot or other property where the treasure was discovered.

In the event of the discovery of a treasure containing a thing relegated to objects of material cultural legacy, it shall be subject to transfer to State ownership. In so doing the owner of the land plot or other property where the treasure was concealed and the person who discovered the treasure shall have the right to receive remuneration in the amount of 50% of the value of the treasure. The remuneration shall be distributed between these persons in equal participatory shares unless established otherwise by an agreement between them [as amended by Law of 18 April 2018, No. 3PY-476].

In the event of the discovery of such treasure by a person who has made diggings or searches for valuables without the consent of the owner of the property where the treasure was concealed, the remuneration shall not be paid to this person and shall go to the owner in full.

The rules of the present Article shall not apply to persons within whose labor or employment duties are the conducting of diggings and searches directed towards the discovery of treasure.

Article 197. Grounds for Termination of Right of Ownership

The right of ownership shall terminate by means of the voluntary performance by the owner of an obligation, the adoption by the owner of a unilateral decision determining the fate of the property, the seizure (or purchase) of property on the basis of a judicial decision, and also of an act of legislation terminating the right of ownership on the basis of a law [as amended by Law of 7 November 2022, No. 3PY-801].

Article 198. Liquidation and Writing Off of Property

The termination of the right of ownership as a result of the destruction of property (or liquidation) shall be permitted in instances if this is not contrary to laws [as amended by Law of 7 November 2022, No. 3PY-801].

The destruction of property by the owner which is of historical, scientific, artistic, or other cultural value shall not be permitted. In exceptional instances the said property may be confiscated by decision of a court or the value thereof recovered if it has been destroyed [as amended by Law of 18 April 2018, No. 3PY-476].

The termination of the right of ownership as a result of the writing off of property from the balance sheet of a juridical person shall be effectuated in the procedure and on the conditions provided for by legislation or by the constitutive documents.

Article 199. Seizure of Property from Owner

The seizure of property from the owner shall be permitted only in the event of the levy of execution against this property with regard to obligations of the owner in the instances and in the procedure provided for by a law, and also by way of nationalization, requisition, and confiscation [as amended by Law of 7 November 2022, No. 3PY-801].

If property proved to be in the ownership of a person which in accordance with a law may not belong to him, the right of ownership to this property shall be terminated in a judicial proceeding with compensation of the value of the seized property to this person.

Article 200. Uncontested Recovery of Indebtedness

The uncontested recovery of indebtedness for obligations, including indebtedness for payments to the budget, shall be permitted in the instances provided for by legislation.

In the event of disagreement with the decision concerning the uncontested recovery, the owner shall have the right to apply to a court.

Article 201. Peculiarities of Acquisition and Termination of Right of Ownership to Precious Metals and Stones

The peculiarities of the acquisition and termination of the right of ownership to precious metals and stones in raw and processed form (except for jewellery and other domestic manufactures) shall be determined by legislation.

Article 202. Nationalization

Nationalization is the compensated transfer of the right of ownership to the property being nationalized, which belongs to citizens and juridical persons, to the State in accordance with a law.

In the event of the subsequent denationalization of the said property, the former owners shall have the right to demand the return of this property unless established otherwise by legislative acts.

Article 203. Requisition

In the event of natural disasters, wrecks, epidemics, epizootic, and other circumstances of an extraordinary character property may, in the interests of society by decision of agencies of State power, be withdrawn from the owner in the procedure and on the conditions established by legislation with payment of the value of the property to him (requisition).

The former owner of the requisitioned property shall have the right, upon the termination of the operation of the circumstances in connection with which the requisition was made, to demand the return to him of the property which has been preserved.

Article 204. Confiscation

In the instances provided for by a law property may be withdrawn without compensation from the owner by decision of a court for the commission of a crime or other violation of law (confiscation).

Article 205. Determination of Value of Property in Event of its Seizure and Right to Compensation of Losses

The value of property seized in the event of the termination of the right of ownership shall be determined by an appraisal organization at the moment of the termination of the right of ownership unless established otherwise by legislation [as amended by Law of 17 September 2010, No. ЗРУ-257. СЗ РУ (2010), no. 37, item 315].

The valuation at which the value of the seized property shall be compensated to the owner may be contested by him in a court.

The owner shall have the right to also demand compensation for other losses caused by the seizure of the property.

Article 206. Termination of Right of Ownership Not Aimed Directly at Withdrawal of Property from Owner

The termination of the right of ownership in connection with a decision of a State agency not aimed directly at the withdrawal of property from the owner, including by a decision concerning the withdrawal of a land plot on which the house, other structures, installations, or plantings that belong to the owner are situated, shall be permitted only in the instances and in the procedure established by a law while granting to the owner property of equal value by right of ownership and compensation of other losses incurred or compensation to him in full of losses caused by the termination of the right of ownership [as amended by Laws of 20 August 2015, No. ЗРУ-391, and of 7 November 2022, No. ЗРУ-801].

The determination of market value of a house, other structures, installations, or plantings situated on the withdrawn land plot, and also the right to the land plot, shall be performed by an appraisal organization in the established procedure. The market value of the withdrawn land plot and the right to the land plot when the right of private ownership is terminated shall be determined by an appraisal organization at the moment directly preceding the withdrawal of this property, or when news concerning the forthcoming withdrawal influenced the market value of the property and the right to the land plot [added by Law of 20 August 2015, No. ЗРУ-391. СЗ РУ (2015), no. 33, item 439].

The demolition of a house, other structure, installations, or plantings on the withdrawn land plot before the preliminary or full compensation of losses at market value shall not be permitted [added by Law of 20 August 2015, No. 3PY-391. C3 PY (2015), no. 33, item 439].

In the event of the failure of the owner to agree with the decision entailing the termination of the right of ownership, it may not be effectuated until the settlement of the dispute by a court. In the event of the consideration of the dispute, all questions of compensation to the owner for losses caused also shall be decided.

Chapter 16. Private Ownership

Article 207. Right of Private Ownership

The right of private ownership is the right of a person to the possession, use, and disposition of property acquired by him in accordance with legislation.

The quantity and value of property in private ownership shall not be limited.

Article 208. Subjects of Right of Private Ownership

Citizens, economic partnerships and societies, cooperatives, social associations, social foundations, and other non-State juridical persons shall be deemed to be subjects of the right of private ownership.

Article 209. Objects of Right of Private Ownership

Any property, except for individual types of property which have been prohibited by a law, may be in private ownership.

Article 210. Procedure for Arising of Right of Ownership in Dwelling House (or Apartment)

The right of ownership in a newly erected dwelling house on a land plot allotted in the established procedure shall arise from the moment of State registration.

[paragraph two repealed by Law of 14 January 2020, No. 3PY-602].

The right of ownership to a dwelling house (or apartment) which belongs to the State shall arise by way of privatization provided for by legislation.

The right of ownership in a cooperative dwelling house, apartment, garage, dacha, and other structure shall ensue after the payment in full of the share contributions by the member of the cooperative.

Article 211. Common Property of Owners of Dwelling and Non-Dwelling Premises in Apartment House [as amended by Law of 8 January 2007, No. ЗРУ-77. СЗ РУ (2007), no. 1-2, item 3]

The common property, including common premises of this house, the supporting and fencing construction, inter-apartment stairwells, stairways, lifts, life and other shafts, corridors, technical floors, basements, attics and roofs, intra-house engineering networks and communications, mechanical, electrical, sanitary-technical, and other equipment and devices beyond the limits or within the premises and servicing more than one premise, shall belong by right of participatory share ownership to the owners of the dwelling and non-dwelling premises in the apartment house [as amended by Law of 8 January 2007, No. ЗРУ-77. СЗ РУ (2007), no. 1-2, item 3].

The extent of the participatory shares of the owners of dwelling and non-dwelling premises in the right of ownership to common property in the apartment house and the procedure for distribution among the owners of the costs relating to the maintenance and preservation of this property shall be determined in accordance with housing legislation [as amended by Law of 8 January 2007, No. ЗРУ-77. СЗ РУ (2007), no. 1-2, item 3].

The participant of participatory ownership in the common property in an apartment house shall not have the right to alienate his participatory share renounce it to the benefit of citizens or juridical persons, nor to perform other actions which entail the transfer thereof separately from the right of ownership to the dwelling or non-dwelling premise belonging to him [as amended by Law of 8 January 2007, No. ЗРУ-77. СЗ РУ (2007), no. 1-2, item 3].

Article 212. Arbitrary Structure and Its Consequences

A dwelling house, other structure, installation, or other immovable property created on a land plot not allotted for these purposes in the procedure established by legislation, and also created without obtaining the necessary authorization for this, or with a material violation of architectural norms and rules, shall be an arbitrary structure.

A person who has effectuated an arbitrary structure shall not acquire the right of ownership in it. He shall not have the right to dispose of the structure — to sell, give, lease out, or conclude other transactions.

The arbitrary structure shall, upon the suit of the person whose right has been violated or respective State agency, be subject by decision of a court to demolition by the person who effectuated it or at his expense, except for the instances provided for by paragraph four of the present Article [as amended by Law of 4 March 2019, No. 3PУ-526].

[paragraph four as amended by Law of 27 August 2004, No. 671-II; repealed by Law of 4 March 2019, No. 3PУ-526].

The right of ownership in an arbitrary structure may be recognized by a court for the person in whose ownership, inheritable possession for life, or permanent possession and use the land plot is where the structure was effectuated. In this event the person whose right of ownership to the structure has been recognized shall compensate the person who effectuated it for the expenses for the structure in the amount determined by the court [as amended by Law of 4 March 2019, No. 3PУ-526].

The right of ownership in the arbitrary structure may not be recognized if retention of the structure violates the rights and the interests protected by a law of the other persons or will create a threat to the life and health of citizens [as amended by Law of 4 March 2019, No. 3PУ-526].

Chapter 17. Public Ownership

Article 213. Concept of Public Ownership

Public ownership is State ownership which consists of Republic ownership and the ownership of administrative-territorial formations (municipal ownership).

Relations of ownership in the Republic Karakalpakstan, including public ownership, shall be regulated by the present Code, and also by legislation of the Republic Karakalpakstan.

Article 214. Republic Ownership

Land, the subsoil, water, airspace, flora and fauna, and other natural resources, the property of Republic agencies of State power and administration, objects of material cultural legacy of State significance, assets of the Republic budget, the gold reserve, currency fund and other State funds shall be in State ownership, and enterprises and other property complexes, educational, scientific, scientific research institutions, and organizations, the results of intellectual activity which have been created or acquired at the expense of budgetary and other assets of the State, and other property also may be [as amended by Law of 18 April 2018, No. 3PУ-476].

The Olii Mazhlis of the Republic Uzbekistan, the President of the Republic Uzbekistan, the Government of the Republic Uzbekistan, or agencies empowered by them, shall dispose of property in Republic ownership unless provided otherwise by legislation.

Property in Republic ownership may be consolidated to juridical persons by right of economic jurisdiction or operative management.

Republic ownership shall be created at the expense of taxes and other obligatory payments to the Republic budget, and also at the expense of other proceeds on the grounds provided by legislative acts [as amended by Law of 31 December 2008, No. 3РУ-197. С3 РУ (2008), no. 52, item 513].

Objects of Republic ownership may be alienated to private ownership in the procedure and on the conditions established by legislation.

Article 215. Municipal Ownership

Property of local agencies of State power, assets of the local budget, the municipal housing fund and municipal economy, enterprises, and other property complexes, institutions of public education, culture, public health, and also other property, shall be in municipal ownership.

Property in municipal ownership shall be disposed of by local agencies of State power or agencies empowered by them unless provided otherwise by legislation.

Property in municipal ownership may be consolidated to juridical persons by right of economic jurisdiction or operative management.

Municipal ownership shall be created at the expense of taxes and other obligatory payments to the local budget, and also at the expense of other proceeds on the grounds provided by legislation [as amended by Law of 31 December 2008, No. 3РУ-197. С3 РУ (2008), no. 52, item 513].

Objects of municipal ownership may be alienated to private ownership in the procedure and on the conditions established by legislation.

Chapter 18. Common Ownership

Article 216. Concept and Grounds of Origin of Common Ownership

Property in the ownership of two or more persons shall belong to them by right of common ownership.

Property may be in common ownership with the determination of the participatory share of each of the owners in the right of ownership (participatory share ownership) or without the determination of such participatory shares (joint ownership).

Common ownership in property shall be participatory share except for instances when the formation of joint ownership to this property has been provided for by a law.

Common ownership shall arise when two or more persons enter into the ownership of property which can not be divided without changing its purpose (indivisible things), or is not subject to division by virtue of a law.

Common ownership in divisible property shall arise in the instances provided for by legislation or contract.

By agreement of the participants of joint ownership, and in the event of not achieving consent, by decision of a court, the participatory share ownership of these persons may be established for common property.

Article 217. Determination of Participatory Share in Right of Participatory Share Ownership

If the participatory shares of the participants of participatory share ownership can not be determined on the basis of a law and were not established by agreement of all of its participants, the participatory shares shall be considered to be equal.

The procedure for the determination and change of their participatory shares may be established by agreement of all the participants of participatory share ownership depending upon the contribution of each of them in the formation and growth of the common property.

A participant of participatory share ownership who has effectuated at his own expense while complying with the established procedure for the use of common property indivisible improvements of this property shall have the right to a corresponding increase of his participatory share in the right to common property.

Divisible improvements of common property, unless provided otherwise by agreement of the participants of the participatory share ownership, shall enter into the ownership of those participants who produced them.

Article 218. Disposition of Property in Participatory Share Ownership

The disposition of property in participatory share ownership shall be effectuated by agreement of all of its participants.

A participant of participatory share ownership shall have the right at his discretion to sell, give, bequeath, or pledge his participatory share or to otherwise dispose of it while complying, in the event of alienation for payment, with the rules provided for by Article 224 of the present Code.

Article 219. Possession and Use of Common Property in Participatory Share Ownership [as amended by Law of 8 January 2007, No. ЗРУ-77. СЗ РУ (2007), no. 1-2, item 3]

The possession and use of common property in participatory share ownership shall be effectuated by the agreement of all of its participants. In the event of the failure to achieve such consent, the possession and use of common property in participatory share ownership shall be effectuated in the procedure established by a court [as amended by Law of 8 January 2007, No. ЗРУ-77. СЗ РУ (2007), no. 1-2, item 3].

A participant of participatory share ownership shall have the right to grant part of the common property in his possession and use commensurate to his participatory share, and if this is impossible, shall have the right to demand of the other participants who possess and use the property respective contributory compensation approximating his participatory share.

Article 220. Fruits, Product, and Revenues from Use of Property in Participatory Share Ownership

The fruits, product, and revenues from the use of property in participatory share ownership shall become part of the common property and be distributed among the participants of participatory ownership commensurately with their participatory shares unless provided otherwise by an agreement between them.

Article 221. Distribution of Expenses for Maintenance of Property in Common Participatory Ownership

Each owner shall be obliged commensurately with his participatory share to participate in the payment of taxes and other obligatory payments relating to the common property, and also the costs for its maintenance and preservation, unless provided otherwise by a contract [as amended by Law of 31 December 2008, No. ЗРУ-197. СЗ РУ (2008), no. 52, item 513].

Expenses which are not necessary and were made by one of the owners without the consent of the others shall fall on him himself. Disputes arising in so doing shall be subject to settlement in a judicial procedure.

Article 222. Moment of Transfer of Participatory Share in Right of Common Ownership to Acquirer Under Contract

The participatory share in the right of common ownership shall pass to the acquirer under a contract from the moment of conclusion of the contract unless provided otherwise by an agreement of the parties.

The moment of transfer of a participatory share in the right of common ownership under a contract subject to State registration shall be determined in accordance with Article 185, paragraph two, of the present Code.

Article 223. Division of Property in Participatory Share Ownership and Partition of Participatory Share Therefrom

Property in participatory share ownership may be divided between its participants by an agreement between them.

A participant of participatory share ownership shall have the right to demand the partition of his participatory share from the common property.

If the participants of participatory share ownership do not reach agreement concerning the means and conditions for the division of common property or partition of the participatory share ownership of one of them, the participant of participatory share ownership shall have the right in a judicial proceeding to demand the partition of his participatory share in kind.

If the partition of a participatory share in kind is not permitted by a law or is impossible without incommensurate damage to property in common ownership, the partitioning owner shall have the right to payment to him of the value of his participatory share by the other participants of participatory share ownership.

The incommensurateness of property partitionable in kind to a participant of participatory share ownership on the basis of the present Article to his participatory share in the right of ownership shall be eliminated by the payment of a corresponding monetary amount or other contributory compensation.

The payment to a participant of participatory share ownership by the remaining owners of contributory compensation in place of the partition of his participatory share in kind shall be permitted with his consent. In instances when the participatory share of the respective owner is insignificant and cannot be truly partitioned and he does not have a material interest in the use of the common property, a court may also, in the absence of the consent of this owner, oblige the other participants of participatory ownership to pay contributory compensation to him.

With the receipt of the contributory compensation in accordance with the present Article the owner shall lose the right to the participatory share in the common property.

Article 224. Right of Preferential Purchase

In the event of the sale by one of the owners of his participatory share to another person the remaining owners shall have the right of preferential purchase of the participatory share being sold at the price for which it is being sold and on other equal conditions, except for sales at public sales.

The seller of a participatory share in common ownership shall be obliged to notify in writing the remaining owners of the intention to sell his participatory share to an outside person, specifying the price and other conditions on which he is selling it.

If the remaining owners refuse to effectuate the right of preferential purchase or do not effectuate this right within a month with respect to immoveable property, and with respect to other property, within ten days from the date of notification, the seller shall have the right to sell his participatory share to any person.

In the event of the sale of a participatory share in violation of the right of preferential purchase, the other owners shall have the right within three months to demand in a judicial proceeding the transfer to them of the rights and duties of the purchaser.

The assignment of a preferential right of purchase of the participatory share shall not be permitted.

In the event of the sale by a State agency or other juridical person of its participatory share in common ownership to a dwelling house (or apartment), the right of preferential purchase shall belong to the citizens residing in the respective part of the house (or apartment) as tenants according to the rules of the present Article, and in the event they waive this right or do not effectuate it, to other owners.

The rules of the present Article shall apply also when alienating a participatory share under a contract of barter.

Article 225. Possession, Use, and Disposition of Property in Joint Ownership

The participants of joint ownership, unless provided otherwise by agreement between them, shall possess and use common property in common.

The disposition of property in joint ownership shall be effectuated by the consent of all the participants, which shall be presupposed irrespective as to which of the participants has concluded the transaction with regard to disposition of the property.

Each of the participants of joint ownership shall have the right to conclude transactions relating to the disposition of common property unless it arises otherwise from the agreement of all the participants. A transaction concluded by one of the participants of joint ownership which is connected with the disposition of common property may be deemed to be invalid at the demand of the remaining participants for reasons that the participant who concluded the transaction lacked the necessary powers only if it is proved that the other party to the transaction knew or should have known about this.

The rules of the present Article shall apply unless established otherwise for individual types of joint ownership by the present Code or other laws.

Article 226. Division of Property in Joint Ownership and Partition of Participatory Share Therefrom

The separation of common property between participants of joint ownership, and also the partition of the participatory share of one of them, may be effectuated after the preliminary determination of the participatory share of each of the participants in the right to common property.

In the event of the separation of common property and the partition of a participatory share therefrom, unless provided otherwise by law or by agreement of the participants, their participatory shares shall be deemed to be equal.

The grounds and procedure for the separation of common property and the partition of the participatory share therefrom shall be determined according to Article 223 of the present Code, and for individual types of joint ownership, by other laws.

Article 227. Levying Execution Against Participatory Share in Common Property

The creditor of a participant of participatory share or joint ownership shall, in the event that the owner's other property is insufficient, have the right to present a demand concerning partition of the participatory share of the debtor in the common property in order to levy execution against it.

If in such instances the apportionment of the participatory share in kind is impossible or the remaining participants of participatory share or joint ownership object to this, the creditor shall have the right to demand the sale by the debtor of his participatory share to the other participants of common ownership at a price commensurate with the value of this participatory share, with the assets received from the sale being applied to repayment of the debt.

In the event of the refusal of the remaining participants of common ownership to acquire the participatory share of the debtor, the creditor shall have the right to demand in court the levy of execution against the participatory share of the debtor in the right of common ownership by means of the sale of this participatory share at a public sale.

Chapter 19. Defense of Right of Ownership and Other Rights to Thing

Article 228. Demanding and Obtaining Property from Another's Illegal Possession (Vindicatio)

The owner shall have the right to demand and obtain his property from another's illegal possession (vindicatio).

Article 229. Demanding and Obtaining Property from a Good-Faith Acquirer

If property has been acquired for compensation from the person who did not have the right to alienate it, of which the acquirer did not know and should not have known (good-faith acquirer), then the owner shall have the right to demand and obtain this property from the acquirer when the property has been lost by the owner or person to whom the property was transferred by the owner in possession, or stolen from one or the other, or left the possession thereof by means other than the will thereof.

The demanding and obtaining of property on the grounds specified in paragraph one of the present Article shall not be permitted if the property was sold in the procedure established for the execution of court decisions.

If property was acquired without compensation from a person who did not have the right to alienate it, the owner shall have the right to demand and obtain the property in all instances.

Money may not be demanded and obtained from a good-faith acquirer [as amended by Law of 22 September 2009, No. 3PY-223. C3 PY (2009), no. 39, item 423].

Article 230. Compensation of Revenues and Expenses When Demanding and Obtaining Property from Another's Illegal Possession

In accordance with Article 228 of the present Code, when demanding and obtaining property the owner also shall have the right to demand and obtain:

from a person who knew or should have known that his possession is illegal (possessor not in good faith) the return or compensation of all revenues which this person derived or should have been derived throughout the entire period of possession;

from a good-faith possessor, all revenues which he derived or should have derived from the time when he knew or should have known about the unlawfulness of the possession or from the moment of receiving a writ relating to the suit of the owner for the demanding and obtaining of the property.

A possessor, both in good faith and not in good faith, in turn shall have the right to demand from the owner compensation for necessary expenditures made by him on the property for that time from which revenues from the property are due to the owner.

A possessor in good faith shall have the right to retain for himself improvements made by him if they can be separated without damaging the thing. If such a separation is impossible, a good-faith possessor shall have the right to demand compensation for expenditures made for the improvement, but not more than the amount of the increase of the value of the thing.

Article 231. Defense of Rights of Owner Against Violations Not Connected with Deprivation of Possession (Nugatory Suit)

An owner may demand the elimination of any violations of his right, even though these violations are not connected with deprivation of possession (nugatory suit).

Article 232. Defense of Rights of Possessor Who is Not the Owner

The rights provided for by Articles 228-231 of the present Code shall belong also to a person who, although not the owner, is the possessor of the property by right of inheritable possession for life, economic jurisdiction or operative management or on another grounds provided for by a law or contract. This person shall have the right to the defense of his possession against the owner as well.

Article 233. Consequences of Termination of Right of Ownership by Virtue of Law

In the event of the adoption of a law terminating the right of ownership the losses caused to the owner as a result of the adoption of this act, including the value of the property, shall be compensated by the State. Disputes concerning compensation of losses shall be settled by a court.

SECTION III. LAW OF OBLIGATIONS

Subsection 1. General Provisions on Obligations

Chapter 20. Concept of and Parties to Obligations

Article 234. Concept of Obligation and Grounds of its Origin

An obligation is a civil-law relation by virtue of which one person (the debtor) shall be obliged to perform to the benefit of another person (the creditor) a specified action, that is, to transfer property, fulfill work, render services, pay money, and the like or to refrain from a specified action, and the creditor shall have the right to demand from the debtor the performance of his duty.

Obligations shall arise from a contract, as a consequence of the causing of harm, and from other grounds specified in the present Code.

Article 235. Parties to Obligation

One or simultaneously several persons may participate as creditor or debtor — the parties of an obligation.

The invalidity of the demands of the creditor with respect to one of the persons participating in the obligation as a debtor, and likewise the expiry of the period of limitations with regard to the demand against such person, shall not in and of itself affect his demands against the remaining such persons.

If the parties to a contract bear a mutual duty with respect to one another, then each of the parties shall be considered to be the debtor of the other party in that which he is obliged to do to its benefit, and simultaneously the creditor thereof in that which it has the right to demand from it.

An obligation shall not create duties for persons who are not participating therein as parties (for third persons).

In the instances provided for by legislation or by agreement of the parties an obligation may create rights for third persons with respect to one or both parties to the obligation.

Chapter 21. Performance of Obligations

Article 236. General Provisions

Obligations must be performed duly in accordance with the conditions of the obligation and the requirements of legislation, and in the absence of such conditions and requirements — in accordance with the customs of business turnover or other usually presented requirements.

Article 237. Inadmissibility of Unilateral Refusal to Perform Obligation

A unilateral refusal to perform an obligation and a unilateral change of conditions of a contract shall not be permitted except for instances provided for by legislation or by a contract.

Article 238. Performance of Obligation by Agreed and Acceptable Means

An obligation must be performed by a means agreed by and acceptable to the parties.

The means of performance of an obligation, unless it arises from the essence of the obligation and has not been established by legislation, must be stipulated in the contract.

Article 239. Performance of Obligation in Parts

A creditor shall have the right not to accept the performance of an obligation in parts unless provided otherwise by legislation or by contract or does not arise from the customs of business turnover or the essence of the obligation.

Article 240. Performance of Obligation to Proper Person

Unless provided otherwise by agreement of the parties and does not arise from the customs of business turnover or the essence of the obligation, the debtor shall have the right when performing the obligation to demand evidence that performance is accepted by the creditor himself or by a person empowered by him and shall bear the risk of the consequences of the failure to present such demand.

Article 241. Placing Performance of Obligation on Third Person

The performance of an obligation which arose from a contract may be placed by in full or in part on a third person if this has been provided for by legislation or by contract, and likewise if the third person is connected with one of the parties by a respective contract.

Unless the duty of the debtor to perform an obligation personally arisen from legislation, a contract, or the essence of the obligation, the creditor shall be obliged to accept performance offered for the debtor by a third person.

Responsibility for the failure to perform an obligation shall be borne by the party under the contract unless it is provided by legislation or by contract that a third person shall bear responsibility.

Article 242. Period for Performance of Obligation

If the period for performance of an obligation has not been established or determined by the moment of demand, the creditor shall have the right to demand performance, and the debtor shall have the right to make performance at any time. The debtor shall be obliged to make performance of such obligation within a seven-day period from the date of presentation of the demand by the creditor if the duty of immediate performance does not arise from a law, contract, or the essence of the obligation.

Article 243. Performance of Obligation Before Time

The debtor shall have the right to perform an obligation before time, and a creditor shall be obliged to accept performance before time if this is provided for by legislation or contract or arises from the essence of the obligation or customs of business turnover or other usually presented requirements.

Article 244. Deferral or Installment Performance of Obligation

The deferral or installment performance of an obligation shall not be permitted unless provided otherwise by legislation or contract.

When there are sufficient grounds a court shall have the right to grant a deferral of performance or [performance] by installment of an obligation to the debtor.

Article 245. Currency of Monetary Obligations

It may be provided in a monetary obligation that it shall be subject to payment in soms in an amount equivalent to a specified amount in foreign currency or in prearranged monetary units (ecu, special borrowing rights, and others). In this event the amount subject to payment in soms shall be determined according to the official exchange rate of the respective currency or prearranged monetary units on the day of payment unless another exchange rate or another date for determining it has been established by legislation or by agreement of the parties.

The use of foreign currency, and also of payment documents in foreign currency, shall be permitted when effectuating the settlement of accounts on the territory of the Republic Uzbekistan with regard to obligations in the instances and on the conditions determined by legislation.

Article 246. Place of Performance of Obligation

If the place of performance has not been determined by legislation or by contract and does not arise from the essence of the obligation or other usually presented requirements, performance must be made:

(1) with regard to an obligation to transfer immovable property: at the location of the property;

(2) with regard to an obligation to transfer a good or other property providing for the carriage thereof: at the place of handing over the good to the first carrier for delivery to the creditor;

(3) with regard to other obligations of a debtor to transfer a good or other property: at the place of manufacture or keeping of the property if this place was known to the creditor at the moment of origin of the obligation;

(4) with regard to a monetary obligation: at the place of residence of the creditor at the moment of origin of the obligation, and if the creditor is a juridical person — at its location at the moment of origin of the obligation; if the creditor at the moment of performance of the obligation has changed place of residence or location and notified the debtor thereof — at the

new place of residence or location of the creditor, relegating the expenses connected with the change of place of performance to his account;

(5) with regard to all other obligations: at the place of residence of the debtor, and if the debtor is a juridical person — at its location.

Article 247. Increase of Amounts Payable for Maintenance of Citizen

An amount payable with regard to a monetary obligation directly for the maintenance of a citizen (in compensation of harm caused to the life or health thereof, under a contract of maintenance for life, and in other instances) shall be increased proportionately with an increase of the minimum amount of payment for labor established by a law.

Article 248. Priority of Payment of Demands Relating to Monetary Obligation

The amount of payment made which is insufficient for the performance of a monetary obligation in full shall in the absence of another agreement pay first of all the costs of the creditor with regard to the receipt of performance and then, interest, and last, the principal amount of the debt.

Article 249. Performance of Obligation by Placing Debt on Deposit

A debtor shall have the right to place money due from him or securities on deposit with a notary, and in the instances established by a law, on deposit with a court if the obligation can not be performed by the debtor as a consequence of:

(1) the absence of the creditor or person empowered by him to accept performance at the place where the obligation must be performed;

(2) the lack of dispositive legal capacity of the creditor and absence of his representative or the consent of the last;

(3) the evident lack of specificity as to who is the creditor with regard to the obligation, in particular, in connection with a dispute in this regard between the creditor and other persons;

(4) avoidance by the creditor of accepting performance or other delay on his part.

The placing of a monetary amount or securities on deposit with a notary or court shall be considered to be performance of the obligation.

The notary or court with whom the deposit has been made of money or securities shall notify the creditor thereof.

Article 250. Performance of Alternative Obligation

The right of choice, unless it follows otherwise from legislation, a contract, or the essence of the obligation, shall belong to the debtor who is obliged to perform one of two or several actions.

Article 251. Performance of Obligation in Which Several Creditors or Several Debtors Participate

If several creditors or several debtors participate in an obligation, each of the creditors shall have the right to demand performance, and each of the debtors shall be obliged to perform the obligation in equal participatory share with the others insofar as it does not follow otherwise from a law or contract.

Article 252. Rights of Creditor in Event of Joint and Several Duty of Debtors

In the event of the joint and several duty of debtors, the creditor shall have the right to demand performance both from all of the debtors jointly or from any of them individually, either for the whole or for part of the debt.

A creditor who has not received full satisfaction from one of the joint and several debtors shall have the right to demand that which has not been received from the other joint and several debtors.

Joint and several debtors shall remain obliged so long as the obligation is not performed in full.

Article 253. Objections of Joint and Several Debtors to Demand of Creditor

In the event of the joint and several duty a debtor shall not have the right to advance objections against the demand of a creditor based on those relations of other debtors with the creditor in which the said debtor does not participate.

Article 254. Performance of Joint and Several Duty by One of Debtors

The performance of a joint and several duty in full by one of the debtors shall relieve the other debtors from performance to the creditor.

The debtor who has performed the joint and several duty shall have the right of a counter (regressive) demand against the remaining debtors in equal participatory shares, deducting the participatory share falling on himself unless established otherwise by legislative acts or contracts.

That unpaid by one of the joint and several debtors to the debtor who has performed the joint and several duty shall fall in equal participatory shares on him and on the remaining debtors.

Article 255. Joint and Several Demands

In the event of the joint and severalness of a demand, any of the joint and several creditors shall have the right to present the demand to the debtor in full.

The debtor shall not have the right to advance against the demand of one of the joint and several creditors objections based on those relations of the debtor with another joint and several creditor in which the particular creditor did not participate.

The performance of the obligation in full to one of the joint and several creditors shall relieve the debtor from performance to the other creditors.

A joint and several creditor who has received performance from the debtor shall be obliged to compensate the other creditors insofar as does not arise otherwise from the relations between them the equal participatory shares which are due to them.

Article 256. Counter Performance of Obligations

The performance of an obligation by one of the parties which in accordance with a contract is conditioned by the performance by the other party of its obligations shall be deemed to be counter performance.

In the event of the failure of an obliged party to provide the performance of an obligation stipulated by the contract or of the existence of circumstances obviously testifying that such performance will not be made within the established period, the party on whom counter performance lies shall have the right to suspend the performance of his obligation or to waive the performance of this obligation and demand compensation of losses.

If the performance of an obligation stipulated by a contract was not made in full, the party on whom the counter performance lies shall have the right to suspend the performance of his obligation or to waive performance in that part corresponding to the performance not provided.

If counter performance of an obligation has been made notwithstanding the failure of the other party to provide performance of its obligation stipulated by the contract, this party shall be obliged to provide such performance.

The rules provided for by paragraphs two, three, and four of the present Article shall apply unless established otherwise by the contract or by a law.

Article 257. Certification of Performance of Obligation

A creditor, in accepting performance of an obligation, shall be obliged upon the demand of the debtor to issue a receipt to him in receipt of the performance of the obligation in full or in part. When transactions are performed between juridical persons and citizens in oral form, the juridical person who has paid for goods or services must receive a document from the other party certifying payment of money or the grounds thereof.

If the debtor issues a debt document to the creditor in certification of the obligation, the creditor, in accepting performance, must return this document, and when it is impossible to return, to specify this in the receipt issued. The receipt may be replaced by an inscription on the returned debt document. The location of the debt document with the debtor shall certify, unless proved otherwise, the termination of the obligation.

Article 258. Consequences of Failure to Perform Demand Concerning Certification of Performance of Obligation

In the event of the refusal of the creditor to issue a receipt, to return the debt document, or to note on the receipt the impossibility of its return, the debtor shall have the right to withhold performance. In these instances the creditor shall be considered to have delayed.

Chapter 22. Securing Performance of Obligations

Article 259. General Provisions

The performance of obligations may be secured by a penalty, pledge, withholding of property from the debtor, suretyship, guarantee, deposit, and other means provided for by legislation or by a contract.

The invalidity of an agreement to secure the performance of an obligation shall not entail the invalidity of this obligation (principal obligation).

The invalidity of the principal obligation shall entail the invalidity of the obligation securing it.

Article 259^{1}. Satisfaction of Demands of Creditors at Expense of Property of Debtor Granted as Security for Performance of Obligations [added by Law of 22 October 2019, No. ЗРУ-572]

Demands of a creditor with regard to obligations secured by property, in the event of the failure of the debtor to perform his obligations, shall be satisfied from the value of this property preferentially before other creditors of the person to whom the particular property belongs. The preferential right of the creditor shall extend also to the fruits, product, and other revenues received from the use or realization of the property of the debtor granted as security for performance of the obligations unless provided otherwise by a contract.

The creditors specified in paragraph one of the present Article who have made an entry in the pledge register of their rights to the property of the debtor shall have a preferential right to satisfaction of their demands before creditors who have not made a respective entry in the pledge register.

The demands of creditors who have made an entry in the pledge register of their rights to one and the same property shall be satisfied in the following priority:

in first priority shall be satisfied demands with regard to obligations secured by withholding the particular property;

in second priority shall be satisfied demands with regard to obligations arising from the acquisition or provision of property by the creditor to the debtor acting as security for performance of the obligations;

in third priority shall be satisfied demands with regard to obligations secured by the property if this property was acquired (or produced) at the expense of means or property provided by the creditor;

in fourth priority are satisfied demands with regard to all remaining obligations secured by the particular property.

The priority of demands of creditors shall be determined by way of chronology (time and date) of the making by them of an entry in the pledge register concerning rights to the respective property. In so doing the demands of creditors of each subsequent priority shall be satisfied after the full satisfaction of demands of creditors of the preceding priority.

The demands of creditors who have not made an entry in the pledge register of their rights to property shall be satisfied from the value of this property in calendar priority of such rights arising after the satisfaction of the demands of creditors who have made an entry in the pledge register on rights to particular property.

A creditor shall have the right to assign the priority of repayment of his demand on condition that the assignment does not prejudice the rights of other creditors.

§ 1. Penalty

Article 260. Concept of Penalty

A penalty shall be deemed to be a monetary amount determined by legislation or by contract which the debtor shall be obliged to pay to the creditor in the event of the failure to perform or the improper performance of an obligation.

With regard to a demand concerning payment of a penalty the creditor shall not be obliged to prove the losses caused to him.

Only a valid demand shall be secured by a penalty.

A creditor shall not have the right to demand payment of a penalty unless the debtor bears responsibility for the failure to perform or the improper performance of the obligation.

Article 261. Forms of Penalty

A penalty shall be in the form of a fine or a forfeit.

A penalty to be paid by the debtor in the event of the failure to perform or the improper performance of obligations and calculated, as a rule, in a firm monetary amount, shall be a fine.

A penalty to be paid by the debtor in the event of delay of performance of obligations and calculated in a percentage of the unperformed part of the obligation for each day of delay shall be deemed to be a forfeit.

Article 262. Form of Agreement on Penalty

An agreement concerning a penalty must be concluded in written form.

Article 263. Legal Penalty

A creditor shall have the right to demand the payment of a penalty specified by a law (legal penalty) irrespective of whether the duty to pay it has been provided for by agreement of the parties.

The amount of a legal penalty may by agreement of the parties be increased if the law does not so prohibit.

§ 2. Pledge

Article 264. Concept and Grounds for Arising of Pledge

The transfer by one person to another of property or rights thereto as security for an obligation shall be considered to be a pledge.

By virtue of a pledge the creditor with regard to an obligation secured by a pledge (pledgeholder) shall have the right, in the event of the nonperformance by the debtor of this obligation, to receive satisfaction from the value of the pledged property preferentially before other creditors of the person to whom this property (pledgor) belongs in the procedure provided by a law [as amended by Law of 22 October 2019, No. ЗРУ-572].

The pledgeholder shall have the right to receive on the same principles satisfaction from insurance compensation for loss or damage of the pledged property irrespective of to whose benefit it was insured unless the loss or damage occurred for reasons for which the pledgeholder is liable.

A pledge shall arise by virtue of a contract or on the basis of a law.

Article 265. Types of Pledge

A pledge may be in the form of a pawn, mortgage, and also a pledge of rights.

A pledge under which the pledged property is transferred from the pledgor to the jurisdiction of the pledgeholder shall be deemed to be a pawn.

A pledge, the subject-matter of which is immoveable property, shall be deemed to be a mortgage.

Article 266. Pledgor

Either the debtor himself or a third person may be a pledgor.

The owner thereof may be the pledgor of a thing.

The person to whom the pledged right belongs may be the pledgor of a right.

The pledge of the right to a thing shall not be permitted without the consent of the owner unless provided otherwise by a law or by the contract.

Article 267. Subject of Pledge

Any property, including things and property rights (or demands), may be the subject of a pledge except for things withdrawn from turnover, demands inextricably connected with the person of the creditor, in particular, demands concerning compensation for harm caused to life or health, alimony, and other demands whose assignment to another person has been prohibited by a law.

The pledge of individual types of property of citizens against which levy of execution is not permitted, may be prohibited or limited by legislation.

Article 268. Demand Secured by Pledge

Unless provided otherwise by a contract, a pledge shall secure a demand in that amount which it has at the moment of satisfaction, in particular, interest, penalty, compensation of losses caused by delay of performance, and also compensation of necessary expenses of the pledgeholder for maintenance of the pledged thing and expenses relating to recovery.

Article 269. Pledge With and Without Transfer of Pledged Property to Pledgeholder

Pledged property shall remain with the pledgor unless provided otherwise by contract.

Pledged goods in turnover shall not be transferred to the pledgeholder [as amended by Law of 5 April 2007, No. ЗРУ-83. СЗ РУ (2007), no. 14, item 132].

The subject-matter of a pledge may be left with the pledgor under lock and seal of the pledgeholder (when there is a seal) [as amended by Law of 20 August 2015, No. ЗРУ-391. СЗ РУ (2015), no. 33, item 439].

The subject-matter of a pledge may be left with the pledgor with the imposition of marks testifying to the pledge (firm pledge).

The subject-matter of a pledge transferred by the pledgor for a time in possession or use to a third person shall be considered to be leaving it with the pledgor.

In the event of the pledge of a property right certified by a security, it shall be transferred to the pledgeholder or on deposit to a notary unless provided otherwise by the contract.

Article 270. Origin of Right of Pledge

The right of pledge shall arise from the moment of conclusion of the contract on pledge or, if the contract is subject to notarial certification, from the moment of notarial certification, and in the event of obligatory registration of the contract — from the moment of the registration thereof.

If the subject of pledge in accordance with a law or contract must be situated with the pledgeholder, the right of pledge shall arise at the moment of the transfer to him of the subject of pledge, and if such transfer was effectuated before the conclusion of the contract, from the moment of its conclusion.

Article 271. Contract on Pledge, Its Form and Registration

In the contract on pledge shall be specified the subject-matter of pledge and its valuation, the essence, amount, and period for performance of the obligation secured by the pledge, or information sufficient for identification of the subject-matter of the pledge and the obligation secured by it. It also must contain an indication of with which of the parties the pledged property is situated [as amended by Law of 22 October 2019, No. 3РУ-572].

The subject-matter of a pledge may be identified by means of a general description of the property, including by means of a description of the particular property as a separate type or class [added by Law of 22 October 2019, No. 3РУ-572].

An obligation secured by a pledge may be identified by means of an indication of the maximum amount of the obligation which may be repaid from the value of this property [added by Law of 22 October 2019, No. 3РУ-572].

A contract on pledge must be concluded in written form.

A contract on mortgage, and also a contract on the pledge of movable property or rights to property to secure obligations under a contract which must be notarially certified, shall be subject to notarial certification, except for contracts on mortgage and pledge in the event of the acquisition of an immoveable and means of transport on the primary market [as amended by Law of 14 January 2020, No. 3РУ-602].

A contract on mortgage must be registered in the procedure established for the registration of transactions with the respective property.

The failure to comply with the rules contained in paragraphs four, five, and six of the present Article shall entail the invalidity of the contract on pledge [as amended by Law of 22 October 2019, No. 3РУ-572].

Article 272. Property to Which Rights of Pledgeholder Extend

The rights of the pledgeholder (right of pledge) to a thing which is the subject of pledge shall extend to its appurtenances unless provided otherwise by contract.

The right of pledge shall extend to fruits, products, and revenues received as a result of the use of the pledged property in the instances provided for by contract.

In the event of the mortgage of an enterprise or other property complex as a whole the right of pledge shall extend to all of the property comprising it, movable and immovable, including the rights of demand and exclusive rights, amongst them those acquired during the period of the mortgage, unless provided otherwise by a law or contract.

The mortgage of a building or installation shall be permitted only with the simultaneous mortgage under the same contract of the land plot on which this building or installation is situated, or the part of this plot functionally ensuring the pledged object, or the right of lease of this plot or corresponding part thereof which belongs to the pledgor.

In the event of the mortgage of a land plot, the right of pledge shall not extend to buildings and installations of the pledgor situated or erected on this plot unless a condition provides otherwise in the contract.

In the absence in the contract of such a condition the pledgor shall in the event execution is levied against the pledged land plot retain the right of limited use (servitude) of that part thereof which is necessary for the use of the building or installation in accordance with its designation. Conditions for the use of this part of the plot shall be determined by agreement of the pledgor with the pledgeholder, and in the event of a dispute, by a court.

If a mortgage has been established on a land plot on which a building or installation is situated which belongs not to the pledgor, but to another person, then when the pledgeholder levies execution against this plot and in the event of its sale at a public sale, to the acquirer of the plot shall pass the rights and duties which the pledgor had with respect to this person.

The pledge of things and property rights which the pledgor acquires in future may be provided for by the contract on pledge, and with respect to a pledge arising on the basis of a law, by the law.

Article 273. Subsequent Pledge

Property under pledge may be granted by the pledgor on pledge to secure other demands (subsequent pledge) [as amended by Law of 22 October 2019, No. 3PY-572].

Subsequent pledge shall be permitted unless it is prohibited by preceding contracts on pledge and on condition of making a respective entry in the pledge register by preceding and subsequent pledgeholders [added by Law of 22 October 2019, No. 3PY-572].

The pledgor shall be obliged to communicate to each subsequent pledgeholder information about all of the existing pledges of the particular property and shall be liable for losses caused to pledgeholders by the failure to fulfill this duty.

If a preceding contract of pledge provides conditions on which a subsequent contract of pledge may be concluded, such contract of pledge must be concluded in compliance with the conditions specified in the preceding contract. In the event of a violation of the said conditions, the preceding pledgeholder shall have the right to demand compensation from the pledgor for losses caused to him [added by Law of 22 October 2019, No. 3PУ-572].

If property under pledge becomes the subject-matter of yet another pledge to secure other demands (subsequent pledge), the demands of the subsequent pledgeholder shall be satisfied from the value of this property in the procedure established by the present Code [added by Law of 22 October 2019, No. 3PУ-572].

Article 274. Content and Preservation of Pledged Property

The pledgor or pledgeholder, depending upon which of them has the pledged property (Article 269 of the present Code), shall be obliged, unless provided otherwise by law or contract, to:

(1) insure pledged property at its full value at the expense of the pledgor against risks of loss and damage, and if the full value of the property exceeds the amount of the demand secured by the pledge, for an amount not lower than the amount of the demand;

(2) take measures necessary in order to ensure the preservation of the pledged property, including to defend it against infringements and demands on the part of third persons;

(3) inform immediately the other party concerning the arising of the threat of loss or damage to the pledged property.

The pledgeholder and the pledgor shall have the right to verify by documents the actual existence, quantity, state, and conditions of keeping the pledged property situated with the other party.

In the event of a flagrant violation by the pledgeholder of the duties specified in paragraph one of the present Article which create a threat of loss or damage of the pledged property, the pledgor shall have the right to demand the termination of the pledge before time.

Article 275. Consequences of Loss of or Damage to Pledged Property

The pledgor shall bear the risk of accidental perishing or accidental damage to pledged property unless provided otherwise by the contract on pledge.

The pledgeholder shall be liable for the full or partial loss of or damage to the subject of pledge transferred to him unless it is proved that he may be relieved of responsibility in accordance with Article 333 of the present Code.

A pledgeholder shall be liable for the loss of the subject of pledge in the amount of its real value, and for the damaging thereof — the amount by which the value was reduced irrespective of the amount at which the subject of pledge was valued when transferring it to the pledgeholder.

If as a result of damage to the subject of pledge it has so changed that it cannot be used for its express designation, the pledgor shall have the right to reject it and to demand compensation for the loss thereof.

The duty of the pledgeholder to compensate the pledgor also for other losses caused by the loss of or damage to the subject-matter of pledge may be provided for by a contract.

The pledgor who is a debtor with regard to the obligation secured by a pledge shall have the right to set off the demand against the pledgeholder concerning compensation of losses caused by the loss of or damage to the subject-matter of pledge in repaying the obligation secured by the pledge.

Article 276. Substitution and Restoration of Subject of Pledge

The replacement of the subject of pledge shall be permitted with the consent of the pledgeholder unless provided otherwise by law or by contract.

If the subject of pledge has perished or is damaged or the right of ownership to it or the right of economic jurisdiction has been terminated on the grounds established by a law, the pledgor shall have the right within a reasonable period (and in the event of a dispute, within the period established by a court) to restore the subject of pledge or substitute other property of equal value unless provided otherwise by the contract.

Article 277. Use and Disposition of Subject of Pledge

The pledgor shall have the right, unless provided otherwise by contract and it follows from the essence of the pledge, to use the subject of pledge in accordance with its designation, including to derive fruits and revenues from it.

Unless provided otherwise by a law or contract and it follows from the essence of the pledge, the pledgor shall have the right to alienate the subject of pledge, to transfer it on lease or for use without compensation to another person, or otherwise to dispose of it only with the consent of the pledgeholder.

An agreement limiting the right of the pledgor to bequeath pledged property shall be void.

The pledgeholder shall have the right to use the subject of pledge transferred to him only in the instances provided for by contract, regularly submitting a report on use to the pledgor. The duty may be placed by contract on the pledgeholder to derive fruits and revenues from the subject of pledge for the purposes of repaying the principal obligation or in the interests of the pledgor.

Article 278. Defense by Pledgeholder of His Rights to Subject of Pledge

The pledgeholder with whom the pledged property is situated or should be situated shall have the right to demand and obtain it from another's illegal possession, including from the pledgor (Articles 228, 229, 230, and 232 of the present Code).

In instances when according to the conditions of the contract the pledgeholder has been granted the right to use a subject of pledge transferred to him, he may demand from other persons, including from the pledgor, the elimination of any violations of his right, even though these violations were not linked with deprivation of possession (Articles 232 and 232 of the present Code).

Article 279. Grounds for Levying Execution Against Pledged Property

Execution may be levied against pledged property in order to satisfy the demands of the pledgeholder (creditor) in the event of the failure to perform or the improper performance by the debtor of an obligation secured by the pledge under circumstances for which he is liable.

Levy of execution against pledged property may be refused if the violation of the obligation secured by the pledge which was permitted by the debtor is extremely insignificant and the amount of the demands of the pledgeholder as a consequence thereof is clearly incommensurate with the value of the pledged property, except for instances established by a law [as amended by Law of 5 April 2007, No. 3PУ-83. C3 PУ (2007), no. 14, item 132].

Article 280. Procedure for Levy of Execution Against Pledged Property

The demands of the pledgeholder (creditor) shall be satisfied from the value of pledged immovable property by decision of a court.

The satisfaction of the demand of a pledgeholder at the expense of the pledged immovable property without recourse to a court shall be permitted, if this is provided for in the contract on pledge or on the basis of a notarially certified agreement of the pledgeholder with the pledgor concluded after the grounds arise to levy execution on the subject-matter of the pledge. Such an agreement may be deemed by a court to be invalid upon the suit of the person whose rights were violated by such agreement [as amended by Law of 5 April 2007, No. 3PУ-83. C3 PУ (2007), no. 14, item 132].

The demands of a pledgeholder at the expense of pledged movable property shall be satisfied according to a judicial act unless provided otherwise by agreement of the pledgor with the pledgeholder. Execution may be levied against the subject of a pledge transferred to the pledgeholder in the procedure established by the contract on pledge unless a different procedure has been established by a law [as amended by Law of 22 October 2019, No. 3PУ-572].

Execution may be levied against the subject of pledge only by decision of a court in instances when:

(1) a requirement has been established by a law concerning the consent or authorization of another person or agency for the conclusion of a contract on pledge [as amended by Law of 22 October 2019, No. 3PУ-572];

(2) property having historical, scientific, artistic, or other cultural value is the subject of pledge [as amended by Law of 18 April 2018, No. 3PУ-476];

(3) the pledgor is absent and it is impossible to establish his whereabouts.

Article 281. Realization of Pledged Property

The compulsory realization of pledged property against which execution is levied in accordance with Article 280 of the present Code shall be made by means of sale at public sale in the form of an electronic online auction in the procedure established by legislation [as amended by Law of 22 October 2019, No. 3PУ-572].

At the request of the pledgor the court shall have the right in the decision concerning levy of execution against pledged property to defer the sale thereof at public sale for a period of up to one year. The deferral shall not affect the rights and duties of the parties with regard to an obligation secured by the pledge of this property and shall not relieve the debtor from compensating the losses of the creditor and penalty which grew during the period of deferral and penalty [as amended by Law of 22 October 2019, No. 3PУ-572].

Pledged property against which execution is levied in an extra-judicial procedure may be realized by means of public sale, direct sale, transfer on credit, finance leasing, lease, installment sale, or through other transactions not prohibited by legislation. When a public sale is declared to be unconstituted (in the event execution is levied against pledged property in an extra-judicial procedure), a pledgeholder shall have the right by agreement with the pledgor to acquire the pledged property and to set off against the purchase price his demands secured by the pledge. The rules concerning the contract of purchase/sale shall apply to such an agreement [as amended by Law of 22 October 2019, No. 3PУ-572].

In the event a second public sale is declared to be unconstituted, the pledgeholder shall have the right to retain the subject-matter of pledge, valuing it in an amount of not more than 10% less that the initial sale price of the unrealized subject-matter of pledge at the second public sale [as amended by Law of 22 October 2019, No. 3PУ-572].

If the pledgeholder does not take advantage of the right to keep the subject-matter of pledge within a month from the day of announcement of the second public sale being unconstituted, the contract on pledge shall terminate.

If the amount received when realizing the pledged property is insufficient to cover the demand of the pledgeholder, he shall have the right in the absence of another indication in a law or the contract to receive the amount in arrears from other property of the debtor which does not enjoy a preference based on the right of pledge.

If the amount received in the event of the realization of the pledged property exceeds the amount of the demands of the pledgeholder secured by the pledge of the particular property, the difference shall be returned to the pledgor [as amended by Law of 22 October 2019, No. 3PУ-572].

A debtor or pledgor who are a third person shall have the right at any time until the realization of the subject-matter of pledge to terminate the levy of execution on it and the realization thereof, having performed the obligation secured by the pledge or that part thereof whose performance has been delayed. An agreement limiting this right shall be null [as amended by Law of 22 October 2019, No. ЗРУ-572].

Article 282. Performance of Obligation Before Time Secured by Pledge and Levy of Execution Against Pledged Property

A pledgeholder shall have the right to demand the performance before time of an obligation secured by pledge in instances of:

(1) the subject of pledge departed from the possession of the pledgor with whom it was left in violation of the conditions of the contract on pledge;

(2) a violation by the pledgor of the rules concerning substitution of the subject of pledge (Article 276 of the present Code);

(3) loss of the subject of pledge under circumstances for which the pledgeholder is not liable if the pledgor has not taken advantage of the right provided for by Article 276, paragraph two, of the present Code.

The pledgeholder shall have the right to demand the performance before time of the obligation secured by pledge and, if this demand is not satisfied, to levy execution against the subject of pledge in instances of:

(1) a violation by the pledgor of rules concerning subsequent pledge (Article 273 of the present Code);

(2) the failure of the pledgor to fulfill the duties relating to the maintenance and preservation of pledged property provided for by Article 274, paragraph one, subpoints (1) and (2), and paragraph two, of the present Code;

(3) a violation by the pledgor of the rules concerning the disposition of pledged property (Article 277, paragraphs two and three, of the present Code);

(4) levy of execution against pledged property by other creditors, including in the event of the enforcement of judicial acts and acts of other agencies [added by Law of 22 September 2010, No. ЗРУ-260, as amended by Law of 22 October 2019, No. ЗРУ-572].

Article 283. Termination of Pledge

A pledge shall terminate:

(1) with the termination of the obligation secured by the pledge;

(2) upon the demand of the pledgor when there exist the grounds provided for by Article 274, paragraph three, of the present Code;

(3) in the event of the perishing of the pledged thing or termination of the pledged right unless the pledgor has taken advantage of the right provided for by Article 276, paragraph two, of the present Code;

(4) in the event of the realization of pledged property, and also when the realization thereof has proved to be impossible (Article 281 of the present Code). A notation in the register in which the contract on mortgage was registered must be made concerning the termination of the mortgage [as amended by Law of 22 October 2019, No. ЗРУ-572];

(5) if the pledgeholder has not taken advantage of the right provided by Article 282, paragraph two, point (4), of the present Code, except for instances when the pledged property was not realized and the creditors whose demands were not secured by the pledge refused to accept this property in order to satisfy their demands [added by Law of 22 September 2010, No. ЗРУ-260. СЗ РУ (2010), no. 38, item 328].

In the event of the termination of pledge as a consequence of the performance of the obligation secured by the pledge or at the demand of the pledgor (Article 274, paragraph three, of the present Code), the pledgeholder with whom the pledged property is situated shall be obliged immediately to return it to the pledgor.

Article 284. Preservation of Pledge in Event of Transfer of Right to Pledged Property to Another Person

In the event of the transfer of the right of ownership to pledged property or the right of economic jurisdiction to it from the pledgor to another person as a result of the compensated or gratuitous alienation of this property or by way of universal legal succession, the right of pledge shall retain force, except for the pledge of goods in turnover and instances when the pledgeholder agrees to the transfer of the right of ownership or right of economic jurisdiction in the pledged property without retention of the pledge to another person [as amended by Law of 22 October 2019, No. ЗРУ-572].

The legal successor of the pledgor shall take the place of the pledgor and shall bear all the duties of the pledgor, unless established otherwise by an agreement with the pledgeholder.

If the property of the pledgor which is the subject-matter of pledge has passed by way of legal succession to several persons, each of the legal successors (or acquirers of the property) shall bear the consequences arising from the pledge for the failure to perform the obligation secured by the pledge commensurate with the part of the said property which has passed to him. If the subject-matter of the pledge is indivisible or on other grounds remains in the common ownership of the legal successors, they shall become joint and several pledgors.

Article 285. Consequences of Compulsory Withdrawal of Pledged Property

If the right of ownership of a pledgor to property which is the subject-matter of pledge terminates on the grounds and in the procedure established by a law as a consequence of the withdrawal (or purchase) thereof for social needs, requisition, or nationalization, other property or respective compensation (or contributory compensation) shall be granted to the pledgor. In this event the right of pledge shall extend to the property granted instead or, respectively, the pledgeholder shall acquire the right of preferential satisfaction of his demand from the amount of compensation (or contributory compensation) due to the pledgor [as amended by Law of 29 June 2022, No. ЗРУ-782].

In the instances when property which is the subject-matter of pledge is withdrawn from the pledgor in the procedure established by a law on the grounds that in reality the owner of this property is another person (Article 228 of the present Code) in the form of a sanction, the pledge with respect to this property shall terminate [as amended by Law of 22 October 2019, No. ЗРУ-572].

In the instances provided for by paragraphs one and two of the present Article the pledgeholder shall have the right to demand performance before time of the obligation secured by the pledge.

Article 286. Assignment of Rights Regarding Contract on Pledge

A pledgeholder shall have the right to transfer his rights under a contract concerning the pledge to another person while complying with the rules on the transfer of the rights of a creditor by means of the assignment of a demand (Articles 313-321 of the present Code).

The assignment by the pledgeholder of his rights under a contract on pledge to another person shall be valid if the rights of demand against the debtor regarding the principal obligation secured by pledge have been assigned to the same person.

Insofar as not proved otherwise, the assignment of rights under a contract on mortgage shall also mean the assignment of rights relating to the obligation secured by the mortgage.

Article 287. Transfer of Debt Regarding Obligation Secured by Pledge

With the transfer of a debt regarding an obligation secured by a pledge to another person, the pledge shall terminate unless the pledgor has given consent to the creditor to be liable for the new debtor (Article 322 of the present Code).

Article 288. Pledge of Goods in Turnover

A pledge of goods while leaving them with the pledgor and granting to the pledgor the right to change the composition and natural form of the pledged property (goods reserves, raw material, materials, semi-fabricates, finished products, and the like) on condition that their total value does not become less than that specified in the contract on pledge, shall be deemed to be a pledge of goods in turnover.

A reduction of the value of the pledged goods in turnover shall be permitted commensurately with the performed part of the obligation secured by pledge unless provided otherwise by the contract.

Goods in turnover alienated by a pledgor shall cease to be the subject of pledge from the moment of their transfer into ownership, economic jurisdiction, or operative management of the acquirer, and goods acquired by the pledgor which are specified in the contract on pledge shall become the subject of pledge from the moment the right of the pledgor arises to ownership therein.

In the event of a violation by the pledgor of the conditions of a pledge of goods in turnover, the pledgeholder shall have the right, by placing his marks and seals (when there is a seal) on the pledged goods, to suspend operations with them until the violation is eliminated [as amended by Law of 20 August 2015, No. ЗРУ-391. СЗ РУ (2015), no. 33, item 439].

Article 289. Pledge of Things in Pawnshop

The acceptance from citizens on pledge of movable property intended for personal consumption to secure short-term micro-loans may be effectuated as entrepreneurial activity by specialized organizations — pawnshops — effectuating activity by way of notification [as amended by Laws of 12 October 2021, No. ЗРУ-721, and of 20 April 2022, No. ЗРУ-765].

A contract on the pledge of things in a pawnshop shall be formalized by the issuance of a pledge ticket by the pawnshop.

The pledged things shall be transferred to the pawnshop.

The pawnshop shall be obliged to insure to the benefit of the pledgor at his expense things accepted on pledge for the full amount of their value as established in accordance with prices for things of this type and quality at the moment of their acceptance on pledge.

The pawnshop shall not have the right to use and dispose of pledged things.

The pawnshop shall bear responsibility for loss of and damage to pledged things unless it is proved that the loss or damage occurred as a consequence of insuperable force.

In the event of the failure to return the amount of the credit within the established period secured by the pledge of things to the pawnshop, the pawnshop shall have the right on the basis of an endorsement of execution of a notary upon the expiry of a grace month's period to sell this property in the procedure established for the realization of pledged property (Article 281 of the present Code). After this demand of the pawnshop against the pledgor (debtor) is paid, even if the amount received when realizing the pledged property is insufficient for the full satisfaction thereof [as amended by Law of 22 October 2019, No. ЗРУ-572].

The rules for granting credits to citizens by pawnshops under pledge of things belonging to citizens shall be established by legislation.

The conditions of a contract on pledge of things in a pawnshop limiting the rights of the pledgor in comparison with the rights granted him by the present Code and by other laws shall be null.

§ 3. Withholding

Article 290. Grounds of Withholding

A creditor with whom a thing is situated which is subject to transfer to a debtor or to another person specified by the debtor shall have the right in the event of the failure of the debtor to perform the obligation relating to payment for this thing within the period or to compensate the creditor for expenses and other losses connected therewith to withhold it so long as the respective obligation is not performed.

The withholding of a thing may also secure demands that, although not connected with the payment for the thing or compensation of costs therefor and other losses, but arose from an obligation, the parties to which act as entrepreneurs.

A creditor may withhold a thing situated with him notwithstanding the fact that after this thing came into the possession of the creditor the rights thereto have been acquired by a third person.

The rules of the present Article shall apply unless provided otherwise by a contract.

Article 291. Satisfaction of Demands at Expense of Withheld Property

The demands of a creditor who is withholding a thing shall be satisfied from the value thereof in the amount and procedure provided for the satisfaction of demands secured by a pledge.

§ 4. Suretyship

Article 292. Contract of Suretyship

Under a contract of suretyship the surety shall be obliged to the creditor of another person to be liable for the performance by the last of his obligation in full or in part.

A contract of suretyship may be concluded also in order to secure an obligation which arises in future.

A contract of suretyship must be concluded in writing. The failure to comply with the written form shall entail the invalidity of the contract of suretyship.

Article 293. Responsibility of Surety

In the event of the failure to perform or the improper performance by the debtor of an obligation secured by a suretyship, the surety and the debtor shall be liable to a creditor jointly and severally unless subsidiary responsibility of the surety has been provided for by a law or by contract.

The surety shall be liable to the creditor in the same amount as the debtor, including the payment of interest, compensation for court costs relating to recovery of the debt, and other losses of the creditor caused by the failure to perform or the improper performance of the obligation by the debtor unless provided otherwise by the contract of suretyship.

Persons who have given a suretyship jointly shall be liable to the creditor jointly and severally unless provided otherwise by the contract of suretyship.

Article 294. Rights and Duties of Surety in Event of Suit Brought Against Him

The surety shall have the right to advance against the demand of the creditor all of those objections which the debtor could present. The surety shall not lose the right to these objections even if the debtor waived them or has acknowledged his obligation.

If suit has been brought against the surety, then he shall be obliged to enlist the debtor to participate in the case. Otherwise the debtor shall have the right to advance against the counter demand of the surety all those objections which he had against the creditor.

Article 295. Rights of Surety Who Has Performed Obligation

To a surety who has performed an obligation shall pass the rights of the creditor with regard to this obligation and the rights which belonged to the creditor as pledgeholder in that amount which the surety satisfied the demand of the creditor. The surety also shall have the right to demand from the debtor the payment of interest on the amount paid to the creditor and compensation for other losses incurred in connection with responsibility for the debtor.

Upon performance by the surety of the obligation the creditor shall be obliged to hand over to the surety the documents certifying the demand against the debtor and to transfer the rights which secure this demand.

The rules established by the present Article shall be applied unless provided otherwise by a law or by the contract of the surety with the debtor.

Article 296. Notification of Surety about Performance of Obligation by Debtor

The debtor who has performed an obligation secured by a suretyship shall be obliged immediately to notify the surety thereof. Otherwise the surety who in turn has performed the obligation shall have the right to recover from the creditor that unjustifiably received or to present a regressive demand against the debtor. In the last instance the debtor shall have the right to recover from the creditor only that unjustly received.

Article 297. Payment for Services of Surety

A surety shall have the right to remuneration for services rendered by him to the debtor unless provided otherwise by the contract.

Article 298. Termination of Suretyship

A suretyship shall terminate with the termination of the obligation secured by it, and also in the event of a change of this obligation which entails an increase of responsibility or other unfavorable consequences for the surety without his consent.

A suretyship shall terminate with the transfer to another person of the debt relating to the obligation secured by the suretyship unless the surety has given consent to the creditor to bear responsibility for the new debtor, and also when the creditor has refused to accept proper performance offered by the debtor or the surety upon the ensuing of the period of performance of the obligation secured by it.

A suretyship shall terminate upon the expiry of the period for which it was given specified in the contract. If such period has not been established, the suretyship shall terminate if the creditor within a year from the date of ensuing of the period of performance of the obligation secured by the suretyship a suit against the surety has not been brought. If the period of performance of the principal obligation has not been specified and can not be determined or is determined by the moment of demand, the suretyship shall terminate if the creditor does not bring suit against the surety within one year from the date of concluding the contract of suretyship.

§ 5. Guarantee

Article 299. Concept of Guarantee

By virtue of a guarantee the bank, other credit institution, or insurance organization (guarantor) gives at the request of another person (principal) a written obligation to pay to the creditor of the principal (beneficiary) a monetary amount in accordance with the conditions of the obligation given by the guarantor upon the presentation by the beneficiary of a written demand concerning the payment thereof.

Article 300. Securing Obligation of Principal by Guarantee

A guarantee shall secure the proper performance by the principal of his obligation to the beneficiary (principal obligation).

The principal shall pay remuneration to the guarantor for the issuance of a guarantee.

Article 301. Independence of Guarantee from Principal Obligation

The obligation of the guarantor to the beneficiary provided for by the guarantee is not dependent in the relations between them upon the principal obligation, to secure the performance of which it was issued even if the guarantee contains a reference to this obligation.

Article 302. Irrevocability of Guarantee

A guarantee may not be revoked by the guarantor unless provided otherwise therein.

Article 303. Nontransferability of Rights Under Guarantee

The right of demand against the guarantor which belongs to the beneficiary under the guarantee may not be transferred to another person unless provided otherwise in the guarantee.

Article 304. Entry of Guarantee into Force

A guarantee shall enter into force from the date of its issuance unless provided otherwise in the guarantee.

Article 305. Presentation of Demand under Guarantee

The demand of a beneficiary concerning the payment of a monetary amount under a guarantee must be submitted to the guarantor in writing with the documents specified in the guarantee appended. In the demand or in the annex thereto the beneficiary must specify what the violation by the principal of the principal obligation consists of, to secure which the guarantee was issued.

The demand of the beneficiary must be submitted to the guarantor before the period specified in the guarantee for which it was issued ends.

Article 306. Duties of Guarantor When Demand of Beneficiary is Considered

Upon receipt of the demand of the beneficiary the guarantor must without delay inform the principal thereof and transfer to him a copy of the demand with all documents relevant thereto.

The guarantor must consider the demand of the beneficiary with the documents appended thereto within the period specified in the guarantee, and in the absence thereof, with a commensurate period to display reasonable care in order to establish whether this demand and the documents appended thereto correspond to the conditions of the guarantee.

Article 307. Refusal of Guarantor to Satisfy Demand of Beneficiary

The guarantor shall refuse to the beneficiary satisfaction of his demand if this demand or the documents appended thereto do not correspond to the conditions of the guarantee or have been submitted to the guarantor at the end of the period specified in the guarantee.

The guarantor must immediately notify the beneficiary about the refusal to satisfy his demand.

If it becomes known to the guarantor before satisfaction of the demand of the beneficiary that the principal obligation secured by the guarantee has been performed fully or in respective part, or has been terminated on other grounds, or is invalid, he must immediately communicate this to the beneficiary and the principal.

Article 308. Limits of Obligations of Guarantor

An obligation of the guarantor to a beneficiary provided for by a guarantee shall be limited to payment of the amount for which the guarantee was issued.

Unless provided otherwise in the guarantee, the responsibility of the guarantor to the beneficiary for the failure to fulfill or the improper fulfillment by the guarantor of the obligation under the guarantee shall not be limited to the amount for which the guarantee was issued.

Article 309. Termination of Guarantee

The obligation of the guarantor to a beneficiary under a guarantee shall be terminated:

(1) by payment to the beneficiary of the amount for which the guarantee was issued;

(2) ending of period specified in the guarantee for which it was issued;

(3) as a consequence of the waiver by the beneficiary of his rights under the guarantee and the return thereof to the guarantor;

(4) as a consequence of the waiver by the beneficiary of his rights under the guarantee by a written statement to release the guarantor from his obligations.

The termination of the obligation of the guarantor on the grounds specified in points 1, 2, and 4, paragraph one, of the present Article shall not depend upon whether the guarantee is returned to him.

A guarantor to whom the termination of a guarantee has become known must without delay notify the principal thereof.

Article 310. Regressive Demands of Guarantor Against Principal

The right of the guarantor to demand from the principal by way of regression the compensation of amounts paid to the beneficiary under a guarantee shall be determined by agreement of the guarantor with the principal for the performance of which the guarantee was issued.

The guarantor shall not have the right to demand from the principal the compensation of amounts paid to the beneficiary not in accordance with the conditions of the guarantee or for a violation of the obligation of the guarantor to the beneficiary unless provided otherwise by agreement of the guarantor with the principal.

§ 6. Deposit

Article 311. Concept of Deposit. Form of Agreement on Deposit

A deposit shall be deemed to be a monetary amount issued by one of the contracting parties as evidence of the conclusion of the contract and to secure its performance.

An agreement on deposit, irrespective of the amount of the deposit, must be concluded in writing.

In the event of doubt as to whether the amount is paid on the account of payments due from a party under the contract as a deposit, in particular as a consequence of the failure to comply with the rule established by paragraph two of the present Article, this amount shall be considered to be paid as an advance unless proved otherwise.

Article 312. Consequences of Termination and Failure to Perform Obligation Secured by Deposit

In the event of the termination of the obligation before the commencement of the performance thereof by agreement of the parties or as a consequence of the impossibility of performance (Article 349 of the present Code) the deposit must be returned.

If for the failure to perform the contract the party which gave the deposit is responsible, it shall remain with the other party. If for the failure to perform the contract the party which received the deposit is responsible, it shall be obliged to pay the other party twice the amount of the deposit.

In addition the party responsible for the failure to perform the contract shall be obliged to compensate the other party for losses, setting off the amount of the deposit unless provided otherwise in the contract.

Chapter 23. Change of Persons in Obligation

Article 313. Grounds and Procedure for Transfer of Rights of Creditor to Other Person

The right (or demand) belonging to a creditor on the basis of an obligation may be transferred by him to another person with regard to the transaction (assignment of demand) or pass to another person on the basis of a law.

The consent of the debtor, unless provided otherwise by law or by contract, shall not be required for the transfer of the rights of the creditor to another person.

If the debtor was not informed in writing about the transfer of the rights of the creditor to another person, the new creditor shall bear the risk of the unfavorable consequences caused by this for him. In this event the performance of the obligation to the initial creditor shall be deemed to be performance to a proper creditor.

The rules concerning the transfer of the rights of a creditor to another person shall not apply to the regressive demands.

Article 314. Rights Which May Not Pass to Other Persons

The transfer to another person of the rights inextricably connected with the person of the creditor, in particular, demands concerning alimony and compensation of harm caused to life or health, shall not be permitted.

Article 315. Amount of Rights of Creditor Passing to Other Person

Unless provided otherwise by a law or by contract, the right of the initial creditor shall pass to the new creditor in that amount and on those conditions which existed at the moment of transfer of the right. In particular, to the new creditor shall pass the rights securing the performance of the obligation, and also other rights connected with the demand, including the right to unpaid interest.

Article 316. Evidence of Rights of New Creditor

The creditor who has assigned a demand to another person shall be obliged to transfer to him the documents certifying the right of demand and to communicate information having significance for the effectuation of the demand.

The debtor shall have the right not to perform the obligation to a new creditor until the submission to him of evidence of the transfer of the demand to this person.

Article 317. Objections of Debtor Against Demand of New Creditor

The debtor shall have the right to advance against the demand of a new creditor objections which he had against the initial creditor at the moment of receipt of notification concerning the transfer of the rights regarding the obligation to the new creditor.

Article 318. Transfer of Rights of Creditor to Another Person on Basis of Law

The rights of a creditor relating to an obligation shall pass to another person:

(1) as a result of universal legal succession to the rights of the creditor;

(2) by decision of a court concerning the transfer of the rights of the creditor to another person;

(3) as a consequence of the performance of the obligation of the debtor by his surety or by a pledgor who is not the debtor with regard to the obligation;

(4) in the event of the subrogation (or transfer) to an insurer of the rights of the creditor with respect to the debtor who is responsible for the ensuing of an insured event;

(5) in the other instances provided for by a law.

Article 319. Conditions of Assignment of Demand

The assignment of a demand by the creditor to another person shall be permitted insofar as this is not contrary to legislation or a contract.

The assignment of the demand regarding the obligation in which the person of the creditor has material significance for the debtor without the consent of the debtor shall not be permitted.

Article 320. Form of Assignment of Demand

The assignment of a demand based on a transaction concluded in simple written or notarial form must be concluded in the same form.

The assignment of a demand relating to a transaction requiring State registration must be registered in the procedure established for registration of this transaction.

The assignment of a demand regarding an order security shall be concluded by means of an endorsement (inscription of transfer) on this security.

Article 321. Responsibility of Creditor Who Has Assigned Demand

The initial creditor who has assigned a demand shall be liable to the new creditor for the invalidity of the demand transferred to him but shall not be liable for the failure to perform this demand by the debtor except when the initial creditor assumed a suretyship for the debtor to the new creditor.

Article 322. Transfer of Debt

The transfer by the debtor of his debt to another person shall be permitted only with the consent of the creditor.

The new debtor shall have the right to advance against the demand of the creditor all of the objections based on relations between the creditor and the initial debtor.

A suretyship or pledge established by a third person shall terminate with the transfer of the debt unless the surety or pledgor has expressed consent to be liable for the new debtor.

The rules contained in Article 320, paragraphs one and two, of the present Code shall apply respectively to the form of the transfer of debt.

Article 323. Parallel Transfer of Debt and Transfer of Performance

The transfer of a debt or part thereof without relieving the debtor from the obligation with regard to payment of the debt shall be authorized. In this event both debtors shall bear joint and several responsibility for the performance of the obligation.

On the basis of a contract of the debtor with a third person, the last shall bear responsibility for the performance of the obligation only with respect to the debtor, but not the creditor.

Chapter 24. Responsibility for Violation of Obligations

Article 324. Duty of Debtor to Compensate Losses

A debtor shall be obliged to compensate the creditor for losses caused by the failure to perform or improper performance of an obligation.

Unless provided otherwise by legislation or by contract, when determining losses the prices which existed in that place where the obligation was to have been performed on the date of voluntary satisfaction by the debtor of the demand of the creditor shall be taken into account, and if the demand was not voluntarily satisfied, on the day of bringing the suit. Proceeding from the circumstances, a court may satisfy the demand to compensate losses by taking into account the prices existing on the day of rendering the decision.

When determining lost advantage the measures undertaken by the creditor to receive it and the preparations made for this purpose shall be taken into account.

Article 325. Penalty and Losses

If a penalty has been established for the failure to perform or for improper performance of an obligation, the losses shall be compensated in the part not covered by the penalty.

Instances may be provided for by a law or by contract: when the recovery of only a penalty is permitted, but not of losses; when losses may be recovered in full above the penalty; when at the choice of the creditor either a penalty or losses may be recovered.

Article 326. Reduction of Penalty

If a penalty subject to payment is clearly incommensurate with the consequences of the violation of an obligation of the creditor, a court shall have the right to reduce the penalty. In so doing the degree of the fulfillment of the obligation by the debtor must be taken into account, the property status of the parties participating in the obligation, and also the interests of the creditor.

A court shall have the right, in exceptional instances, taking into account the interests of the debtor and the creditor, to reduce the penalty subject to payment to the creditor.

Article 327. Responsibility for Failure to Perform Monetary Obligation

For the use of another's monetary assets as a consequence of their unlawful withholding, avoidance of the return thereof, other delay in the payment thereof or the unjustified receipt or savings thereof at the expense of another person interest shall be subject to payment on the amount of these assets.

The amount of interest shall be determined as the rate of bank interest on the day of performance of the monetary obligation or respective part thereof which existed at the place of residence of the creditor, and if the creditor is a juridical person, at the place of its location. In the event of the recovery of a debt in a judicial proceeding the court may satisfy the demand of the creditor by proceeding from the bank interest rate on the date of presenting the suit or on the date of rendering the decision. These rules shall apply unless another amount of interest has been established by a law or by the contract.

If the losses caused to a creditor by the unlawful use of his monetary assets exceed the amount of interest due him on the basis of paragraphs one and two of the present Article, he shall have the right to demand from the debtor compensation of losses in that part exceeding this amount.

Article 328. Performance of Obligation at Expense of Debtor

In the event of the failure to perform an obligation by a debtor to manufacture and transfer a thing in ownership, economic jurisdiction, or operative management, or to transfer a thing for use to a creditor, or to fulfill specified work or to render a service for him, the creditor shall have the right within a reasonable period to commission the fulfillment of the obligation to third persons for a reasonable price or to fulfill it by his own efforts unless it follows otherwise from legislation, the contract, or the essence of the obligation, and to demand from the debtor compensation for necessary expenses and other losses incurred.

Article 329. Subsidiary Responsibility

Until demands are brought against the person who in accordance with legislation or with the conditions of an obligation bears responsibility additionally to the responsibility of another person who is the principal debtor (subsidiary responsibility), the creditor must present the demand to the principal debtor.

If the principal debtor refused to satisfy the demand of the creditor or the creditor has not received a reply from him within a reasonable period to the demand presented, this demand may be presented to the person who bears subsidiary responsibility.

A creditor shall not have the right to demand satisfaction of his demand against the principal debtor from a person bearing subsidiary responsibility if this demand can be satisfied by means of the set-off of the counter demand against the principal debtor, or by the uncontested recovery of assets from the principal debtor.

The person who bears subsidiary responsibility must until satisfaction of the demand presented to him by the creditor warn the principal debtor thereof, and if suit is brought against such person, to involve the principal debtor in the case. Otherwise the principal debtor shall have the right to advance against the regressive demand of the person subsidiarily liable objections which he had against the creditor.

Article 330. Responsibility and Performance of Obligation in Kind

The payment of a penalty and compensation of losses in the event of the improper performance of an obligation shall not relieve the debtor from performance of the obligation in kind unless provided otherwise by a law or by contract.

The compensation of losses in the event of the failure to perform an obligation and the payment of a penalty for the failure to perform shall relieve the debtor from the performance of the obligation in kind unless provided otherwise by a law or by contract.

The refusal of a creditor to accept performance which as a consequence of delay has lost interest for him (Article 337, paragraph two, of the present Code), and also the payment of a penalty established as release-money (Article 342 of the present Code), shall relieve the debtor from performance of the obligation in kind.

Article 331. Consequences of Failure to Perform Obligation to Transfer Individually-Specified Thing

In the event of the failure to perform an obligation to transfer an individually-specified thing in ownership, economic jurisdiction, operative management, or use to a creditor, the last shall have the right to demand that this thing be taken away from the debtor and the transfer thereof to the creditor on the conditions provided for by the obligation. This right shall disappear if the thing already has been transferred to a third person having the same kind of right. If the thing has not yet been transferred, those creditors to whose benefit the obligation arose earlier shall have priority, and if this is impossible to establish, then he who has brought suit earlier.

The creditor shall have the right to demand compensation of losses instead of a demand to transfer the thing to him which is the subject of the obligation.

Article 332. Limitation of Amount of Responsibility for Obligations

The right to full compensation of losses may be limited (limited responsibility) by a law with regard to individual types of obligations and with regard to obligations connected with the specified nature of activity.

An agreement concerning the limitation of the amount of responsibility of a debtor under a contract of adhesion or other contract in which the citizen acting as a consumer is a creditor shall be invalid if the amount of responsibility for the particular type of obligations or for the particular violation has been determined by a law and if the agreement was concluded before the circumstances ensue which entail responsibility for the failure to perform or the improper performance of the obligation.

Article 333. Grounds of Responsibility for Violation of Obligations

A debtor shall be liable for the failure to perform or the improper performance of an obligation when there is fault unless provided otherwise by legislation or a contract.

The absence of fault shall be proved by the person who violated the obligation.

Unless provided otherwise by a law or by contract, the person who has not performed or who has improperly performed an obligation shall, when effectuating entrepreneurial activity, bear responsibility unless it is proved that proper performance proved to be impossible as a consequence of insuperable force, that is, extraordinary and unavertable circumstances (force majeure) under the particular conditions. There shall not be relegated to such circumstances, in particular, a violation of duties on the part of the contracting parties of the debtor, the absence in the market of goods necessary for performance, and the lack of necessary cash assets on the part of the debtor.

An agreement concluded beforehand concerning the elimination or limitation of responsibility for an intentional violation of an obligation shall be void.

Article 334. Responsibility of Debtor for Actions of Third Persons

A debtor shall be liable for the failure to perform or the improper performance of the obligation by third persons on whom performance has been placed unless it has been established by legislation or a contract that responsibility shall be borne by the third person who is the immediate performer.

Article 335. Fault of Creditor

If a creditor has intentionally or through negligence facilitated the ensuing of the impossibility of the performance of an obligation or an increase of the amount of losses caused by the failure to perform, and also if a creditor intentionally or through negligence has not taken measures to reduce losses from the failure to perform, a court shall have the right, depending upon the circumstances of the case, to reduce the amount of compensation or to refuse compensation entirely to the creditor.

Article 336. Consequences of Failure to Perform Bilateral Contract

If performance has become impossible in a bilateral contract for one party by virtue of a circumstance for which it is liable, the other party, insofar as not provided otherwise by a law or contract, shall have the right to repudiate the contract and to recover losses caused by the failure to perform the contract.

Article 337. Delay of Performance by Debtor and Creditor

A debtor who has delayed performance shall be liable to the creditor for losses caused by the delay and for the impossibility of performance which incidentally ensued during the delay.

If as a consequence of delay of the debtor the performance has lost interest for the creditor, he may refuse to accept performance and demand compensation of losses.

The creditor shall be considered to have delayed if he refused to accept proper performance offered by the debtor or did not perform actions which he should have performed before the performance of which the debtor could not perform his obligation.

Article 338. Consequences of Delay of Creditor

Delay on the part of a creditor in the acceptance of that which is due under a contract shall give to the debtor the right to compensation for losses caused by the delay and relieve him from responsibility for the impossibility of performance, except for instances of intent or gross negligence of the debtor.

A debtor shall not be obliged under a monetary obligation to pay interest for the period of delay of the creditor.

Article 339. Relieving Creditor from Responsibility for Delay

A creditor shall be relieved from responsibility for delay if it is proved that it was caused by the intent or negligence of those persons on whom by virtue of a law or commission of the creditor the acceptance of performance was placed.

Chapter 25. Termination of Obligations

Article 340. Grounds for Termination of Obligations

An obligation shall terminate wholly or in part on the grounds provided for by the present Code, other legislative acts, or contract.

The termination of an obligation relating to the demand of one of the parties shall be permitted only in the instances provided for by legislation or by contract.

Article 341. Termination of Obligation by Performance

An obligation shall be terminated, as a rule, by the proper performance thereof.

Article 342. Release-Money

By agreement of the parties an obligation may be terminated by granting release-money in place of performance (payment of money, transfer of property, etc.). The amount, periods, and procedure for granting release-money shall be established by the parties.

Article 343. Termination of Obligation by Set-Off

An obligation shall be terminated wholly or in part by the set-off of a counter demand of the same type, the period for which has ensued or the period of which has not been specified or is determined by the moment of demand.

The statements by one party are sufficient for set-off.

Article 344. Inadmissibility of Set-Off

The set-off of demands shall not be permitted:

with regard to which the period of limitations has expired;

concerning compensation of harm which has given rise to the impairment of health or causing the death of a citizen;

concerning the recovery of alimony;

concerning the alienation of a house on condition of maintenance for life;

in other instances provided for by a law or by a contract.

Article 345. Set-Off in Event of Assignment of Demand

In the event of the assignment of a demand the debtor shall have the right to set-off against the demand of the new creditor his counter demand against the initial creditor.

The set-off shall be made if the demand arose on a grounds which existed at the moment of receipt by the debtor of information concerning the assignment of the demand and the period of the demand ensued before receiving it or this period was not specified or is determined by the moment of demand.

Article 346. Termination of Obligation by Coincidence of Debtor and Creditor in One Person

An obligation shall terminate by the coinciding of the debtor and the creditor in one person.

Article 347. Termination of Obligation by Novation

An obligation shall be terminated by agreement of the parties concerning the substitution of the initial obligation which existed between them by another obligation between the same persons providing for another subject or means of performance (novation).

Novation shall not be permitted with respect to obligations relating to compensation for harm caused to life or health and relating to the payment of alimony.

Novation shall terminate additional obligations connected with the initial one unless provided otherwise by agreement of the parties.

Article 348. Forgiveness of Debt

An obligation shall be terminated by the release of the debtor by the creditor from the duties on him unless this violates the rights of other persons with respect to the property of the creditor.

Article 349. Termination of Obligation for Impossibility of Performance

An obligation shall be terminated by the impossibility of performance if it was caused by a circumstance for which none of the parties is liable.

In the event of the impossibility of performance by a debtor of an obligation caused by the guilty actions of the creditor, the last shall not have the right to demand the return of that which has been performed under the obligation.

Article 350. Termination of Obligation on Basis of Act of State Agency

If as a result of the publication of an act of a State agency the performance of an obligation becomes impossible wholly or partially, the obligation shall terminate wholly or in respective part. The parties who have incurred losses as a result thereof shall have the right to demand compensation thereof in accordance with Articles 12 and 15 of the present Code.

In the event of the .act of the State agency being deemed in the established procedure to be invalid on the basis of which an obligation has terminated, the obligation shall be restored unless it follows otherwise from an agreement of the parties or the essence of the obligation and performance has not lost interest for the creditor.

Article 351. Termination of Obligation by Death of Citizen

An obligation shall be terminated by the death of the debtor if performance can not be made without the personal participation of the debtor or the obligation is otherwise inextricably connected with the person of the debtor.

An obligation shall be terminated by the death of the creditor if the performance was intended personally for the creditor or the obligation was otherwise inextricably connected with the person of the creditor.

Article 352. Termination of Obligation by Liquidation of Juridical Person

An obligation shall be terminated by the liquidation of a juridical person (debtor or creditor) except for instances when by legislation the performance of an obligation of a liquidated juridical person is placed on another person (relating to demands concerning compensation of harm caused to life or health, and others).

Subsection 2. General Provisions on Contract

Chapter 26. Concept and Conditions of Contract

Article 353. Concept of Contract

A contract shall be deemed to be an agreement of two or several persons concerning the establishment, change, or termination of civil rights and duties.

The rules concerning bilateral and multilateral transactions provided for by Chapter 9 of the present Code shall apply to contracts.

The general provisions on obligations (Articles 234-352 of the present Code) shall apply to obligations which arose from a contract unless provided otherwise by rules of the present Chapter and by rules on individual types of contracts contained in the present Code.

The general provisions on contract shall apply to contracts concluded by more than two parties unless this is contrary to the multilateral character of such contracts.

Article 354. Freedom of Contract

Citizens and juridical persons shall be free in concluding a contract.

Coercion to conclude a contract shall not be permitted except for instances when the duty to conclude a contract has been provided for by the present Code, other law, or by an obligation voluntarily accepted.

The parties may conclude a contract which is not provided for by legislation.

The parties may conclude a contract which contains elements of various contracts (mixed contract). The rules on contracts whose elements are contained in a mixed contract shall apply to the relations of the parties under a mixed contract unless it follows otherwise from the agreement of the parties or the essence of the mixed contract.

The conditions of a contract shall be determined by discretion of the parties except for instances when the content of the respective condition has been prescribed by legislation.

In instances when a condition of a contract has been provided for by a norm which applies insofar as not established otherwise by agreement of the parties (dispositive norm), the parties may by their agreement exclude the application thereof or establish a condition which differs from that provided therein. In the absence of such agreement, the condition of the contract shall be determined by the dispositive norm.

If the condition of a contract has not been determined by the parties or by a dispositive norm, the respective conditions shall be determined by the customs of business turnover applicable to the relations of the parties.

Article 355. Contract For and Without Compensation

A contract under which a party must receive payment or other counter-giving for the performance of his duties shall be for compensation.

A contract under which one party is obliged to grant something to the other party without receiving payment from him or other counter-giving shall be deemed to be without compensation.

A contract shall be presupposed to be for compensation unless it follows otherwise from legislation or the content or essence of the contract.

Article 356. Price

The performance of a contract shall be paid for at the price established by agreement of the parties.

In the instances provided for by a law the prices (or tariffs, price scales, rates, etc.) established or regulated by duly empowered State agencies shall be applied.

The change of the price after the conclusion of a contract shall be permitted in the instances and on the conditions provided for by legislation or contract.

In instances when in a contract for compensation the price has not been provided for and can not be determined by proceeding from the conditions of the contract, the performance of the contract must be paid for at the price which under comparable circumstances usually was recovered for analogous goods, work, or services.

Article 357. Operation of Contract

A contract shall enter into force and become binding for the parties from the moment of its conclusion.

The parties shall have the right to establish that the conditions of a contract concluded by them shall apply to their relations which arose before the conclusion of the contract.

It may be provided by a law or by contract that the end of the period of operation of a contract shall entail the termination of the obligations of the parties under the contract.

A contract which lacks such a condition shall be deemed to be in force until the moment of the ending of performance of the obligation by the parties.

The ending of the period of operation of a contract shall not relieve the parties from responsibility for the violation thereof.

Article 358. Public Contract

A contract concluded by an organization and establishing its duties relating to the sale of goods, fulfillment of work, or rendering of services which this organization by the character of its activity must effectuate with respect to everyone who has recourse to it (retail trade, carriage by common-use transport, communications services, electric power supply, medical, hotel servicing, and so forth) shall be deemed to be a public contract. Such organization shall not have the right to prefer one person to others with respect to the conclusion of a public contract except for the instances provided for by legislation.

The price of goods, work, and services, and also other conditions of a public contract, shall be established identically for all consumers except for instances when the granting of privileges for individual categories of consumers is permitted by legislation.

A refusal of an organization to conclude a public contract when it is possible to grant the respective goods or services to the consumer or to fulfill the respective work for him shall not be permitted.

In the event of an unjustified evasion by an organization from the concluding of a public contract the provisions provided for by Article 377, paragraphs six and seven, of the present Code shall apply.

In instances provided for by a law the rules issued by the Government of the Republic Uzbekistan which are binding upon the parties when concluding and performing public contracts (standard contracts, statutes, etc.) shall apply.

The conditions of a public contract which do not correspond to the requirements established by paragraphs two and five of the present Article shall be invalid.

Article 359. Model Conditions of Contracts

It may be provided in a contract that its individual conditions shall be determined by model conditions worked out for contracts of the respective type.

In instances when a reference to the model conditions is not contained in the contract, such model conditions shall apply to the relations of the parties as customs of business turnover.

Model conditions may be set out in the form of a model contract or other document containing these conditions.

Article 360. Contract of Adhesion

A contract of adhesion shall be deemed to be a contract whose conditions have been determined by one of the parties in records or other standard forms and which can be accepted by the other party not other than by means of adhering to the contract as a whole being offered.

A party which has adhered to the contract shall have the right to demand dissolution or change of the contract if the contract of adhesion, although not contrary to legislation, deprives this party of the rights usually granted under contracts of that type, excludes or limits the responsibility of the other party for a violation of obligations, or contains other conditions clearly burdensome for the adhering party which it, proceeding from its own interests, would not accept if it has the opportunity to participate in determining the conditions of the contract.

When the circumstances provided for in paragraph two of the present Article are present, the demand concerning dissolution or change of the contract presented by a party which has adhered to a contract in connection with the effectuation of its entrepreneurial activity shall not be subject to satisfaction, if the adhering party knew or should have known on what conditions the contract is concluded.

Article 361. Preliminary Contract

Under a preliminary contract the parties shall be obliged to conclude in future a contract concerning the transfer of property, fulfillment of work, or rendering of services (principal contract) on the conditions provided for by the preliminary contract.

The preliminary contract shall be concluded in the form established for the principal contract, and if the form of the principal contract has not been established, then in written form. The failure to comply with the rules concerning the form of the preliminary contract shall entail its invalidity.

A preliminary contract must contain conditions enabling the establishment of the subject, and also the other material conditions, of the principal contract.

A preliminary contract shall specify the period in which the parties are obliged to conclude the principal contract. If such period has not been determined in the preliminary contract, the principal contract shall be subject to conclusion within a year from the moment of concluding the preliminary contract.

In instances when a party which has concluded a preliminary contract evades the conclusion of the principal contract, the provisions established by Article 377, paragraphs six and seven, of the present Code shall apply.

The obligations provided for by a preliminary contract shall terminate if before the ending of the period in which the parties must conclude the principal contract it has not been concluded or one of the parties does not send to the other party an offer to conclude this contract.

Article 362. Contract to Benefit of Third Person

A contract to the benefit of a third person shall be deemed to be a contract in which the parties have established that a debtor is obliged to make performance not to the creditor, but to a third person specified or not specified in the contract and having the right to demand performance of the obligation to his benefit from the debtor.

Unless provided otherwise by legislation or a contract, from the moment of the expression by the third person to the debtor of an intention to take advantage of his right under the contract, the parties may not dissolve or change the contract concluded by them without the consent of the third person.

The debtor in the contract shall have the right to advance against the demand of the third person objections which he could have advanced against the creditor.

When a third person waives a right granted to him under the contract, the creditor may take advantage of this right unless this is contrary to legislation and the contract.

Article 363. Interpretation of Contract

In the event of the interpretation of the conditions of a contract by a court the literal meaning of the words and expressions contained therein shall be taken into account. The literal meaning of the condition of a contract in the event of its ambiguity shall be established by means of comparing with the other conditions and with the sense of the contract as a whole.

If the rules contained in paragraph one of the present Article do not enable the content of the contract to be determined, the true common will of the parties must be elicited by taking into account the purpose of the contract. In so doing all the respective circumstances, including negotiations preceding the contract and correspondence, practice being established in the mutual relations of the parties, the customs of business turnover, and the subsequent conduct of the parties, shall be taken into account.

Chapter 27. Conclusion of Contract

Article 364. Basic Provisions on Conclusion of Contract

A contract shall be considered to be concluded if agreement regarding all the material conditions of the contract has been reached in the form required in appropriate instances.

Conditions concerning the subject of the contract, conditions which have been named in legislation as material or necessary for contracts of the particular type, and also all those conditions relative to which agreement must be reached according to the statement of one of the parties, shall be material.

A contract shall be concluded by means of sending an offer (proposal to conclude a contract) by one party and its acceptance (acceptance of the proposal) by the other party.

Article 365. Moment of Conclusion of Contract

A contract shall be deemed to be concluded at the moment of receipt by the person who has sent an offer of its acceptance.

If in accordance with a law the transfer of property also is necessary in order to conclude a contract, the contract shall be considered to be concluded from the moment of the transfer of the respective property (Article 185 of the present Code).

Article 366. Form of Contract

A contract may be concluded in any form provided for in order to conclude transactions unless a specified form has been established by a law for contracts of the particular type.

A contract subject to notarial certification or State registration shall be considered to be concluded from the moment of notarial certification or registration, and when notarial certification and registration are necessary, from the moment of registration of the contract.

If the parties have agreed to conclude a contract in a specified form, it shall be considered to be concluded after imparting the stipulated form to it even though such form has not been required by a law for contracts of the particular type.

A contract in writing may be concluded by means of drawing up one document signed by the parties, and also by means of the exchange of documents by means of postal, telegraph, teletype, telephone, electronic, or other communications enabling it to be reliably established that the document emanates from the parties with regard to a contract.

The written form of the contract shall be considered to be complied with if the written offer to conclude a contract has been accepted in the procedure provided for by Article 370, paragraph four, of the present Code.

Article 367. Offer

A proposal addressed to one or several specific persons which is sufficiently definite and expresses the intention of the person who has made the proposal to consider himself to have concluded a contract with the addressee who will accept the proposal shall be deemed to be an offer.

An offer must contain the material conditions of the contract.

An offer shall bind the person who sent it from the moment of its receipt by the addressee.

If notice of the revocation of an offer has been received earlier than or simultaneously with the offer itself, the offer shall be considered to be not received.

Article 368. Irrevocability of Offer

An offer received by the addressee may not be revoked within the period established for its acceptance unless otherwise stipulated in the offer itself or does not arise from the essence of the proposal or situation in which it was made.

Article 369. Invitation to Make Offers. Public Offer

An advertisement and other proposals addressed to an indefinite group of persons shall be regarded as an invitation to make offers unless expressly specified otherwise in the proposal.

A proposal containing all the material conditions of a contract from which the will of the person making the proposal is seen to conclude a contract on the conditions specified in the proposal with anyone who responds shall be deemed to be an offer (public offer).

Article 370. Acceptance

The reply of a person to whom an offer has been addressed concerning the acceptance thereof shall be deemed to be an acceptance.

An acceptance must be full and unconditional.

Silence shall not be an acceptance unless it follows otherwise from a law, custom of business turnover, or former business relations of the parties.

The performance by a person who has received an offer within the period established for its acceptance of actions relating to the fulfillment of the conditions of the contract specified therein (shipment of goods, provision of services, fulfillment of work, payment of respective amount, etc.) shall be considered to be an acceptance unless provided otherwise by legislation or specified in the offer.

Article 371. Revocation of Acceptance

If notice of the revocation of an acceptance has been received by the person to whom the offer was sent earlier than or simultaneously with the acceptance itself, the acceptance shall be considered to be not received.

Article 372. Conclusion of Contract on Basis of Offer Determining Period for Acceptance

When an offer contains a period for acceptance, a contract shall be considered to be concluded if the acceptance was received by a person who has sent the offer within the limits of the period specified therein.

Article 373. Conclusion of Contract on Basis of Offer Not Containing Period for Acceptance

When a written offer does not determine the period for acceptance, the contract shall be considered to be concluded if the acceptance was received by the person who has sent the offer before the end of the period established by legislation, and if such a period has not been established, during the time normally necessary for this.

When an offer has been made orally without specifying the period for acceptance, the contract shall be considered to be concluded if the other party immediately declared its acceptance thereof.

Article 374. Acceptance Received Late

In the instances when a notification of acceptance sent in good time has been received late, the acceptance shall not be considered to be late if a party who has sent the offer immediately does not inform the other party about the late receipt of the acceptance.

If a party who has sent an offer immediately communicates to the other party the accepting of its acceptance which has been received late, the contract shall be considered to be concluded.

Article 375. Acceptance on Other Conditions

A reply concerning consent to conclude a contract on conditions other than those proposed in the offer shall not be an acceptance. Such a reply shall be deemed to be a refusal to accept and, at the same time, a new offer.

Article 376. Place of Conclusion of Contract

Unless the place of conclusion has been specified in the contract, a contract shall be deemed to be concluded at the place of residence of a citizen or location of the juridical person which sent the offer.

Article 377. Conclusion of Contract in Obligatory Procedure

In instances when in accordance with the present Code or other laws the conclusion of a contract for a party to whom an offer (or draft contract) is obligatory, this party must send to the other party a notification concerning acceptance or rejection of acceptance or acceptance of the offer (or draft contract) on other conditions (protocol of disagreements to draft contract) within 30 days from the date of receipt of the offer.

A party who has sent an offer and received from the party for whom the conclusion of the contract is obligatory a notification of its acceptance on other conditions (protocol of disagreements to draft contract) shall have the right to transfer disagreements which have arisen when concluding the contract for consideration of a court within 30 days from the date of receipt of such notification or the expiry of the period for acceptance.

In instances when in accordance with the present Code or other laws the conclusion of a contract is obligatory for the party who has sent an offer (or draft contract) and a protocol of disagreements to the draft contract is sent to it within 30 days, this party shall be obliged within 30 days from the date of receipt of the protocol of disagreements to notify the other party about acceptance of the contract in the recension thereof or about rejection of the protocol of disagreements.

In the event the protocol of disagreements is rejected or of the failure to receive notice concerning the results of the consideration thereof within the specified period, the party which sent the protocol of disagreements shall have the right to transfer the disagreements which arose when concluding the contract for the consideration of a court.

The rules concerning the periods provided for by paragraphs one, two, three, and four of the present Article shall apply unless other periods have been established by legislation or have not been agreed by the parties.

If a party for which in accordance with the present Code or other laws the conclusion of the contract is obligatory evades the conclusion thereof, the other party shall have the right to apply to a court with a demand to compel the contract to be concluded.

The party which has unjustifiably evaded the conclusion of the contract must compensate the other party for losses caused by this.

Article 378. Precontractual Disputes

In the instances of the transfer of disagreements which arose when concluding a contract for the consideration of a court on the basis of Article 377 of the present Code, the conditions of the contract with regard to which the parties had disagreements shall be determined in accordance with the decision of the court.

Article 379. Conclusion of Contract at Public Sale

A contract may, unless it follows otherwise from the essence thereof, be concluded by means of holding a public sale. The contract shall be concluded with the person who has won the public sale.

The owner of the thing or the possessor of the property right or a specialized organization may act as the organizer of a public sale. A specialized organization shall operate on the basis of a contract with the owner of the thing or the possessor of the property right and shall act in its name or in his own name.

In the instances specified in the present Code or in another law, contracts concerning the sale of a thing or property right may be concluded only by means of holding public sales.

A public sale shall be held in the form of an auction or a competition.

The form of public sale shall be determined by the owner of the thing being sold or the possessor of the property right being realized unless provided otherwise by a law.

An auction or competition in which only one participant took part shall be deemed to be unconstituted.

The rules provided for by Articles 380 and 381 of the present Code also shall apply to a public sale held by way of execution of the decision of a court unless provided otherwise by legislation.

Article 380. Organization and Procedure for Holding Public Sale

Auctions and competitions may be open and closed. Any person may participate in an open auction or open competition. Only persons specially invited for this purpose shall participate in a closed auction or closed competition.

Unless provided otherwise by a law, a notice concerning a forthcoming public sale must be made by the organizer not less than thirty days before holding it. The notice must contain in any event information concerning the time, place, and form of the public sale, the subject thereof and the procedure for holding it, including the formalization of participation in the public sale, and also information concerning the starting price.

If the subject of the public sale is only the right to conclude a contract, the period granted for this must be specified in the notice of the forthcoming public sale.

Unless provided otherwise in a law or in the notice on holding the public sale, the organizer of an open public sale who has given notice shall have the right to refuse to hold an auction at any time, but not later than three days before the date ensues for holding it, and to hold a competition, not later than thirty days before holding the competition.

In instances when the organizer of open a public sale refuses to hold it in violation of the specified periods, he shall be obliged to compensate participants for real damage incurred.

The organizer of a closed auction or closed competition shall be obliged to compensate the invited participants for real damage irrespective of precisely when the sending of the notice followed the refusal to hold the public sale.

The participants of a public sale shall make a deposit in the amount, within the periods, and in the procedure specified in the notice on holding the sale. If the public sale is unconstituted, the deposit shall be subject to return. A deposit shall also be returned to persons who participated in the public sale, but did not win it.

When concluding a contract with a person who has won a public sale, the amount of the deposit made by him shall be deducted from the performance of the obligations under the contract concluded.

A person who has won a public sale and the organizer of the public sale shall sign a protocol on the day of holding the auction or competition concerning the results of the public sale, which shall have the force of a contract. In the event of the person who won the public sale evading the signature of the contract, he shall lose the deposit made by him. The organizer of a public sale who has evaded the signature of the protocol shall be obliged to return the deposit in double the amount, and also to compensate the person who won the public sale for losses caused by participation in the public sale in that part exceeding the amount of the deposit.

If only the right to conclude a contract was the subject of a public sale, such contract must be signed by the parties not later than twenty days or other period specified in the notice after the completion of the public sale and formalization of the protocol. In the event of one of them evading the conclusion of the contract, the other party shall have the right to apply to a court with a demand to compel the contract to be concluded, and also for compensation of losses caused by evading the conclusion thereof.

Article 381. Consequences of Violation of Rules for Holding Public Sale

A public sale held in violation of the rules established by a law may be deemed by a court to be invalid upon the suit of an interested person.

The deeming of a public sale to be invalid shall entail the invalidity of the contract concluded with the person who won the public sale.

Chapter 28. Change and Dissolution of Contract

Article 382. Grounds for Change and Dissolution of Contract

A change and dissolution of a contract shall be possible by agreement of the parties unless provided otherwise by the present Code, by other laws, or by contract.

Upon the demand of one of the parties a contract may be changed or dissolved by decision of a court only:

(1) in the event of a material violation of the contract by the other party;

(2) in other instances provided for by the present Code, by other laws, or by contract.

A violation of a contract by one of the parties which entails for the other party such damage that it is deprived in significant degree of that which it had the right to count on when concluding the contract shall be deemed to be material.

In the event of a unilateral refusal to perform a contract wholly or partially when such refusal is permitted by a law or by agreement of the parties, the contract shall be considered to be dissolved or changed respectively.

Article 383. Change and Dissolution of Contract in Connection with Material Change of Circumstances

A material change of circumstances from which the parties proceeded when concluding a contract shall be a grounds for the change or dissolution thereof unless provided otherwise by the contract or it follows from the essence thereof.

A change of circumstances shall be deemed to be material when they have changed such that if the parties could reasonably foresee this, the contract would not have been concluded at all by them or it would have been concluded on significantly differing conditions.

If the parties have not reached agreement concerning the bringing of the contract into conformity with the materially changed circumstances or the dissolution thereof, the contract may be dissolved, and on the grounds provided for by paragraph five of the present Article, changed by a court at the demand of the interested party when the following conditions simultaneously exist:

(1) at the moment of concluding the contract the parties proceeded from the fact that such a change of circumstances would not occur;

(2) the change of circumstances has been caused by reasons which the interested party could not overcome after they arose with that degree of good faith and attentiveness which are required of him by the character of the contract and the conditions of turnover;

(3) the performance of the contract without a change of its conditions would so violate correlation of property interests of the parties which correspond to the contract and entail for the interested party such damage that it would be deprived to a significant degree of that which it had the right to count on when concluding the contract;

(4) it does not follow from the customs of business turnover or the essence of the contract that the risk of the change of circumstances is borne by the interested party.

In the event of the dissolution of a contract as a consequence of materially changed circumstances the court at the demand of any of the parties shall determine the consequences of the dissolution of the contract by proceeding from the need for a just distribution between the parties of the expenses incurred by them in connection with the performance of this contract.

The change of a contract in connection with a material change of circumstances shall be permitted by decision of a court in exceptional instances when dissolution of the contract is contrary to social interests or entails damage for the parties which significantly exceeds the costs needed to perform the contract on the conditions changed by the court.

Article 384. Procedure for Change of and Dissolution of Contract

An agreement concerning a change of or dissolution of a contract shall be concluded in the same form as the contract unless it follows otherwise from legislation, the contract, or the customs of business turnover.

A demand concerning a change of or dissolution of a contract may be made by a party in court only after receipt of a refusal of the other party to the proposal to change or dissolve the contract or of not receiving a reply within the period specified in the proposal or established by law or by contract, and in the absence thereof, within a thirty-day period.

Article 385. Consequences of Dissolution of and Change of Contract

In the event of the change of a contract, the obligations of the parties shall be preserved in the changed form.

In the event of the dissolution of the contract the obligations of the parties shall terminate.

In the event of the change of or the dissolution of a contract, the obligations shall be considered to be changed or terminated from the moment of the conclusion of an agreement of the parties concerning the change of or dissolution of the contract unless it follows otherwise from the agreement or the character of the change of the contract, and in the event of the change of or the dissolution of a contract in a judicial procedure, from the moment of the entry into legal force of the decision of the court on the change of or the dissolution of the contract.

The parties shall not have the right to demand the return of that which was performed by them under the obligation before the moment of change or dissolution of the contract, unless established otherwise by a law or by agreement of the parties.

If a material violation of the contract by one of the parties has served as the grounds for change of or the dissolution of a contract, the other party shall have the right to demand compensation of losses caused by the change of or the dissolution of the contract.

PART TWO

[Confirmed by Law No. 256-I, 29 August 1996; entered into force: 1 March 1997]

Subsection 3. Individual Types of Obligations

Chapter 29. Purchase-Sale

§ 1. General Provisions on Purchase-Sale

Article 386. Contract of Purchase-Sale

Under a contract of purchase-sale one party (seller) shall be obliged to transfer a good to the ownership of the other party (purchaser), and the purchaser shall be obliged to accept this good and to pay for it the determined monetary amount (price).

Unless special rules have been established for the purchase-sale thereof by a law, the provisions provided for by the present paragraph shall apply to the sale of securities and currency valuables.

In the instances provided for by the present Code or other law, the peculiarities of the purchase and sale of goods of individual types shall be determined by legislation.

The contract of purchase-sale of motor vehicle means subject in the procedure established by legislation to State registration must be notarially certified, except for instances established by the Government of the Republic Uzbekistan [as amended by Law of 7 December 2001, No. 320-II. Ведомости Олий Мажлиса (2002), no. 1, item 20].

The provisions provided for by the present paragraph shall apply to the sale of property rights unless it arises otherwise from the content or character of these rights.

Unless provided otherwise by rules of the present Code and contracts of these types, the provisions provided for by the present paragraph shall apply to individual types of contract for purchase-sale (retail purchase-sale, delivery of goods, delivery of goods, electric power supply, sale of enterprise, and others).

Article 387. Condition of Contract on Good

Any things may be a good under a contract of purchase-sale in compliance with the rules provided for by Article 82 of the present Code.

A contract may be concluded for the purchase-sale of a good which the seller has at the moment of concluding the contract, and also a good which will be created or acquired by the seller in the future, unless established otherwise by a law or unless it so arises from the character of the good.

The condition of a contract of purchase-sale concerning a good shall be considered to be agreed if the contract enables the name and quantity of the good to be determined.

Article 388. Duties of Seller Relating to Transfer of Good

The seller shall be obliged to transfer to the purchaser the good provided for by the contract of purchase-sale.

Unless provided otherwise by the contract of purchase-sale, the seller shall be obliged simultaneously with the transfer of the thing to transfer to the purchaser the appurtenances thereto, as well as the documents relating thereto (technical passport, certificate of quality, instructions relating to operation, and so forth) provided for by legislation or the contract.

Article 389. Period for Performance of Duty to Transfer Good

The period for the performance by the seller of the duty to transfer the good to the purchaser shall be determined by the contract of purchase-sale, and if the contract does not enable this period to be determined, in accordance with the rules provided for by Article 242 of the present Code.

A contract of purchase-sale shall be deemed to be concluded with a condition of the performance thereof within a strictly determined period if it clearly arises from the contract that in the event of a violation of this period the purchaser loses interest in the contract. The seller shall have the right to perform such contract before the ensuing or after the expiry of the period determined therein only with the consent of the purchaser.

Article 390. Moment of Performance of Duty of Seller to Transfer Good

Insofar as not provided otherwise by the contract of purchase-sale, the duty of the seller to transfer the good to the purchaser shall be considered to be performed at the moment of:

handing over the good to the purchaser or person specified by him if the duty of the seller relating to the delivery of the good has been provided for by the contract;

placing the good at the disposition of the purchaser if the good must be transferred to the purchaser or person specified by him at the location of the good. A good shall be considered to be placed at the disposition of the purchaser when within the period provided for by the contract the good is ready for transfer to the proper place and the purchaser in accordance with the conditions of the contract has knowledge of the readiness of the good for transfer. A good shall not be deemed to be ready for transfer if it is not identified for the purposes of the contract by means of marking or in other form.

In the instances when the duty relating to delivery of a good or transfer of a good at its location to the purchaser does not arise from a contract of purchase-sale, the duty of the seller to transfer the good to the purchaser shall be considered to be performed at the moment of handing over the good to the carrier or communications organization for delivery to the purchaser, unless provided otherwise by the contract.

Article 391. Duty of Seller Relating to Preservation of Sold Property

When the right of ownership or other right to a thing passes to the purchaser before the transfer of the property, the seller shall be obliged until the transfer to preserve the property, not allowing the deterioration thereof. The purchaser shall be obliged to compensate the seller for the costs necessary for this unless provided otherwise by agreement of the parties.

Article 392. Transfer of Risk of Accidental Perishing or Accidental Damaging of Good

Unless provided otherwise by the contract of purchase-sale, the risk of accidental perishing or accidental damage of a good shall pass to the purchaser from the moment when in accordance with a law or the contract the seller is considered to have performed his duty relating to transfer of the good to the purchaser.

The risk of accidental perishing or accidental damage of a good sold while en route shall pass to the purchaser from the moment of the conclusion of the contract unless provided otherwise by agreement of the parties.

The condition of the contract of purchase-sale that the risk of accidental perishing or accidental damage of the good passes to the purchaser from the moment of handing over the good to the first carrier may, at the demand of the purchaser, be deemed by a court to be invalid if at the moment of concluding the contract the seller knew or should have known that the good has been lost or damaged and did not communicate this to the purchaser.

Article 393. Duty of Seller to Transfer Good Free of Rights of Third Persons

The seller shall be obliged to transfer a good to the purchaser free from any rights of third persons, except for the instance when the purchaser has agreed to accept the good encumbered by the rights of third persons. The failure of the seller to perform this rule shall give the purchaser the right to demand a reduction of the price of the good or dissolution of the contract of purchase-sale unless it is proved that the purchaser knew or should have known about the rights of third persons to this good.

The rules provided for by the present Article shall apply respectively also when with respect to the good at the moment of its transfer to the purchaser there are claims of third persons, which were known to the seller if these claims subsequently were deemed to be lawful in the established procedure.

Article 394. Duties of Purchaser and Seller in Event of Filing of Suit Concerning Seizure of Good

If a third person on grounds which arose before performance of the contract of purchase-sale files suit against the purchaser concerning seizure of the good, the purchaser shall be obliged to involve the seller in the case, and the seller shall be obliged to appear in this case on the side of the purchaser.

The failure of the purchaser to involve the seller in the case shall relieve the seller from responsibility to the purchaser if the seller proves that, having accepted to participate in the case, he would have averted the seizure of the good sold from the purchaser.

The seller involved by the purchaser in a case but who has not taken part therein shall be deprived of the right to prove the incorrectness of the conducting of the case by the purchaser.

Article 395. Responsibility of Seller in Event of Seizure of Good from Purchaser

In the event of the seizure of the good from the purchaser by third persons on grounds which arose before the performance of the contract of purchase-sale, the seller shall be obliged to compensate the purchaser for losses incurred by him except for the instance when the purchaser knew or should have known about the existence of these grounds.

An agreement of the parties concerning relieving the seller from responsibility or limitation thereof in the event a good acquired is demanded and obtained from the purchaser by third persons shall be invalid.

Article 396. Consequences of Refusal of Seller to Transfer Good

If the seller refuses to transfer the good sold to the purchaser, the purchaser shall have the right to refuse to perform the contract of purchase-sale.

In the event of the refusal of the seller to transfer an individually-determined thing, the purchaser shall have the right to present the demand to the seller provided for by Article 331 of the present Code.

Article 397. Consequences of Failure to Perform Duty to Transfer Appurtenances and Documents Relating to Good

If the seller does not transfer or refuses to transfer to the purchaser appurtenances or documents relating to the good which he should transfer in accordance with legislation or the contract of purchase-sale (Article 388, paragraph 2, of the present Code), the purchaser shall have the right to designate a reasonable period to him for the transfer thereof.

When appurtenances or documents relating to a good have not been transferred by the seller within the specified period, the purchaser shall have the right to refuse the good unless provided otherwise by the contract of purchase-sale.

Article 398. Quantity of Good

The quantity of a good subject to transfer to a purchaser shall be provided for by the contract of purchase-sale in respective units of measurement or in monetary expression. The condition concerning the quantity of a good may be agreed by means of establishing in the contract the procedure for determining it.

If the contract of purchase-sale does not enable the quantity of the good subject to transfer to be determined, the contract shall be considered to be not concluded.

Article 399. Consequences of Violation of Condition Concerning Quantity of Good

If the seller has transferred to the purchaser in violation of the conditions of the contract of purchase-sale a lesser quantity of the good that has been determined by the contract, the purchaser shall have the right, unless provided otherwise by the contract, either to demand to transfer the short quantity of the good or to refuse the good transferred and the payment thereof, and if it has been paid for, to demand the return of the monetary amount paid.

When the seller has transferred to the purchaser a good in a quantity exceeding that specified in the contract of purchase-sale, the purchaser shall be obliged to notify the seller thereof in the procedure provided for by Article 416, paragraph one, of the present Code. If within a reasonable period after receipt of the notice of the purchaser the seller does not dispose of the respective good, the purchaser shall have the right, unless provided otherwise by the contract, to accept the entire good.

In the event of the acceptance of the good by the purchaser in a quantity exceeding that specified in the contract of purchase-sale, the respective good shall be paid for at the price established by the contract unless another price has been determined by agreement of the parties.

Article 400. Assortment of Goods

If under the contract of purchase-sale goods are subject to transfer in a determined correlation with regard to types, models, dimensions, colors, or other indicia (assortment), the seller shall be obliged to transfer the goods to the purchaser in the assortment agreed by the parties.

If the assortment in a contract of purchase-sale is not determined and the procedure for the determination thereof has not been established in the contract but it follows from the essence of the obligation that the goods must be transferred to the purchaser in an assortment, the seller shall have the right to transfer the goods to the purchaser in an assortment by proceeding from the requirements of the purchaser which were known to the seller at the moment of conclusion of the contract, or to refuse to perform the contract.

Article 401. Consequences of Violation of Condition of Contract on Assortment of Good

In the event of the transfer by the seller of goods provided for by the contract of purchase-sale in an assortment which does not correspond to the contract, the purchaser shall have the right to refuse to accept and to pay for them, and if they have been paid for, to require the return of the monetary amount paid.

If the seller has transferred to the purchaser, together with goods whose assortment corresponds to the contract of purchase-sale, goods in violation of the conditions concerning the assortment, the purchaser shall have the right at his choice to:

accept the goods corresponding to the conditions concerning the assortment and refuse the other goods;

refuse all of the goods transferred;

require the replacement of the goods which do not correspond to the conditions of the contract concerning the assortment with goods in the assortment provided for by the contract;

accept all the goods transferred.

In the event of the refusal of goods whose assortment does not correspond to the conditions of the contract of purchase-sale, or of presenting a demand concerning replacement of the goods which do not correspond to the conditions concerning the assortment, the purchaser shall have the right also to refuse to pay for these goods, and if they have been paid for, to require the return of the monetary amount paid.

Goods which do not correspond to the conditions of the contract concerning the assortment shall be considered to be accepted if the purchaser within a reasonable period after the receipt thereof does not notify the seller concerning his refusal of the goods.

If the purchaser has not refused goods whose assortment does not correspond to the contract, he shall be obliged to pay for them at the price agreed with the seller. When necessary measures have not been taken by the seller to agree the price within a reasonable period, the purchaser shall pay for the goods at the price which at the moment of concluding the contract under comparable circumstances is usually recovered for analogous goods.

The rules of the present Article shall apply unless provided otherwise by the contract of purchase-sale.

Article 402. Quality of Good

The seller shall be obliged to transfer a good to the purchaser whose quality corresponds to the contract of purchase-sale.

In the absence in a contract of purchase-sale of conditions concerning the quality of a good the seller shall be obliged to transfer to the purchaser a good fit for the purposes for which a good of such nature is usually used.

If the seller when concluding the contract was given notice by the purchaser of the specific purposes for the acquisition of the good, the seller shall be obliged to transfer to the purchaser a good fit for use in accordance with these purposes.

In the event of the sale of a good according to a model and/or description, the seller shall be obliged to transfer a good to the purchaser which corresponds to the model and/or description.

If in accordance with the procedure established by a law obligatory requirements have been provided for the quality of a good being sold, the seller effectuating entrepreneurial activity shall be obliged to transfer to the purchaser a good corresponding to these obligatory requirements.

By agreement between the seller and the purchaser a good may be transferred which corresponds to higher quality requirements in comparison with the obligatory requirements established in the procedure provided for by a law.

Article 403. Guarantee of Quality of Good

A good which a seller is obliged to transfer to a purchaser must correspond to the requirements provided for by Article 402 of the present Code at the moment of the transfer thereof to the purchaser unless another moment of determining the conformity of the good to these requirements has been provided for by the contract of purchase-sale and within the limits of a reasonable period must be fit for the purposes intended.

When by a contract of purchase-sale the granting by the seller of a guarantee of the quality of a good has been provided for, the seller shall be obliged to transfer to the purchaser a good which must correspond to the requirements provided for by Article 402 of the present Code during the time established by the contract (guarantee period).

A guarantee of the quality of a good also extends to all sets of manufacture unless provided otherwise by the contract of purchase-sale.

Article 404. Calculation of Guarantee Period of Good

A guarantee period shall begin to run from the moment of the transfer of the goods to the purchaser unless provided otherwise by the contract of purchase-sale.

If a purchaser is deprived of the possibility to use the good with respect to which a guarantee period has been established by the contract under circumstances dependent upon the seller, the guarantee period shall not run until the elimination of the respective circumstances by the seller.

Unless provided otherwise by the contract of purchase-sale, a guarantee period shall be extended for the time during which the good could not be used because of defects discovered therein, on condition of the notification of the seller about the defects of the good in the procedure established by Article 416 of the present Code.

Unless provided otherwise by the contract of purchase-sale, a guarantee period for a set of manufactures shall be considered to be equal to the guarantee period for the principal manufacture and shall begin to run simultaneously with the guarantee period on the principal manufacture.

In the event of the replacement of a good (or set of manufactures) the guarantee shall begin to run anew.

Article 405. Period of Fitness of Good

The period of time upon the expiry of which a good is considered to be unfit for use for its designation (period of fitness) may be determined by legislation, including national standards [as amended by Law of 22 October 2019, No. ЗРУ-572] [as amended by Law of 3 November 2022, No. ЗРУ-800].

A good for which a period of fitness has been established the seller shall be obliged to transfer to the purchaser so calculated that it may be used for its designation until the expiry of the period of fitness.

Article 406. Calculation of Period of Fitness of Good

The period of fitness of a good shall be determined by the period of time calculated from the date of its manufacture during which the good is fit for use or by the date until the ensuing of which the good is fit for use.

Article 407. Verification of Quality of Good

If the verification of the quality of a good has been provided for by legislation or by the contract of purchase-sale, it must be effectuated in accordance with the requirements established therein.

In instances when standards establish requirements for control of the quality of goods, the quality must be verified inn accordance with the instructions thereof [as amended by Law of 3 Novemiber 2022, No. ЗРУ-800].

If the conditions for the verification of the quality have not been provided for in the procedure established by paragraphs one and two of the present Article, the quality of a good must be verified in accordance with the customs of business turnover or other ordinarily used conditions for the verification of a good subject to transfer under a contract of purchase-sale.

If the duty of the seller to verify the quality of a good transferred to the purchaser (test, analysis, inspection, and so forth) has been provided for by legislation, including State standards, or by the contract of purchase-sale, the seller must grant to the purchaser at his demand evidence of the effectuation of the verification of the quality of the good.

The quality of a good must be verified by the seller and the purchaser under identical conditions.

Article 408. Consequences of Transfer of Good of Improper Quality

If the defects of a good were not stipulated by the seller, the purchaser to whom the good of improper quality was transferred shall acquire the rights provided for by Article 434 of the present Code.

In the event of the improper quality of part of a good which is part of a set, the purchaser shall have the right to effectuate with respect to this good the rights provided for by Article 434 of the present Code.

In the event the seller of a good of improper quality is not the manufacturer thereof, the demands concerning replacement or uncompensated elimination of the defects of the good may be presented to the seller or to the manufacturer.

The rules provided for by the present Article shall apply unless established otherwise by the present Code or other law.

Article 409. Defects of Good for Which Seller is Liable

The seller shall be liable for the defects of a good if the purchaser proves that the defects of the good arose before the transfer thereof to the purchaser or for reasons which arose before this moment.

With respect to a good for which a guarantee of quality has been granted by the seller the seller shall be liable for defects of the good unless it is proved that the defects of the good arose after the transfer thereof to the purchaser as a consequence of a violation by the purchaser of the rules for the use of the good or the keeping thereof, or the actions of third persons, or insuperable force.

Article 410. Periods for Discovery of Defects in Transferred Good

Unless provided otherwise by a law or by a contract of purchase-sale, the purchaser shall have the right to present demands connected with the defects of a good on condition that they were discovered within the periods established by the present Article.

When a guarantee period or a period of fitness has not been established for a good, demands connected with defects may be presented by the purchaser on condition that the defects in the good sold were discovered within a reasonable period, but within the limits of two years from the date of the transfer of the good to the purchaser, unless other periods ware established by a law or by a contract of purchase-sale. The period for eliciting the defects of a good subject to carriage or to despatch by a communications organization shall be calculated from the date of receipt of the good at the place of its destination.

If a guarantee period has been established for a good, the purchaser shall have the right to present demands connected with defects of the good in the event the defects are discovered during the guarantee period.

If a guarantee period has been in a contract of purchase-sale for sets of manufactures which is less in duration than the principal manufacture, the purchaser shall have the right to present demands concerning the defects of the sets of manufactures in the event of their discovery during the guarantee period for the principal manufacture.

If a guarantee period has been established in a contract for the purchase-sale of a set of manufactures which is of greater duration than for the principal manufacture, the purchaser shall have the right to present demands concerning defects of the set of manufactures if the defects in the set of manufactures are discovered during the guarantee period for it irrespective of the expiry of the guarantee period for the principal manufacture.

With respect to a good for which a period of fitness has been established, the purchaser shall have the right to present demands concerning defects of the good if they were discovered within the period of fitness of the good.

If the defects of a good have been discovered by the purchaser outside the limits of the guarantee period or the period of fitness, the seller shall bear responsibility if the purchaser proves that the defects of the good arose before the transfer of the good to the purchaser or for reasons which arose before this moment.

Article 411. Completeness of Good

The seller shall be obliged to transfer to the purchaser a good which corresponds to the conditions of the contract of purchase-sale concerning completeness.

When the completeness of a good has not been determined by a contract of purchase-sale, the seller shall be obliged to transfer to the purchaser a good whose completeness is determined by the customs of business turnover or other usually presented requirements.

Article 412. Complete Set of Goods

If the duty of the seller to transfer to the purchaser a determined selection of goods in a complete set (complete set of goods) has been provided for by a contract of purchase-sale, the obligation shall be considered to be performed from the moment of the transfer of all goods included in the complete set.

Unless otherwise provided for by the contract of purchase-sale and does not arise from the essence of the obligation, the seller shall be obliged to transfer simultaneously to the purchaser all goods which comprise the complete set.

Article 413. Consequences of Transfer of Incomplete Good

In the event of the transfer of an incomplete good the purchaser shall have the right at his choice to require from the seller:

commensurate reduction of the purchase price;

making the good complete within a reasonable period.

If the seller within a reasonable period has not fulfilled the demand of the purchaser to make the good complete, the purchaser shall have the right at his choice to:

require replacement of the incomplete good for a complete [one];

refuse to perform the contract of purchase-sale and require the return of the monetary amount paid for it, and also compensation of losses.

The consequences provided for by paragraphs one and two of the present Article shall also apply in the event of a violation by the seller of the duty to transfer a complete set of goods to the purchaser unless provided otherwise by the contract of purchase-sale and does not arise from the essence of the obligation.

Article 414. Packaging and Packing

Unless provided otherwise by the contract of purchase-sale and does not arise from the essence of the obligation, the seller shall be obliged to transfer the good to the purchaser in packaging and/or packing, except for a good which by its character does not require packaging and/or packing.

Unless the requirements for packaging and packing have been determined by the contract of purchase-sale, the good must be packaged and/or packed by the means usual for such good, and in the absence of such, by a means ensuring the preservation of goods of such nature under the usual conditions for storage and transportation.

If in the procedure established by a law obligatory requirements for packaging and/or packing have been provided for, the seller who effectuates entrepreneurial activity shall be obliged to transfer to the purchaser the good in packaging and/or packing which corresponds to these obligatory requirements.

Article 415. Consequences of Transfer of Good Without Packaging and/or Packing or in Improper Packaging and/or Packing

In instances when a good which is subject to packaging and/or packing is transferred to the purchaser without packaging and/or packing or in improper packaging and/or packing, the purchaser shall have the right to demand of the seller to package and/or to pack the good or to replace the improper packaging and/or packing unless arises otherwise from the essence of the obligation or the character of the good. Instead of presenting the said demands to the seller, the purchaser shall have the right to present to him other demands also which arise from the transfer of a good of improper quality provided for by Article 434 of the present Code.

Article 416. Notification of Seller About Improper Performance of Contract of Purchase-Sale

The purchaser shall be obliged to notify the seller about a violation of the conditions of the contract of purchase-sale concerning quantity, assortment, quality, completeness, packaging and/or packing of the good within the period provided for by legislation or the contract, and if such period is not established, within a reasonable period after such violation of the respective condition of the contract should have been discovered by proceeding from the character and designation of the good.

In the event of the failure of the purchaser to fulfill the duty specified in paragraph one of the present Article, the seller shall have the right to refuse satisfaction wholly or partially of the respective demands of the purchaser, if it is proved that this has entailed the impossibility of satisfying his demands or entails for the seller incommensurate expenses in comparison with those which he would bear if he had been notified in good time about the violation of the contract of purchase-sale.

If the seller knew or should have known that the goods transferred to the purchaser do not correspond to the conditions of the contract of purchase-sale, he shall not have the right to refer to the failure of the purchaser to fulfill the duty provided for by paragraph one of the present Article.

Article 417. Duty of Purchaser to Accept Good

The purchaser shall be obliged to accept a good transferred to him except for instances when he has the right to demand the replacement of the good or to refuse performance of the contract of purchase-sale.

Unless provided otherwise by legislation or the contract of purchase-sale, the purchaser shall be obliged to perform the actions which in accordance with requirements usually presented are necessary on his part in order to ensure the transfer and receipt of the respective good.

In instances when the purchaser in violation of legislation or the contract of purchase-sale does not accept or refuses to accept a good, the seller shall have the right to refuse performance of the contract and to demand compensation of losses.

Article 418. Price of Good

The purchaser shall be obliged to pay for a good at the price determined in accordance with Article 356 of the present Code, and also to perform at his expense actions which according to legislation, the contract of purchase-sale, or requirements usually presented are necessary in order to effectuate payment.

When the price has been established by dependence on the weight of the good, it shall be determined according to net weight unless provided otherwise by the contract of purchase-sale.

If the contract of purchase-sale provides that the price of a good is subject to change depending upon indicators which condition the price of the good (cost of production, expenditures, and so forth) but in so doing does not determine the means for revision of the price, the price shall be determined by proceeding from the correlation of these indicators at the moment of conclusion of the contract and at the moment of transfer of the good. In the event of delay by the seller of performance of the duty to transfer the good, the price shall be determined by proceeding from the correlation of these indicators at the moment of conclusion of the contract and at the moment of transfer of the good provided for by the contract, and if the moment of transfer of the good is not provided for by the contract, at the moment determined in accordance with Article 242 of the present Code.

The rules provided for by paragraph three of the present Article shall apply unless established otherwise by legislation or the contract of purchase-sale and does not arise from the essence of the obligation.

Article 419. Payment for Good

Unless the duty arises from legislation or the conditions of the contract of purchase-sale to pay the price within a determined period, the purchaser shall be obliged to pay it without delay after the transfer of the good to him by the seller or of the goods-disposition documents for this good.

Unless payment by installment for a good has been provided by the contract of purchase-sale, the purchaser shall be obliged to pay to the seller the amount of the price of the transferred good in full.

If the purchaser does not pay in a timely way for the good transferred in accordance with the contract of purchase-sale, the seller shall have the right to require payment of the good and the payment of interest for the use of another's monetary means.

If the purchaser in violation of the contract of purchase sale refuses to accept and to pay for the good, the seller shall have the right at his choice to require payment of the good or to refuse performance of the contract.

In instances when the seller in accordance with the contract of purchase-sale is obliged to transfer to the purchaser not only goods which are not paid for but also other goods, he shall have the right to suspend the transfer of these goods until the full payment of all goods previously transferred unless provided otherwise by legislation or contract.

Article 420. Preliminary Payment for Good

In instances when the duty of the purchaser to pay the price wholly or partially before the transfer of the good by the seller (preliminary payment) has been provided for by the contract of purchase-sale, the purchaser must make payment within the period provided for by the contract, and if such period has not been provided by the contract, within the period determined in accordance with Article 242 of the present Code.

In the event of the failure of the purchaser to perform the duty to pay in advance for the good, the rules provided for by Article 256 of the present Code shall apply.

In instances when a seller who has received the amount of preliminary payment does not perform the duty to transfer the good, the purchaser shall have the right to require the transfer of the good paid for or the return of the amount of preliminary payment for the good not transferred by the seller.

Unless provided otherwise by the contract of purchase-sale, in instances when the seller does not perform the duty relating to the transfer of the good paid for in advance the amount of preliminary payment shall be subject to the payment of interest in accordance with Article 327 of the present Code from the date when under the contract the transfer of the good should have been made up to the date of the transfer of the good to the purchaser or the return to him of the amount paid in advance by him. The duty of the seller to pay interest on the amount of the preliminary payment, from the date of receipt of this amount from the purchaser, may be provided for by the contract.

Article 421. Payment for Good Sold on Credit

In an instance when payment for a good over a determined time after the transfer thereof to the purchaser (sale of good on credit) has been provided for by the contract of purchase-sale, the purchaser must make payment within the period provided for by the contract, and if such period is not provided for by the contract, within the period determined in accordance with Article 242 of the present Code.

In the event of the failure of the seller to perform the duty to transfer the good, the rules provided for by Article 256 of the present Code shall apply.

In an instance when the purchaser which received the good does not perform the duty with regard to payment within the period established by the contract of purchase-sale, the seller shall have the right to require payment of the good transferred or return of the good not paid for.

Unless provided otherwise by the present Code or by the contract of purchase-sale, in an instance when the purchaser does not perform the duty with regard to payment of the good transferred within the period established by the contract, interest shall be subject to payment on the delayed amount in accordance with Article 327 of the present Code from the date when under the contract the good should have been paid for up to the date of payment for the good by the purchaser.

The duty of the purchaser to pay interest on the amount corresponding to the price of the good, commencing from the date of transfer of the good by the seller, may be provided for by the contract.

A good shall be sold on credit at the prices prevailing on the date of sale unless provided otherwise by legislation or by the contract.

From the moment of transfer of good to the purchaser and up to the payment for it in full a good sold on credit shall be deemed to be under pledge to the seller in order to secure performance by the purchaser of its duty with regard to payment for the good.

Article 422. Payment for Good by Installment

Payment for a good by installment may be provided for by a contract concerning the sale of a good on credit.

A contract concerning the sale of a good on credit with a condition concerning installment payment shall be considered to be concluded if, together with the other material conditions of the contract of purchase-sale, the price of the good and the procedure, periods, and amounts of payments have been specified.

When a purchaser does not make a regular payment within the period established by the contract for a good sold by installment and transferred to him, the seller shall have the right to refuse performance of the contract and to levy execution against the good in the procedure provided for recovery of the subject-matter of a pledge [as amended by Law of 22 October 2019, No. ЗРУ-572].

In the instance provided by a contract on the sale of a good on credit, the purchaser shall have the right to provide as security for performance of obligations the paid part of the participatory share of the good received [added by Law of 22 October 2019, No. ЗРУ-572].

Article 423. Insurance of Good

If the duty of the seller or purchaser to insure a good has been provided for by the contract, but the conditions of insurance and minimum amount for which the good is to be insured have not been determined in so doing, the amount of insurance compensation provided for by the contract of insurance may not be less than the price of the good.

In instances when a party obliged to insure a good does not effectuate insurance in accordance with the conditions of the contract, the other party shall have the right to insure the good and require from the obliged party compensation of expenses for the insurance or to refuse performance of the contract.

Article 424. Preservation of Right of Ownership for Seller

In instances when it is provided by a contract of purchase-sale that the right of ownership in a good transferred to the purchaser shall be preserved by the seller until payment for the good or the ensuing of other circumstances, the purchaser shall not have the right before transfer of the right of ownership to him to alienate the good or otherwise dispose of it unless provided otherwise by a law or contract or unless it arises otherwise from the designation and properties of the good.

In instances when within the period provided for by the contract of purchase-sale the transferred good is not paid for or other circumstances do not ensue under which the right of ownership passes to the purchaser, the seller shall have the right to require from the purchaser to return the good to him unless provided otherwise by the contract.

§ 2. Retail Purchase-Sale

Article 425. Contract of Retail Purchase-Sale

Under a contract of retail purchase-sale the seller effectuating entrepreneurial activity shall be obliged to transfer to the purchaser a good intended for personal, home, or other use which is not connected with entrepreneurial activity.

A contract of retail purchase-sale shall be a public [contract].

Article 426. Public Offer of Good

The proposal of a good which contains all the material conditions of the contract of retail purchase-sale specified in an advertisement of the good, catalogues, and also other descriptions of the good addressed to an indefinite group of persons shall be deemed to be a public offer (Article 369, paragraph two).

Exhibition of goods and demonstration of models thereof or the granting of information concerning the goods to be sold (descriptions, catalogues, photographs, and so forth) at the place of sale thereof shall be deemed to be a public offer irrespective of whether the price and other material conditions of the contract of retail purchase-sale have been specified, except for instances when the seller visibly determined that the respective goods are not intended for sale.

Article 427. Granting of Information Concerning Good to Purchaser

The seller shall be obliged to grant to the purchaser necessary and reliable information concerning the good proposed for sale which corresponds to the requirements established by legislation or those usually presented in retail trade for the content and means of granting such information.

The purchaser shall have the right before the conclusion of a contract of retail purchase-sale to inspect the good and require the conducting in his presence of a verification of the properties or demonstration of the use of the good unless this is precluded in view of the character of the good and is not contrary to the rules accepted in retail trade.

If the purchaser has not been granted the possibility at once to receive information at the place of sale concerning the good specified in paragraphs one and two of the present Article, he shall have the right to require from the seller the compensation of losses caused by unfounded avoidance of conclusion of the contract of retail purchase-sale, and if the contract has been concluded, within a reasonable period to refuse performance of the contract and to require the return of the amount paid for the good and compensation of other losses.

A seller who has not granted the purchaser the possibility to receive respective information concerning a good shall bear responsibility also for defects of the good which arose after its transfer to the purchaser with respect to which the purchaser proves that they arose in connection with the absence of such information.

Article 428. Sale of Good with Condition Concerning Acceptance Thereof by Purchaser Within Determined Period

A contract of retail purchase-sale may be concluded by the parties with a condition concerning acceptance by the purchaser of the good within a period determined by the contract during which this good may not be sold to another purchaser.

Unless provided otherwise by the contract of retail purchase-sale, the failure of the purchaser to appear or the failure to perform other necessary actions in order to accept the good within the period determined by the contract may be considered by the seller as the refusal of the purchaser to perform the contract.

Additional expenses of the seller relating to ensuring the transfer of the good to the purchaser within the period determined by the contract of retail purchase-sale shall be included in the price of the good unless provided otherwise by legislation or the contract.

Article 429. Sale of Good by Sample

A contract of purchase-sale for a good may be concluded by the parties on the basis of a sample (or description, catalogue, and so forth).

The performance of a contract of sale for a good by a sample shall be effectuated in accordance with the rules of Article 431 of the present Code.

A purchaser before the transfer of the good shall have the right to refuse performance of a contract of retail purchase-sale on condition of compensation to the seller for necessary expenses incurred in connection with the performance of actions relating to fulfillment of the contract.

Article 430. Sale of Good With Use of Automatic Machine

In the instances when goods are sold with the use of an automatic machine, the possessor of the automatic machine shall be obliged to bring to the information of the purchaser concerning the seller of the good by means of placing on the automatic machine or granting to the purchaser by other means information concerning the name (or firm name) of the seller, location, work regime, and also actions which are necessary to be performed by the purchaser in order to receive the good.

A contract of retail purchase-sale with the use of an automatic machine shall be considered to be concluded from the moment of the performance of actions by the purchaser which are necessary in order to receive the good.

If the purchaser has not been granted a good paid for, the seller shall be obliged to grant the good at once to the purchaser or to return the amount paid by him. In the event of the failure to perform this duty the purchaser shall have the right to require compensation from the seller for losses caused.

In instances when an automatic machine is used to change money or for the acquisition of banknotes for payment or the exchange of currency, the rules concerning retail purchase-sale shall apply unless it arises otherwise from the essence of the obligation.

Article 431. Sale of Good with Condition of Delivery Thereof to Purchaser

In instances when a contract of retail purchase-sale has been concluded with a condition concerning delivery of the good to the purchaser, the seller shall be obliged within the period established by the contract to deliver the good at the place specified by the purchaser, and if the place of delivery is not specified by the purchaser, at the place of residence of the citizen or location of the juridical person which is the purchaser.

A contract of retail purchase-sale shall be considered to be performed from the moment of handing of the good over to the purchaser, and in the event of his absence, to any person presenting the receipt or other document testifying to the conclusion of the contract or formalization of the delivery of the good, unless provided otherwise by legislation or the contract or does not arise from the essence of the obligation.

In instances when the time for delivery of a good for handing over to its purchaser is not determined by the contract, the good must be delivered within a reasonable period after receipt of the demand of the purchaser.

Article 432. Price and Payment for Good

The purchaser shall be obliged to pay for a good at the price declared by the seller at the moment of concluding the contract of retail purchase-sale unless provided otherwise by legislation or does not arise from the essence of the obligation.

In instances when preliminary payment for a good has been provided for by the contract of retail purchase-sale, the failure of the purchaser to pay for the good within the period established by the contract shall be deemed to be a refusal of performance of the contract by the purchaser unless provided otherwise by agreement of the parties.

The rules provided for by Article 421, paragraphs four and five, of the present Code shall not be subject to application to contracts of retail purchase-sale for goods on credit, including with a condition for payment by the purchaser for the goods by installment.

The purchaser shall have the right to pay up for the good at any time in full within the limits of the installment period for payment for the good established by the contract.

Article 433. Exchange of Good of Proper Quality

The purchaser shall have the right within ten days from the moment of the transfer to him of a non-foodstuff good, unless a longer period is declared by the seller, to exchange a good of proper quality bought at the place of purchase or other places declared by the seller for an analogous good of another size, form, dimension, style, color, or complement, and the like, making the necessary settlement with the seller in the event of a difference in price.

If the seller does not have the good necessary for the exchange, the purchaser shall have the right to return the acquired good to the seller and to receive the monetary amount paid for it.

The demand of the purchaser concerning an exchange or return of the good shall be subject to satisfaction if the good was not used, has retained its consumer properties, and there is evidence of its acquisition from the particular seller.

A list of goods which are not subject to exchange or return on the grounds specified in the present Article shall be determined in the procedure established by legislation.

Article 434. Rights of Purchaser in Event of Sale to Him of Good of Improper Quality

A purchaser to whom a good of improper quality was sold, unless its defects were stipulated when concluding the contract, shall have the right at his choice to require:

replacement by a good of proper quality of an analogous brand (or model, article);

replacement by a similar good of another brand (or model, article) with a respective recalculation of the purchase price;

elimination without compensation of the defects of the good or compensation of expenses for rectification of the defects by the purchaser or by a third person;

commensurate reduction of the purchase price;

dissolution of the contract with compensation of losses incurred.

In the event of the return to the purchaser of the monetary amount paid for the good, the seller shall not have the right to withhold from it the amount by which the value of the good was lowered because of the full or partial use of the good, loss of goods appearance, or other similar circumstances.

Article 435. Compensation of Difference in Price in Event of Replacement of Good, Reduction of Purchase Price, and Return of Good of Improper Quality

In the event of the replacement of a poor-quality good with a good of proper quality, the seller shall not have the right to demand compensation of the difference between the price of the good established by the contract of retail purchase-sale and the price of the good existing at the moment of replacement of the good or rendering by a court of a decision concerning replacement of the good.

In the event of the replacement of a poor-quality good by an analogous good of proper quality but different in dimension, style, quality, or other indicia, the difference between the price of the good being replaced at the moment of replacement and the price of the good being transferred in place of the good of improper quality shall be subject to compensation. If the demand of the purchaser is not satisfied by the seller, these prices shall be determined at the moment of the rendering by a court of the decision concerning replacement of the good.

In the event a demand is presented concerning a commensurate reduction of the purchase price of the good in settlement, the price of the good at the moment of presenting the demand concerning the price reduction shall be used, and if the demand of the purchaser is not satisfied voluntarily, at the moment of the rendering by a court of a decision concerning the commensurate reduction of the price.

In the event of the return to the seller of a good of improper quality the purchaser shall have the right to require compensation for the difference between the price of the good established by the contract of retail purchase-sale and the price of the respective good at the moment of voluntary satisfaction of his demand, and if the demand is not satisfied voluntarily, at the moment of the rendering of a decision by the court.

Article 436. Responsibility of Seller and Performance of Obligation in Kind

In the event of the failure of the seller to perform an obligation under the contract of retail purchase-sale, compensation of losses and the payment of a penalty shall not relieve the seller from performance of the obligation in kind.

§ 3. Delivery

Article 437. Contract of Delivery

Under a contract of delivery the supplier-seller effectuating entrepreneurial activity shall be obliged to transfer goods produced or purchased by him within the stipulated period or periods to the purchaser for use in entrepreneurial activity or for other purposes not connected with personal, family, home, and other analogous use, and the purchaser shall be obliged to accept the goods and to pay for them.

Article 438. Period of Operation of Contract of Delivery

A contract of delivery may be concluded for one year, for a period of more than one year (long-term contract), or for another period provided for by agreement of the parties.

If the period of its operation is not determined in a contract of delivery, the contract shall be deemed to be concluded for one year.

If in a long-term contract the quantity of goods subject to delivery or other conditions of the contract have been determined for a good or for a longer period, the procedure for agreeing these provisions by the parties for subsequent periods before the end of the period of operation of the contract must be established in the contract. In the absence of such procedure in the contract, the contract shall be deemed to be concluded respectively for one year or for the period for which the conditions of the contract have been agreed.

In the event of the refusal or evasion by one of the parties to a long-term contract to agree the quantity of goods subject to delivery or other conditions of the contract for subsequent periods in the procedure established by the contract, the other party shall have the right to apply to a court with a demand concerning determination of the conditions for the delivery of goods for the respective periods or dissolution of the contract.

Article 439. Settlement of Disagreements When Concluding Contract of Delivery

In an instance when a proposal by one party to conclude a contract of delivery of goods is sent in the form of a draft contract to the other party, which agreeing to conclude a contract on other conditions shall draw up a protocol of disagreements not later than thirty days after receipt of the draft and return it with the signed contract, the party which received the protocol of disagreements being obliged within a thirty day period to take measures (when possible jointly with the other party) to agree the conditions of the contract or inform the other party in writing of its refusal to conclude it.

The party which received the protocol of disagreements regarding the conditions of the contract of delivery but did not take measures to agree the conditions of the contract and did not inform the other party about the refusal to conclude the contract within the period established by paragraph one of the present Article shall be obliged to compensate the losses caused by the avoidance of agreeing the conditions of the contract.

Article 440. Periods for Delivery

When the delivery of goods has been provided for by the parties within the period of operation of the contract by individual lots and the periods of delivery of the individual lots (or delivery periods) have not been determined therein, the goods must be delivered in lots of equal measure monthly insofar as it does not arise otherwise from a legislation or the essence of the obligation or the customs of business turnover.

Together with the determination of the periods of delivery, a delivery schedule for the goods (ten-day, twenty-four hour, hour, and so forth) may be established in the contract.

Goods may be delivered before time with the consent of the purchaser. Goods delivered before time and accepted by the purchaser shall be credited to the quantity of goods subject to delivery within the following period.

Article 441. Procedure for Delivery of Goods

The delivery of goods shall be effectuated by the supplier by means of shipment (or transfer) of the goods to the purchaser according to the contract or to the person specified in the contract as the recipient.

When the right of the purchaser has been provided for by the contract of delivery to give an instruction to the supplier concerning the shipment of the goods to the recipients (shipment order), the shipment (or transfer) of the goods shall be effectuated by the supplier to the recipients specified in the shipment order.

The content of a shipment order and the period for sending it by the purchaser to the supplier shall be determined by the contract of delivery. If the period for sending the shipment order is not provided for by the contract, it must be sent to the supplier not later than thirty days before the ensuing of the delivery period.

The failure of the purchaser to present the shipment order within the established period shall give the supplier the right either to refuse performance of the contract of delivery or to require payment for the goods from the recipient. In addition, the supplier shall have the right to require compensation of losses caused in connection with the failure to present the shipping order.

Article 442. Delivery of Goods

The delivery of goods shall be effectuated by the supplier by means of the shipment thereof by transport provided for by the contract of delivery and on the conditions determined by it.

If what type of transport or on what conditions the delivery shall be effectuated is not determined in the contract, the right of choice of the type of transport or determination of the conditions of delivery of the goods shall belong to the supplier unless it arises otherwise from legislation, the essence of the obligation, or customs of business turnover.

Article 443. Augmentation of Short Deliveries of Goods

The supplier who has permitted a short delivery of goods in an individual period of delivery shall be obliged to augment the short-delivered quantity of goods within the following period(s) within the limits of the period of operation of the contract of delivery unless provided otherwise by the contract.

Under a long-term contract the quantity of goods short delivered by the supplier in an individual period of delivery shall be subject to augmentation in the next period(s) within the limits of that year in which the short delivery of goods was permitted unless provided otherwise by the contract of delivery.

When goods have been shipped by the supplier to several recipients specified in the contract of delivery or shipment order of the recipient, the goods delivered to one recipient in excess of the quantity provided for in the contract or shipment order shall not be credited to cover the short delivery to other purchasers and shall be subject to augmentation by the supplier unless provided otherwise in the contract.

Article 444. Refusal to Accept Goods Whose Delivery is Delayed

The purchaser shall have the right, having informed the supplier, to refuse acceptance of the goods whose delivery has been delayed unless provided otherwise by the contract. The goods delivered before receipt of the notice by the supplier the purchaser shall be obliged to accept and to pay for.

Article 445. Assortment of Goods When Augmenting Short Delivery

The assortment of goods whose short delivery is subject to augmentation shall be determined by agreement of the parties. In the absence of such agreement the supplier shall be obliged to augment the short-delivered quantity of the goods in the assortment established for that period in which the short delivery was permitted.

The delivery of goods of one name in a larger quantity than is provided for the contract of delivery shall not be credited towards covering the short delivery of goods of another name within the same assortment and shall be subject to augmentation except for instances when such delivery was made with the prior written consent of the purchaser.

Article 446. Acceptance of Goods by Purchaser

The purchaser (or recipient) shall be obliged to perform all necessary actions ensuring the acceptance of goods delivered in accordance with the contract.

A good accepted by the purchaser (or recipient) must be inspected by him within the period determined by legislation, the contract of delivery, or the customs of business turnover.

The purchaser (or recipient) shall be obliged within the same period to verify the quantity and quality of the goods accepted in the procedure established by legislation, the contract of delivery, or the customs of business turnover and to inform the supplier about elicited nonconformities or short deliveries of goods immediately in writing.

In the event of the receipt of goods delivered from a transport organization, the purchaser (or recipient) shall be obliged to verify the conformity of the goods to the information specified in the transport and accompanying documents, and also to accept these goods from the transport organization in compliance with the established rules.

Article 447. Custody of Good Not Accepted by Purchaser

When the purchaser (or recipient) in accordance with legislation or the contract of delivery refuses a good transferred by the supplier, he shall be obliged to ensure the preservation of this good (custody) and immediately notify the supplier.

The supplier shall be obliged to remove the good accepted by the purchaser (or recipient) for custody or to dispose of it within a reasonable period. If the supplier within this period does not dispose of the good, the purchaser shall have the right to realize the good or to return it to the supplier.

Necessary expenses incurred by the purchaser in connection with the acceptance of the good for custody, realization of the good, or the return thereof to the seller shall be subject to compensation by the supplier. In so doing the monetary amount received from the realization of the good shall be transferred to the supplier, deducting that due to the purchaser.

In instances when the purchaser does not accept a good from the supplier or refuses the good without grounds established by legislation or the contract, the supplier shall have the right to require payment for the good from the purchaser.

Article 448. Selection of Goods

If the selection of goods by the purchaser (or recipient) has been provided for by the contract of delivery at the location of the supplier, the purchaser (or recipient) must inspect the goods to be transferred to the place of their transfer. In the event of eliciting the nonconformity of the goods to the contract, he shall have the right to refuse to accept them.

The failure of the purchaser (or recipient) to select goods within the period established by the contract of delivery, and in the absence thereof within a reasonable period after receipt of the notice of the supplier concerning the readiness of the goods shall give the supplier the right to refuse performance of the contract or to require payment for the goods from the recipient.

Article 449. Settlement of Accounts for Goods to be Delivered

The purchaser shall pay for delivered goods in compliance with the procedure and form for the settlement of accounts provided for by the contract. If the procedure and form for the settlement of accounts has not been determined by agreement of the parties, the settlement of accounts shall be effectuated by payment orders.

When the delivery of goods by individual parts within a set is provided for in a contract, payment for the goods by the purchaser shall be made after the shipment (or selection) of the last part within the set unless established otherwise by the contract.

If it has been provided by a contract of delivery that payment for the goods shall be effectuated by the recipient (or payer) and the last unfoundedly refuses to pay or has not made payment for the goods within the period established by the contract, the supplier shall have the right to require payment for the goods delivered from the purchaser.

Article 450. Return of Packaging and Packing

Unless provided otherwise by the contract of delivery, the purchaser (or recipient) shall be obliged to return to the supplier nondisposable packaging and means of packing in which the good arrived in the procedure and within the periods established by legislation.

Other packaging and packing shall be subject to return to the supplier only in the instances provided for by the contract of delivery.

Article 451. Consequences of Delivery of Goods of Improper Quality

The purchaser (or recipient) to whom the goods of improper quality are delivered shall have the right to present demands to the supplier provided for by Article 434 of the present Code except for the instance when the supplier who received the notice of the purchaser concerning defects of the delivered goods replaces without delay the goods delivered with goods of the proper quality.

The purchaser (or recipient) effectuating the sale of goods delivered to him at retail shall have the right to demand the replacement of a good of improper quality within a reasonable period returned by a consumer unless provided otherwise by the contract of delivery.

Article 452. Consequences of Delivery of Incomplete Goods

The purchaser (or recipient) to whom goods have been delivered in violation of the conditions of a contract of delivery, the requirements of legislation, or requirements usually presented for completeness shall have the right to present the demands to the supplier provided for by Article 413 of the present Code, except for an instance when the supplier who has received notice of the purchaser concerning the incompleteness of the delivered goods without delay makes the goods complete or replaces them with complete goods.

The purchaser (or recipient) effectuating the sale of goods at retail shall have the right to demand replacement of the incomplete goods within a reasonable period returned by a consumer with complete ones unless provided otherwise by the contract of delivery.

Article 453. Rights of Purchaser in Event of Failure to Deliver Goods, Failure to Fulfill Requirements Concerning Elimination of Defects of Goods or Completing Sets of Goods

If the supplier does not deliver the quantity of goods provided for by the contract of delivery or did not fulfill the demands of the purchaser (or recipient) concerning the replacement of poor-quality goods or concerning the completion of the sets of goods within the established period, the purchaser shall have the right to acquire the nondelivered goods from other persons, relegating to the supplier all necessary and reasonable expenses for the acquisition thereof.

The calculation of the expenses of the purchaser for the acquisition of goods from other persons in instances of the short delivery thereof by the supplier or the failure to fulfill the demands of the purchaser concerning elimination of the defects of the goods or concerning the completion of sets of the goods shall be made according to the rules provided for by Article 456, paragraph one, of the present Code.

The purchaser (or recipient) shall have the right to refuse to pay for goods of improper quality and incomplete goods, and if such goods have been paid for, to require the return of the paid amounts until elimination of the defects and completion of the sets of the goods or the replacement thereof.

Article 454. Penalty for Short Delivery of Goods

The penalty established by a law or contract for the short delivery or delay of delivery of goods shall be recovered from the supplier until the actual performance of the obligation within the limits of the period of operation of the contract unless another procedure for recovery of the penalty has been established by a law or the contract.

Article 455. Unilateral Refusal of Performance of Contract of Delivery

A unilateral refusal of performance of a contract of delivery (wholly or partially) shall be permitted in the event of a material violation of the contract by one of the parties.

A violation of a contract of delivery by the supplier may be deemed to be material in instances of:

the delivery of goods of improper quality with defects which can not be eliminated within a period acceptable to the purchaser;

the repeated violation of the periods for delivery of goods.

The violation of a contract of delivery by the purchaser may be deemed to be material in instances of:

the repeated violation of the periods for the payment of goods;

the repeated failure to select goods.

By agreement of the parties it may be provided that the other party may unilaterally refuse performance of the contract of delivery or unilaterally change it.

A contract of delivery shall be considered to be changed or dissolved from the moment of receipt by one party of notice by the other party concerning the unilateral refusal of performance of the contract wholly or partially unless another period of dissolution or change of the contract is provided for in the notice or has not been determined by agreement of the parties.

Article 456. Calculation of Losses in Event of Dissolution of Contract

If within a reasonable period after dissolution of the contract as a consequence of a violation of an obligation by the seller the purchaser has bought from another person a good at a higher but reasonable price in place of that provided for by the contract, the purchaser may present a demand to the seller concerning compensation of losses in the form of the difference between the price established in the contract and the price of the transaction concluded in lieu.

If within a reasonable period after dissolution of the contract as a consequence of a violation of an obligation by the purchaser the seller has sold the good to another person at a lower but reasonable price than that provided for by the contract, the seller may present a demand to the purchaser concerning compensation of losses in the form of the difference between the price established in the contract and the price for the transaction concluded in lieu.

If after the dissolution of a contract on the grounds provided for by paragraphs one and two of the present Article a transaction has not been concluded in place of the dissolved contract and for the particular good there is a current price, a party may present a demand concerning compensation of losses in the form of the difference between the price established in the contract and the current price at the moment of dissolution of the contract.

The current price shall be deemed to be the price usually recovered under comparable circumstances for an analogous good at the place where the transfer of the good should have been effectuated. If a current price does not exist at that place, the current price applied in another place may be used which may serve as a reasonable replacement, taking into account the difference in expenses for the transportation of the good.

Satisfaction of the demands provided for by the present Article shall not relieve the party which did not perform or which improperly performed the obligation from compensation of other losses caused to the other party on the basis of Article 14 of the present Code.

§ 4. State Contract for Delivery of Goods

Article 457. Delivery of Goods for State Needs

The delivery of goods for State needs shall be effectuated on the basis of a State contract for the delivery of goods for State needs, and also contracts for the delivery of goods concluded in accordance therewith for State needs. State needs shall be deemed to be requirements of the Republic Uzbekistan determined in the procedure established by legislation which are ensured at the expense of assets of the State budget and extrabudgetary sources of financing.

The rules of Articles 437-456 of the present Code also shall apply to relations relating to the delivery of goods for State needs.

Other legislation regulating the delivery of goods for State needs shall apply to relations not regulated by the present Code.

Article 458. State Contract for Delivery of Goods for State Needs

Under a State contract for the delivery of goods for State needs (hereinafter: State contract), the supplier (or executor) shall be obliged to transfer within the stipulated period the goods to the State customer or at his instruction on the basis of a contract of delivery to another person, and the State customer shall be obliged to ensure the established periods for payment of the goods delivered.

Article 459. Grounds for Conclusion of State Contract

A State contract shall be concluded on the basis of the order of a State customer for the delivery of goods for State needs accepted by the supplier (or executor).

The conclusion of a State contract shall be obligatory for the State customer which placed the order accepted by the supplier (or executor).

The conclusion of a State contract shall be obligatory for the supplier (or executor) only in the instances established by legislation and on condition that the State customer will compensate all losses which may be caused to the supplier (or executor) in connection with the fulfillment of the State contract.

The condition concerning compensation of losses provided for in paragraph three of the present Article shall not apply with respect to a State enterprise.

If the order for the delivery of goods for State needs is placed by a competition, the conclusion of a State contract with the supplier (or executor) who is declared the winner of the competition shall be obligatory for the State customer.

Article 460. Procedure for Conclusion of State Contract

The draft State contract shall be worked out by the State customer and sent to the supplier (or executor) unless provided otherwise by agreement between them.

The party who has received the draft State contract shall sign it within not later than a thirty-day period and return one example of the State contract to the other party, and if there are disagreements regarding the conditions of the State contract shall draw up within the same period a protocol of disagreements and send it together with the signed State contract to the other party or inform it of the refusal to conclude the State contract.

The party who has received the State contract with the protocol of disagreements must within thirty days consider the disagreements, take measures to agree the conditions of the contract with the other party, and inform it about the acceptance of the State contract in the agreed version or reject the protocol of disagreements. Upon the expiry of this period, all unsettled disagreements may be transferred by the other party within a thirty-day period for the consideration of a court.

In instances when a State contract is concluded according to the results of a competition for the placement of an order for the delivery of goods for State needs, the State contract must be concluded not later than thirty days from the date of holding the competition.

If the party for which the conclusion of a State contract is obligatory evades the conclusion thereof, the other party shall have the right to apply to a court with the demand to compel the other party to conclude the State contract.

Article 461. Performance of State Contract

In instances when in accordance with the conditions of the State contract the delivery of goods is effectuated directly to the State customer or at his instruction (or shipment order) to another person (recipient), the relations of the parties with regard to the performance of the State contract shall be regulated by the rules provided for by Articles 437-456 of the present Code.

If it is provided by a State contract that the delivery of goods is effectuated by the supplier (or executor) to the purchasers with regard to contracts for the delivery of goods for State needs, the State customer shall not later than thirty days from the date of signature of the State contract send to the supplier-executor notice concerning the attachment of the purchaser to the supplier (or executor).

The notice concerning attachment of the purchaser to the supplier (or executor) shall be grounds for the conclusion of the contract for the delivery of goods for State needs.

In instances when the delivery of goods for State needs is effectuated by the recipient specified in the shipment orders, the goods shall be paid for by the State customer unless another procedure for the settlement of accounts is provided for by the State contract.

In the event of delivery of goods to purchasers according to contract for the delivery of goods for State needs the goods shall be paid for by the purchasers at the prices to be determined in accordance with the State contract unless another procedure for determining the prices and settlement of accounts not provided for by the State contract.

In the event of payment by the purchaser for goods under a State contract for the delivery of goods for State needs the State customer shall be deemed to be surety of the purchaser with regard to this obligation.

Article 462. Conclusion of Contract of Delivery of Goods for State Needs

Unless another procedure is provided for the preparation of a draft contract or the draft contract is not submitted by the purchaser, the supplier (or executor) shall be obliged to send the draft contract for the delivery of goods for State needs to the purchaser specified in the notice concerning attachment not later than thirty days from the moment of receipt of the notice from the State customer.

The party who has received the draft contract of delivery of goods for State needs shall sign it within not later than a thirty-day period and return one example of the contract to the other party, and if there are disagreements with regard to the conditions of the contract to draw up within this same period a protocol of disagreements and send it together with the signed contract to the other party.

The party who has received the contract of delivery of goods for State needs with the protocol of disagreements must within thirty days consider the disagreements, take measures to agree the conditions of the contract with the other party, and notify the other party about the acceptance of the contract in the version thereof — or reject the protocol of disagreements. The unsettled disagreements within a thirty-day period may be transferred by the interested party for consideration of a court.

If the supplier (or executor) evades conclusion of the contract of delivery of goods for State needs, the purchaser shall have the right to apply to a court with a demand concerning compelling the supplier (or executor) to conclude the contract on conditions of the draft contract worked out by the purchaser.

Article 463. Refusal of Purchaser to Conclude Contract of Delivery of Goods for State Needs

The purchaser shall have the right wholly or partially to refuse goods specified in the notice concerning attachment and to conclude the contract for the delivery thereof. In this event the supplier (or executor) must immediately inform the State customer and shall have the right to demand from the State customer the issuance of a notice concerning attachment of another purchaser to it.

The State customer shall not later than thirty days from the date of receipt of the notification of the supplier (or executor) either issue the notice concerning attachment of another purchaser to the supplier (or executor) or to send to the supplier (or executor) a shipment order specifying the recipient of the goods or communicate his consent to accept and to pay for the goods.

In the event of the failure to fulfill the duties provided for by paragraph two of the present Article by the State customer, the supplier (or executor) shall have the right either to require the State customer to accept and pay for the goods or to realize the goods at his discretion, relegating reasonable expenses connected with the realization thereof to the State customer.

Article 464. Compensation of Losses Caused in Connection with Fulfillment or Dissolution of State Contract

Unless provided otherwise by legislation on the delivery of goods for State needs or by the State contract, losses which were caused to the supplier (or executor) in connection with the fulfillment of the State contract (Article 459. paragraph two, of the present Code) shall be subject to compensation by the State customer not later than thirty days from the date of transfer of the good in accordance with the State contract.

When losses caused to the supplier (or executor) in connection with the fulfillment of a State contract are not compensated in accordance with the State contract, the supplier (or executor) shall have the right to refuse performance of the State contract and require compensation of losses caused by the dissolution of the State contract.

In the event of the dissolution of the State contract with regard to the grounds specified in paragraph two of the present Article, the supplier shall have the right to refuse performance of the contract of the delivery of the good for State needs. Losses caused to the purchaser by such refusal of the supplier shall be compensated by the State customer.

§ 5. Agricultural Procurement Contract

Article 465. Contract of Agricultural Procurement

Under a contract of agricultural procurement the producer of agricultural products shall be obliged to transfer the agricultural products to the procurer — the person effectuating the purchase of such products for processing or sale, and the procurer shall be obliged to accept this product and to pay for it within the stipulated periods at the determined price.

The rules concerning the contract of delivery, and in respective instances concerning the State contract for the delivery of goods for State needs, shall apply to the contract of agricultural procurement unless established otherwise by the present Code or does not arise from the essence of the obligation.

Article 466. Duties of Producer of Agricultural Product

The producer of an agricultural product shall be obliged to transfer to the procurer the agricultural product grown (or produced) in a quantity or assortment provided for by the contract of agricultural procurement.

If it becomes knowingly known that as a consequence of the failure of a producer of a product to fulfill the duty specified in paragraph one of the present Article, the agricultural product can not be received in a quantity and assortment provided for by the contract of agricultural product, the procurer shall have the right to require dissolution or change of the contract and the compensation of losses.

Article 467. Duties of Procurer

Unless established otherwise by the contract of agricultural procurement, the procurer shall be obliged to accept the agricultural product from the producer at the location thereof and to ensure the carriage thereof.

If the acceptance of an agricultural product is effectuated at the location of the procurer or other place specified by him, the procurer shall not have the right to refuse to accept the agricultural product delivered by the producer thereof in accordance with the contract of agricultural procurement within the period stipulated by it.

In the event the procurer has not ensured the carriage or acceptance of the agricultural product, he shall pay to the producer thereof the cost of the agricultural product and the expenses for the delivery thereof.

The procurer effectuating the processing of an agricultural product received under the contract of agricultural procurement shall be obliged to return to the producer at his demand the wastes from the processing of the agricultural product with payment at the price agreed by the parties.

§ 6. Electric Power Supply

Article 468. Contract of Electric Power Supply

Under a contract of electric power supply the electric power supply organization shall be obliged to provide electric power to the subscriber (or consumer) through the connecting network, and the subscriber shall be obliged to pay for the electric power accepted, and also to comply with the consumption regime provided for by the contract, ensure the safety of operation of the electric power networks within its jurisdiction and the good repair of the instruments and equipment connected with the consumption of electric power used by it.

Article 469. Conclusion and Extension of Contract of Electric Power Supply

A contract of electric power supply shall be concluded with a subscriber when there is an electrical device connected to the networks of the electric power supply organization in the procedure established by legislation, and also the necessary equipment and instruments for recording the consumption of electric power.

In the event when the subscriber under a contract of electric power supply is a citizen who is using electric power for domestic consumption, the contract shall be considered to be concluded from the moment of first actual connection of the subscriber in the established procedure to the connecting network.

In the absence of an application by one of the parties concerning the termination or change of the contract of electric power supply at the end of the period, it shall be considered to be prolonged for the same period and on the same conditions as were provided for by the contract. When prolonging the contract for a new period, the conditions thereof may be changed by agreement of the parties.

If one of the parties before the end of the period of operation of the contract has made a proposal to conclude a new contract, the relations of the parties until the conclusion of the new contract shall be regulated by the previously concluded contract.

Article 470. Quantity of Electric Power

The electric power supply organization shall be obliged to provide the subscriber with electric power through the connecting network in the quantity provided for by the contract of electric power supply and in compliance with the provision regime agreed by the parties. The quantity provided by the electric power supply organization and accepted by the subscriber of electric power shall be determined by the indicators of the recording instruments.

The right of the subscriber to change the quantity of electric power used by him as determined by the contract may be provided for by the contract of electric power supply on condition of compensation by him of expenses incurred by the electric power supply organization in connection with ensuring the provision of electric power in a quantity not stipulated by the contract.

In the event when a citizen is the subscriber under the contract of electric power supply who used electric power for domestic consumption, he shall have the right to use electric power in the quantity necessary for him.

Article 471. Consequences of Violation of Condition of Contract of Electric Power Supply on Quantity of Electric Power

If a lesser quantity of electric power has been provided by the electric power supply organization through the connecting network to the subscriber than is provided by the contract of electric power supply, the rules provided for by Article 399 of the present Code shall apply unless provided otherwise by legislation, the contract, or does not arise from the essence of the obligation.

Article 472. Quality of Electric Power

The quality of electric power provided by the electric power supply organization must correspond to the requirements established by legislation relating to standardization or the contract of electric power supply.

In the event of a violation by the electric power supply organization of the requirements for quality of electric power, the rules provided for by Article 408 of the present Code shall apply unless provided otherwise by legislation, the contract of electric power supply, or does not arise from the essence of the obligation.

Article 473. Duties of Subscriber for Maintenance and Operation of Networks, Instruments, and Equipment

The subscriber shall be obliged to ensure the proper technical state and safety of electric power networks being operated, instruments, and equipment, to comply with the established consumption regime for electric power, and also immediately to notify the electric power supply organization about accidents, fires, the disrepair of instruments for recording electric power, and other violations arising when using electric power.

When a citizen is a subscriber under a contract of electric power supply who is using electric power for domestic consumption, the duty to ensure the proper technical state and safety of the electric power networks, and also the instruments for recording the consumption of electric power, shall be placed on the electric power supply organization unless established otherwise by legislation.

The requirements for the technical state and operation of electric power networks, instruments, and equipment, and also the procedure for effectuating control over compliance therewith, shall be determined by legislation.

Article 474. Payment for Electric Power

Payment for electric power shall be made for the quantity of electric power actually accepted by the subscriber in accordance with Article 470 of the present Code, unless provided otherwise by legislation or a contract.

Article 475. Transfer by Subscriber of Electric Power to Another Person

A subscriber may transfer electric power accepted by him from the electric power supply organization through the connecting network to another person (sub-subscriber) only with the consent of the electric power supply organization.

The rules of the present paragraph shall apply to the contract regarding the transfer by the subscriber of electric power to the sub-subscriber unless provided otherwise by legislation or by the contract of electric power supply.

In the event of the transfer of electric power to a sub-subscriber, the subscriber shall remain responsible to the electric power supply organization unless established otherwise by legislation.

Article 476. Change and Dissolution of Contract of Electric Power Supply

An interruption in provision, the termination, or limitation of provision of electric power shall be permitted by agreement of the parties, except for instances when the unsatisfactory state of electric power devices of the subscriber certified by a State electric power supervision agency threatens an accident or creates a threat to the life and safety of citizens. The electric power supply organization must warn the subscriber about an interruption in provision or the termination or limitation of provision of electric power.

An interruption in provision or termination or limitation of provision of electric power without the agreement of the subscriber and without a warning thereof but with immediate notification thereof shall be permitted when necessary to take urgent measures relating to the prevention or liquidation of an accident in the system of the electric power supply organization.

When a citizen is a subscriber under a contract of electric power supply who is using electric power for domestic consumption, he shall have the right to dissolve the contract unilaterally on condition of informing the electric power supply organization thereof and of payment in full for the electric power used.

When a citizen is a subscriber under a contract of electric power supply who is using electric power for domestic consumption, the electric power supply organization shall have the right unilaterally to refuse performance of the contract in connection with the failure of the subscriber to pay for the electric power used by him on condition of warning the subscriber not later than a month before refusal to perform the contract.

When a juridical person is a subscriber under the contract of electric power supply, the electric power supply organization shall have the right to refuse performance of the contract unilaterally on the grounds provided for by Article 455 of the present Code, except for instances established by legislation.

Article 477. Responsibility Under Contract of Electric Power Supply

In the event of the failure to perform or the improper performance of obligations under a contract of electric power supply, the electricity supply organization shall be obliged to compensate these losses, and the subscriber shall be obliged to compensate real damage caused [as amended by Law of 20 April 2012, No. 3PY-325. C3 PY (2012), no. 16, item 176].

If interruptions in the provision of electric power were the result of the regulation of the consumption regime by the electric power organization in connection with a shortage of capacity and electric power effectuated on the basis of legislation, the electric power supply organization shall bear responsibility for the failure to perform or the improper performance of contractual obligations only when there is fault thereof.

Article 478. Application of Rules of Contract of Electric Power Supply to Other Relations Relating to Supply Through Connecting Network

The rules of the present paragraph shall apply to relations relating to the supply of heating electric power through a connecting network unless established otherwise by legislation.

The rules of the present paragraph shall apply to relations relating to the supply through a connecting network of gas, oil and oil products, water, and other goods unless established otherwise by legislation or does not arise from the essence of the obligation.

§ 7. Sale of Immoveable

Article 479. Contract of Sale of Immoveable

Under a contract of purchase-sale of immoveable property (contract of sale of immoveable) the seller shall be obliged to transfer to the ownership of the purchaser a land plot, building, installation, apartment, or other immoveable property (Article 83 of the present Code).

The rules provided for by the present paragraph shall apply to the sale of enterprises insofar as not provided otherwise by the rules concerning the contract of sale of an enterprise (Articles 489-496 of the present Code).

Article 480. Form of Contract of Sale of Immoveable

A contract of sale of an immoveable shall be concluded in written form by means of drawing up one document signed by the parties (Article 366, paragraph four, of the present Code) [as amended by Laws of 11 October 2018, No. 3PY-497, and of 20 March 2019, No. 3PY-531].

The failure to comply with the form of the contract of sale of an immoveable shall entail its invalidity.

Article 481. State Registration of Transfer of Right of Ownership to Immoveable

The transfer of the right of ownership to an immoveable under a contract of sale of an immoveable to a purchaser shall be subject to State registration.

The performance of a contract of sale of an immoveable by the parties before State registration of the transfer of the right of ownership shall not be grounds for a change of their relations with third persons.

When one of the parties evades State registration of the transfer of the right of ownership to an immoveable a court shall have the right at the demand of the other party to render a decision concerning State registration of the transfer of the right of ownership. The party who unfoundedly evaded State registration of the transfer of the right of ownership must compensate the other party for losses caused by the delay of registration.

Article 482. Rights to Land Plot in Event of Sale of Building, Installation, or Other Immoveable Situated Thereon

Under a contract for the sale of a building, installation, or other immoveable the rights shall pass to the purchaser simultaneously with the transfer of the right of ownership to such immoveable to that part of the land plot which is occupied by this immoveable and necessary in order to use it.

In an event when the seller is an owner of the land plot on which an immoveable being sold is situated, the right of ownership shall be transferred to the purchaser or the right of lease shall be granted, or other right provided for by the contract of sale of an immoveable to the corresponding part of the land plot.

If the right to the corresponding land plot is not determined by the contract for the immoveable being transferred to the purchaser, to the purchaser shall pass the right of ownership to that part of the land plot which is occupied by the immoveable and necessary in order to use it.

The sale of an immoveable situated on a land plot which does not belong to the seller by right of ownership shall be permitted without the consent of the owner of this plot if this is not contrary to the conditions of use of such plot established by a law or by the contract. In the event of the sale of such immoveable, the purchaser shall acquire the right of use of the respective part of the land plot on the same conditions as the seller of the immoveable.

Article 483. Right to Immoveable in Event of Sale of Land Plot

In instances when the land plot on which a building, installation, or other immoveable belonging to the seller is situated is sold without the transfer of this immoveable to the ownership of the purchaser, the right of use of the part of the land plot which is occupied by the immoveable and necessary for its use shall be retained for the seller on the conditions determined by the contract of sale.

If the conditions for the use of the respective part of the land plot have not been determined by the contract for the sale thereof, the seller shall retain the right of limited use (servitude) of that part of the land plot which is occupied by the immoveable and is necessary for its use in accordance with its designation.

Article 484. Determination of Subject in Contract of Sale of Immoveable

Data must be specified in a contract of sale of an immoveable enabling the immoveable property subject to transfer to the purchaser under the contract to be established definitely, including data determining the location of the immoveable on the respective land plot or as part of other immoveable property.

In the absence of such data in the contract, the condition concerning immoveable property subject to transfer shall be considered to be not agreed by the parties, and the respective contract shall not be considered to be concluded.

Article 485. Price in Contract of Sale of Immoveable

The contract of sale of an immoveable must provide for the price of this property.

In the absence in the contract of a condition concerning the price of the immoveable agreed by the parties in written form, the contract concerning the sale thereof shall be considered to be not concluded. In so doing the rules for determining the price provided for by Article 356, paragraph four, of the present Code shall not apply.

Unless provided otherwise by a law or contract for the sale of an immoveable, the price established therein of the building, installation, or other immoveable property situated on the land plot shall include the price of the immoveable property transferred therewith of the respective part of the land plot or rights thereto.

In instances when the price of the immoveable in a contract of sale of an immoveable is established per unit of the space thereof or other indicator of its dimension, the total price of such immoveable property subject to payment shall be determined by proceeding from the actual dimension of the immoveable property transferred to the purchaser.

Article 486. Transfer of Immoveable

The transfer of an immoveable by the seller and the acceptance thereof by the purchaser shall be effectuated under the act of transfer or other document concerning the transfer signed by the parties.

Unless provided otherwise by a law or contract, the obligation of the seller to transfer the immoveable to the purchaser shall be considered to be performed after the handing over of this property to the purchaser and the signature by the parties of the respective document concerning transfer.

The evasion by one of the parties of signature of the document concerning transfer of the immoveable on the conditions provided for by the contract shall be considered to be a refusal respectively of the seller to perform the duty to transfer the property and of the purchaser, the duty to accept the property.

The acceptance by the purchaser of an immoveable which does not correspond to the conditions of the contract of sale of an immoveable, including when such nonconformity is stipulated in the document concerning the transfer of the immoveable, shall not be grounds for relieving the seller of responsibility for improper performance of the contract.

Article 487. Consequences of Transfer of Immoveable of Improper Quality

In the event of the transfer by the seller to the purchaser of an immoveable which does not correspond to the conditions of the contract of sale of an immoveable concerning the quality thereof, the rules of Article 434 of the present Code shall apply except for the provisions concerning the right of the purchaser to require replacement of the good of improper quality for a good corresponding to the contract.

Article 488. Peculiarities of Sale of Dwelling Premises

A material condition of the contract of sale of a dwelling house, apartment, or part of a dwelling house or apartment in which persons reside who retain in accordance with a law the right of use of this dwelling premise after its acquisition by the purchaser shall be the list of such persons specifying their rights to use the dwelling premise being sold.

[paragraph two repealed by Law of 11 October 2018, No. 3PY-497].

The contract of sale of a dwelling house, apartment, or part of a dwelling house or apartment shall be subject to notarial certification and State registration [added by Law of 20 March 2019, No. 3PY-531].

§ 8. Sale of Enterprise

Article 489. Contract of Sale of Enterprise

Under a contract of sale of an enterprise the seller shall be obliged to transfer the enterprise as a whole as a property complex to the ownership of the purchaser, except for the rights and duties which the seller does not have the right to transfer to other persons.

The rights to the use of a firm name, trademarks, service marks, and other means of individualization of the seller and its products, work fulfilled, or services rendered shall pass to the purchaser unless provided otherwise by the contract of sale of the enterprise.

The rights of the seller received by it on the basis of a special authorization (or license) to engage in the respective activity shall not be subject to transfer to the purchaser of the enterprises unless established otherwise by legislation. The inclusion in the composition of the enterprise being transferred under the contract of sale of obligations whose performance by the purchaser is impossible in the absence of a special authorization (or license) for this shall not relieve the seller from the respective obligations to creditors. The seller and the purchaser shall bear joint and several responsibility to creditors for the failure to perform such obligations.

Article 490. Form and State Registration of Contract of Sale of Enterprise

The contract of sale of an enterprise shall be concluded in written form by means of drawing up one document signed by the parties with the obligatory appending thereto of the documents specified in Article 491, paragraph two, of the present Code, and shall be subject to notarial certification and State registration. The contract of sale of an enterprise concluded on a competitive (or tender) basis shall, by decision of an empowered State agency, not be subject to notarial certification except for instances provided for by Article 110, paragraph two, point (2) of the present Code [as amended by Laws of 20 August 1999, No. 832-I, and of 20 August 2021, No. ЗРУ-709].

The failure to comply with the requirements provided for by paragraph one of the present Article shall entail the invalidity of the contract. Such contract shall be considered to be null, the performance thereof shall not be permitted, and the rules provided for by Articles 112, paragraphs two and three, of the present Code shall not apply to it.

Article 491. Establishment of Composition and Valuation of Value of Enterprise Subject to Sale

The composition and valuation of the value of the enterprise subject to sale shall be determined in the contract of sale of an enterprise on the basis of the full inventorization of the enterprise conducted in accordance with the established rules of such inventorization.

Before signature of the contract of sale of an enterprise there must be drawn up and considered by the parties: the act of inventorization, the bookkeeping balance sheet, the opinion of an auditor, the appraisal report, and also a list of all the debts (or obligations) included within the enterprise, specifying the creditors and the character, amount, and periods of their demands. The property, rights, and duties specified in the named documents shall be subject to transfer by the seller to the purchaser unless it arises otherwise from Article 489 of the present Code or is established otherwise by agreement of the parties [as amended by Law of 17 September 2010, No. ЗРУ-257. СЗ РУ (2010), no. 37, item 315].

Article 492. Rights of Creditors in Event of Sale of Enterprise

The creditors with regard to obligations included within the enterprise being sold must be informed in writing by the seller about the sale of the enterprise before the transfer thereof to the purchaser.

The creditor who in writing has not communicated to the seller his consent to the transfer of the debt shall have the right within three months from the date of receipt of the notice concerning the sale of the enterprise to require either the termination or performance before time of the obligation and compensation by the seller of the losses or recognition of the contract of sale of the enterprise to be invalid wholly or in respective part.

The creditor who was not informed about the sale of the enterprise in the procedure provided for by paragraph one of the present Article may bring suit concerning satisfaction of the demands provided for by paragraph two of the present Article within a year from the date when he knew or should have known about the transfer of the enterprise by the seller to the purchaser.

After the transfer of the enterprise to the purchaser, the seller and the purchaser shall bear joint and several responsibility for debts included within the enterprise being transferred which were transferred to the purchaser without the consent of the creditor.

Article 493. Transfer of Enterprise

The transfer of an enterprise by the seller to the purchaser shall be effectuated under the act of transfer, in which shall be specified data concerning the composition of the enterprise and notice of the creditors concerning the sale of the enterprise, and also information concerning defects elicited in the property being transferred and list of property, the duties with regard to the transfer of which have been impossible in view of its loss.

The preparation of the enterprise for transfer, including the drawing up and submission for signature of the act of transfer, shall be the duty of the seller and shall be effectuated at his expense unless provided otherwise by the contract.

An enterprise shall be considered to be transferred to the purchaser from the date of signature of the act of transfer by both parties. From this moment the risk of accidental perishing or accidental damage of property being transferred within the enterprise shall pass to the purchaser.

Article 494. Transfer of Right of Ownership to Enterprise

The right of ownership to an enterprise shall pass to the purchaser from the moment of State registration of this right.

Unless provided otherwise by the contract of sale of an enterprise, the State registration of the right of ownership of the purchaser to the enterprise shall be effectuated directly after the transfer of the enterprise to the purchaser.

In instances when the retention by the seller of the right of ownership to an enterprise transferred to the purchaser has been provided for by the contract until the payment for the enterprise or until the ensuing of other obligations, the purchaser shall have the right until the transfer of the right of ownership to him to dispose of the property within the enterprise being transferred, and also to use the rights, to that extent as is necessary in order to ensure the activity of the enterprise as a property complex.

Article 495. Consequences of Transfer and Acceptance of Enterprise with Defects

The consequences of the transfer by the seller and acceptance by the purchaser under an act of transfer of an enterprise the composition of which does not correspond to the contract of sale of the enterprise provided for by the contract, including with respect to the quality of the property being transferred, shall be determined on the basis of the rules provided for by Articles 393-395, 399, 402, 408, and 412 of the present Code unless it arises otherwise from the contract and is not provided for by paragraphs two, three, and four of the present Article.

When an enterprise has been transferred and accepted under the act of transfer in which information concerning elicited defects of the enterprise and lost property have been specified, the purchaser shall have the right to demand a corresponding reduction of the purchase price of the enterprise unless the right to present other demands in such instances has been provided for by the contract of sale of the enterprise.

The purchaser shall have the right to demand a reduction of the purchase price in the event of the transfer to it within the enterprise of debts (or obligations) of the seller which were not specified in the contract of sale of the enterprise or act of transfer unless the seller proves that the purchaser knew of such debts (or obligations) during the conclusion of the contract and transfer of the enterprise.

The seller in the event of receiving notice of the purchaser concerning defects of the property being transferred within the enterprise, or the absence of individual types of property in such composition which are subject to transfer, may without delay replace the property of improper quality or grant short-delivered property to the purchaser.

The purchaser shall have the right in a judicial proceeding to demand dissolution or change of the contract of sale of an enterprise and the return of that which was performed by the parties under the contract if it is established that the enterprise, in view of the defects for which the seller is liable, is unfit for the purposes named in the contract of sale of the enterprise and these defects have not been eliminated by the seller on the conditions, in the procedure, and within the periods which have been established in accordance with the present Code, legislation, or the contract, or the elimination of such defects is impossible.

Article 496. Application to Contract of Sale of Enterprise of Rules Concerning Consequences of Invalidity of Transactions and Concerning Change or Dissolution of Contract

The rules of the present Code concerning the consequences of the invalidity of transactions and a change or dissolution of the contract of purchase-sale providing for the return or recovery in kind of that received under the contract from one party or from both parties shall apply to the contract of sale of an enterprise unless such consequences materially violate the rights and the interests protected by a law of the creditors of the seller and purchaser, of other persons, and are not contrary to the rules of Article 116 of the present Code.

Chapter 30. Barter

Article 497. Contract of Barter

Under a contract of barter, each of the parties shall be obliged to transfer to the ownership of the other party one good in exchange for another.

To the contract of barter shall apply respectively the rules concerning purchase-sale if this is not contrary to the rules of the present Chapter and the essence of the barter. In so doing each of the parties shall be deemed to be the seller of the good which he is obliged to transfer and the purchaser of the good which he is obliged to accept in exchange.

The contract of barter of motor vehicle means of transport subject in the procedure established by legislation to State registration must be notarially certified [added by Law of 7 December 2001, No. 320-II. Ведомости Олий Мажлиса (2001), no. 1, item 20].

Article 498. Prices and Expenses Under Contract of Barter

Unless it arises otherwise from the contract of barter, goods subject to exchange shall be proposed of equal value and expenses for the transfer thereof and acceptance shall be effectuated in each instance by that party which bears the respective duties.

When in accordance with the contract of barter the goods being exchanged are deemed not to be of equal value, the party obliged to transfer a good whose price is lower than the price of the good being granted in exchange must pay for the difference in prices without delay after the transfer the good or goods-disposition documents for it unless another procedure of payment has been paid for by the contract.

Article 499. Counter Performance of Obligation to Transfer Good Under Contract of Barter

When in accordance with a contract of barter the periods for the transfer of the goods being exchanged do not coincide, the rules concerning counter performance of obligations shall apply to the performance of the obligation to transfer the good by the party which must perform it after the transfer of the good by the other party.

Article 500. Transfer of Right of Ownership to Goods Being Exchanged

Unless provided otherwise by a law or by the contract of barter, the right of ownership to the goods being transferred shall pass to the parties acting under the contract of barter as purchasers simultaneously after the performance of the obligations to transfer the respective goods by both parties.

Article 501. Responsibility for Seizure of Good Acquired Under Contract of Barter

The party from whom a good is seized by third persons which was acquired under a contract of barter shall have the right when there are grounds provided for by Article 395 of the present Code to require from the other party the return of the good received by the last in the exchange and/or compensation of losses.

Chapter 31. Gift

Article 502. Contract of Gift

Under a contract of gift one party (donor) transfers without compensation or is obliged to transfer to the other party (donee) a thing in ownership or transfers or is obliged to transfer to it a property right (or demand) against himself or against a third person or relieves or is obliged to relieve him of a property duty to himself or to a third person.

When there exists a counter transfer of a thing or right or a counter obligation the contract shall not be deemed to be a gift. The rules of Article 124, paragraph two, of the present Code shall apply to such contract.

The promise to transfer without compensation any thing or property right whatever or to relieve someone of a property duty (promise of gift) shall be deemed to be a contract of gift if it was made in the proper form and contains a clearly expressed intention to perform in the future the transfer of the thing or property right without compensation to a specific person or to relieve him from a property duty.

The promise to give all of his property or part of all of his property without specifying the specific subject of gift in the form of a thing, property right, or relief from a property duty shall be null.

A contract providing for the transfer of a gift to the donee after the death of the donor shall be null. The rules of the present Code concerning inheriting shall apply to such kind of gift.

Article 503. Refusal of Donee to Accept Gift

The donee shall have the right at any time before the transfer of the gift to him to refuse it. In this event the contract of gift shall be considered to be dissolved.

If the contract of gift is concluded in written form, the refusal of the gift must also be concluded in written form. When the contract of gift has been registered, the refusal to accept the gift also shall be subject to State registration.

If the contract of gift was concluded in written form, the donor shall have the right to demand from the donee compensation of real damage caused by the refusal to accept the gift.

Article 504. Form of Contract of Gift

A gift accompanied by the transfer of the gift to the donee may be concluded orally, except for instances provided for by paragraphs three and five of the present Article.

The transfer of the gift shall be effectuated by means of handing it over, by symbolic transfer (handing over keys, and so forth) or by handing over right-establishing documents.

A contract of gift of immoveable property must be concluded in simple written form in instances when:

the donor is a juridical person;

the contract is concluded between citizens for an amount of more than ten minimum base calculation amounts [as amended by Law of 3 December 2019, No. ЗРУ-586];

the contract contains a promise of a gift in the future.

In the instances provided for in paragraph three of the present Article a contract of gift concluded orally shall be null.

A contract of gift of immoveable property must be notarially certified and shall be subject to State registration.

A contract of gift of motor vehicle means subject in the procedure established by legislation to State registration must be notarially certified [added by Law of 7 December 2001, No. 320-II. Ведомости Олий Мажлиса (2002), no. 1, item 20].

Article 505. Limitations of Gift

A juridical person to whom a thing belongs by right of economic jurisdiction or operative management shall have the right to gift it with the consent of the owner unless provided otherwise by a law. This limitation shall not extend to ordinary gifts of small value.

The gift of property in common joint ownership shall be permitted by consent of all the participants of joint ownership in compliance with the rules provided for by Article 225 of the present Code.

The gift of a right of demand belonging to the donor against a third person shall be effectuated in compliance with the rules provided for by Articles 313-317, 319, and 320 of the present Code.

A gift of the right of lease or other right to another's thing without the consent of the owner thereof or the person having the right of economic jurisdiction or operative management to it shall be permitted unless by a law or by a contract on which such right is based the alienation thereof is prohibited without the consent of the said persons.

A gift by means of the performance for the donee of his duty to a third person shall be effectuated in compliance with the rules provided for by Article 241, paragraphs one and two, of the present Code.

A gift by means of the transfer by the donor to himself of the debt of the donee to a third person shall be effectuated in compliance with the rules provided for by Articles 322, paragraphs one and two, of the present Code.

A power of attorney to perform a gift by a representative in which the donee is not named and the subject of the gift is not specified shall be null.

Article 506. Refusal of Performance of Contract of Gift

The donor shall have the right to refuse performance of a contract which contains a promise to transfer a thing or property right in the future to a donee, or to relieve the donee from a property duty, if after conclusion of the contract his property status has materially worsened.

The donor shall have the right to refuse performance of a contract which contains a promise to transfer a thing or property right to the donee in the future or to relieve the donee from a property duty on the grounds provided for by Article 507, paragraph one, of the present Code.

The refusal of the donor of performance of the contract of gift on the grounds provided for by the present Article shall not give a right of demand for compensation of losses to the donee.

Article 507. Revocation of Gift

The revocation of a gift shall be permitted in a judicial proceeding in the event of the commission by the donee of an intentional crime against the life or health of the donor, the members of his family or close relatives.

In the event of the intentional deprivation of life of the donor by the donee, the right to demand revocation of the gift in court shall belong to the heirs of the donor.

The donor shall have the right to require revocation of the gift in a judicial proceeding if the treatment by the donee of the thing given was of great nonproperty value to the donor and creates a threat of its irretrievable loss.

Upon the demand of an interested person a court may revoke a gift made by an individual entrepreneur or juridical person in violation of the provisions of the legislation on bankruptcy at the expense of means connected with its entrepreneurial activity within the year which preceded the declaration of such person to be bankrupt.

The right of the donor to revoke the gift in the event he outlives the donee may be stipulated in the contract of gift.

In the event of revocation of a gift the donee shall be obliged to return the thing given if it has been preserved in kind at the moment of revocation of the gift.

Article 508. Instances in Which Refusal of Performance of Contract of Gift and Revocation of Gift are Impossible

The rules concerning the refusal of performance of a contract of gift and revocation of a gift shall not apply to contracts of gift to be performed in oral form.

Article 509. Consequences of Gift of Property with Defects

Harm caused to the life, health, or property of a donee as a consequence of defects of the thing given shall be subject to compensation by the donor in accordance with the rules provided for by Chapter 57 of the present

Code if it is proved that these defects arose before the transfer of the thing to the donee and were not obvious and the donor, although he knew about them, did not warn the donee about them.

Article 510. Legal Succession in Event of Promise of Gift

The rights of a donee to whom a gift was promised under a contract of gift shall not pass to his heirs (or legal successors) unless provided otherwise by the contract of gift.

The duties of the donor who promised the gift under a contract of gift shall pass to his heirs (or legal successors) unless provided otherwise by the contract of gift.

Article 511. Donations

A gift for generally useful purposes shall be deemed to be a donation.

Donations may be made to citizens, treatment and nurturing institutions, institutions of social defense, and other analogous institutions, philanthropic, scientific, and educational institutions, foundations, museums, and other institutions of culture, social associations and religious organizations, and also to the State and other subjects of civil law.

No authorizations or consents whatever shall be required to accept donations.

The donation of property to a citizen must be, and to juridical persons may be, conditioned by the donor by the use of this property for a determined designation. In the absence of such a condition the donation of the property to a citizen shall be considered to be an ordinary gift, and in other instances the donated property shall be used by the donee in accordance with the designation thereof.

A juridical person which has accepted a donation for whose use a determined designation has been established must carry out a solitary recording of all operations relating to the use of the donated property.

If the use of donated property in accordance with the designation specified by the donor becomes as a consequence of changed circumstances impossible, it may be used for another designation only with the consent of the donor, and in the event of the death of a citizen who has donated property or the reorganization or liquidation of a juridical person which has donated property, by decision of a court.

The use of donated property not in accordance with the designation specified by the donor or a change of such designation in violation of the rules provided for by paragraph six of the present Article shall give the right to the donor, his heirs, or other legal successor to demand revocation of the donation.

The provisions of Articles 507 and 510 of the present Code shall not apply to donations.

Chapter 32. Rent

§ 1. General Provisions

Article 512. Contract of Rent

Under a contract of rent one party (recipient of the rent) shall transfer immoveable or moveable property in ownership to the other party (payer of rent), and the payer of rent shall be obliged in exchange for the property received periodically to pay to the recipient rent in the form of a determined monetary amount or of granting means for his maintenance in other form.

Under a contract of rent the establishment of the duty to pay rent in perpetuity (permanent rent) or for the period of life of the recipient of the rent (rent for life) shall be permitted. Rent for life may be established on conditions of the maintenance for life of a dependent citizen.

Article 513. Form of Contract of Rent

The contract of rent shall be subject to notarial certification, and a contract providing for the alienation of immoveable property under payment of rent shall also be subject to State registration.

Article 514. Alienation of Property Under Payment of Rent

Property which is alienated under payment of rent may be transferred by the recipient of the rent to the ownership of the payer of rent for payment or free of charge.

In the event when the transfer of property for payment is provided for by the contract of rent, the rules concerning the contract of purchase-sale shall apply to relations of the parties relating to the transfer and payment, and in instances when such property is transferred free of charge, the rules concerning the contract of gift insofar as not established otherwise by the rules of the present Chapter and is not contrary to the essence of the contract of rent.

Article 515. Encumberment of Immoveable Property by Rent

Rent shall encumber a land plot, enterprise, building, installation, or other immoveable property transferred under payment thereof. In the event of the alienation of such property by the payer of the rent, his obligations under the contract of rent shall pass to the acquirer of the property.

The person who has transferred immoveable property encumbered by rent to the ownership of another person shall bear subsidiary responsibility with him with regard to the demands of the recipient of the rent which arose in connection with a violation of the contract of rent unless joint and several responsibility for this obligation has been provided for by the present Code, other law, or the contract.

Article 516. Securing Payment of Rent

In the event of the transfer of a land plot or other immoveable property under payment of rent, the recipient of the rent shall acquire the right of pledge on this property to secure the obligation of the payer of the rent.

The condition establishing the duty of the payer of rent to grant security for the performance of his obligations or to insure to the benefit of the recipient of rent the risk of the failure to perform or the improper performance of these obligations shall be a material condition of a contract providing for the transfer of a monetary amount or other moveable property as payment of rent.

In the event of the failure of the payer of the rent to fulfill the duties provided for by paragraph two of the present Article, and also in the event of the loss of the security or worsening of the conditions of the security under circumstances for which the recipient of rent is not liable, the recipient of rent shall have the right to dissolve the contract of rent and require compensation of losses caused by the dissolution of the contract.

Article 517. Responsibility for Delay of Payment of Rent

For a delay of payment of rent the payer of rent shall pay interest to the recipient of rent provided for by Article 327 of the present Code unless another amount of interest has been established by the contract of rent.

§ 2. Permanent Rent

Article 518. Recipient of Permanent Rent

Only citizens and noncommercial organizations may be recipients of permanent rent if this is not contrary to a law and corresponds to the purposes of their activity.

The rights of the recipient of rent under a contract of permanent rent may be transferred to the persons specified in paragraph one of the present Article by means of assignment of a demand and transfer by inheritance or in the event of the reorganization of juridical persons, unless provided otherwise by a law or by a contract.

Article 519. Form and Amount of Permanent Rent

Permanent rent shall be paid in money in the amount established by the contract within the limits of the average rate of payment for the use of property applicable when hiring out property analogous to that transferred as payment of rent, and in the event of the transfer of a monetary amount as payment of rent, within the limits of the properly established bank interest rate provided for by Article 327 of the present Code.

The payment of rent by means of the granting of things, fulfillment of work, or rendering of services which correspond to the value of the monetary amount of rent may be provided for by the contract.

Unless provided otherwise by the contract of permanent rent, the amount of rent to be paid shall be changed in proportion to the change of the respective rate of payment for the use of property or bank interest rate.

Article 520. Periods for Payment of Permanent Rent

Unless provided otherwise by the contract, permanent rent shall be paid at the end of each calendar quarter.

Article 521. Right of Payer to Purchase Permanent Rent

The payer of permanent rent shall have the right to refuse the further payment of rent by means of purchasing it. Such refusal shall be valid on condition that it is declared by the payer of rent in written form not later than three months before the termination of the payment of rent or longer period provided for by the contract. In so doing the obligation relating to the payment of rent shall not terminate until the receipt of the entire amount of the purchase by the recipient of the rent unless another procedure of purchase has been provided for by the contract.

The condition of a contract concerning the waiver of the payer of permanent rent to purchase it shall be null.

It may be provided by a contract that the right of purchase of permanent rent may not be effectuated during the life of the recipient of rent or during another period not exceeding thirty years from the moment of conclusion of the contract.

Article 522. Purchase of Permanent Rent at Demand of Recipient of Rent

The recipient of permanent rent shall have the right to demand the purchase of rent by the payer in instances when:

the payer of rent delayed the payment thereof by more than one year, unless established otherwise by the contract;

the payer of rent violated his obligations relating to ensuring the payment of rent;

the payer of rent is deemed to be insolvent or other obligations have arisen which testify that the rent will not be paid in the amount and within the periods which have been established by the contract;

the immoveable property transferred under payment of rent has ensued to common ownership or been divided among several persons;

and in other instances provided for by the contract.

Article 523. Purchase Price of Permanent Rent

The purchase of permanent rent in the instances provided for by Articles 521 and 522 of the present Code shall be made at the price established by the contract.

In the absence of a condition concerning the purchase price in a contract of permanent rent under which property has been transferred for payment as payment of permanent rent, the purchase shall be effectuated at the price corresponding to the yearly amount of rent payments.

In the absence of a condition concerning the purchase price in a contract of permanent rent under which property has been transferred as payment of rent free of charge, the price of the transferred property determined according to the rules provided for by Article 356, paragraph three, of the present Code shall be included in the purchase price together with the yearly amount of rent payments.

Article 524. Risk of Accidental Perishing or Accidental Damaging of Property Transferred as Payment of Permanent Rent

The risk of accidental perishing or accidental damage of property transferred free of charge as payment of permanent rent shall be borne by the payer of rent.

In the event of the accidental perishing or accidental damaging of property transferred for payment as payment of permanent rent, the payer shall have the right to demand respectively termination of the obligation relating to the payment of rent or a change of the conditions for the payment thereof.

§ 3. Rent for Life

Article 525. Recipient of Rent for Life

Rent for life may be established for the period of life of a citizen transferring property as payment of rent or for the period of life of another citizen specified by him.

The establishment of rent for life to the benefit of several citizens whose participatory share in the right to receive rent shall be presupposed to be equal shall be permitted unless provided otherwise by the contract.

In the event of the death of one of the recipients of rent his participatory share in the right to receive rent shall pass to the recipients of rent who survive him unless provided otherwise by the contract, and in the event of the death of the last recipient of rent, the obligation to pay the rent shall terminate.

The contract establishing rent for life to the benefit of a citizen who is deceased at the moment of concluding the contract shall be null.

Article 526. Amount of Rent for Life

Rent for life shall be determined in the contract as a monetary amount periodically to be paid to the recipient of rent during his life.

The amount of rent for life determined in the contract calculated per month must be not less than the base calculation amount established by legislation, and in the instances provided for by Article 247 of the present Code, shall be subject to increase [as amended by Law of 3 December 2019, No. 3PY-586].

Article 527. Period for Payment of Rent for Life

Unless provided otherwise by the contract, the rent for life shall be paid at the end of each calendar month.

Article 528. Dissolution of Contract of Rent for Life at Demand of Recipient of Rent

In instances of a material violation of a contract of rent for life by the payer, the recipient of rent shall have the right to demand from the payer of rent the purchase of rent on the conditions provided for by Article 523 of the present Code or dissolution of the contract and compensation of losses.

If an apartment, dwelling house, or other property as payment of rent for life has been alienated free of charge, the recipient of the rent shall have the right in the event of a material violation of the material conditions of the contract by the payer of the rent to require the return of this property, setting off the value thereof at the expense of the purchase of the rent.

Article 529. Risk of Accidental Perishing or Accidental Damaging of Property Transferred as Payment of Rent for Life

The accidental perishing or accidental damaging of property transferred as payment of rent for life shall not relieve the payer of rent from the obligation to pay it on the conditions provided for by the contract.

Chapter 33. Alienation of Dwelling House (or Apartment) with Condition of Maintenance for Life

Article 530. Contract of Alienation of Dwelling House (or Apartment) with Condition of Maintenance for Life

Under a contract of alienation of a dwelling house (or part of a house) or apartment with a condition of maintenance for life, one party (the acquirer) shall be obliged to grant to the other party who lacks capacity to labor by reason of age or state of health (the alienator) material provision for life in kind (in the form of housing, nourishment, care, and necessary assistance), and the alienator, to transfer to the ownership of a dwelling house (or part of the house) or apartment of the acquirer.

Article 531. Form and Conditions of Contract of Alienation of Dwelling House (or Apartment) with Condition of Maintenance for Life

In a contract of alienation of a dwelling house (or apartment) with a condition of maintenance for life it must be specified which types of material provision shall be granted to the alienator, the monetary value thereof per month, and the value of the dwelling house (or part of house) or the apartment must be specified.

The valuation of the dwelling house (or part of house) or the apartment being transferred and of the material provision shall be determined by agreement of the parties.

The contract of alienation of a dwelling house (or part of house) or apartment with condition of maintenance for life must be concluded in written form and notarially certified in compliance with the rules of Article 110 of the present Code.

Article 532. Rights and Duties of Parties

Under a contract of alienation of a dwelling house (or part of house) or apartment with a condition of maintenance for life the acquirer shall not have the right during the operation of the contract to sell this house, give, pledge, or perform other actions encumbering the right of ownership to the house (or part of house) or apartment. Execution shall not be levied on this house (or part of house) or apartment with regard to debts of the acquirer.

The accidental perishing of the house (or part of house) or apartment received from the alienator under the contract of alienation of the dwelling house (or apartment) with a condition of maintenance for life shall not relieve the acquirer from the duties assumed under the contract.

Article 533. Change or Dissolution of Contract of Alienation of Dwelling House (or Apartment) with Condition of Maintenance for Life

If the acquirer of a dwelling house (or part of house) or apartment does not perform his duties under the contract of alienation of a dwelling house (or apartment) with a condition of maintenance for life or fulfils them improperly, the alienator may require the replacement of maintenance with periodic payments or dissolution of the contract.

The contract of alienation of a dwelling house (or apartment) with a condition of maintenance for life may be dissolved at the demand of the acquirer if for circumstances beyond his control the material position has changed to such a degree that he can not grant to the alienator the stipulated maintenance or if the alienator has restored his capacity to labor.

In the event of the dissolution of a contract of alienation of a dwelling house (or apartment) with a condition of maintenance for life on the grounds provided for by paragraphs one and two of the present Article, the house (or part of house) or apartment shall be subject to return to the alienator.

In the event of the dissolution of a contract of alienation of a dwelling house (or apartment) with a condition of maintenance for life at the demand of the alienator, the acquirer shall have the right to demand compensation of expenses incurred by him for the maintenance of the alienator and the house (or part of house) or apartment during the operation of the contract.

Article 534. Transfer of Duties Under Contract of Alienation of Dwelling House (or Apartment) with Condition of Maintenance for Life to Heirs

In the event of the death of the acquirer, the duties under the contract of alienation of a dwelling house (or part of house) or apartment with a condition of maintenance for life shall pass to his heirs. In the absence of heirs of the acquirer or in the event of their refusal to perform the contract of alienation of the dwelling house (or part of house) or apartment with a condition of maintenance for life, the house (or part of house) or apartment transferred to the acquirer shall be returned to the alienator.

Chapter 34. Property Rental (Lease)

§ 1. General Provisions

Article 535. Contract of Property Rental

Under a contract of property rental (or lease) the renter shall be obliged to grant to the rentee property for payment in temporary possession and use or use.

Article 536. Right of Ownership of Rentee to Products, Fruits, and Revenues from Rented Property

The products, fruits, and other revenues received by the rentee as a result of the use of the rented property shall be his ownership unless provided otherwise by a law or by the contract of property rental.

Article 537. Objects of Property Rental

Land plots, subsoil plots, and other solitary natural objects, enterprises, and other property complexes, buildings, installations, equipment, means of transport, and other things which do not lose their natural properties in the process of their use (nonconsumable things) may be transferred on property rental.

Types (or groups) of enterprises and types of property, the renting out of which is not permitted or is limited, may be established by legislation.

Article 538. Renter

The right to rent out property shall belong to its owner. Persons empowered by a law or by the owner to rent out property also may be renters.

Article 539. Form of Contract of Property Rental

A contract of property rental for a period of more than one year, and if one of the parties of the contract is a juridical person, irrespective of the period, must be concluded in written form.

A contract of property rental for immoveable property shall be subject to State registration.

A contract of property rental which provides for the transfer thereafter of the right of ownership to this property to the rentee shall be concluded in the form provided for by the contract of purchase-sale of such property.

Article 540. Period of Contract of Property Rental

A contract of property rental shall be concluded for the period determined by the contract.

If the period of the property rental has not been determined in the contract, the contract shall be considered to be concluded for an indefinite period. In this event each of the parties shall have the right at any time to repudiate the contract, having warned the other party thereof in writing one month in advance, and in the event of the rental of immoveable property, three months. Another period may be established by a law or by a contract for warning of the termination of a contract of property rental concluded for an indefinite period.

Maximum periods for a contract for individual types of property rental may be established by a law, and also for the rental of individual types of property. In these instances if the period of the rental is not determined in the contract and neither of the parties has repudiated the contract before the expiry of the maximum period established by a law, the contract shall terminate upon the expiry of the maximum period. A contract of rental of such property concluded for a period exceeding the maximum period established by a law shall be considered to be concluded for the period equal to the maximum.

Article 541. Granting Property to Rentee

The renter shall be obliged to grant property to the rentee in a state corresponding to the conditions of the contract and designation of the property.

The preparation of the property for transfer, including the drawing up and submission for signature of the act of transfer, shall be the duty of the renter and shall be effectuated at his expense.

Property shall be rented out together with all of its appurtenances and documents relating thereto (technical passport, certificate of quality, and so forth), unless provided otherwise by the contract. If such appurtenances and documents were not transferred and without them the rentee can not use the property in accordance with its designation or is to a significant degree deprived of that which he had the right to count upon when concluding the contract, he may require the granting to him by the renter of such appurtenances and documents or dissolution of the contract, and also compensation of losses.

If the renter did not grant to the rentee property rented out within the period specified in the contract, and if in the contract such period is not specified, within a reasonable period, the rentee shall have the right to demand and obtain this property from him in accordance with Article 331 of the present Code and to require compensation of losses caused by the delay of performance or to require dissolution of the contract and compensation of losses caused by his failure to perform.

Article 542. Responsibility of Renter for Defects of Property Rented Out

The renter shall be liable for defects of property rented out which wholly or partially obstruct the use thereof even if during the conclusion of the contract he did not know about these defects. In the event of the discovery of such defects the rentee shall have the right at his choice to:

require of the renter either the elimination of the defects of the property without compensation or a commensurate reduction of the rental payment for the use of the property, or compensation of his expenses for elimination of the defects of the property;

directly withhold the amount of expenses incurred by him for elimination of the said defects from the payment for the use of the property, having informed the renter in advance thereof;

require the dissolution of the contract before time.

The renter who is notified about the demands of the rentee or about his intention to eliminate the defects of the property at the expense of the renter may without delay replace the property granted on rent to the rentee with other analogous property in a proper state or eliminate the defects of the property without compensation.

If satisfaction of the demands of the rentee or withholding of expenses by him for elimination of defects from the payment for the use of the property does not cover the losses caused to the rentee, he shall have the right to require compensation of the uncovered part of the losses.

The renter shall not be liable for those defects of property rented out which were stipulated by him when concluding the contract or were previously known to the rentee or should have been discovered by the rentee during the inspection of the property or verification of its good repair when concluding the contract or transferring the property on rental.

Article 543. Rights of Third Persons to Property Rented Out

The transfer of property on rental shall not be grounds for termination or change of the rights of third persons to this property.

When concluding a contract the renter shall be obliged to warn the rentee about all the rights of third persons to the property being rented out (servitude, right of pledge, and so forth). The failure of the renter to perform this duty shall give the rentee the right to demand a reduction of payment for the use of the property or dissolution of the contract and compensation of losses.

Article 544. Payment for Use of Property

The rentee shall be obliged to make payment in a timely way for the use of property.

The procedure, conditions, and periods of making the payment for the use of the property shall be determined by the contract of property rental. In instances when they have not been determined by the contract, it shall be considered that the procedure, conditions, and periods have been established which are usually applied when renting analogous property under comparable circumstances.

The payment for the use of property shall be established for the entire rented property as a whole or individually for each of the constituent parts in the form of:

payments determined in a fixed amount to be made periodically or one time;

the established participatory share of the products, fruits, or revenues received as a result of the use of the rented property;

the granting of specified services by the rentee;

the transfer by the rentee to the renter of things stipulated by the contract in ownership or on rental;

imposing on the rentee expenditures stipulated by the contract for the improvement of the rented property.

The parties may provide in the contract of property rental for combining the forms of payment for the use of property specified in paragraph three of the present Article or other forms of payment.

Unless provided otherwise by the contract of property rental, the amount of payment for the use of the property may be changed by agreement of the parties within the periods provided for by the contract, but not more often than once a year. Other minimum periods for review of the amount of payment for individual types of property rental, and also for the rental of individual types of property, may be provided for by legislation.

Unless provided otherwise by legislation, the rentee shall have the right to require a respective reduction of the payment for the use of property if by virtue of circumstances for which he is not liable the conditions of use provided for by the contract or the state of the property materially has worsened.

Unless provided otherwise by the contract, in the event of a material violation of the rentee of the periods for making the payment for the use of property the renter shall have the right to require the making of payment by him before time within the period established by the renter. In so doing the renter shall not have the right to demand the making of payment for the use of property before time for more than two periods in succession.

Article 545. Use of Rented Property

The rentee shall be obliged to use the property in accordance with the conditions of the contract, and if such conditions have not been determined in the contract, in accordance with the purpose of the property.

If a rentee uses property not in accordance with the conditions of the contract of lease or the purpose of the property, notwithstanding the written warning of the renter, the last shall have the right to require dissolution of the contract before time and compensation of losses.

Article 546. Disposition of Rented Property

The rentee shall have the right with the consent of the renter to sub-rent the rented property (sublease) and to transfer his rights and duties under the contract of lease to another person (re-rent), to grant the rented property for use without compensation, and also to pledge these rights and contribute them as a contribution to the charter fund (or capital) of economic partnerships and societies or a share contribution to the production cooperative unless established otherwise by the present Code or other legislation. In the said instances, except for re-rent, the rentee shall remain responsible under the contract to the lessor. The contract on the transfer of property to other persons may not be concluded for a period exceeding the period of the contract of rental.

The rules concerning the contract of property rental, unless established otherwise by legislation, shall apply to the contract of sub-rent.

Article 547. Duties of Renter With Regard to Maintenance of Rented Property

The renter shall be obliged to perform at his own expense capital repair to the property transferred on rental unless provided otherwise by legislation or the contract.

The renter shall be obliged to perform at his own expense a repair caused by urgent necessity which arose by virtue of circumstances for which the rentee is not liable.

Capital repair must be performed within the period established by the contract of property rental, and if it is not determined by the contract or called for by urgent necessity, within a reasonable period.

A violation by the renter of the duty with regard to the performance of capital repair shall give the rentee the right at his choice to:

perform the capital repair provided for by the contract or called for by urgent necessity and to recover from the renter the value of the repair or to set it off from the account of the payment for the use of the property;

require a corresponding reduction of the payment;

require dissolution of the contract before time and compensation of losses.

Article 548. Duties of Rentee With Regard to Maintenance of Rented Property

The rentee shall be obliged to maintain the property in a proper state, to perform current repair at his own expense, and to bear expenses for the maintenance of the property unless otherwise established by a law or by the contract.

Article 549. Preservation of Contract of Property Rental in Force in Event of Change of Parties

Transfer of the right of ownership (or economic jurisdiction, operative management, inheritable possession for life) to property leased out to another person shall not be grounds for a change of or dissolution of the contract of property rental.

In the event of the death of a citizen who is the rentee of immoveable property, his rights and duties under the contract of rental of this property shall pass to the heir unless provided otherwise by a law or by the contract. The renter shall not have the right to refuse the heir from entering into the contract for the remaining period of its operation except for instances when the conclusion of the contract was conditioned by the personal qualities of the rentee.

Article 550. Termination of Contract of Subrent in Event of Termination of Contract of Property Rental Before Time

Unless provided otherwise by the contract of property hire, the termination of the contract of property hire before time shall entail the termination of the contract of subrent concluded in accordance with it. A contract of rental of the property in his use may be concluded with the subrentee in this event in accordance with the contract of subrent within the limits of the remaining period of subrent on the conditions corresponding to the conditions of the terminated contract of property rental.

If the contract of property rental is deemed to be invalid on the grounds provided for by the present Code, the contracts of subrent concluded in accordance with it also shall be deemed to be invalid.

Article 551. Dissolution of Contract of Property Rental Before Time at Demand of Renter

At the demand of the renter the contract of property hire may be dissolved before time by a court in instances when the rentee:

uses the property with material violation of the conditions of the contract or the designation of the property or with repeated violations despite the written warning of the renter;

materially worsens the property;

does not make payment for the use of the property more than two times in succession upon the expiry of the period established by the contract;

does not make capital repair of the property within the periods established by the contract, and in the absence thereof in the contract within reasonable periods in those instances when in accordance with legislation or the contract the performance of capital repair is the duty of the rentee.

Other grounds for the dissolution of the contract before time also may be established by the contract of property rental upon the demand of the renter in accordance with Article 382, paragraph two, of the present Code.

The renter shall have the right to demand dissolution of the contract before time only after sending written warning to the rentee and granting him the possibility to perform his obligation.

Article 552. Dissolution of Contract of Property Rental Before Time Upon Demand of Rentee

Upon the demand of the rentee the contract of property rental may be dissolved before time by a court in instances when:

the renter does not grant property for use to the rentee or creates obstacles to the use of the property in accordance with the conditions of the contract or the designation of the property;

the property transferred to the rentee has defects which obstruct its use by him which were not stipulated by the renter when concluding the contract, were not known to the rentee in advance, and could not have been discovered by him during the inspection of the property or verification of its good condition when concluding the contract;

the renter does not make capital repair of the property which is his duty within the periods established by the contract, and in the absence thereof in the contract, within reasonable periods;

the property by virtue of circumstances for which the rentee is not liable turns out to be in a state not fit for use.

Other grounds of dissolution of the contract before time also may be established by the contract of property rental at the demand of the rentee in accordance with Article 382, paragraph two, of the present Code.

Article 553. Preferential Right of Rentee to Conclude Contract of Property Rental for New Period

Unless provided otherwise by a law or by the contract, the rentee who has properly performed his duties shall have upon the expiry of the period of the contract a preferential right under equal conditions before other persons to conclude a contract of property rental for a new period. The rentee shall be obliged to inform the renter in writing about the wish to conclude such contract within the period specified in the contract of property hire, and if such period is not specified in the contract, within a reasonable period before the end of the operation of the contract.

When concluding a contract of property rental for a new period, the conditions of the contract may be changed by agreement of the parties.

If the renter has refused the rentee to conclude a contract for a new period, but within a year from the date of expiry of the period of the contract with him concluded a contract of property rental with another person, the rentee shall have the right at his choice to require in court the transfer to himself of the rights and duties under the contract concluded and compensation of losses caused by the refusal to renew the contract with him or only compensation of such losses.

If the rentee continues to use the property after the expiry of the period of the contract of property rental in the absence of objections on the part of the renter, the contract shall be considered to be renewed on the same conditions for an indefinite period.

Article 554. Return of Property to Renter

In the event of the termination of the contract of property hire the rentee shall be obliged to return property to the renter in that state in which he received it, taking into account normal wear and tear or in the state stipulated by the contract.

If the rentee has not returned the rented property or returned it not in good time, the renter shall have the right to require the making of payment for the use of the property for the entire time of the delay. In an event when the said payment does not cover the losses caused to the renter, he may demand the compensation thereof.

In an event when a penalty has been provided for by the contract for the untimely return of the rented property, losses may be recovered in the full amount above the penalty unless provided otherwise by the contract.

Article 555. Improvement of Rented Property

Separable improvements of property made by the rentee shall be his ownership unless provided otherwise by the contract of property rental.

In an event when a rentee has made improvements of rented property at the expense of own means and with the consent of the renter which are not separable without harm to the property, the rentee shall have the right after termination of the contract to compensation of the cost of these improvements unless provided otherwise by the contract.

The cost of inseparable improvements of rented property made by the rentee without the consent of the renter shall not be subject to compensation unless provided otherwise by a law.

Improvements of rented property, both separable and inseparable, made at the expense of amortization deductions from this property shall be the ownership of the renter.

Article 556. Purchase of Rented Property

It may be provided in a contract of property rental that rented property passes to the ownership of the rentee upon the expiry of the period of the property rental or before the expiry thereof on condition of the rentee making the entire purchase price stipulated by the contract.

If the condition concerning the purchase of rented property is not provided for in the contract, it may be established by an additional agreement of the parties, who in so doing shall have the right to agree on the set-off of the payment for the use of property previously paid against the purchase price.

Instances of the prohibition of the purchase of rented property may be established by legislative acts.

Article 557. Peculiarities of Individual Types of Property Rental and Rental of Individual Types of Property

The provisions provided for by the present paragraph shall apply to individual types of contract of property rental and to contracts of rental of individual types of property (rental, lease of means of transport, lease of enterprises, finance lease, and others) unless provided otherwise by the rules of the present Code.

§ 2. Rental

Article 558. Contract of Rental

Under a contract of rental the renter effectuating the rental of property as a permanent entrepreneurial activity shall be obliged to grant moveable property to the rentee in temporary possession and use for payment.

Property granted under a contract of rental shall be used for consumption purposes unless provided otherwise by the contract or does not arise from the essence of the obligation.

A contract of rental shall be concluded in written form. A contract of rental shall be a public [contract].

Article 559. Period of Contract of Rental

A contract of rental shall be concluded for a period of up to one year.

The rules concerning renewal of a contract of property rental for an indefinite period and concerning the preferential right of the rentee to renewal of the contract of property rental shall not apply to the contract of rental.

The rentee shall have the right to refuse performance of the contract of rental at any time.

Article 560. Granting of Property to Rentee

A renter who has concluded a contract of rental shall be obliged in the presence of the rentee to verify the good state of the property being rented, and also to familiarize the rentee with the rules for the operation of the property or to issue him written instructions concerning the use of this property.

Article 561. Elimination of Defects of Property Rented

In defects in the property rented have appeared as a consequence of a violation by the rentee of the rules for operation and maintenance of the property, the rentee shall pay the renter the cost of the repair and transportation of the property.

Article 562. Payment for Use of Property Under Contract of Rental

Payment for the use of property under a contract of rental shall be established in the form of payments determined in a lump sum to be made periodically or at one time.

In the event of the return of the property before time by the rentee, the renter shall return to him the corresponding part of the payment received for the use of the property, calculating it from the day following the day of the actual return of the property.

The recovery of indebtedness from the rentee with regard to a payment for the use of property shall be made in an uncontested proceeding on the basis of the endorsement of execution of a notary.

Article 563. Use of Rented Property

The capital and current repair of property rented under a contract of rental shall be the duty of the renter.

The subrent of property granted to a rentee under a contract of rental, the transfer by the rentee of his rights and duties under the contract of rental to another person, the granting of this property for uncompensated use, the pledge of the rights of the rentee, and the contribution thereof as a contribution to the charter fund (or capital) of economic partnerships and societies or as a share contribution to cooperatives shall not be permitted.

§ 3. Lease of Means of Transport

Article 564. Contract of Lease of Means of Transport

Under a contract of lease of a means of transport with a crew the lessor shall grant the means of transport to the lessee in temporary possession and use for payment and render services with his own forces with regard to the management and technical operation thereof.

Under a contract of lease of a means of transport without a crew the lessor shall grant the means of transport to the lessee in temporary possession and use for payment without rendering services with regard to the management and technical operation thereof.

The rules of the present Chapter concerning renewal of a contract of lease for an indefinite period and concerning the preferential right of the lessee to a renewal of the contract of lease for a new period shall not apply to the contract of lease of means of transport.

Article 565. Form of Contract of Lease of Means of Transport

A contract of lease of means of transport must be concluded in written form irrespective of the period thereof except powers of attorney for the driving and disposition of means of motor vehicle transport [as amended by Law of 27 September 2006, No. ЗРУ-56. СЗ РУ (2006), no. 39, item 385].

A contract of lease of means of motor vehicle transport subject in the procedure established by legislation to State registration must be notarially certified, except for instances provided by paragraph three of the present Article [added by Law of 7 December 2001, No. 320-II, as amended by Law of 26 July 2018, No. 3РУ-488].

Juridical persons rendering services with regard to the lease of light motor vehicles and means of motor transport may conclude contracts of lease with natural persons for light motor vehicles and means of motor transport in simple written form for a period of up to thirty days [as amended by Law of 26 July 2018, No. 3РУ-488].

Article 566. Duties of Lessor in Event of Lease of Means of Transport With Granting of Services Relating to Maintenance, Management, and Technical Operation

The lessor throughout the entire period of operation of the contract shall be obliged to maintain the means of transport leased in a proper state, including the effectuation of current and capital repair and the granting of necessary appurtenances.

The amount of services with regard to management and technical operation of means of transport to be granted by the lessor to the lessee must ensure its normal and safe operation in accordance with the purposes of the lease specified in the contract. A more extensive group of services to be granted to the lessee may be provided for by the contract of lease.

The composition of the crew of means of transport and the skills thereof must correspond to the rules and conditions of the contract which are binding upon the parties, and if such requirements have not been established by rules which are binding upon the parties, the requirements of usual practice for the operation of means of transport of the particular type and the conditions of the contract.

Members of the crew shall retain labor relations with the lessor. They shall be subordinate to the regulations of the lessor with respect to the management and technical operation and to the regulations of the lessee affecting the commercial operation of the means of transport.

Unless provided otherwise by the contract of lease of means of transport, expenses relating to the payment for services of members of the crew, and also expenses for the maintenance thereof, shall be borne by the lessor.

Unless provided otherwise by the contract of lease of means of transport, the duty to insure the means of transport and/or to insure the responsibility for damage which may be caused to it or in connection with the operation thereof shall be placed on the lessor in those instances when such insurance is obligatory by virtue of a law or the contract.

Article 567. Duty of Lessee Relating to Payment of Expenses Connected with Commercial Operation of Means of Transport

Unless provided otherwise by the contract of lease of means of transport, the lessee shall bear expenses for the payment of fuel and other materials expended in the process of operation, for the payment of fees, and other expenses arising in connection with the commercial operation of means of transport.

Article 568. Duties of Lessee in Event of Lease of Means of Transport Without Granting of Services for Maintenance, Management, and Technical Operation

The lessee during the entire period of operation of the contract of lease of means of transport shall be obliged to maintain the proper state of the leased means of transport, including the effectuation of current repair, and also, unless provided otherwise by the contract, capital repair.

The lessee shall by his own forces effectuate the management of leased means of transport and also the commercial and technical operation thereof.

Unless provided otherwise by the contract, the lessee shall bear expenses for the maintenance of leased means of transport, the insurance thereof, including insurance of its responsibility, and also expenses connected with the operation thereof.

Article 569. Contracts With Third Persons Concerning Use of Means of Transport

Unless provided otherwise by the contract of lease, the lessee shall have the right with the consent of the lessor to sublease the leased means of transport on the conditions of the contract of lease with or without a crew.

The lessee shall have the right without the consent of the lessor to conclude in his own name with third persons contracts of carriage and other contracts unless they are contrary to the purposes of the use of means of transport specified in the contract of lease, and if such purposes have not been established, the designation of the means of transport.

Article 570. Responsibility for Harm Caused to Means of Transport

In the event of the perishing or damage of leased means of transport, the lessee shall be obliged to compensate the lessor for losses caused if the last proves that the perishing or damage of the means of transport occurred with regard to circumstances for which the lessee is liable in accordance with a law or the contract.

Article 571. Responsibility for Harm Caused by Means of Transport

Responsibility for harm caused to third persons by leased means of transport, mechanisms thereof, devices, equipment, and the like in the event of a lease with a crew shall be borne by the lessor in accordance with the rules provided for by Chapter 57 of the present Code. He shall have the right to present a regressive demand against the lessee concerning compensation of amounts paid to third persons if it is proved that the harm arose through the fault of the lessee.

Responsibility for harm caused to third persons by means of transport, mechanisms thereof, devices, equipment, and the like in the event of a lease without granting services relating to maintenance, management, and technical operation shall be borne by the lessee in accordance with the rules of Chapter 57 of the present Code.

Article 572. Peculiarities of Lease of Individual Types of Means of Transport

The peculiarities of the lease of individual types of means of transport, besides those provided for by the present paragraph, may be established by legislation.

§ 4. Lease of Buildings and Installations

Article 573. Contract of Lease of Building or Installation

Under the contract of lease of a building or installation the lessor shall be obliged to transfer a building or installation in temporary possession and use or temporary use to the lessee.

The rules of the present paragraph shall apply to the lease of enterprises unless provided otherwise by the rules of the present Code concerning the lease of an enterprise.

Article 574. Form and State Registration of Contract of Lease of Building or Installation

A contract of lease of a building or installation shall be concluded in written form by means of drawing up one document signed by the parties.

The failure to comply with the form of the contract of lease of a building or installation shall entail its invalidity.

The contract of lease of a building or installation or parts thereof between citizens shall be subject to recording in State tax agencies [added by Law of 30 December 2011, No. 3PY-313, as amended by Law of 11 October 2018, No. 3PY-497].

The contract of lease of a building or installation concluded for a period of not less than a year shall be subject to State registration and shall be considered to be concluded from the moment of such registration.

Article 575. Rights to Land Plot in Event of Lease of Building or Installation Situated Thereon

Under a contract of lease of a building or installation, to the lessee shall pass simultaneously with the transfer of the rights of possession and use of such immoveable the rights to that part of the land plot which is occupied by this immoveable and is necessary for its use.

In instances when the lessor is the owner of the land plot on which the building or installation to be leased is situated, the right of lease shall be granted to the lessee or other right to the respective part of the land plot provided for by the contract of lease of the building or installation.

Unless the right to the respective land plot to be transferred to the lessee has been determined by the contract, to him shall pass for the period of the lease of the building or installation the right to use that part of the land plot which is occupied by the building or installation and is necessary for its use in accordance with its designation.

The lease of a building or installation situated on the land plot which does not belong to the lessor by right of ownership shall be permitted without the consent of the owner of this plot unless this is contrary to the conditions of the use of this plot established by a law or by contract with the owner of the land plot.

Article 576. Preservation by Lessee of Building or Installation of Right to Use Land Plot in Event of Sale Thereof

In instances when the land plot on which the leased building or installation is situated is sold to another person, the right of use of the part of the land plot which is occupied by the building or installation and is necessary for its use shall be preserved for the lessee of this building or installation on the conditions which operated before the sale of the land plot.

Article 577. Amount of Lease Payment

The contract of lease of a building or installation must provide for the amount of lease payment. In the absence of the condition concerning the amount of lease payment agreed by the parties in written form, the contract of lease of a building or installation shall be considered to be not concluded. In so doing the rules for determining the price provided for by Article 356, paragraph four, of the present Code shall not apply.

The payment established in the contract of lease of a building or installation for the use of the building or installation shall include payment for use of the land plot on which it is situated or the respective part of the plot transferred together with it, unless provided otherwise by a law or the contract.

In instances when the payment for lease of a building or installation has been established in the contract per unit of space of the building (or installation) or other indicator of the dimension thereof, the lease payment shall be determined by proceeding from the actual dimension of the building or installation transferred to the lessee.

Article 578. Transfer of Building or Installation

The transfer of a building or installation by the lessor and the acceptance thereof by the lessee shall be effectuated under an act of transfer or other document concerning the transfer signed by the parties.

Unless provided otherwise by a law or the contract of lease of the building or installation, the obligation of the lessor to transfer the building or installation to the lessee shall be considered to be performed after the granting thereof to the lessee in possession or use and signature by the parties of the respective document concerning transfer.

The avoidance by one party of signature of the document concerning the transfer of the building or installation on the conditions provided for by a contract shall be considered as a refusal respectively of the lessor to perform the duties with regard to the transfer of property and of the lessee to accept the property.

In the event of the termination of the contract of lease of a building or installation, the leased building or installation must be returned to the lessor in compliance with the rules provided for by the present Article.

§ 5. Lease of Enterprise

Article 579. Contract of Lease of Enterprise

Under the contract of lease of an enterprise the lessor shall be obliged to grant to the lessee for payment in temporary possession and use the enterprise as a whole as a property complex or part thereof, except for those rights and duties which the lessor does not have the right to transfer to other persons.

The lessor shall be obliged in writing to inform its creditors concerning the transfer of debts to the lessee, who in the event of disagreement with such transfer shall have the right within three months from the date of receipt of the notification to require from the lessor the termination or performance before time of the respective obligations and compensation of losses caused by this. If within the said period such demands have not been presented, the creditor shall be deemed to have given consent to the transfer of the respective debt to the lessee.

The enterprise may be transferred to the lessee only after the completion of the settlement of accounts with creditors which have required of the lessor the termination or performance before time of the obligations and compensation of losses.

After the transfer of an enterprise as a property complex on lease, the lessor and the lessee shall bear joint and several responsibility for the debts included within the transferred enterprise which were transferred to the lessee without the consent of the creditor.

The rights of the lessor received by him on the basis of a special authorization (or license) to engage in a respective activity shall not be subject to transfer to the lessee unless established otherwise by legislation. The inclusion in the composition of the enterprise to be transferred under the contract of obligations whose performance by the lessee is impossible in the absence of such special authorization (or license) shall not relieve the lessor from the respective obligations to creditors.

Article 580. Form of Contract of Lease of Enterprise

The contract of lease of an enterprise shall be concluded in written form by means of drawing up one document signed by the parties and shall be subject to State registration [as amended by Law of 14 January 2020, No. ЗРУ-602].

The contract of lease of an enterprise shall be considered to be concluded from the moment of State registration.

The failure to comply with the form of the contract of lease of an enterprise shall entail its invalidity.

Article 581. Transfer of Leased Enterprise

The transfer of an enterprise to the lessee shall be effectuated under an act of transfer.

The preparation of the leased enterprise for transfer, including the drawing up and granting for signature of the act of transfer, shall be the duty of the lessor and shall be effectuated at his expense unless provided otherwise by the contract of lease.

Article 582. Duties of Lessee with Regard to Maintenance of Enterprise and Payment of Expenses for Operation Thereof

The lessee of an enterprise shall be obliged within the entire period of operation of the contract of lease to maintain the enterprise in a proper technical state, including the current and, in the instances provided for by the contract, the capital repair thereof.

Expenses connected with the operation of the leased enterprise shall be placed on the lessee unless provided otherwise by the contract, and also the payment of payments for insurance of the leased property, taxes, and other obligatory payments.

Article 583. Use of Property of Leased Enterprise

Unless provided otherwise by a law or the contract, the lessee shall have the right with the consent of the lessor to sell, exchange, or without his consent grant for temporary use, or loan material valuables which are part of the property of the leased enterprise, sublease them, and transfer its rights and duties under the contract of lease with respect to such valuables to another person on condition that this does not entail a reduction of the value of the enterprise and does not violate other provisions of the contract.

Unless provided otherwise by the contract of lease of an enterprise, the lessee shall have the right without the consent of the lessor to conduct the conversion of the leased enterprise, expansion, or technical re-equipping which increases its value.

Article 584. Making of Improvements by Lessee in Leased Enterprise

The lessee of an enterprise shall have the right to compensation for the cost to him of inseparable improvements of the leased property irrespective of the authorization of the lessor for such improvements unless provided otherwise by the contract of lease of the enterprise.

The lessor may be relieved by a court from the duty to compensate the lessee for the cost of such improvements if it is proved that the costs of the lessee for such improvements exceeds the value of the leased property incommensurately to the improvement of its quality and/or operational properties or when effectuating such improvements the principles of good faith and reasonableness were violated.

Article 585. Application to Contract of Lease of Enterprise of Rules Concerning Consequences of Invalidity of Transactions and Changes and Dissolution of Contract

The rules of the present Code concerning the consequences of the invalidity of the transactions and changes and dissolution of a contract providing for the return or the recovery in kind of that received under the contract from one or from both parties shall apply to a contract of lease of an enterprise if such consequences do not violate the material rights and the interests protected by a law of creditors of the lessor and lessee and other persons and are not contrary to the rules of Article 116 of the present Code.

Article 586. Return of Leased Enterprise

In the event of the termination of a contract of lease of an enterprise, the leased property complex must be returned to the lessor in compliance with the rules provided for by Articles 579 and 581 of the present Code.

§ 6. Finance Leasing

[as amended by Law of 28 December 2007, No. ЗРУ-138. СЗ РУ (2007), no. 52, item 533]

Article 587. Contract of Finance Leasing

Under a contract of finance leasing one party, the finance lessor (or lessor), shall on behalf of the other party, the finance lessee (or lessee) be obliged to enter into an agreement with a third party, as seller in order to acquire from the last property for the finance lessee, and the finance lessee shall be obliged to pay finance lease payments to the finance lessor for this [as amended by Law of 13 December 2002, No. 447-II. Ведомости Олий Мажлиса (2003), no. 1, item 8].

Article 588. Object of Finance Leasing

Any non-consumer things to be used for entrepreneurial activity, except land plots and other natural objects, may be the object of finance lease.

Article 589. Subject of Finance Lease

The person acquiring property in ownership for the purpose of the subsequent transfer thereof to the finance lessee under a finance lease shall be deemed to be the finance lessor.

The person acquiring the object of finance lease in his possession and use and be deemed to be the finance lessee.

The person from whom the finance lessor acquires the object of the finance lease shall be deemed to be the seller [as amended by Law of 13 December 2002, No. 447-II. Ведомости Олий Мажлиса (2003), no. 1, item 8].

The combining of the finance lessee and seller in one person shall be permitted if the finance lessor acquires the property from a future user or when the finance lessor finances the producer for the purpose of acquiring property from him for subsequent finance leasing out to this same person [as amended by Law of 13 December 2002, No. 447-II. Ведомости Олий Мажлиса (2003), no. 1, item 8].

Article 590. Finance Leasing Payment

The finance leasing payment is compensation by the finance lessee to the finance lessor for the value of the object of finance leasing, and also interest revenue to the finance lessor [as amended by Laws of 13 December 2002, No. 447-II, and of 28 December 2007, No. ЗРУ-138. Ведомости Олий Мажлиса (2003), no. 1, item 8; СЗ РУ (2007), no. 52, item 533].

Article 591. Notification of Seller Concerning Finance Lease of Property

The finance lessor must, in acquiring the property for the finance lessee, notify the seller that the property is intended for transfer to a determined person on a finance lease.

Article 592. Transfer to Finance Lessee of Subject of Contract of Finance Lease

Unless provided otherwise by the contract of finance lease, the property which is the object of this contract shall be transferred by the seller directly to the finance lessee at the location of the last.

When property which is the subject of a contract of finance lease is not transferred to the finance lessee within the period specified in this contract, and if such period has not been specified in this contract, within a reasonable period, the finance lessee shall have the right if the delay was permitted under circumstances for which the finance lessor is liable to require dissolution of the contract and compensation of losses.

Article 593. Transfer to Finance Lessee of Risk of Accidental Perishing or Accidental Damaging of Property

The risk of accidental perishing or accidental damaging of leased property under a finance lease shall pass to the finance lessee at the moment of the transfer of this property to him unless provided otherwise by the contract of finance lease.

Article 594. Duties and Responsibility of Finance Lessor

The finance lessor shall be obliged to grant the object of finance lease to the finance lessee in a state corresponding to the conditions of the contract and within the periods stipulated by it.

The finance lessor shall bear responsibility to the finance lessee for failure to deliver, short delivery, delay of delivery, and the delivery of property of improper quality if they are a consequence of the guilty actions and omissions thereof.

Article 595. Rights of Finance Lessee

In the event of a failure to deliver, short delivery, delay of delivery, or the delivery of property of improper quality, the finance lessee shall have right unless provided otherwise by the contract to [as amended by Law of 13 December 2002, No. 447-II. Ведомости Олий Мажлиса (2003), no. 1, item 8]:

withhold the payment of finance lease payments;

refuse the property delivered and demand dissolution of the contract of finance lease.

In the event of the dissolution before time of the contract of finance lease, the finance lessee shall have the right to demand the return of the payments paid by him earlier as an advance payment, deducting the cost of those advantages which he derived for the use of the object of the finance lease [as amended by Law of 13 December 2002, No. 447-II. Ведомости Олий Мажлиса (2003), no. 1, item 8].

In the instance provided by a contract of finance leasing, the finance lessee may grant the object of finance leasing to secure the performance of other obligations in that part by which the value of the object of finance leasing exceeds the residual amount of finance leasing payments subject to payment to the finance lessor [added by Law of 22 October 2019, No. ЗРУ-572].

Upon the expiry of the period of the contract of finance lease, the object of finance lease shall pass to the ownership of the finance lessee unless stipulated otherwise by the contract.

Article 596. Sub-Finance Lease

The finance lessee shall have the right to sublease the property received under the contract of finance lease with the consent of the finance lessor while remaining responsible to him under the contract.

Article 597. Duties and Responsibility of Finance Lessee

The finance lessee shall be obliged in a timely way to make finance lease payments, use the property in accordance with the conditions on which it was delivered, maintain it in a proper state, make current repair at his own expense, and bear other expenses for the maintenance thereof unless established otherwise by the contract of finance lease [as amended by Law of 13 December 2002, No. 447-II. Ведомости Олий Мажлиса (2003), no. 1, item 8].

In the event of the termination of the contract of finance lease the finance lessee shall be obliged to return the property in the state in which he received it from the finance lessor taking into account normal wear and tear and the changes stipulated by the agreement of the parties.

In the event of the failure by the finance lessee to perform his obligations with regard to payment of the finance lease payments, the finance lessor may receive the payments due to him together with interest [as amended by Law of 13 December 2002, No. 447-II. Ведомости Олий Мажлиса (2003), no. 1, item 8].

In the event of the finance lessee permitting a material violation of his duties, the finance lessor may require an accelerated payment of future finance lease payments unless provided otherwise by the contract of finance lease, or require the dissolution of the contract by levy of execution against the object of finance leasing in the procedure provided for levy against the subject-matter of pledge and the recovery of losses [as amended by Laws of 13 December 2002, No. 447-II, and of 22 October 2019, No. 3PY-572].

Article 598. Responsibility of Seller

The finance lessee shall have the right to present demands directly to the seller of the property which is the subject of the contract of finance lease and which arise from the contract of purchase-sale concluded between the seller and the finance lessor, in particular, with respect to the quality and completeness of the property, the periods for the delivery thereof, and in other instances of improper performance of the contract by the seller. In so doing the finance lessee shall have the rights and bear the duties provided for by the present Code for a purchaser (except the duty to pay for the property acquired) as if he were a party to the contract of purchase-sale of the said property. However, the finance lessee may not dissolve the contract of purchase-sale with the seller without the consent of the finance lessor.

In relations with the seller the finance lessee and finance lessor shall act as joint and several creditors.

Unless provided otherwise by the contract of finance lease, the finance lessor shall not be liable to the finance lessee for the fulfillment by the seller of demands arising from the contract of purchase-sale, except for instances when responsibility for the choice of the seller lies on the finance lessor. In the last instance the finance lessee shall have the right at his choice to present demands arising from the contract of purchase-sale both directly to the seller of the property and to the finance lessor, who shall bear joint and several responsibility.

Article 599. Preservation of Force of Contract of Finance Lease in Event of Transfer of Object of Finance Lease to Another Owner

In the event of the transfer of the right of ownership to property under finance lease from the finance lessor to another person, the contract of finance lease shall retain force for the new owner.

Chapter 35. Rental of Dwelling Premise

Article 600. Contract of Rental of Dwelling Premise

Under a contract of rental of a dwelling premise one party – the owner of the dwelling premise or person empowered by him (landlord) – shall be obliged to grant to the other party (tenant) a dwelling premise for payment in possession and use in order to reside therein.

A dwelling premise may be granted to juridical persons in possession and/or use on the basis of a contract of lease or other contract. A juridical person may use the dwelling premise only for the residing of citizens.

Article 601. Contract of Rental of Dwelling Premise in Municipal Housing Fund of Special-Purpose Designation

Dwelling premises shall be granted to citizens by a contract of rental of dwelling premise in the municipal dwelling fund of special-purpose designation. Members of his family residing jointly with the tenant under such contract of social rental of a dwelling premise shall enjoy all the rights and bear all the duties under the contract of rental of dwelling premise equally with the tenant.

At the demand of the tenant and members of his family the contract may be concluded with one of the members of the family. In the event of the death of the tenant or of his departure from the dwelling premise the contract shall be concluded with one of the members of the family residing in the dwelling premise.

The contract of rental of a dwelling premise in a municipal housing fund of special-purpose designation shall be concluded on the grounds, on the conditions, and in the procedure provided for by housing legislation. The rules of Articles 603, 604, 607, 609, 610, and also 613, paragraphs one, two, and three, of the present Code shall apply to such contract. Other provisions of the present Code shall apply to the contract of rental of dwelling premise in municipal housing fund of special purpose-designation unless provided otherwise by housing legislation.

Article 602. Object of Contract of Rental of Dwelling Premise

An isolated dwelling premise fit for permanent residing (apartment, dwelling house, part of apartment or dwelling house) may be the object of a contract of rental of a dwelling premise.

The fitness of a dwelling premise for residing shall be determined in the procedure provided for by housing legislation.

The tenant of a dwelling premise in an apartment house shall have the right, together with the use of the dwelling premise, to use the property specified in Article 211 of the present Code.

Article 603. Form of Contract of Rental of Dwelling Premise

A contract of rental of dwelling premise shall be concluded in written form.

A contract of rental of a dwelling premise between citizens shall be subject to recording in State tax agencies [added by Law of 30 December 2011, No. ЗРУ-311, as amended by Law of 11 October 2018, No. ЗРУ-497].

Article 604. Preservation of Contract of Rental of Dwelling Premise in Event of Transfer of Right of Ownership to Dwelling Premise

The transfer of the right of ownership to a dwelling premise occupied under a contract of rental shall not entail the change or dissolution of the contract. The new owner shall become the landlord on the conditions of the contract of rental previously concluded.

Article 605. Duties of Landlord of Dwelling Premise

The landlord shall be obliged to grant to the tenant a vacant dwelling premise in a state fit for permanent residing.

The landlord shall be obliged to effectuate the proper operation of the dwelling house in which the rented dwelling premise is situated, to grant or to ensure the granting of the necessary municipal services to the tenant for payment, ensure the conducting of the repair of the common property of an apartment house and devices for rendering municipal services situated in the dwelling premise, and also take mesures for ensuring use of the premise only for the purposes specified in the contract of rental [as amended by Law of 25 April 2016, No. ЗРУ-405. СЗ РУ (2016), no. 17, item 173].

Article 606. Tenant and Citizens Permanently Residing Together With Him

Only a citizen may be a tenant under a contract of rental of a dwelling premise.

The citizens permanently residing in the dwelling house together with the tenant must be specified in the contract. In the absence of such indications in the contract these citizens shall be evicted in accordance with the rules of Article 608 of the present Code.

Citizens permanently residing jointly with the tenant shall have equal rights with him with regard to the use of the dwelling premise. Relations between the tenant and such citizens shall be determined by a law.

The tenant shall bear responsibility to the landlord for the actions of citizens permanently residing jointly with him which violate the conditions of the contract of rental of the dwelling premise.

Citizens permanently residing together with the tenant may, having notified the landlord, conclude with the tenant a contract that all citizens permanently residing in the dwelling premise shall bear jointly with the tenant joint and several responsibility to the landlord. In this event such citizens shall be co-tenants.

Article 607. Duties of Tenant of Dwelling Premise

The tenant shall be obliged to use the dwelling premise only for its designation, ensure the preservation of the dwelling premise, and maintain it in a proper state.

The tenant shall not have the right to rebuild and convert a dwelling premise without the consent of the landlord.

The tenant shall be obliged to make payment in good time for the dwelling premise in a timely way. Unless established otherwise by the contract, the tenant shall be obliged autonomously to make payment for municipal services.

Article 608. Inclusion of New Members of Family of Tenant in Contract of Rental of Dwelling Premise

The tenant of a dwelling premise, and likewise the members of his family, shall have the right to require the inclusion in the contract of rental of dwelling premise of other citizens as a member of the family. The procedure and conditions for the inclusion of such citizens in the contract of rental of dwelling premise shall be determined by legislation.

Article 609. Temporary Inhabitants

The tenant and citizens permanently residing with him shall have the right by common consent and with prior notification of the landlord to authorize the uncompensated residing in the dwelling premise of temporary inhabitants (users). The landlord may prohibit the residing of temporary inhabitants on condition of the failure to comply with the requirements of legislation concerning the norm of dwelling space per person. The period of residing of temporary inhabitants may not exceed six months.

Temporary inhabitants shall not possess an autonomous right of use of the dwelling premise. The tenant shall bear responsibility to the landlord for their actions.

Temporary inhabitants shall be obliged to vacate the dwelling premise upon the expiry of the period of residing agreed with them, and if the period is not agreed, not later than seven days from the date of the respective demand being presented by the tenant or by any citizen permanently residing with them.

Article 610. Repair of Rented Dwelling Premise

The current repair of a rented dwelling premise shall be the duty of the tenant unless established otherwise by the contract of rental of the dwelling premise.

The capital repair of a rented dwelling premise shall be the duty of the landlord unless established otherwise by the contract of rental of the dwelling premise.

The re-equipping of a dwelling house in which a rented dwelling premise is situated, if such re-equipping materially changes the conditions of use of the dwelling premise, shall not be permitted without the consent of the tenant.

Article 611. Payment for Dwelling Premise

The amount of payment for a dwelling premise shall be established by agreement of the parties in the contract of rental of a dwelling premise. If in accordance with a law the maximum amount of payment for the dwelling premise is established, the payment established in the contract must not exceed this amount.

A unilateral change of the amount of payment for the dwelling premise shall not be permitted except for instances provided for by a law or by the contract.

Payment for the dwelling premise must be made by the tenant within the periods provided for by the contract of rental of the dwelling premise. Unless the periods have been provided for by the contract, the payment must be made by the tenant monthly in the procedure established by legislation.

Article 612. Period in Contract of Rental of Dwelling Premise

The contract of rental of a dwelling premise shall be concluded for a period not exceeding five years. If the period is not determined in the contract, it shall be considered to be concluded for five years.

The rules provided for by Article 606, paragraphs two and three, Article 609, paragraph three of the present Article, and Articles 613 and 614 of the present Code shall not apply to the contract of the rental of a dwelling premise concluded for a term of up to one year (short-term rental) unless provided otherwise by the contract.

The tenant shall have a preferential right to conclude a contract for a new period.

The landlord may refuse to conclude a contract for a new period if he has adopted a decision not to rent the premise for less than a year.

Article 613. Sub-Rental of Dwelling Premise

Under a contract of sub-rental of a dwelling premise the tenant shall with the consent of the landlord transfer for a period part or all of the premise rented by him to the use of the subtenant. The subtenant shall not acquire autonomously the right of use of the dwelling premise. The tenant shall remain responsible to the landlord under the contract of rental of the dwelling premise.

The contract of sub-rental of a dwelling premise may be concluded on condition of compliance with the requirements of legislation concerning the norm of dwelling space per person.

The contract of sub-rental of a dwelling premise shall be for compensation.

The period of the contract of sub-rental of a dwelling premise may not exceed the period of the contract of rental of a dwelling premise.

In the event of the termination before time of the contract of rental of a dwelling premise the contract of sub-rental of the dwelling premise shall terminate simultaneously with it.

The rules concerning the preferential right to conclude a contract for a new period shall not extend to the contract of sub-rental of a dwelling premise.

Article 614. Replacement of Tenant in Contract of Rental of Dwelling Premise

Upon the demand of the tenant and other citizens permanently residing with him and with the consent of the landlord, the tenant in a contract of rental of a dwelling premise may be replaced by one of the citizens who has reached majority permanently residing with the tenant.

In the event of the death of the tenant or of his departure from the dwelling premise, the contract shall continue to operate on those same conditions and one of the citizens permanently residing with the previous tenant shall become the tenant by general consent among them. If such consent is not reached, all the citizens permanently residing in the dwelling premise shall become co-tenants.

Article 615. Dissolution of Contract of Rental

The dissolution of a contract of rental of a dwelling premise shall be made by agreement of the parties.

The tenant of a dwelling premise shall have the right with the consent of other citizens permanently residing with him at any time to dissolve the contract of rental with a warning in writing to the landlord three months beforehand.

The contract of rental of a dwelling premise may be dissolved in a judicial proceeding upon the demand of the landlord in instances of:

the failure of the tenant to make payment for the dwelling premise for six months unless a longer period has been established by the contract, and in the event of a short-term rental in the event of the failure to make payment more than twice upon the expiry of the period of payment established by the contract;

destruction or spoilage of the dwelling premise by the tenant or other citizens for whose actions he is liable;

use of the dwelling premise for the commission of unlawful acts [as amended by Law of 25 April 2016, No. 3PУ-405. C3 PУ (2016), no. 17, item 173].

The contract of rental of a dwelling premise may be dissolved in a judicial proceeding upon the demand of any of the parties to the contract:

if the premise ceases to be fit for permanent habitation, and also in the event of the damaged state thereof;

in other instances provided for by housing legislation.

If the tenant of a dwelling premise or other citizens for whose actions he is liable uses the dwelling premise not for the designation or systematically violates the rights and interests of neighbors, the landlord may warn the tenant about the need to eliminate the violations.

If the tenant or other citizens for whose actions he is liable continues after a warning to use the dwelling premise not for the designation or to violate the rights and interests of neighbors, the landlord shall have the right in a judicial proceeding to dissolve the contract of rental of the dwelling premise.

The procedure and periods for eliminating violations which served as the grounds for dissolution of the contract of rental of a dwelling premise shall be established by a law.

Article 616. Consequences of Dissolution of Contract of Rental of Dwelling Premise

In the event of the dissolution of a contract of rental of a dwelling premise the tenant and other citizens residing in the dwelling premise at the moment of dissolution of the contract shall be subject to eviction from the dwelling premise on the basis of the decision of a court.

Chapter 36. Uncompensated Use

Article 617. Concept of Contract of Uncompensated Use

Under a contract of uncompensated use (or contract of loan) one party (the lender) is obliged to transfer or transfers a thing for temporary uncompensated use to the other party (loan recipient), and the last is obliged to return this thing in the same state in which it was received, taking into account normal wear and tear, or in a state stipulated by the contract.

The rules provided for by Article 537, Article 540, paragraphs one and two, Article 545, Article 553, paragraph four, and Article 555, paragraphs one and three, of the present Code shall apply respectively to the contract of uncompensated use.

Article 618. Lender

The right to transfer a thing to the uncompensated use shall belong to the owner thereof and to other persons empowered to do so by a law or by the owner.

A commercial organization shall not have the right to transfer a thing for uncompensated use to a person who is the founder, participant (or stockholder), director, or member of the management or control organs thereof.

Article 619. Granting Thing for Uncompensated Use

The lender shall be obliged to grant a thing in a state corresponding to the conditions of the contract of uncompensated use and the designation thereof.

A thing shall be granted for uncompensated use with all of its appurtenances and documents relating thereto (instruction manuals for use, technical passport, and so forth) unless provided otherwise by the contract.

If such appurtenances and documents were not transferred and without them the thing can not be used for the designation or its use to a significant degree loses value for the loan recipient, the last shall have the right to require such appurtenances and documents be granted to him or to dissolve the contract and compensation for real damage incurred by him.

Article 620. Consequences of Failure to Grant Thing for Uncompensated Use

If the lender does not grant a thing to the loan recipient, the last shall have the right to require dissolution of the contract of uncompensated use and compensation of the real damage incurred by him.

Article 621. Responsibility for Defects of Thing Transferred for Uncompensated Use

The lender shall be liable for defects of a thing which he intentionally or through gross negligence did not stipulate when concluding the contract of uncompensated use.

In the event of the discovery of such defects the loan recipient shall have the right at his choice to demand of the lender the uncompensated elimination of the defects of the thing or compensation of expenses for elimination of the defects of the thing or dissolution before time of the contract and compensation of real damage.

The lender notified about the demands of the loan recipient or of his intention to eliminate the defects of the thing at the expense of the lender may without delay replace the thing in disrepair with another analogous thing which is in a proper state.

The lender shall not be liable for defects of a thing which were stipulated by him when concluding the contract for uncompensated use or were known to the recipient of the loan beforehand or should have been discovered by the loan recipient during the inspection of the thing or verification of its good repair when concluding the contract or when transferring the thing.

Article 622. Rights of Third Persons to Thing Being Transferred for Uncompensated Use

The transfer of a thing for uncompensated use shall not be grounds for the change or termination of the rights of third persons to this thing.

When concluding a contract of uncompensated use the lender shall be obliged to warn the loan recipient about all the rights of third persons to this thing (servitude, right of pledge, and so forth). The failure to perform this duty shall give the loan recipient the right to demand dissolution of the contract and compensation of real damage.

Article 623. Duties of Loan Recipient With Regard to Maintenance of Thing

The loan recipient shall be obliged to maintain the thing received for uncompensated use in a correct state of repair. The loan recipient shall be obliged to make current and capital repair of the thing and bear all expenses for the maintenance thereof unless provided otherwise by the contract.

Article 624. Risk of Accidental Perishing or Accidental Damaging of Thing

The loan recipient shall bear the risk of accidental perishing or accidental damage of a thing received for uncompensated use if the thing perished or was spoiled in connection with the fact that he used it not in accordance with the contract or designation of the thing or transferred it to a third person without the consent of the lender. The loan recipient also shall bear the risk of accidental perishing or accidental damage of the thing if he could prevent the perishing or spoilage thereof by having sacrificed his thing.

Article 625. Responsibility for Harm Caused to Third Person as Result of Use of Thing

The lender shall be liable for harm caused to a third person by the use of the thing unless it is proved that the harm was caused as a consequence of the intent or gross negligence of the loan recipient or person from whom this thing is situated with the consent of the lender or if the harm was caused by use of the thing which had left the possession of the loan recipient without the consent of the lender.

Article 626. Transfer of Thing Received for Uncompensated Use to Third Person

The loan recipient shall have the right to transfer for the use of a third person a thing received for uncompensated use only with the consent of the lender, remaining responsible to him.

Article 626[1]. Form of Contract on Granting Dwelling Premise for Uncompensated Use [added by Law of 25 April 2016, No. 3PY-405]

A contract on granting a dwelling premise for uncompensated use shall be concluded in written form, except for instances when the dwelling premise in uncompensated use is granted to close relatives (parents, blood and step-brothers and sisters, spouses, children, including adopted, grandfathers, grandmothers, grandchildren, and also parents, blood and step-brothers and sisters of spouses).

[paragraph two repealed by Law of 11 October 2018, No. 3PY-497].

The rules provided by Article 606, paragraph two, Article 607, paragraphs one and two, Articles 609 and 610, Article 612, paragraph one, Article 615, paragraph one, paragraph three, indentations three and four, paragraphs four and five, and Article 616 of the present Code shall apply to the contract on granting a dwelling premise for uncompensated use.

Article 627. Dissolution Before Time of Contract of Uncompensated Use

The lender shall have the right to require dissolution before time of a contract of uncompensated use in instances when the loan recipient:

uses the thing not in accordance with the contract or designation of the thing;

does not fulfill duties with regard to maintenance of the thing in a proper state of repair or the maintenance thereof;

materially worsens the state of the thing;

has transferred the thing without the consent of the lender to a third person.

The loan recipient shall have the right to demand the dissolution before time of the contract of uncompensated use:

in the event of the discovery of defects making the normal use of the thing impossible or encumbered, concerning the existence of which he did not know and could not have known at the moment of concluding the contract;

if the thing by virtue of circumstances for which he is not liable proves to be in a state not fit for use;

if when concluding the contract the lender did not warn him about the rights of third persons to the thing being transferred;

in the event of the lender's failure to perform the duty to transfer the thing or appurtenances thereof and documents relating to it.

Article 628. Renunciation of Contract of Uncompensated Use

Each of the parties shall have the right at any time to renounce the contract if the period of uncompensated use of the thing is not determined in the contract, having notified the other party thereof one month in advance unless a different period of notice has been provided for by the contract.

Unless provided otherwise by the contract of uncompensated use, the loan recipient shall have the right at any time to renounce the contract concluded with specification of the period in the procedure provided for by paragraph one of the present Article.

Article 629. Change of Parties in Contract of Uncompensated Use

The lender shall have the right to alienate the thing or transfer it for compensated use to a third person. In so doing to the new owner or user shall pass the rights relating to the previously concluded contract of uncompensated use, and his rights with respect to the thing shall be encumbered by the rights of the loan recipient.

In the event of the death of a citizen-lender or the reorganization or liquidation of a juridical person-lender the rights and duties thereof under the contract of uncompensated use shall pass to the heir or other legal successor or to another person to whom the right of ownership has passed to the thing or other right on the basis of which the thing was transferred for uncompensated use.

In the event of the reorganization of a juridical person-loan recipient its rights and duties under the contract shall pass to the legal successor thereof unless provided otherwise by the contract for uncompensated use.

Article 630. Termination of Contract of Uncompensated Use

A contract of uncompensated use shall terminate in the event of the death of the citizen-loan recipient or liquidation of the juridical person-loan recipient unless provided otherwise by the contract.

Chapter 37. Independent Work

§ 1. General Provisions on Independent Work

Article 631. Contract of Independent-Work

Under a contract of independent-work one party the (independent-work contractor) shall be obliged to fulfill according to the planning task of the other party (customer) determined work and to hand over the result to the customer, and the customer shall be obliged to accept and to pay for the result of the work. The work shall be fulfilled at the risk of the independent-work contractor unless provided otherwise by legislation or by agreement of the parties.

The provisions provided for by the present paragraph shall apply to individual types of contract of independent-work (domestic independent-work, construction independent-work, independent-work for the fulfillment of design and survey work, independent-work for scientific-research, experimental construction design, and technological work) unless established otherwise by the rules of the present Code concerning these types of contracts.

Article 632. Work to be Fulfilled Under Contract of Independent-Work

A contract of independent-work shall be concluded for the manufacture or converting (or processing) of a thing or for the fulfillment of other work with the transfer of its results or giving thereof otherwise to the customer.

Unless provided otherwise by the contract of independent-work, the work shall be fulfilled from the materials, forces, and means of the independent-work contractor.

Unless provided otherwise by the contract of independent-work, the independent-work contractor autonomously shall determine the means of fulfillment of the planning task of the customer.

The independent-work contractor shall bear responsibility for the improper quality of the materials and equipment granted by him, and also for the granting of materials and equipment encumbered by the rights of third persons.

Article 633. Risk of Accidental Perishing or Accidental Damaging of Materials

The risk of accidental perishing or accidental damage of materials before the ensuing of the period for handing over the work by the independent-work contractor stipulated by the contract of independent-work shall be borne by the party which granted the materials, and after the ensuing of this period, by the party which delayed, unless established otherwise by legislation or by the contract.

Article 634. General Independent-Work Contractor and Subindependent-Work Contractor

Unless the duty of the independent-work contractor to fulfill the work provided for in the contract personally arises from legislation or the contract of independent-work, the independent-work contractor shall have the right to recruit other persons to perform part of his obligation (subindependent-work contractor). In this event the independent-work contractor shall act in the role of general independent-work contractor.

The independent-work contractor shall bear responsibility to the subindependent-work contractor for the failure of the customer to perform or improper performance of his obligations under the contract of independent-work, and to the customer, responsibility for the consequences of the failure of the independent-work contractor to perform or the improper performance of his obligation in accordance with Article 241, paragraphs two and three, and Article 334 of the present Code.

Unless provided otherwise by the law or contract of independent-work, the customer and the subindependent-work contractor shall not have the right to present to one another demands connected with a violation of the contracts concluded by each of them with the general independent-work contractor.

An independent-work contractor who has enlisted a subindependent-work contractor to perform the contract in violation of the provisions of paragraph one of the present Article or the contract of independent-work shall bear responsibility to the customer for losses caused by the participation of such subindependent-work contractor in the performance of the contract.

With the consent of the general independent-work contractor the customer shall have the right to conclude a contract for the fulfillment of individual work with other persons. In this event the said persons shall bear responsibility for the failure to perform or the improper performance of work directly to the customer.

Article 635. Periods for Fulfillment of Work

The beginning and ending periods of fulfillment of the work shall be specified in the contract of independent-work. By agreement between the parties periods for completing individual stages of work (intermediate periods) also may be provided for in the contract.

Unless provided otherwise by the contract of independent-work, the independent-work contractor shall bear responsibility for a violation of both the beginning and ending, and also the intermediate, periods for the fulfillment of work.

The beginning, ending, and intermediate periods for the fulfillment of work specified in the contract of independent-work may be changed in the instances and in the procedure provided for by the contract.

The consequences of delay of performance specified in Article 337, paragraph two, of the present Code shall ensue in the event of a violation of the ending of the period for the fulfillment of the work.

Article 636. Price of Work

In the contract of independent-work the price of the work subject to fulfillment and the means of determining it shall be specified. In the absence of such specifications in the contract the price shall be determined in accordance with Article 356, paragraph four, of the present Code.

The price of work in the contract of independent-work shall include contributory compensation for the costs of the independent-work contractor and the remuneration due to it.

The price of the work may be determined by means of drawing up an estimate.

In an event when work is fulfilled in accordance with the estimate drawn up by the independent-work contractor, the estimate shall acquire force and become part of the contract of independent-work from the moment of the confirmation thereof by the customer.

The price of the work (or estimate) may be approximate or firm. In the absence of such indications in the contract of independent-work the price of the work shall be considered to be firm.

If the necessity arises for carrying out additional work and for this reason the price of the work determined approximately materially increases (approximate price), the independent-work contractor shall be obliged to warn the customer thereof in good time. The customer who has not agreed to the increase of the price of the work (or estimate) specified in the contract of independent-work shall have the right to repudiate the contract. In this event the independent-work contractor may demand payment from the customer to him of the price for the part of the work fulfilled.

An independent-work contractor who has not warned the customer in good time about the necessity of increasing the price of the work (or estimate) specified in the contract shall be obliged to fulfill the contract, retaining the right to payment for the work at the price determined in the contract.

An independent-work contractor shall not have the right, as a rule, to demand an increase of a firm price (or firm estimate), nor the customer to reduce it, including also in the event when at the moment of concluding the contract of independent-work the possibility to provide for the full amount of work subject to fulfillment or the expenses necessary for this was excluded.

In the event of the material growth of the cost of materials and equipment which must be granted by the independent-work contractor, and also of services rendered to him by third persons which could not be provided for when concluding the contract, the independent-work contractor shall have the right to demand an increase of the established price for the work (or estimate), and in the event of the refusal of the customer to fulfill this demand, dissolution of the contract in accordance with Article 383 of the present Code.

Article 637. Economies of Independent-Work Contractor

In instances when the actual expenses of the independent-work contractor prove to be less than those which were taken into account when determining the price of the work, the independent-work contractor shall retain the right to payment for the work at the price provided for by the contract of independent-work unless the customer proves that the economies received by the independent-work contractor influenced the quality of the work fulfilled.

A distribution of the economies received by the independent-work contractor between the parties may be provided for in the contract of independent-work.

Article 638. Procedure for Payment of Work

Unless preliminary payment for work fulfilled or individual stages thereof has been provided for by the contract of independent-work, the customer shall be obliged to pay the independent-work contractor the stipulated price after the final handing over of the results of the work, on condition that the work is properly fulfilled and within the agreed period, or with the consent of the customer, before time.

The independent-work contractor shall have the right to demand the payment to him of an advance or a deposit only in the instances and in the amount specified in legislation or in the contract of independent-work.

Article 639. Right of Independent-Work Contractor to Withholding

In the event of the failure of the customer to fulfill the duty to pay the established price or other amount due to the independent-work contractor in connection with the fulfillment of the contract, the independent-work contractor shall have the right to withholding in accordance with Articles 290 and 291 of the present Code the result of the work, and also the equipment belonging to the customer transferred for converting (or processing) the thing, the balance of the unused material, and other property of the customer which proves to be with him until the payment by the customer of the respective amounts.

Article 640. Fulfillment of Work with Use of Material of Customer

The independent-work contractor shall be obliged to use the material granted by the customer economically and carefully, after the ending of the work to submit a report to the customer concerning the expenditure of the material, and also to return the balance thereof or with the consent of the customer to reduce the price of the work by taking into account the cost of the unused material remaining with the independent-work contractor.

The independent-work contractor shall bear responsibility for the improper fulfillment of work caused by defects of the material granted by the customer unless it is proved that the defenses could not be discovered by him in the event of the proper acceptance of this material.

Article 641. Responsibility of Independent-Work Contractor for Non-Preservation of Property Granted by Customer

The independent-work contractor shall bear responsibility for the non-preservation of material, equipment, the thing transferred for conversion (or processing), or other property granted by the customer which turned out to be in the possession of the independent-work contractor in connection with the performance of the contract of independent-work.

Article 642. Rights of Customer During Fulfillment of Work by Independent-Work Contractor

The customer shall have the right at any time to verify the course and quality of the work being fulfilled by the independent-work contractor without interfering in the activity of the independent-work contractor.

If the independent-work contractor does not embark upon the timely performance of the contract of independent-work or fulfils the work so slowly that the ending thereof within the period clearly becomes impossible, the customer shall have the right to repudiate the contract and to require compensation of losses. In so doing the customer must prove the loss to him of interest in the contract if it were to be fulfilled with delay.

If during the fulfillment of work it becomes evident that it will not be properly fulfilled, the customer shall have the right to designate a reasonable period to the independent-work contractor for elimination of the defects and in the event of the failure to perform this demand by the independent-work contractor within the designated period to repudiate the contract of independent-work or to commission rectification of the work to another person at the expense of the independent-work contractor, and also to require compensation of losses.

Unless provided otherwise by the contract of independent-work, the customer may at any time before the handing to him of the results of the work to repudiate the contract, having paid to the independent-work contractor the part of the established price in proportion to the part of the work fulfilled before receipt of the notice concerning the repudiation of the contract by the customer. The customer also shall be obliged to compensate the independent-work contractor for losses caused by the termination of the contract within the limits of the difference between the part of the price to be paid for the work fulfilled and the price determined for all of the work.

Article 643. Circumstances of Which Independent-Work Contractor is Obliged to Warn Customer

The independent-work contractor shall be obliged immediately to warn the customer and until receiving instructions from him to suspend the work in the event of discovering:

the unfitness or poor quality of the material, equipment, technical documentation, or thing transferred for conversion (or processing) granted by the customer;

possible consequences unfavorable for the customer of the fulfillment of his instructions concerning the means of performance of the work;

other circumstances beyond the control of the independent-work contractor which threaten the fitness or stability of the results of the work being fulfilled or create the impossibility of completing it within the period.

An independent-work contractor who has not warned the customer about the circumstances specified in paragraph one of the present Article or who has continued the work without awaiting the expiry of the period specified in the contract, and in the absence thereof of a reasonable period for a reply to the warning or notwithstanding the timely instruction of the customer concerning termination of the work, shall not have the right to refer to the said circumstances in the event of the presentation to him or by him to the customer of respective demands.

If the customer, notwithstanding a timely and substantiated warning on the part of the independent-work contractor concerning the circumstances specified in paragraph one of the present Article, within a reasonable period does not replace unfit or poor-quality material, does not change instructions concerning the means of fulfilling the work, or does not take other necessary measures in order to eliminate the circumstances threatening the fitness or stability of the work, the independent-work contractor shall have the right to refuse performance of the contract and to require compensation of losses.

Article 644. Failure of Customer to Perform Counter Duties Under Contract of Independent-Work

An independent-work contractor shall have the right not to embark upon the work, and to suspend work begun, in instances when a violation by the customer of his counter duties under the contract of independent-work, in particular the failure to grant material, equipment, technical documentation, or thing subject to converting (or processing) obstructs the performance of the contract by the independent-work contractor, and also when there are circumstances which obviously testify to the fact that performance of the said duties will not be made within the established period (Article 256 of the present Code).

Unless provided otherwise by the contract of independent-work, the independent-work contractor shall have the right, when the circumstances specified in paragraph one of the present Article are present, to refuse performance of the contract and require compensation of losses.

Article 645. Assistance of Customer

The customer shall be obliged in the instances, in the amount, and in the procedure provided for by the contract of independent-work to render assistance to the independent-work contractor in the fulfillment of the work.

In the event of the failure of the customer to perform this duty the independent-work contractor shall have the right to demand compensation of losses caused, including additional costs caused by idle-time, or to carry over the periods for performance of the work, or to increase the price of the work specified in the contract of independent-work.

In instances when performance of the work under the contract of independent-work has become impossible as a consequence of actions or omissions of the customer, the independent-work contractor shall retain the right to payment to him of the price specified in the contract taking into account the part of the work fulfilled.

Article 646. Acceptance by Customer of Work Fulfilled

The customer shall be obliged within the periods and in the procedure which are provided for by the contract of independent-work to inspect and accept, with the participation of the independent-work contractor, the work fulfilled (or result thereof), and in the event of discovering deviations from the contract which worsen the result of the work or other defects in the work, to immediately declare this to the independent-work contractor.

The customer who has discovered defects in the work when receiving it shall have the right to refer to them in the event when in the act or in the other document certifying acceptance these defects or the possibility of subsequent presentation of a demand concerning their elimination were stipulated.

The customer who has accepted work without verification shall be deprived of the right to refer to defects of the work which could have been established by ordinary means of the acceptance thereof (obvious defects).

The customer who has discovered after acceptance of the work deviations therein from the contract of independent-work or other defects which could not be established by ordinary means of acceptance (latent defects), including those which were intentionally concealed by the independent-work contractor, shall be obliged to notify the independent-work contractor thereof within a ten-day period with regard to the discovery thereof.

In the event a dispute arises between the customer and the independent-work contractor on the occasion of defects of the work fulfilled or the reasons therefor, an expert examination must be designated at the demand of any of the parties. The expenses with regard to the expert examination shall be borne by the independent-work contractor except for instances when the expert examination established the absence of violations of the contract of independent-work or a causal link between the actions of the independent-work contractor and the defects discovered. In these instances the expenses for the expert examination shall be borne by the party which required the designation thereof, and if it was designated by agreement between the parties, both parties equally.

Unless provided otherwise by the contract of independent-work, in the event the customer evades accepting the work fulfilled, the independent-work contractor shall have the right upon the expiry of one month from the date when according to the contract the result of the work should have been transferred to the customer, and on condition of a subsequent warning twice of the customer, to sell the result of the work, and to deposit the amount received less all payments due to the independent-work contractor in the name of the customer on deposit in a notarial office. The independent-work contractor shall have the right instead of the sale of the subject of independent-work to take advantage of the right to withhold it or to recover losses caused from the customer.

If the evasion of the customer of acceptance of the work fulfilled entailed delay in handing over the work, the risk of accidental perishing of the manufactured (or converted) thing shall be deemed to have passed to the customer at the moment when the transfer of the thing should have occurred.

Article 647. Quality of Work

The work fulfilled by the independent-work contractor must correspond to the conditions of the contract of independent-work, and in the absence or incompleteness thereof, to the requirements ordinarily presented for work of the respective nature. Unless provided otherwise by legislation or contract, the result of work fulfilled must at the moment of transfer to the customer possess the properties specified in the contract or determined requirements usually presented, and within the limits of a reasonable period be fit for the use established by the contract, and if such use is not provided for by the contract, for ordinary use of the result of work of this nature.

If obligatory requirements for work to be fulfilled under a contract of independent-work have been provided for by legislation, the independent-work contractor acting as an entrepreneur shall be obliged to fulfill the work while complying with these obligatory requirements.

The independent-work contractor may accept the duty to fulfill work under the contract of independent-work which meets the requirements for quality that are higher in comparison with the established obligatory requirements.

Article 648. Guarantee of Quality of Work

In the event when the granting of a guarantee of the quality of the work is provided for by legislation or by the contract of independent-work, the independent-work contractor shall be obliged to transfer to the customer the result of the work which must correspond during the entire guarantee period to the requirements of Article 647, paragraph one, of the present Code.

The guarantee of quality of the result of work, unless provided otherwise by the contract of independent-work, shall extend to everything comprising the result of the work.

Article 649. Procedure for Calculating Guarantee Period

Unless provided otherwise by the contract of independent-work, the guarantee period shall begin to run from the moment when the result of the work fulfilled was accepted or should have been accepted by the customer.

The rules contained in Article 404, paragraphs two, three, four, and five, of the present Code shall apply respectively to calculating the guarantee period under a contract of independent-work unless provided otherwise by legislation or by agreement of the parties or does not arise from the peculiarities of the contract of independent-work.

Article 650. Responsibility of Independent-Work Contractor for Improper Quality of Work

In instances when work is fulfilled by an independent-work contractor with deviations from the contract of independent-work which worsen the result of the work, or with other defects which make it unfit for the use provided for in the contract or in the event of the absence in the contract of a corresponding condition of unfitness for ordinary use, the customer shall have the right, unless established otherwise by a law or the contract, at his choice to require from the independent-work contractor:

elimination of the defects without compensation within a reasonable period;

commensurate reduction of the price established for the work;

compensation of his expenses for elimination of the defects when the right of the customer to eliminate them has been provided for in the contract.

The independent-work contractor shall have the right instead of eliminating the defects of the work for which he is liable to fulfill the work without compensation anew with compensation to the customer of losses caused by the delay of performance. In this event the customer shall be obliged to return the result of the work previously transferred to him to the independent-work contractor if by the character of the work such return is possible.

If deviations in the work from the conditions of the contract of independent-work or other defects of the result of the work are material and ineradicable or the defects discovered have not been eliminated within a reasonable period established by the customer, the customer shall have the right to refuse performance of the contract and to require compensation of losses caused.

The condition of the contract of independent-work concerning relieving the independent-work contractor of responsibility for determined defects shall not relieve him from responsibility if it is proved that such defects arose as a consequence of guilty actions or the failure to act of the independent-work contractor.

The independent-work contractor who has granted material to fulfill work shall be liable for its quality according to the rules concerning responsibility of the seller for goods of improper quality.

Article 651. Periods of Discovery of Improper Quality of Result of Work

Unless established otherwise by a law or the contract of independent-work, the customer shall have the right to present demands connected with the improper quality of the result of work on condition that it is elicited within the periods established by the present Article.

In the event when a guarantee period is not established for the result of the work, demands connected with defects of the result of the work may be presented by the customer on condition that they were discovered within a reasonable period, but within the limits of two years from the date of transfer of the result of the work, unless other periods have been established by a law, the contract, or the customs of business turnover.

The customer shall have the right to present demands connected with defects of the result of the work discovered during the guarantee period.

In the event when the guarantee period provided for by the contract constitutes less than two years and the defects of the result of the work are discovered by the customer upon the expiry of the guarantee period but within the limits of two years from the moment provided for by paragraph five of the present Article, the independent-work contractor shall bear responsibility if the customer proves that the defects arose before the transfer of the result of the work to the customer or for reasons which arose before that moment.

Unless provided otherwise by the contract of independent-work, the guarantee period shall commence to run from the moment when the result of the work fulfilled was accepted or should have been accepted by the customer.

The rules contained in Article 404, paragraphs two, three, four, and five, of the present Code respectively shall apply to calculating the guarantee period under the contract of independent-work unless provided otherwise by legislation, agreement of the parties, or does not arise from the peculiarities of the contract of independent-work.

Article 652. Limitation With Regard to Suits Concerning Improper Quality of Work

The period of limitations for demands caused by improper quality of work shall be determined according to the rules of Article 150 of the present Code.

If the granting by the independent-work contractor of a guarantee of the quality of work has been provided for by legislation or the contract of independent-work, the guarantee period is established and the statement with regard to defects of the result of the work was made within the limits of the guarantee period, the running of the periods of limitations shall commence from the date of the statement concerning the defects.

If in accordance with the contract of independent-work the work was accepted by the customer in parts, the running of the period of limitations shall commence from the date of acceptance of the work as a whole.

Article 653. Duty of Independent-Work Contractor to Transfer Information to Customer

The independent-work contractor shall be obliged to transfer to the customer together with the result of the work information affecting the operation or other use of the subject of the contract of independent-work if this is provided for by the contract or the character of the information such that without it the use of the result of the work is impossible for the purposes specified in the contract.

Article 654. Confidentiality of Information Received by Parties

If a party thanks to the performance of its obligation under the contract of independent-work has received information from the other party concerning new solutions and technical knowledge, including not enjoying legal protection, and also information which might be considered as a commercial secret, it shall not have the right to communicate it to third persons without the consent of the other party. The procedure and conditions for the use of such information shall be determined by agreement of the parties.

Article 655. Return to Customer of Materials and Equipment

In instances when the customer on the basis of Article 642, paragraph four, or Article 650, paragraph three, of the present Code refuses performance of a contract of independent-work, the independent-work contractor shall be obliged to return the materials, equipment, thing transferred for conversion (or processing), and other property granted by the customer or to transfer them to the person specified by the customer, and if this proves to be impossible, to compensate the cost of the materials, equipment, thing, and other property.

§ 2. Domestic Independent-Work

Article 656. Contract of Domestic Independent-Work

Under a contract of domestic independent-work the independent-work contractor effectuating entrepreneurial activity shall be obliged to fulfill according to the planning task of a citizen-customer the work determined which is intended to satisfy the domestic or other personal requirements of the customer, and the customer shall be obliged to accept and to pay for the work.

Unless provided otherwise by legislation or the contract, including the conditions of standard contracts or other standard forms to which the customer accedes, the contract of domestic independent-work shall be considered to be concluded from the moment of the issuance by the independent-work contractor to the customer of a receipt or other document confirming acceptance of the order.

The absence of the said documents with the customer shall not deprive him of the right to refer to witness testimony in confirmation of the fact of conclusion of the contract of domestic independent-work or the conditions thereof.

The contract of domestic independent-work shall be a public contract.

Article 657. Guarantees of Rights of Customer

An independent-work contractor shall not have the right to bind the customer to include additional compensated work or services in the contract of domestic independent-work. In the event of a violation of this requirement, the customer shall have the right to refuse to pay for the respective work or services.

The customer shall have the right at any time before the work is handed over to him to refuse performance of the contract of domestic independent-work, having paid to the independent-work contractor the part of the established price in proportion to the part of the work fulfilled before receipt of the notice concerning the refusal of performance of the contract of the customer and having compensated him for expenses made until this moment for the purposes of performance of the contract unless they are within the said part of the price of the work. Conditions of a contract depriving the customer of this right shall be null.

Article 658. Granting Information to Customer About Proposed Work

The independent-work contractor shall be obliged before conclusion of the contract of domestic independent-work to grant to the customer necessary and reliable information concerning the proposed work, the types thereof, and peculiarities, the price and form of payment, and also notify the customer at his request of other information relating to the contract and respective work. If by the character of the work this has significance, the independent-work contractor must indicate to the customer the specific person who will fulfill it.

The customer shall have the right to demand dissolution of a concluded contract of domestic independent-work without payment of the work fulfilled, and also compensation of losses in instances when as a consequence of the incompleteness or unreliability of information received from the independent-work contractor the contract was concluded for the fulfillment of work not possessing the properties which the customer had in view.

Article 659. Warning of Customer About Conditions of Use of Work Fulfilled

When handing work over to the customer, the independent-work contractor shall be obliged to notify him about the requirements which it is necessary to comply with for the effective and safe use of the result of the work, and also possible consequences for the customer himself and other persons of the failure to comply with the respective requirements.

Article 660. Fulfillment of Work from Material of Independent-Work Contractor

If work under the contract of domestic independent-work is fulfilled from material of the independent-work contractor, the material shall be paid for by the customer when concluding the contract wholly or in the part specified in the contract, with the final settlement of accounts when the work fulfilled by the independent-work contractor is received by the customer.

In accordance with the contract of domestic independent-work the material may be granted by the independent-work contractor on credit, including with a condition of payment for the material by the customer on installment.

A change of price of the material granted by the independent-work contractor after the conclusion of a contract of domestic independent-work shall not entail a recalculation of accounts.

Article 661. Fulfillment of Work from Material of Customer

If work under the contract of domestic independent-work is fulfilled from the material of the customer, the precise name, description, and price of the material determined by agreement of the parties must be specified on the receipt or other document issued by the independent-work contractor to the customer when concluding the contract. A valuation of the material on the receipt or other analogous document may be consequently contested by the customer in a court.

Article 662. Price and Payment for Work

The price of work in a contract of domestic independent-work shall be determined by agreement of the parties and may not be higher than that specified in a pricelist announced by the independent-work contractor. The work shall be paid for by the customer after the final handing over thereof by the independent-work contractor. By agreement of the parties the work may be paid for by the customer when concluding the contract in full or by means of issuance of an advance.

Article 663. Consequences of Discovery of Defects in Work Fulfilled

In the event he has discovered defects during the acceptance of the result of the work or during the use of the subject of independent-work the customer may within the general periods provided for by Article 652, paragraph one, of the present Code, and when there are guarantee periods, during these periods effectuate one of the rights provided for in Article 650 of the present Code.

The requirement concerning the elimination without compensation of defects of the work fulfilled under a contract of domestic independent-work which may represent a danger to the life or health of the customer himself and other persons may be presented by the customer or his legal successor within ten years from the moment of acceptance of the result of the work unless longer periods (or service periods) have been provided in the procedure established by a law. Such requirement may be presented irrespective of when these defects were discovered, including when discovering them at the end of the guarantee period. In the event of the failure of the independent-work contractor to fulfill the said requirement, the customer shall have the right within this same period to require either the return of part of the price paid for the work or compensation of expenses incurred in connection with the elimination of defects by his forces or with the assistance of third persons.

Article 664. Consequences of Failure of Customer to Appear for Receipt of Result of Work

In the event of the failure of the customer to appear for the receipt of the result of the work fulfilled or other evasion of the customer from acceptance thereof, the independent-work contractor shall have the right, having warned the customer in writing, upon the expiry of two months from the date of such warning to sell the result of the work and to place the amount received, less all payments due to the independent-work contractor, on deposit in accordance with Article 249 of the present Code.

In the instances specified in paragraph one of the present Article, the independent-work contractor may, instead of the sale of the result of the work, take advantage of the right to withhold it or to recover losses caused from the customer.

Article 665. Rights of Customer in Event of Improper Fulfillment or Failure to Fulfill Work Under Contract of Domestic Independent-Work

In the event of the improper fulfillment or the failure to fulfill work under a contract of domestic independent-work, the customer may take advantage of the rights granted to the purchaser in accordance with Articles 434-436 of the present Code.

§ 3. Construction Independent-Work

Article 666. Contract of Construction Independent-Work

Under a contract of construction independent-work the independent-work contractor shall be obliged within the period established by the contract to built a determined object according to the planning task of the customer or to fulfill other construction work, and the customer shall be obliged to create necessary conditions for the independent-work contractor in order to fulfill the work, accept the result thereof, and to pay the stipulated price.

The contract of construction independent-work shall be concluded for the construction or reconstruction of an enterprise, building (including dwelling house), installation, or other object, and also for the fulfillment of assembly, launching, and other work inextricably connected with the object being built. The rules concerning the contract of construction independent-work shall also apply to work relating to the capital repair of buildings and installations unless provided otherwise by the contract.

In the instances provided for by the contract of construction independent-work, the independent-work contractor shall assume the duty to ensure the operation of the object after its acceptance by the customer during the period specified in the contract.

The independent-work contractor shall be the owner of uncompleted construction until the handing over thereof to the customer and payment to him.

Article 667. Risk of Accidental Perishing or Accidental Damaging of Object of Independent-Work

The risk of accidental perishing or accidental damaging of the object before the acceptance thereof shall be borne by the independent-work contractor if the object of independent-work has perished or been damaged.

Article 668. Responsibility for Safety of Work Conducted

Responsibility for the safety of work conducted shall be borne by the independent-work contractor.

Article 669. Insurance of Object of Construction

The independent-work contractor shall be obliged at his expense to make the insurance of the object provided for by the contract or complex of work unless a different procedure and conditions have been determined by the parties in the contract.

The party on whom the duty is placed with regard to insurance must grant to the other party evidence of the conclusion by it of the contract of insurance in accordance with the conditions of the contract in the procedure provided for by the contract of construction independent-work, including data concerning the insurer, the amount of the insured amount, and the risks insured.

Insurance shall not relieve the respective party from the duty to take necessary measures in order to prevent the ensuing of the insured event.

Article 670. Project-Estimate Documentation

The independent-work contractor shall be obliged to effectuate construction and work connected therewith in accordance with the project-estimate documentation determining the amount and content of the work and other requirements presented to him.

In the absence of other instructions in the contract of construction independent-work it shall be presupposed that the independent-work contractor is obliged to fulfill all the work specified in the project-estimate documentation.

The composition and content of the project-estimate documentation must be determined by the contract of construction independent-work, and it also must be provided which of the parties and within what period must grant the respective documentation.

An independent-work contractor who has discovered in the course of construction work which is not clarified in the project-estimate documentation and in connection therewith the need for additional work and an increase of the estimate cost of the construction shall be obliged to inform the customer thereof.

In the event of the failure to receive a reply from the customer to his communication within ten days, unless another period has been provided by a law or by the contract of construction independent-work, the independent-work contractor shall be obliged to suspend the respective work with relegation of the losses caused by the idleness to the account of the customer. The customer shall be relieved from compensation of such losses if the absence of the necessity to conduct the additional work is proved.

An independent-work contractor who has not fulfilled the duties established by paragraphs four and five of the present Article shall be deprived of the right to demand payment from the customer for the additional work fulfilled by him and compensation of losses caused thereby unless it is proved that the necessity for immediate actions in the interests of the customer, in particular in connection with the fact that the suspension of work could lead to the perishing or damaging of the object of construction.

In the event of the consent of the customer to the additional work and to pay for it, the independent-work contractor shall have the right to refuse to fulfill the said work only in instances when such is not within the sphere of the professional activity of the independent-work contractor or may not be fulfilled by the independent-work contractor for reasons beyond his control.

Article 671. Making Changes in Design-Estimate Documentation

The customer shall have the right to make changes in the technical documentation on condition that the additional work caused by this does not exceed in cost 10% of the total cost of the construction specified in the estimate and does not change the character of the work provided for in the contract of construction independent-work.

The making of changes in the technical documentation greater than those specified in paragraph one of the present Article shall be effectuated on the basis of an additional estimate agreed by the parties.

The independent-work contractor shall have the right to demand in accordance with Article 382 of the present Code a review of the estimate if for reasons beyond his control the cost of the work exceeded the estimate by not less than 10%.

The independent-work contractor shall have the right to demand compensation of reasonable expenses which were incurred by him in connection with the establishment and elimination of defects in the design-estimate documentation.

Article 672. Provision of Construction with Materials and Equipment

The duties relating to provision of the construction with materials, including parts and construction designs, and also equipment, shall be borne by the independent-work contractor unless it is provided by the contract that the material provision of construction as a whole or in determined part shall be effectuated by the customer.

The party within those duty is the provision of the construction shall bear responsibility for the impossibility being discovered of using the materials, and also the equipment, granted by it without worsening the quality of the work to be fulfilled unless it is proved that the impossibility of the use arose through circumstances for which the other party is liable.

In the event of the impossibility being discovered of the use of the materials or equipment granted by the customer without worsening the quality of the work to be fulfilled and of the refusal of the customer to replace them, the independent-work contractor shall have the right to repudiate the contract of construction independent-work and to demand from the customer the payment of the price of the contract in proportion to the fulfilled part of the work.

Article 673. Payment for Work

Payment for the work fulfilled by the independent-work contractor shall be made by the customer in the amount provided for by the estimate, within the periods, and in the procedure which has been established by a law or by the contract of construction independent-work. In the absence of respective instructions in a law or in the contract the payment for work fulfilled by the independent-work contractor shall be made in accordance with Article 638 of the present Code.

Payment for work at one time and in full after acceptance of the object by the customer may be provided for by the contract of construction independent-work.

Article 674. Granting of Land Plot for Construction

The customer shall be obliged in a timely way to grant a land plot for construction of such expanse and in such state as is specified in the contract of construction independent-work. In the absence of such conditions in the contract, the expanse and state of the land plot must ensure the timely commencement of work, the normal conducting thereof, and completion within the period.

Article 675. Additional Duties of Customer in Contract of Construction Independent-Work

The customer shall be obliged in the instances and procedure provided for by the contract of construction independent-work to transfer for use to the independent-work contractor buildings and installations necessary in order to effectuate the work, ensure transport of goods to his address, the temporary laying of the network for electricity supply, water, and steam and to render other services.

Article 676. Control and Supervision Over Fulfillment of Work under Contract of Construction Independent-Work

The customer shall have the right to effectuate control and supervision over the course and quality of work being fulfilled, compliance with the periods thereof for the fulfillment (or schedule), the quality of materials granted by the independent-work contractor, and also the correctness of the use of the materials of the customer by the independent-work contractor without interfering in so doing in the operational-economic activity of the independent-work contractor.

The customer who has discovered when effectuating control and supervision over the fulfillment of work deviations from the conditions of the contract of construction independent-work which may worsen the quality of work or other defects thereof shall be obliged immediately to state this to the independent-work contractor. The customer who has not made such statement shall lose the right thereafter to refer to the defects discovered by him.

The independent-work contractor shall be obliged to perform instructions of the customer received in the course of the construction if such instructions are not contrary to the conditions of the contract of construction independent-work and do not represent interference in the operational-economic activity of the independent-work contractor.

The independent-work contractor who has improperly fulfilled work shall not have the right to refer to the fact that the customer did not effectuate control and supervision over the fulfillment thereof except for instances when the duty to effectuate such control and supervision is placed on the customer by legislation.

Article 677. Cooperation of Parties in Contract of Construction Independent-Work

If when fulfilling construction and work connected therewith obstacles are discovered to the proper performance of the contract of construction independent-work, each of the parties shall be obliged to take all reasonable measures within its control to eliminate such obstacles. The party who does not perform this duty shall lose the right to compensation of losses caused by the fact that the respective obstacles were not eliminated.

The expenses of the party connected with the performance of the duties specified in paragraph one of the present Article shall be subject to compensation by the other party when this is provided for by the contract of construction independent-work.

Article 678. Duties of Independent-Work Contractor Relating to Protection of Environment and Safety of Conducting Construction Work

The independent-work contractor when effectuating construction and work connected therewith shall be obliged to comply with the requirements of legislation concerning protection of the environment and the safety of construction work and shall bear responsibility to third persons for a violation of these requirements.

The independent-work contractor shall not have the right to use materials and equipment (parts, construction designs) in the course of effectuating work provided by the customer or to fulfill his instructions if this may lead to a violation of requirements for the protection of the environment and safety of conducting construction work which are obligatory for the parties.

Article 679. Duties of Customer in Event of Shutting Down of Construction

If for reasons beyond the control of the parties the work under the contract of construction independent-work is suspended and the object of construction shut down, the customer shall be obliged to pay the independent-work contractor in full for the work fulfilled up to the moment of the shutting down, and also to compensate expenses caused by the necessity to terminate work and shut down the construction.

Article 680. Handing Over and Acceptance of Work

The customer who has received the communication of an independent-work contractor concerning the readiness for handing over the result of the work fulfilled under the contract of construction independent-work shall be obliged or, if this is provided for by the contract, stage of work fulfilled, immediately to embark upon the acceptance thereof.

The customer shall organize and effectuate the acceptance of the result of work at his expense unless provided otherwise by the contract of construction independent-work. In the instances provided for by legislation the representatives of State agencies and agencies of self-government of citizens must participate in the acceptance of the result of the work.

The customer, having accepted the result of individual stages of work in advance, shall bear the risk of the perishing or damaging thereof which is not the fault of the independent-work contractor, including also in instances when the fulfillment of work at the risk of the independent-work contractor has been provided for by the contract of construction independent-work.

The handing over of the result of the work by the independent-work contractor and its acceptance by the customer shall be formalized by an act signed by both parties. In the event of the refusal of one of the parties to sign the act, a notation shall be made thereon concerning this and the act shall be signed by the other party.

A unilateral act of handing over or acceptance of the result of work may be deemed by a court to be invalid only if the reasons for the refusal to sign the act are deemed by it to be substantiated.

In instances when this has been provided for by a law or contract of construction independent-work or arises from the character of the work to be fulfilled under the contract, preliminary tests must precede acceptance of the result of the work. In these instances acceptance may be effectuated only in the event of a positive result of the preliminary tests.

The customer shall have the right to refuse to accept the result of the work in the event of the discovery of defects which exclude the possibility of using it for the purpose specified in the contract of construction independent-work and can not be eliminated by the independent-work contractor, by the customer, or by a third person.

Article 681. Responsibility of Independent-Work Contractor for Quality of Work

The independent-work contractor shall bear responsibility to the customer for deviations permitted from the requirements provided for by the contract of construction independent-work, technical design, and construction norms and rules obligatory for the parties, and also for the failure to achieve the indicators of the object of construction specified in the design-estimate documentation, including those such as the production capacity of the enterprise.

In the event of the reconstruction (renewal, restructuring, restoration, and so forth) of a building or installation, the responsibility shall be placed on the independent-work contractor for a reduction or the loss of firmness, stability, or reliability of the building, installation, or part thereof.

The independent-work contractor shall not bear responsibility for petty deviations permitted by him without the consent of the customer from the design documentation if it is proved that they did not influence the quality of the object of construction.

Article 682. Guarantees of Quality in Contract of Construction Independent-Work

The independent-work contractor, unless provided otherwise by the contract of construction independent-work, shall guarantee the achievement by the object of construction of the indicators specified in the project-estimate documentation and the possibility of operation of the object in accordance with the contract throughout the extent of the guarantee period. The guarantee period shall comprise ten years from the date of acceptance of the object by the customer unless another guarantee period has been provided for by a law or by the contract.

The independent-work contractor shall bear responsibility for defects discovered within the limits of the guarantee period unless it is proved that they arose as a consequence of normal wear and tear of the object or parts thereof, the incorrect operation thereof or the incorrectness of the instructions for its operation worked out by the customer himself or by third persons involved by him, or improper repair of the object made by the customer himself or third persons involved by him.

The running of the guarantee period shall be interrupted for the entire time during the extent of which the object could not be operated as a consequence of the defects for which the independent-work contractor is liable.

In the event of the discovery during the guarantee period of the defects specified in Article 681, paragraphs one and two, of the present Code, the customer must state them to the independent-work contractor within a reasonable period upon the discovery thereof.

Article 683. Elimination of Defects at Expense of Customer

The duty of the independent-work contractor to eliminate defects at the demand of the customer and defects at the expense of the customer for which the independent-work contractor does not bear responsibility may be provided for by the contract of construction independent-work.

The independent-work contractor shall have the right to refuse fulfillment of the duty specified in paragraph one of the present Article in instances when the elimination of the defects is not connected directly with the subject of the contract of construction independent-work or can not be fulfilled by the independent-work contractor for reasons beyond his control.

Article 684. Mortgage of Land Plot

Together with the right of withholding in instances provided for by the contract of construction independent-work, the performance of any obligations of the customer under the contract, including payment for work fulfilled, may be secured also by a mortgage of the land plot on which construction is effectuated or work connected therewith.

Article 685. Legal Regulation of Construction Independent-Work

Relations under the contract of construction independent-work shall be regulated by the present Code, and also by legislation on construction independent-work.

§ 4. Independent-Work Contract for Design and Survey Work

Article 686. Contract of Independent-Work for Design and Survey Work

Under a contract of independent-work for design and survey work the independent-work contractor (or designer, surveyor) shall within the established periods be obliged to work out design-estimate documentation according to the planning task of the customer and/or to fulfill the survey work, and the customer shall be obliged to accept and to pay for the result thereof.

Unless provided otherwise by a law or the contract, the risk of accidental impossibility of performance of the contract for design and survey work shall lie on the customer.

Article 687. Base Data for Fulfillment of Design and Survey Work

Under a contract of independent-work for design and survey work the customer shall be obliged to transfer to the independent-work contractor a planning task for the design, and also other base data necessary in order to draw up the design-estimate documentation. The planning task for the designing may be prepared on behalf of the customer by the independent-work contractor. In this event the planning task shall become obligatory for the parties from the moment of its confirmation by the customer.

The independent-work contractor shall be obliged to comply with the requirements contained in the planning task and other base data for the fulfillment of the design and survey work and shall have the right to deviate from such only with the consent of the customer.

Article 688. Duties of Customer

Under an independent-work contract for design and survey work the customer shall be obliged, unless provided otherwise by the contract, to:

pay the independent-work contractor the established price in full after the completion of all work or to pay for it in parts after the completion of individual stages of work;

use design-estimate documentation received from the independent-work contractor only for the purposes provided for by the contract, not transfer the design-estimate documentation to third persons, and not divulge the data contained therein without the consent of the independent-work contractor;

render assistance to the independent-work contractor in the fulfillment of design and survey work to the extent and on the conditions provided for in the contract;

participate together with the independent-work contractor in agreeing the finished design-estimate documentation with the respective State agencies and agencies of self-government of citizens;

compensate the independent-work contractor for additional expenses caused by a change of base data for the fulfillment of design and survey work as a consequence of the circumstances not dependent on the independent-work contractor;

involve the independent-work contractor to participate in the case with regard to a suit brought against the customer by a third person in connection with shortcomings in the design-estimate documentation drawn up or survey work fulfilled.

Article 689. Duties of Independent-Work Contractor

Under a contract of independent-work for design and survey work the independent-work contractor shall be obliged to:

fulfill work in accordance with the planning task and other base data for the design;

agree the finished project-estimate documentation with the customer, and also together with the customer, with respective State agencies and agencies of self-government of citizens;

transfer the finished project-estimate documentation to the customer and the results of the survey work.

not transfer project-estimate documentation to third persons without the consent of the customer.

Article 690. Guarantees of Independent-Work Contractor

The independent-work contractor under a contract of independent-work for design and survey work shall guarantee to the customer the absence with third persons of the right to obstruct the fulfillment or limit the fulfillment of the work on the basis of the project-estimate documentation prepared by the independent-work contractor.

Article 691. Responsibility of Independent-Work Contractor for Defects of Documentation and Work

The independent-work contractor under a contract of independent-work for design and survey work shall bear responsibility for the defects of project-estimate documentation and survey work, including defects discovered subsequently in the course of construction, and also in the process of operation of the object created on the basis of project-estimate documentation and the data of survey work.

In the event of the discovery of defects in the project-estimate documentation or in the survey work the independent-work contractor shall be obliged at the demand of the customer to redo the project-estimate documentation without compensation and respectively make necessary additional survey work, and also to compensate the customer for losses caused unless established otherwise by a law or by the contract.

Article 692. Legal Regulation of Independent-Work for Design and Survey Work

Relations with regard to a contract of independent-work for design and survey work shall be regulated by the present Code, and also by legislation on independent-work for design and survey work.

§ 5. Independent-Work for Scientific-Research, Experimental-Construction Design, and Technological Work

Article 693. Contracts of Independent-Work for Scientific-Research Work and Experimental-Construction Design and Technological Work

Under a contract of independent-work for scientific-research work, the independent-work contractor (or executor) shall be obliged to carry on the scientific research stipulated by the planning task of the customer, and under a contract of independent-work for experimental construction design and technological work – to work out the model of a new manufacture, construction design documentation for it, new technology, or to manufacture the model. The customer shall be obliged in so doing to issue a technical planning task to the independent-work contractor (or executor), accept the work and to pay for it.

A contract with the independent-work contractor may encompass both the entire cycle of conducting the research, development, and manufacture of the models, or individual stages (or elements) thereof.

Article 694. Fulfillment of Work

The independent-work contractor shall be obliged to conduct scientific research personally. Unless provided otherwise by the contract of independent-work for scientific research work, he shall have the right to involve third persons to perform the contract with the consent of the customer.

In the event of the fulfillment of experimental-construction design or technological work the independent-work contractor shall have the right, unless provided otherwise by the contract, to involve third persons in the performance thereof as subindependent-work contractors. The rules provided for by Article 634 of the present Code shall apply to relations of the executor with third persons.

Article 695. Confidentiality of Information Concerning the Contract

Unless provided otherwise by the contract for scientific-research work, or for experimental-construction design, and technological work, the parties shall be obliged to ensure the confidentiality of information affecting the subject of the contract, the course of its performance, and the results received. The amount of information deemed to be confidential shall be determined in the contract. The independent-work contractor shall have the right with the written consent of the customer to effectuate the patenting of the results of the work received with regard to the said contract.

Article 696. Rights of Parties to Results of Work

The parties to contracts for scientific-research, experimental-construction design, and technological work shall have the right to use the results of the work, including that capable of legal protection, within the limits and on the conditions provided for by the contract.

Unless provided otherwise by the contract, the customer shall have the right to use the results of work transferred to him by the independent-work contractor, including that capable of legal protection, and the independent-work contractor shall have the right to use the results of the work received by him for own needs.

Article 697. Duties of Customer

The customer under contracts of independent-work for scientific-research, experimental-construction design, and technological work shall be obliged to:

issue to the independent-work contractor a technical planning task and agree the program or theme of work with him (technical-economic parameters);

transfer information to the independent-work contractor necessary for the fulfillment of work;

accept the work fulfilled and pay for it.

Article 698. Duties of Independent-Work Contractor

The independent-work contractor under contracts for scientific-research work, experimental-construction design, and technological work shall be obliged to:

fulfill work in accordance with the program (technical-economic parameters) or theme agreed with the customer and transfer to the customer the results thereof within the period provided for by the contract;

comply with the requirements connected with the legal protection of intellectual property;

eliminate with his own forces and at his expense defects permitted through his fault in the work fulfilled which might entail deviations from the technical-economic parameters provided for in the technical planning task of the customer or in the contract;

immediately inform the customer about the impossibility discovered of receiving the anticipated results or the inadvisability of continuing the work;

guarantee to the customer the absence with third persons of exclusive rights to the results transferred on the basis of such contracts.

Unless provided otherwise by contracts for scientific research or for experimental-construction design and technological work, the independent-work contractor shall be obliged to:

refrain from the publication of the scientific-technical results received when fulfilling the work without the consent of the customer;

take measures in order to defend the results received when fulfilling the work which are capable of legal protection and inform the customer thereof;

grant to the customer an exclusive license for the use of the scientific-technical results which have legal protection applied in the work fulfilled.

Article 699. Consequences of Impossibility of Achieving Result in Contract for Scientific Research Work

If in the course of scientific research work the impossibility is discovered of achieving the results as a consequence of circumstances beyond the control of the independent-work contractor, the customer shall be obliged to pay for the cost of the work conducted until the eliciting of the impossibility of receiving the results provided for by the contract, but not higher than the respective part of the price of the work specified in the contract.

Article 700. Consequences of Impossibility of Achieving Result in Contract for Experimental-Construction Design and Technological Work

If in the course of the fulfillment of experimental-construction design and technological work the impossibility or inadvisability of continuing work is discovered which arose not through the fault of the independent-work contractor, the customer shall be obliged to pay for the expenditures incurred by the independent-work contractor.

Article 701. Responsibility of Independent-Work Contractor for Violation of Contract

The independent-work contractor shall bear responsibility to the customer for the failure to perform or the improper performance of a contract for scientific-research work, experimental-construction design, and technological work unless it is proved that such violation of the contract occurred not through its fault.

The independent-work contractor shall be obliged to compensate losses of the customer in the form of real damage within the limits of the cost of the work unless provided otherwise by the contract.

Article 702. Legal Regulation of Contracts of Independent-Work for Scientific-Research Work, Experimental-Construction Design, and Technological Work

Relations under a contract for scientific-research work or experimental-construction design and technological work shall be regulated together with the present Code by legislation on contracts for scientific-research, experimental-construction design, and technological work.

Chapter 38. Compensated Rendering of Services

Article 703. Contract of Compensated Rendering of Services

Under a contract of compensated rendering of services the performer shall be obliged under the planning task of the customer to render services (or perform determined actions or effectuate a determined activity) not having a material form, and the customer shall be obliged to pay for these services.

The rules of the present Chapter shall apply to contracts for the rendering of communications, medical, veterinary, auditor, consulting, and informational services, services relating to teaching, tourist servicing, and others, except for services rendered under contracts provided for by Chapters 37, 39, 40, 43, 44, 45, 46, 48, 49, and 51 of the present Code.

Article 704. Performance of Contract of Compensated Rendering of Services

In the absence in the contract of other instructions, the executor shall be obliged to render the service(s) provided for by the contract personally.

Article 705. Payment for Services

The customer shall be obliged to pay for services rendered to him within the periods and in the procedure which has been specified in the contract of compensated rendering of services.

In the event of the impossibility of performance which arose not through the fault of the executor, the customer shall be obliged to compensate the executor for expenses incurred by him less the advantages which the executor acquired or could acquire as a consequence of being relieved from the rendering of the service(s). In an event when the impossibility of performance arose through the fault of the customer, the price of the services shall be subject to payment in full unless provided otherwise by legislation or by the contract.

Article 706. Responsibility of Executor for Violation of Contract of Compensated Rendering of Services

In instances of the failure of the executor to fulfill or of the improper fulfillment of a contract of compensated rendering of services the performer shall be obliged to compensate the customer for losses caused in full but not higher than twice the amount of the price of services provided for by the contract.

In instances when the executor has not performed or improperly performed the obligation when effectuating entrepreneurial activity, higher responsibility than specified in paragraph one of the present Article may be provided for by the contract for compensated rendering of services.

Article 707. Dissolution of Contract of Compensated Rendering of Services

The customer shall have the right to demand dissolution of the contract of compensated rendering of services on condition of the payment in full of the established price thereof, except for instances when dissolution of the contract is caused by the guilty actions of the executor.

The executor shall have the right to demand dissolution of the contract of compensated rendering of services only on condition of the full compensation to the customer of losses caused by dissolution of the contract, except when this occurred through the fault of the customer.

Article 708. Legal Regulation of Contract of Compensated Rendering of Services

The general provisions on independent-work contract and the provisions on domestic independent-work contract shall apply to the contract of compensated rendering of services unless this is contrary to the rules of the present Chapter.

Chapter 39. Carriage

Article 709. General Provisions on Carriage

The carriage of passengers, baggage, and goods shall be effectuated on the basis of the contract of carriage.

The general conditions of carriage shall be determined by the present Code, transport charters and codes, other laws, and rules issued in accordance with them.

The conditions for the carriage of passengers, baggage, and goods by individual types of transport, and also responsibility of the parties for these carriages, shall be determined by agreement of the parties unless established otherwise by the present Code, transport charters and codes, other laws, and rules issued in accordance with them.

Article 710. Contract of Carriage of Passenger

Under the contract of carriage of a passenger, the carrier shall be obliged to carry the passenger to the point of destination, and in the event of the passenger handing over baggage, also to deliver the baggage to the point of destination and to issue it to the person empowered to receive the baggage. The passenger shall be obliged to pay the established payment for the travel, and in the event of handing over baggage, also for the carriage of the baggage.

The conclusion of a contract of carriage of a passenger and baggage shall be certified respectively by a ticket and by a baggage receipt.

The passenger shall have the right in the procedure provided for by the respective transport charter or code to:

carry children with him free of charge or on privileged conditions;

carry free of charge his baggage within the limits of established norms;

hand over baggage for carriage free of charge within the limits of established norms, and in the event of exceeding the norms, for payment according to the tariff.

Article 711. Contract of Carriage of Goods

Under a contract for the carriage of goods the carrier shall be obliged to deliver the goods entrusted to him by the consignor at the point of destination and to issue them to the person (or recipient) empowered to receive the goods, and the consignor shall be obliged to pay the established payment for the carriage of the goods.

The conclusion of the contract of carriage of goods shall be confirmed by drawing up and issuing to the consignor of the goods a document (transport waybill, bill of lading or other document for goods) provided for by the respective transport charter or code.

Article 712. Contract of Charter

Under a contract of charter one party (charterer) shall be obliged to grant to the other party (charteree) for payment all or part of the capacity of one or several means of transport for one or several voyages for the carriage of passengers, baggage, and goods.

The procedure for the conclusion of the contract of charter, and also the form and types thereof, shall be established by transport charters and codes.

Article 713. Direct Mixed Transport

The mutual relations of transport organizations in the event of the carriage of passengers, baggage, and goods by various types of transport under a single transport document (direct mixed transport), and also the procedure for the organization of these carriages, shall be determined by agreements between the organizations of the respective types of transport concluded in accordance with legislation on direct mixed (or combined) carriages.

Article 714. Carriage by Transport of Common Use

Carriage being effectuated by a commercial organization shall be deemed to be carriage by transport of common use if from legislation or the authorization (or license) issued to this organization it arises that this organization is obliged to effectuate the carriage of passengers, baggage, and/or goods upon the recourse of any citizen or juridical person.

A contract of carriage by transport of common use shall be a public contract.

Article 715. Fare

The fare established by agreement of the parties, unless provided otherwise by legislation, shall be recovered for the carriage of passengers, baggage, and goods.

Payment for the carriage of passengers, baggage, and goods by transport of common use shall be determined on the basis of tariffs confirmed in the procedure established by transport charters and codes.

Work and services being fulfilled by the carrier at the demand of the goods possessor and not provided for by the tariffs shall be paid by agreement of the parties.

The carrier shall have the right to withhold goods transferred to him for carriage to secure the fare due to him and other payments relating to carriage unless established otherwise by legislation, the contract of carriage, or does not arise from the essence of the obligation.

Article 716. Supply of Means of Transport, Loading (or Unloading) of Goods

The carrier shall be obliged to supply to the consignor of goods for loading within the period established by the application (or order) accepted from him, by the contract of carriage, or by the contract concerning the organization of carriages, means of transport in good repair in a state fit for carriage of the respective goods.

The consignor of goods shall have the right to refuse the means of transport supplied which are not fit for the carriage of the respective goods.

The loading (or unloading) of the goods shall be effectuated by the transport organization or consignor (or consignee) in the procedure provided for by the contract of carriage in compliance with the rules established by the transport charters and codes and by the rules issued in accordance with them.

The loading (or unloading) of goods effectuated by the forces and means of the consignor (or consignee) of the goods must be done within the periods provided for by the contract unless such periods have been established by the transport charters and codes and with the rules issued in accordance therewith.

Article 717. Periods of Delivery of Passenger, Baggage, and Goods

The carrier shall be obliged to deliver the passenger, baggage, or goods to the point of destination within the periods determined in the procedure provided for by the transport charters and codes, and in the absence of such periods, within a reasonable period.

Article 718. Responsibility for Violation of Obligations Arising from Carriage

In the event of the failure to perform or the improper performance of obligations arising from carriage, the parties shall bear responsibility established by the present Code, transport charters and codes, and also by agreement of the parties.

The agreements of transport organizations with passengers and goods possessors concerning the limitation or elimination of the responsibility of the carrier established by a law shall be invalid.

Article 719. Responsibility of Carrier for Failure to Supply Means of Transport and of Consignor for Failure to Use Means of Transport Supplied

The carrier shall bear the responsibility established by transport charters and codes, and also by agreement of the parties, for the failure to supply means of transport for the carriage of goods in accordance with an accepted application (or order) or other contract of carriage, and the consignor for the failure to present the goods or failure to use the means of transport supplied for other reasons.

The carrier and the consignor of goods shall be relieved from responsibility in the event of the failure to supply or the untimely supply of means of transport or the failure to use the means of transport supplied if this occurred as a consequence of:

insuperable force or other phenomena of a natural character, and also military actions;

termination or limitation of the carriage of goods in determined directions established in the procedure provided for by the respective transport charter or code.

Article 720. Responsibility of Carrier for Delay of Departure of Passenger

For a delay of the departure of the means of transport for the carriage of a passenger, or for the late arrival of such means of transport at the point of destination, except for carriages on city and suburban transport, the carrier shall pay to the passenger a penalty in the form of a fine unless it is proved that the delay or lateness occurred as a consequence of insuperable force, or other circumstances beyond the control of the carrier. The amount and procedure for payment of the fine shall be established by transport charters and codes.

The payment of a fine to the passenger shall not relieve the carrier from the duty to compensate the passenger for losses incurred by him as a consequence of delay of the departure of a means of transport or the lateness of arrival at the point of destination.

In the event of the refusal of the passenger of carriage by reason of delay of the departure of the means of transport, the carrier shall be obliged to return the fare and other expenses incurred by him to the passenger.

Article 721. Responsibility of Carrier for Loss, Shortage, and Damage (or Spoilage) of Goods or Baggage

The carrier shall bear responsibility for the loss, shortage, or damage (or spoilage) of goods and baggage accepted unless it is proved that the loss, shortage, or damage (or spoilage) of the goods or baggage occurred not through his fault.

Damage caused during the carriage of goods or baggage shall be compensated by the carrier in the following amount:

in the event of the loss or shortage of goods or baggage – in the amount of the value of the lost or short delivered goods or baggage;

in the event of damage (or spoilage) of the goods or baggage – in the amount by which its value was reduced, and if it is impossible to restore the damaged (or spoiled) good or baggage – in the amount of its value;

in the event of the loss of the goods or baggage handed over to the carrier with a declaration of the value thereof – in the amount of the declared value of the goods or baggage.

The transport organization shall together with compensation of the real damage return to the consignor (or recipient) the carriage payment recovered for carriage of the lost, short delivered, or damaged (or spoiled) goods unless this payment is part of the price of the goods.

The consignor shall have the right to demand from the carrier compensation and other losses caused by the loss, short delivery, or damage (or spoilage) of the goods.

The carriers in direct mixed transport shall be liable to the goods consignor (or goods consignee) jointly and severally for the loss, short delivery, or damaging (or spoilage) of the goods.

Responsibility for delay shall be borne by the last carrier unless it is proved that the delay occurred not through the fault of the carrier.

Article 722. Contracts on Organization of Carriages

The carrier and goods possessor may, in the event of the necessity to effectuate the systematic carriages of goods, conclude long-term contracts concerning the organization of carriages.

Under a contract of the organization of carriage of goods the carrier shall be obliged within the established periods to accept, and the goods possessor to present goods for carriage in the stipulated amount. The amounts, periods, and other conditions for granting means of transport and presenting goods for carriage, the procedure for the settlement of accounts, and also other conditions for the organization of carriage, shall be determined in the contract concerning the organization of the carriage of goods.

Article 723. Contracts Between Transport Organizations

Contracts concerning the organization of work relating to ensuring the carriage of goods (junction agreements, contracts for centralized delivery (or export) of goods and others) may be concluded between organizations of various types of transport. The procedure for the conclusion of such contracts shall be determined by transport charters and codes, and other legislation.

Article 724. Claims and Suits With Regard to Carriages of Goods

Before bringing suit against a carrier arising from the carriage of goods the presentation to him of a claim in the procedure provided for by the respective transport charter or code shall be obligatory.

A suit against the carrier may be brought by the consignor or consignee in the event of the full or partial refusal of the carrier to satisfy the claim or the failure to receive a reply from the carrier within a thirty-day period.

The period of limitations with regard to demands arising from the carriage of goods shall be established at one year from the moment determined in accordance with Article 154 of the present Code.

The rules of the present Article shall not extend to demands arising from the carriage of a passenger or baggage.

Article 725. Responsibility of Carrier for Causing Harm to Life or Health of Passenger

The responsibility of a carrier for harm caused to the life or health of a passenger shall be determined according to the rules of Chapter 57 of the present Code unless increased responsibility of the carrier has been provided for by a law or by the contract.

Chapter 40. Transport Expediting

Article 726. Contract of Transport Expediting

Under a contract of transport expediting the expeditor shall be obliged for remuneration and at the expense of the client (consignor or consignee) to fulfill or organize the fulfillment of the services connected with the carriage of goods determined by the contract of expediting.

The duties of the expeditor to organize the carriage of goods by transport and according to the route selected by the expeditor or the client, the duty of the expeditor to conclude a contract(s) for the carriage of goods in the name of the client or in his own name, to ensure the sending and receipt of the goods, and also other duties connected with carriage may be provided for by the contract of transport expediting.

The effectuating of such operations necessary for the delivery of goods as the receipt of documents required for export or import, the fulfillment of customs and other formalities, verification of the quantity and state of cargo, the loading and unloading thereof, the payment of duties, charges, and other expenses placed on the client, the keeping of goods, the receipt thereof at the point of destination, and also the fulfillment of other operations and services provided for by the contract, may be provided for by the contract of transport expediting as additional services.

The rules of the present Chapter shall extend also to instances when in accordance with the contract of transport expediting the duties of expeditor are performed by the carrier.

The conditions of the fulfillment of the contract of transport expediting shall be determined by agreement of the parties unless established otherwise by legislation on transport-expediting activity.

Article 727. Form of Contract

The contract of transport expediting shall be concluded in written form.

The client must issue a power of attorney to the expeditor if it is necessary for the fulfillment of his duties.

Article 728. Responsibility of Expeditor Under Contract of Transport Expediting

For the failure to perform or the improper performance of duties under the contract of expediting the expeditor shall bear responsibility on the grounds and in the amounts which are determined in accordance with the rules of Chapter 24 of the present Code.

If the expeditor proves that a violation of the obligation has been caused by the improper performance of the contracts of carriage, the responsibility of the expeditor to the client shall be determined according to the same rules under which the respective carrier is liable to the expeditor.

Article 729. Documents and Other Information Granted to Expeditor

The client shall be obliged to grant to the expeditor documents and other information concerning the properties of the goods, conditions of carriage thereof, and also other information necessary for the performance of the duty by the expeditor provided for by the contract of transport expediting.

The expeditor shall be obliged to communicate to the client information received about defects discovered, and in the event of the incompleteness of the information to request necessary additional data from the client.

In the event of the failure of the client to grant the necessary information, the expeditor shall have the right not to commence performance of the respective duties until such information is granted.

The client shall bear responsibility for losses caused to the expeditor in connection with the violation of the duty relating to the granting of the information specified in paragraph one of the present Article.

Article 730. Performance of Duties of Expeditor by Third Person

Unless the duty of the expeditor arises from the contract of transport expediting to perform his duties personally, the expeditor shall have the right to involve other persons in the performance of his duties.

The imposition of the performance of an obligation on a third person shall not relieve the expeditor from responsibility to the client for the performance of the contract of transport expediting.

Article 731. Repudiation of Contract of Transport Expediting

The client or expeditor shall have the right to refuse performance of a contract of transport expediting, having warned the other party thereof ten days in advance.

In the event of the unilateral refusal to perform the contract of transport expediting, the party which has declared the refusal shall compensate the other party for losses caused by the termination of the contract.

Chapter 41. Loan and Credit

§ 1. Loan

Article 732. Contract of Loan

Under a contract of loan one party (lender) shall transfer to the ownership of the other party (borrower) money or other things determined by generic indicators, and the borrower shall be obliged to return to the lender in a lump sum or by installment the same amount of money or equal quantity of other things received by him of the same kind and quality.

The contract of loan shall be considered to be concluded from the moment of transfer of the money or things.

Article 733. Form of Contract of Loan

A contract of loan between citizens must be concluded in simple written form if the amount thereof exceeds ten times the established base calculation amount, and when the party to the contract is a juridical person, irrespective of the amount [as amended by Law of 3 December 2019, No. 3PУ-586].

The failure to comply with the written form of the contract of loan shall entail the consequences provided for by Article 109 of the present Code.

The contract of loan shall be deemed to be concluded in written form when there is a receipt of the borrower or other document certifying the transfer to him by the lender of the determined amount or determined quantity of things.

The written form of the contract of loan shall be considered to be complied with if the loan obligation is certified by a bill of exchange, bond, or other security issued by the borrower determining the amount of the loan and the rights of the lender to recover it.

Article 734. Interest Under Contract of Loan

Unless provided otherwise by a law or by the contract of loan, the lender (juridical person or citizen) shall have the right to receive interest from the borrower on the amount of the loan in the amounts and in the procedure determined by the contract.

If under the contract of loan things are transferred to the borrower which are determined by generic indicia, interest shall be subject to payment in the event when the amount thereof and the form (monetary or in kind) has been provided for by the contract.

The procedure and periods for the payment of interest shall be established by the contract of loan. If the procedure and periods for the payment of interest have not been established by the contract, then they shall be paid in the procedure and within the periods provided for by the contract for return of the principal debt.

Article 735. Duty of Borrower to Return Amount of Loan

The borrower shall be obliged to return to the lender the amount of loan received within the period and in the procedure provided for by the contract of loan.

If the period of return of the amount of the loan is not established, it must be returned by the borrower within thirty days from the date of presentation by the lender of the demand therefor.

The amount of an interest-free loan may be returned by the borrower before time.

The amount of the loan granted under interest may be returned before time if this is permitted by the contract of loan or with the consent of the lender.

Article 736. Consequences of Violation by Borrower of Contract of Loan

Unless provided otherwise by legislation or by the contract of loan, in instances when the borrower does not return the amount of the loan within the period interest shall be subject to payment on this amount in the amount provided for by Article 327, paragraphs one and two, of the present Code from the day when it should have been returned until the day of its return to the lender irrespective of the payment of interest provided for by Article 734, paragraph one, of the present Code.

If return of the loan has been provided for by the contract of loan in parts (or installment), then in the event of a violation of the period established for return of the regular part of the loan by the borrower, the lender shall have the right to demand the return of the entire amount remaining before time together with the interest due.

If payment of interest on the loan within the periods outstrips the period for return of the loan itself which have been provided for by the contract of loan, then in the event of the violation of this duty the lender shall have the right to require return of the amount of the loan before time by the borrower together with the interest due.

Article 737. Contesting Contract of Loan

The borrower shall have the right to contest a contract of loan, proving that the money or other things in reality were not received by him from the lender or were received in a lesser quantity than specified in the contract.

A contract of loan which must be concluded in written form may not be contested with the assistance of witness testimony, except for instances when the contract was concluded under the influence of fraud, coercion, threat, or ill-intentioned agreement of a representative of the borrower with the lender or the confluence of grave circumstances.

If in the process of the contesting of a contract of loan by the borrower it is established that the money or other things in reality were not received from the lender, the contract of loan shall be considered to be not concluded. When money or other things in reality were received by the borrower from the lender in a lesser quantity than is specified in the contract, the contract shall be considered to be concluded for this quantity of money or things.

Article 738. Securing Performance of Obligations of Borrower

In the event of the failure of the borrower to fulfill the duties provided for by the contract of loan with regard to securing the return of the amount of the loan, and also in the event of the loss of security or a worsening of its conditions under circumstances for which the lender is not liable, the lender shall have the right to require from the borrower the repayment of the amount of the loan before time and the payment of interest due unless provided otherwise by the contract.

Article 739. Special-Purpose Loan

If a contract of loan was concluded with a condition of the use by the borrower of means received for specified purposes (special-purpose loan), the borrower shall be obliged to ensure the possibility of the effectuation by the lender of control over the special-purpose use of the amount of the loan.

In the event of the failure to fulfill the conditions of the contract of loan by the borrower concerning the special-purpose use of the amount of the loan, the lender shall have the right to require from the borrower repayment of the amount of the loan before time and the payment of interest due unless provided otherwise by the contract.

Article 740. Bill of Exchange

In instances when in accordance with an agreement of the parties a bill of exchange is issued by the borrower certifying the unconditional obligation of the issuer (promissory note) or other payer specified in the bill of exchange (bill of exchange) to pay the monetary amounts upon the ensuing of the period provided for by the bill of exchange, the relations of the parties shall be regulated by legislation.

Article 741. Bond

In instances provided for by legislation a contract of loan may be concluded by means of the issuance and sale of bonds.

A bond shall be deemed to be a security certifying the right of its holder to receive from the person who issued the bond the par value of the bond within the period provided for therein or other property equivalent. A bond shall grant to its holder also the right to receive the interest fixed therein on the par value of the bond or other property rights.

Article 742. Novation of Debt and Loan Obligation

By agreement of the parties any debt which has arisen from purchase-sale, rental of property, or other grounds may be replaced by a loan obligation.

The replacement of a debt by a loan obligation shall be effectuated in compliance with the rules concerning novation provided for by Article 347 of the present Code and concluded in the form established for a contract of loan.

Article 743. Contract of State Loan

Under a contract of State loan the borrower is the State, and the lender is a citizen or juridical person.

State loans shall be voluntary.

The contract of State loan shall be concluded by means of the acquisition by the lender of issued State bonds or other State securities certifying the right of the lender to receive from the borrower the monetary means granted to it on loan or, depending upon the conditions of the loan, other property, established interest, or other property rights within the periods provided for by the conditions of the issuance of the loan into circulation.

A change of the conditions of a loan issued into circulation (converting of loan), including on the grounds provided for by Article 383 of the present Code, shall not be permitted, except for instances provided for by legislation.

The State shall bear responsibility under the contract of State loan in accordance with the rules of the present Code.

§ 2. Credit

Article 744. Credit Contract

Under a credit contract one party – a bank or other credit organization (creditor) – shall be obliged to grant monetary means (credit) to the other party (borrower) in the amount and on the conditions provided for by the contract, and the borrower shall be obliged to return the monetary amount received and to pay interest on it.

In instances when in accordance with legislation the effectuation of granting credits by commercial organizations is permitted which are not credit organizations, the rules concerning the credit contract shall apply to relations relating to the granting of credits effectuated by such commercial organizations.

The rules of paragraph 1 of the present Chapter shall apply to relations under the credit contract unless provided otherwise by the rules of the present paragraph and does not arise from the essence of the credit contract.

Article 745. Form of Credit Contract

A credit contract must be concluded in written form.

The failure to comply with the written form shall entail the invalidity of the credit contract. Such contract shall be considered null.

Article 746. Refusal to Grant or Receive Credit

A creditor shall have the right to refuse to grant a credit to the borrower provided for by a credit contract wholly or partially in the event the borrower is deemed to be insolvent, of the failure to fulfill the duties relating to securing the credit, of a violation of the duty provided for by the contract of special-purpose use of the credit, and also in other instances provided for by the contract.

The borrower shall have the right to refuse to receive a credit wholly or partially. He must inform the creditor thereof before the period established by the contract for granting the credit unless provided otherwise by legislation or the credit contract. In the event of a violation by the borrower of the duties provided for by the credit contract for the special-purpose use of the credit, the creditor shall have the right to refuse further granting of credits to the borrower under the contract.

Article 747. Contract on Granting Things on Credit

A contract may be concluded by the parties which provides for the duty of one party to grant to the other party things determined by generic indicia on the conditions of a credit contract.

Unless provided otherwise by the contract on granting things on credit, the conditions thereof concerning the quantity, assortment, sets, quality, packing and/or packaging of the things being granted must be performed in accordance with the rules on the contract of purchase-sale of goods.

Article 748. Commercial Credit

The granting of a credit, including in the form of an advance, preliminary payment, deferral, and installment payment of goods, work, or services (commercial credit) may be provided for by contracts whose performance is connected with the transfer to the ownership of the other party of monetary amounts or other things determined by generic indicia, unless established otherwise by legislation.

The rules of the present Chapter shall apply to the commercial credit respectively unless provided otherwise by the rules on the contract from which the respective obligation arose and is not contrary to the essence of such obligation.

Chapter 42. Financing Under Assignment of Monetary Demand

Article 749. Contract of Financing Under Assignment of Monetary Demand

Under a contract of financing under assignment of a monetary demand one party (financial agent) shall transfer or shall be obliged to transfer to the other party (client) monetary means at the expense of a monetary demand of the client (creditor) to a third person (debtor) arising from goods granted by the client, the fulfillment of work by him, or the rendering of services to a third person, and the client shall assign or shall be obliged to assign this monetary demand to the financial agent.

A monetary demand against a debtor may be assigned by the client to a financial agent also for the purpose of securing the performance of an obligation of the client to the financial agent.

The obligations of the financial agent under a contract of financing under assignment of monetary demand may include the keeping of bookkeeping records for the client, and also the granting to the client of other financial services connected with monetary demands which are the subject of the assignment.

Article 750. Financial Agent

Banks and other credit organizations may in the capacity of a financial agent conclude contracts of financing under assignment of monetary demand [as amended by Law of 20 April 2022, No. ЗРУ-765].

Article 751. Monetary Demand Assigned for Purposes of Receiving Financing

Both a monetary demand, the period for the payment of which has already ensued (existing demand) and the right to receive monetary means which arise in the future (future demand) may be the subject of an assignment under which financing is granted.

A monetary demand which is the subject of an assignment must be determined in the contract of the client with the financial agent such that it enables the existing demand to be identified at the moment of conclusion of the contract, and a future demand, not later than at the moment it arises.

When assigning a future monetary demand, it shall be considered to have passed to the financial agent after the right itself arose to receive the monetary means from the debtor which are the subject of assignment of the demand provided for by the contract. If the assignment of a monetary demand is conditioned by a determined event, it shall enter into force after the ensuing of this event. In these instances additional formalization of the assignment of the monetary demand shall not be required.

Article 752. Responsibility of Client to Financial Agent

Unless provided otherwise by the contract of financing under assignment of monetary demand, the client shall bear responsibility to the financial agent for the validity of the monetary demand which is the subject of the assignment.

A monetary demand which is the subject of assignment shall be valid if the client possesses the right to transfer the monetary demand and at the moment of assignment of this demand circumstances were not known to him as a consequence of which the debtor has the right not to perform it.

A client shall not be liable for the failure to perform or the improper performance by the debtor of a demand which is the subject of an assignment in the event of the presentation thereof by the financial agent for performance unless provided otherwise by the contract between the client and the financial agent.

Article 753. Invalidity of Prohibition of Assignment of Monetary Demand

The assignment of a monetary demand to a financial agent shall be valid even if an agreement exists between the client and the debtor thereof concerning the prohibition or limitation thereof.

The provision established by paragraph one of the present Article shall not relieve the client from obligations or responsibility to the debtor in connection with the assignment of the demand in violation of an agreement existing between them concerning the prohibition or limitation thereof.

Article 754. Subsequent Assignment of Monetary Demand

Unless the contract of financing under assignment of monetary demand provides otherwise, subsequent assignment of the monetary demand by the financial agent shall not be permitted.

In instances when subsequent assignment of a monetary demand is permitted by the contract, the provisions of the present Chapter shall apply to it respectively.

Article 755. Performance of Monetary Demand by Debtor to Financial Agent

The debtor shall be obliged to make payment to a financial agent on condition that he received from the client or from the financial agent written notification concerning the assignment of the monetary demand to the particular financial agent and the monetary demand subject to performance has been determined in the notification, and also the financial agent to whom payment must be made has been specified.

At the request of the debtor, the financial agent is obliged within a reasonable period to submit evidence to the debtor that the assignment of the monetary demand to the financial agent has actually occurred. If the financial agent does not fulfill this duty, the debtor shall have the right to make payment with regard to the particular demand to the client in performance of his obligation to the last.

The performance of a monetary demand by the debtor to the financial agent in accordance with the rules of the present Article shall relieve the debtor from the respective obligation to the client.

Article 756. Rights of Financial Agent to Amounts Received from Debtor

If under the conditions of a contract of financing under assignment of a monetary demand the financing of a client is effectuated by means of the purchase from him of this demand by the financial agent, the last shall acquire the right to all the amounts which he received from the debtor in performance of the demand, and the client shall not bear responsibility to the financial agent for the amounts received by him which prove to be less than the price for which the agent acquired the demand.

If the assignment of a monetary demand to a financial agent is effectuated for the purpose of securing the performance to him of an obligation of the client and it is not provided otherwise by the contract of financing under assignment of monetary demand, the financial agent shall be obliged to submit a report to the client and to transfer to him the amount exceeding the amount of the debt of the client securing the assignment of the demand. If the monetary means received by the financial agent from the debtor prove to be less than the amount of the debt of the client to the financial agent secured by the assignment of the demand, the client shall remain responsible to the financial agent for the balance of the debt.

Article 757. Counter Demands of Debtor

In the event of the financial agent applying to the debtor with a demand to make payment, the debtor shall have the right in accordance with Articles 343-345 of the present Code to present his own monetary demands as set-off which are based on the contract with the client that the debtor already had at the time when notification was received by him concerning the assignment of the demand to the financial agent.

Demands which the debtor might present to the client in connection with a violation by the last of the agreement concerning the prohibition or limitation of the assignment of a demand shall not have force with respect to the financial agent.

Article 758. Return to Debtor of Amounts Received by Financial Agent

In the event of a violation by the client of his obligations under the contract concluded with the debtor, the last shall not have the right to demand from the financial agent the return of amounts already paid to him under the demand transferred to the agent if the debtor has the right to receive such amounts directly from the client.

A debtor who has the right to receive amounts directly from the client paid to the financial agent as a result of the assignment of a demand nonetheless shall have the right to demand the return of these amounts by the financial agent if it is proved that the last did not perform his obligation to effectuate the promised payment to the client connected with the assignment or the demand or made such payment knowing about the violation by the client of the obligation to the debtor to which the payment relates connected with the assignment of the demand.

Chapter 43. Bank Deposit

Article 759. Contract of Bank Deposit

Under a contract of bank deposit one party (bank), having accepted a monetary amount (deposit) from the other party (depositor) or received for him, shall be obliged to return the amount of the deposit and to pay interest on it on the conditions and in the procedure provided for by the contract.

The contract of bank deposit shall be considered to be concluded from the day of receipt of the amount of the deposit in the bank.

The contract of bank deposit in which the depositor is a citizen shall be deemed to be a public contract.

To relations of the bank and depositor with regard to an account to which a deposit has been made the rules concerning the contract of bank account shall apply unless provided otherwise by the rules of the present Chapter or does not arise from the essence of the contract of bank deposit.

The rules of the present Chapter relating to banks also shall apply to other credit organizations accepting deposits from juridical persons in accordance with legislation.

Article 760. Right to Attract Monetary Means as Deposits

Banks shall have the right to attract monetary means as deposits to whom such right has been granted by a license issued in the procedure established by legislation.

In the event of the acceptance of a deposit from a citizen by a person not having this right, the depositor may require the immediate return of the amount of the deposit, and also payment of the interest on it provided for by Article 327 of the present Code and compensation of all losses caused to the depositor above the amount of the interest.

If the monetary means of a juridical person have been accepted by such person on the conditions of a contract of bank deposit, the respective rules of the present Code on the grounds and consequences of the invalidity of transactions shall be applied.

Unless established otherwise by a law, the consequences provided for by paragraphs two and three of the present Article shall also apply in instances of attracting monetary means of citizens and juridical persons for the deposit of:

a bill of exchange or other securities not permitting the possibility of the receipt by their holders of the deposit at first demand and the effectuation by the depositor of other rights provided for by the rules of the present Chapter

by means of the sale of stocks and other securities to them whose issuance is deemed to be illegal.

Article 761. Form of Contract of Bank Deposit

A contract of bank deposit must be concluded in written form.

The written form of a contract of bank deposit shall be considered to be complied with if the making of the deposit is certified by a savings book, savings (or deposit) certificate, or other document issued by the bank to the depositor which meets the requirements provided for such documents by a law, by banking rules established in accordance therewith, and customs of business turnover used in banking practice.

The failure to comply with the written form of the contract of bank deposit shall entail the invalidity of this contract. Such contract shall be null.

Article 762. Types of Deposits

A contract of bank deposit shall be concluded on the conditions of the issuance of the deposit at first demand (demand deposit) or on conditions of the return of the deposit upon the expiry of a period determined by the contract (time deposit).

The making of deposits on other conditions of their return which are not contrary to legislation may be provided for by the contract of bank deposit.

Under a contract of bank deposit, irrespective of the type of deposit, the bank shall be obliged to issue the amount of the deposit or part thereof at the demand of the depositor except for deposits made by juridical persons on other conditions of return provided for by the contract [as amended by Law of 30 August 2002, No. 405-II. Ведомости Олий Мажлиса (2002), no. 9, item 165].

The condition of a contract of bank deposit concerning the waiver by the citizen of the right to receive the demand deposit at first demand, and a fixed-term or other deposit – upon the expiry of the period of notice established by legislation, shall be null [as amended by Law of 30 August 2002, No. 405-II. Ведомости Олий Мажлиса (2002), no. 9, item 165].

If a depositor intended to demand the return of a fixed-term or other deposit, except for a demand deposit, before the expiry of the period or ensuing of other circumstances specified in the contract of bank deposit, he shall be obliged not later than one month in advance before the propose date of withdrawal to notify the bank of his intention [added by Law of 30 August 2002, No. 405-II. Ведомости Олий Мажлиса (2002), no. 9, item 165].

In instances when a fixed-term or other deposit, except a demand deposit, is returned to the depositor at his demand before the expiry of the period or before the ensuing of other circumstances specified in the contract of bank deposit, interest on the deposit shall not be paid on the deposit unless provided otherwise by the contract [as amended by Law of 30 August 2002, No. 405-II. Ведомости Олий Мажлиса (2002), no. 9, item 165].

In instances when the depositor does not demand the return of the amount of a time deposit upon the expiry of the period or the amount of the deposit made on other conditions of return, upon the ensuing of the circumstances provided for by the contract, the contract shall be considered to be extended on the conditions of a demand deposit unless provided otherwise by the contract.

Article 763. Interest on Deposit

The bank shall pay interest to the depositor on the amount of the deposit determined by the contract of bank deposit.

In the absence in the contract of bank deposit of a condition concerning the amount of interest to be paid, the bank shall be obliged to pay interest in the amount to be paid by the bank for demand deposits.

Unless provided otherwise by the contract of bank deposit, the bank shall have the right to change the amount of interest to be paid on demand deposits.

In the event of a reduction by the bank of the amount of interest, the new amount of interest shall apply to deposits made after depositors are notified about the reduction of interest. To deposits made before this notification the reduced amount of interest shall apply upon the expiry of a month from the moment of the respective notification unless another period has been provided for by the contract of bank deposit.

The amount of interest determined by the contract of bank deposit on a deposit made on conditions of the return thereof upon the expiry of a determined period or upon the ensuing of the circumstances provided for by the contract may not be unilaterally reduced by the bank unless provided otherwise by the contract.

Article 764. Procedure for Calculating and Payment of Interest on Deposit

Interest on the amount of a bank deposit shall be calculated from the day following the day of its receipt in the bank up to the day preceding the return thereof to the depositor or withdrawn from the account of the depositor on other grounds. Interest shall not be calculated for the period when the bank as a consequence of the imposition of arrest on the account of the depositor could not use the monetary means available in this account.

Unless provided otherwise by the contract of bank deposit, interest shall be paid on the amount of a bank deposit to the depositor at his demand upon the expiry of each month separately from the amount of the deposit, and interest not demanded within this period shall increase the amount of the deposit on which the interest is calculated.

In the event of the return of the deposit all interest calculated to this moment shall be paid.

Article 765. Ensuring Return of Deposit

The means and methods which the bank is obliged to use in order to ensure the return of deposits received by it shall be determined by a law and by the contract of bank deposit.

A bank shall be obliged to grant upon the demand of the depositor information concerning the provision for the return of the deposit.

In the event of the failure of a bank to fulfill the duties relating to ensuring the return of the deposit, and also in the event of the loss of security or worsening of its conditions, the depositor shall have the right to require from the bank the immediate return of the amount of the deposit, payment of interest thereon, and compensation of losses caused to it in accordance with Article 327 of the present Code.

Article 766. Responsibility for Failure to Fulfill Demand Concerning Return of Deposit

In the event of the failure of a bank to fulfill the demand of a depositor concerning return of the deposit or part thereof within the periods provided for by Article 762 of the present Code, the bank shall be obliged irrespective of the payment of interest on the deposit to compensate the losses caused in accordance with Article 327 of the present Code.

Article 767. Deposit of Monetary Means by Third Persons to Account of Depositor

Unless provided otherwise by the contract of bank deposit, monetary means received at a bank in the name of the depositor from third persons shall be credited to the deposit with an indication of the necessary data concerning his account on deposit. In so doing it shall be presupposed that the depositor has expressed consent to receipt of the monetary means from such persons, having granted them the necessary data concerning the account on deposit.

Article 768. Deposit to Benefit of Third Person

A deposit may be made to a bank in the name of a determined third person.

An indication of the name of the citizen or name of the juridical person to whose benefit the deposit is made shall be a material condition of the respective contract of bank deposit.

Unless provided otherwise by the contract, the third person in whose name the deposit was made shall acquire the rights of a depositor from the moment of the receipt of money in his account.

In instances when the third person in whose name the deposit was made has refused it, the person who concluded the contract of bank deposit in the name of the third person shall have the right to demand and obtain the deposit back or to transfer it to his own name.

Article 769. Savings Book

Unless provided otherwise by agreement of the parties, the conclusion of a contract of bank deposit with a citizen and the deposit of monetary means in his account on deposit shall be certified by a savings book.

In the savings book must be specified and certified by the bank the name and location of the bank or its respective branch, the number of the account on deposit, and also all the amounts of monetary means credited to the account, all amounts of monetary means withdrawn from the account, and the balance of monetary means in the account at the moment of presentation of the savings book to the bank.

Unless a different state of the deposit is proved, the data concerning the deposit specified in the savings book shall be the grounds for the settlement of accounts regarding the deposit between the bank and the depositor.

The issuance of an inscribed savings book shall be provided for by the contract of bank deposit [as amended by Law of 22 September 2009, No. ЗРУ-223. СЗ РУ (2009), no. 39, item 423].

The issuance of the deposit, payment of interest on it, and performance of the instructions of the depositor concerning the transfer of monetary means from the deposit account to other persons shall be effectuated by the bank upon the presentation of the savings book.

If an inscribed savings book is lost or is in a state unfit for presentation, the bank upon the application of the depositor shall issue him a new savings book.

[paragraph seven lost force by Law of 22 September 2009, No. ЗРУ-223. СЗ РУ (2009), no. 39, item 423].

Article 770. Savings (or Deposit) Certificate

A savings (or deposit) certificate shall be an inscribed security certifying the amount of the deposit made in a bank and the rights of the depositor (or holder of the certificate) to receive the amount of the deposit upon the expiry of the established period and the interest stipulated on the certificate at the bank which issued the certificate or any branch of this bank [as amended by Law of 22 September 2009, No. ЗРУ-223. СЗ РУ (2009), no. 39, item 423].

[paragraph two repealed by Law of 22 September 2009, No. ЗРУ-223. СЗ РУ (2009), no. 39, item 423].

In the event of the presentation of a savings (or deposit) certificate for payment before time, the amount of the deposit and the interest to be paid on the deposit on demand shall be paid by the bank unless another amount of interest is established by the conditions of the certificate.

Chapter 44. Bank Account

Article 771. Contract of Bank Account

Under a contract of bank account, one party – the bank or other credit institution (hereinafter: the bank) – shall be obliged to accept and credit monetary means entering the account opened of the other party – the client (or possessor of the account), fulfill instructions of the client concerning the transfer and issuance of respective amounts from the account and the conducting of other operations with regard to the account.

The rules of the present Chapter relating to banks also shall apply to other credit organizations when they conclude and perform a contract of bank account in accordance with an authorization (or license) issued.

Article 772. Use by Bank of Monetary Means of Client

The bank may use monetary means available in the bank account, guaranteeing their availability when demands are presented against the account and the right of the possessor thereof to dispose of these means without obstruction within the limits of the amounts situated in the account.

Article 773. Disposition by Client of Monetary Means

The client autonomously shall dispose of his monetary means situated in the account in the bank.

The bank shall not have the right to determine and control the orientations of use of the monetary means of the client nor establish other limitations of his rights to dispose of monetary means at his discretion which are not provided for by a law or by the contract of bank account.

The monetary means of a client in an account at a bank may be received in the form of cash money in the procedure established by legislation [paragraph added by Law of 15 December 2000, No. 175-II. Ведомости Олий Мажлиса (2001), no. 1-2, item 23].

Article 774. Form of Contract of Bank Account

A contract of bank account must be concluded in written form.

The failure to comply with the written form of a contract of bank account shall entail the invalidity of this contract. Such contract shall be considered to be null.

Article 775. Conclusion of Contract of Bank Account

A contract of bank account shall be concluded by means of the opening by the bank for a client or person specified by him an account in the bank on the conditions agreed by the parties.

Juridical persons and citizens autonomously shall select banks for their account and cashier servicing [as amended by Law of 30 August 1997, No. 485-I. Ведомости Олий Мажлиса (1997), no. 9, item 241].

The bank shall be obliged to conclude a contract of bank account with the client who has applied with a proposal to open the account on conditions announced by the bank for opening accounts of the particular type which correspond to the requirements provided for by a law and banking rules established in accordance therewith.

The bank shall not have the right to refuse to open the account and to perform respective operations which have been provided for by a law, the constitutive documents of the bank, and license issued to it, except for instances when such refusal is caused by the lack of the possibility for the bank to accept for bank servicing.

In the event of the unsubstantiated avoidance of a bank to conclude a contract of bank account the client shall have the right to present a demand to it provided for by Article 377, paragraphs six and seven, of the present Code.

Article 776. Certification of Right of Disposition of Monetary Means in Account

The rights of persons effectuating in the name of the client instructions concerning the debiting and issuance of means from the account shall be certified by the client by means of submitting to the bank documents provided for by a law, banking rules established in accordance therewith, and by the contract of bank account.

The client may give an instruction to the bank concerning the withdrawal of monetary means from the account at the demand of third persons, including connected with the performance by the client of his duties to these persons. The bank shall accept these instructions on condition of specifying therein in written form the necessary data enabling it when the respective demand is presented to identify the person having the right to present it and to establish the character and grounds of such demand.

The certification of the rights of disposition of monetary means in the account by electronic means of payment and other documents with the use of analogues of handwritten signatures thereon, codes, passwords, and other means confirming that the disposition is given by the person empowered for this may be provided for by the contract of bank account.

Article 777. Operations With Regard to Account to be Fulfilled by Bank

The bank shall be obliged to accept and credit monetary means coming to the account and to fulfill instructions of the client concerning the transfer and issuance of monetary means by means of performing operations provided for accounts of the particular type by a law, banking rules established in accordance therewith, and customs of business turnover applied in banking practice unless provided otherwise by the contract of bank account.

Article 778. Periods for Operations With Regard to Account

The bank shall be obliged to credit monetary means coming to the account, issue or transfer them from the account at the instruction of the client no later than the day following the day of receipt at the bank of the respective payment document unless other periods have been provided for by a law or by the contract of bank account. A violation of the established periods of operations with regard to the account shall entail for the bank the consequences provided for by Article 327 of the present Code [as amended by Law of 22 September 2009, No. 3РУ-223. С3 РУ (2009), no. 39, item 423].

Article 779. Overdrawing of Account

In instances when in accordance with the contract of bank account the bank effectuates payments with regard to demands against the client notwithstanding the absence of monetary means in his account, the bank shall be considered to have granted a credit to the client for the respective amount from the date of effectuation of such payment (overdrawing of account).

The rights and duties of the parties connected with overdrawing the account shall be determined by the rules concerning loan and credit, unless provided otherwise by the contract of bank account.

Article 780. Payment of Expenses of Bank for Performance of Operations With Regard to Account

The client shall pay for services of the bank with regard to the performance of operations with the monetary means in the account on the conditions provided for by the contract of bank account. In instances when the price of services of the bank with regard to the performance of the said operations is not determined in the contract of bank account, the payment for the services shall be determined in accordance with Article 356 of the present Code.

Payment for services of the bank provided for by paragraph one of the present Article shall be recovered by the bank upon the expiry of each month from the monetary means of the client in his account unless provided otherwise by the contract of bank account.

Article 781. Interest for Use by Bank of Monetary Means in Account

Unless provided otherwise by the contract of bank account, the bank shall pay the client interest for the use of monetary means in the account, the amount of which shall be credited to the account.

Interest specified in paragraph one of the present Article shall be paid by the bank in the amount determined by the contract of bank account, and in the absence in the contract of a respective condition, in the amount usually paid by the bank for demand deposits.

The amount of interest shall be credited to the account within the periods provided for by the contract of bank account, and when such periods have not been provided for by the contract, upon the expiry of each quarter.

Article 782. Set-off of Counter Demands of Bank and Client

Monetary demands of the bank against the client connected with overdrawing the account and the payment for services of the bank, and also demands of the client against the bank concerning the payment of interest for the use of monetary means, shall be terminated by set-off unless provided otherwise by the contract of bank account.

Set-off of the demands specified in paragraph one of the present Article shall be effectuated by the bank, which shall be obliged to inform the client about the set-off made in the procedure and within the periods which are established by the contract of bank account, and if the respective conditions have not been agreed by the parties, in the procedure and within the periods which are usual for banking practice of granting information to clients concerning the state of monetary means in the respective account.

Article 783. Grounds for Withdrawal of Monetary Means from Account

The withdrawal of monetary means from the account shall be effectuated by the bank on the basis of the instruction of the client.

Without the instruction of the client the withdrawal of monetary means in the account shall be permitted by decision of a court, and also in other instances established by the present Code or other law or provided for by the contract between the bank and the client.

Article 784. Priority of Withdrawal of Monetary Means from Account

When there are monetary means in the account, the amount of which is sufficient in order to satisfy all demands presented to the account, the withdrawal of these means from the account shall be effectuated in the sequence of receipt of instructions of the client and other documents for withdrawal (calendar priority) unless provided otherwise by a law.

In the event the monetary means in the account are insufficient for the satisfaction of all demands presented to it, the withdrawal of monetary means shall be effectuated in the following priority:

in first priority shall be made the withdrawal proportionally with regard to documents of payment (or execution) which provide for payments to the budget, to extrabudgetary funds, and the issuance of monetary means from the account in order to satisfy demands concerning the recovery of alimony, with regard to payment of remuneration under authors' contracts, and also compensation of harm caused to life or health, ensuring an equal degree of the fulfillment of obligations of economic subjects with regard to payment to the budget and demands arising from labor violations and violations equated thereto;

in second priority shall be made the withdrawal with regard to payment documents of execution which provide for the satisfaction of other monetary demands;

in third priority shall be made the withdrawal with regard to payment documents by way of calendar priority.

The withdrawal of monetary means for urgent needs connected directly with production activity in the amount established by legislation shall be effectuated outside calendar priority [as amended by Law of 1 May 1998, No. 621-I. Ведомости Олий Мажлиса (1998), no. 5-6, item 102].

Article 785. Responsibility of Bank for Untimely Effectuation of Operations With Regard to Account and Unsubstantiated Withdrawal of Monetary Means

In instances of the untimely crediting to an account of monetary means received by a client or the unsubstantiated withdrawal of means by the bank from the account, the bank shall be obliged to immediately credit the respective amount to the account at the demand of the client, except for instances provided by a law [as amended by Law of 22 September 2009, No. 3PY-223. C3 PY (2009), no. 39, item 423].

The bank shall be obliged also to pay interest for the untimely crediting or unsubstantiated withdrawn amount and to compensate losses in accordance with Article 327 of the present Code. The bank also shall bear such responsibility for the untimely issuance of means from the account and the untimely fulfillment of instructions of the client concerning the transfer of means from the account, except for instances provided by a law [as amended by Law of 22 September 2009, No. 3PY-223. C3 PY (2009), no. 39, item 423].

Article 786. Bank Secret

A bank shall guarantee the secrecy of a bank account and bank deposit, operations relating to the account, and information concerning the client.

Information constituting a bank secret may be granted only to the clients themselves or their representatives. Such information may be granted to State agencies and their officials in the instances and in the procedure provided for by a law.

In the event of the divulgence by a bank of information constituting a bank secret, the client whose rights were violated shall have the right to require compensation of losses caused from the bank.

Article 787. Limitation of Disposition of Account

Limitation of the rights of the client to dispose of monetary means in the account shall not be permitted except for the imposition of arrest on the monetary means in the account or the suspension of operations with regard to the account in the instances provided for by a law.

Article 788. Dissolution of Contract of Bank Account

A contract of bank account shall be dissolved upon the application of the client at any time.

At the demand of the bank the contract of bank account may be dissolved by a court in the following instances:

when the amount of monetary means kept in the account of the client proves to be lower than the minimum amount provided for by banking rules or the contract if such amount is not reinstated within a month from the date of the warning of the bank thereof;

in the absence of operations with regard to this account during a year unless provided otherwise by the contract.

The balance of monetary means in the account shall be issued to the client or upon his instruction credited to another account not later than seven days after receipt of the respective written application of the client.

Dissolution of a contract of bank account shall be grounds for closing the account of the client.

Article 789. Accounts of Banks

The rules of the present Chapter shall extend to correspondent accounts, correspondent subaccounts, and other accounts of banks unless provided otherwise by legislation.

Chapter 45. Settlement of Accounts

§ 1. General Provisions on Settlement of Accounts

Article 790. Cash and Noncash Settlement Accounts

Settlement of accounts between citizens and settlement of accounts with the participation of citizens not connected with the effectuation by them of entrepreneurial activity may be performed with cash money without limitation of the amount or in a noncash procedure.

Settlement of accounts between juridical persons, and also settlement of accounts with the participation of citizens connected with the effectuation by them of entrepreneurial activity, shall be performed in a noncash procedure. Settlement of accounts between the named persons may be performed also by cash money unless established otherwise by a law.

Noncash settlements of accounts shall be performed through banks and other credit organizations (hereinafter: banks) in which accounts of the persons participating in the settlement of accounts have been opened unless it arises otherwise from a law or is stipulated by the form of settlement of accounts being used.

Article 791. Forms of Noncash Settlement of Accounts

When effectuating noncash settlements of accounts, the settlement of accounts by payment orders, letters of credit, cheques, and encashment shall be permitted, and also the settlement of accounts in other forms provided for by a law and by banking rules issued in accordance with it, and customs of business turnover applicable in banking practice.

The parties under a contract shall have the right to choose and provide in the contract any of the forms of settlement of accounts specified in paragraph one of the present Article.

§ 2. Settlements of Accounts by Payment Orders

Article 792. General Provisions on Settlements of Accounts by Payment Orders

When settling accounts by a payment order the bank shall be obliged on behalf of the client at the expense of means in his account to transfer the determined monetary amount to the account of the person specified by the client in that or in another bank within the period provided for by legislation unless a shorter period has been provided by the contract of bank account or is determined by the customs of business turnover used in banking practice.

The person specified in the payment order as recipient of the means shall not acquire the right to demand performance of the payment from the bank except for instances when such right is provided for by a law or by the contract of the client with the bank.

Article 793. Conditions of Acceptance by Bank of Payment Order

The content of a payment order and settlement of account documents submitted together with it and the form thereof must correspond to the requirements established by banking rules.

The order of the client shall be accepted by the bank for performance only when there are means in the account of the client unless provided otherwise by the contract between the client and the bank.

Article 794. Performance of Order

A bank which has accepted a payment order of the client shall be obliged to transfer the respective monetary amount to the bank of the recipient of the means in order to credit it to the account of the person specified in the order within the period established by Article 792, paragraph one, of the present Code.

The bank shall have the right to involve other banks in order to fulfill operations with regard to transferring the monetary means to the account specified in the order of the client.

The bank shall be obliged immediately to inform the client at his demand about the performance of the order unless established otherwise by the contract.

Article 795. Responsibility for Failure to Perform or Improper Performance of Order

In the event of the failure to perform or the improper performance of the order of the client the bank shall bear responsibility for this violation in accordance with Article 327 of the present Code.

Banks participating in the conducting of a settlement operation with regard to a payment order shall bear joint and several responsibility to the person who gave this order.

§ 3. Settlement of Accounts by Letter of Credit

Article 796. General Provisions on Settlements of Accounts by Letter of Credit

In the event of the settlements of accounts under a letter of credit, the bank which has opened a letter of credit on behalf of the client (payer) and in accordance with his instructions (emitent-bank) shall be obliged to make payments of means in the event of the presentation by the recipient or person specified by him (hereinafter: recipient of means) of documents and the fulfillment of other conditions provided for by the letter of credit.

In the event of the opening of a covered (or deposited) letter of credit the emitent-bank shall be obliged when opening it to transfer own means of the client or the credit granted to him to the disposition of the performing bank for the entire period of operation of the obligation of the emitent-bank.

In the event of the opening of an uncovered letter of credit the emitent bank shall grant to the performing bank the right to withdraw the entire amount of the letter of credit from the account of the emitent-bank kept in the performing bank.

Article 797. Period of Operation and Procedure for Settlement of Accounts Under Letter of Credit

The period of operation and procedure for the settlement of accounts under a letter of credit shall be established in the contract between the payer and the recipient of the monetary means.

The contract also must contain:

the name of the emitent-bank;

the type of letter of credit and means of performance thereof;

the method of notice of the recipient of means concerning the opening of the letter of credit;

the full list and precise description of documents granted by the recipient in order to receive the means under the letter of credit;

the periods for granting of documents after the shipment of goods (or rendering of services, fulfillment of work) and the requirements for the formalization thereof.

Article 798. Revocable Letter of Credit

A letter of credit which may be changed or revoked by the emitent-bank without prior notice of the recipient of the means shall be deemed to be revocable. Revocation of the letter of credit shall not create any obligations of the emitent-bank to the recipient of the means.

The performing bank shall be obliged to effectuate payment and other operations with regard to a revocable letter of credit if at the moment of the performance thereof notice has not been received concerning the change of conditions or revocation of the letter of credit.

The letter of credit shall be revocable unless provided otherwise in the text thereof.

Article 799. Irrevocable Letter of Credit

A letter of credit which may not be revoked without the consent of the recipient of the means shall be deemed to be irrevocable.

At the request of the emitent-bank the performing bank participating in the conducting of letter of credit operations may confirm an irrevocable letter of credit (confirmed letter of credit). Such confirmation shall mean the acceptance by the performing bank of an obligation additional to the obligation of the emitent-bank to make payment in accordance with the conditions of the letter of credit.

An irrevocable letter of credit confirmed by the performing bank may not be changed or revoked without the consent of the performing bank.

Article 800. Performance of Letter of Credit

In order to perform a letter of credit the recipient of means shall submit to the performing bank documents which confirm the fulfillment of all conditions of the letter of credit. In the event of a violation of even one of these conditions, performance of the letter of credit shall not be effectuated.

If the performing bank has made payment or effectuated another operation in accordance with the conditions of the letter of credit, the emitent-bank shall be obliged to compensate it for expenses incurred. The said expenses, and also all other expenses of the emitent-bank connected with the performance of the letter of credit, shall be compensated by the client.

Article 801. Refusal to Accept Documents

If the performing bank refused to accept documents which by external indicia do not correspond to the conditions of the letter of credit, it shall be obliged immediately to inform the recipient of the means and the emitent-bank thereof, specifying the reasons for the refusal.

If the emitent-bank, having received the documents accepted by the performing bank, considers that they do not correspond by external indicia to the conditions of the letter of credit, it shall have the right to refuse to accept them and to require from the performing bank the amount of means paid to the recipient in violation of the conditions of the letter of credit, and with regard to an uncovered letter of credit, to refuse to compensate the amounts paid.

Article 802. Responsibility of Bank for Violation of Conditions of Letter of Credit

Responsibility for a violation of the conditions of a letter of credit to the client shall be borne by the emitent-bank, and to the emitent-bank by the performing bank except for instances provided for by the present Article.

In the event of the unsubstantiated refusal of the performing bank to pay the monetary means under a covered or confirmed letter of credit responsibility to the recipient of the means may be placed on the performing bank.

In the event of the incorrect payment by the performing bank of monetary means under a covered or confirmed letter of credit as a consequence of a violation of the conditions of the letter of credit responsibility to the client may be placed on the performing bank.

Article 803. Closure of Letter of Credit

A letter of credit in the performing bank shall be closed upon:

the expiry of the period of the letter of credit;

the statement of the recipient of the means concerning a refusal to use the letter of credit before the expiry of the period of its operation if the possibility of such refusal has been provided for by the conditions of the letter of credit;

the demand of the payer concerning the full or partial revocation of the letter of credit if such revocation is possible under the conditions of the letter of credit.

The performing bank must bring the closure of the letter of credit to the notice of the emitent-bank.

The unused amount of a deposited letter of credit shall be subject to return to the emitent-bank simultaneously with the closure of the letter of credit. The emitent-bank shall be obliged to credit the returned amounts to the account of the payer with which the means were deposited.

§ 4. Settlements of Accounts by Encashment

Article 804. General Provisions on Settlements of Accounts by Encashment

In the event of the settlements of accounts by encashment the client shall send to its bank (or emitent-bank) an order concerning the effectuation at the expense of the client of the receipt from the payer of a payment and/or acceptance of the payment.

The emitent-bank which has received an encashment order shall have the right to involve another bank (performing bank) in order to fulfill it.

The procedure for the effectuation of the settlement of accounts by encashment shall be regulated by legislation and customs of business turnover applicable in banking practice.

In the event of the failure to perform or improper performance of the commission of the client the emitent-bank shall bear responsibility to him on the grounds and in the amount which has been provided for by Chapter 24 of the present Code.

If the failure to perform or the improper performance of the commission of the client occurred in connection with a violation of the rules for performing settlement of account operations by the performing bank, responsibility to the client may be placed on this bank.

Article 805. Performance of Encashment Commission

In the absence of any document or nonconformity of documents by external indicia to an encashment commission the performing bank shall be obliged immediately to notify the person thereof from whom the encashment commission was received. In the event of the failure to eliminate the said defects the bank shall have the right to return the documents without performance.

Documents shall be submitted to the payer in that form in which they were received except for notations and inscriptions of banks necessary in order to formalize the encashment operation.

If documents are subject to payment upon presentation, the performing bank must make the submission for payment immediately upon receipt of the encashment commission.

If the documents are subject to payment within a different period, the performing bank must in order to receive acceptance of the payer submit the documents for acceptance immediately upon receipt of the encashment commission, and the demand for payment must be made not later than the day of the ensuing of the period of payment specified in the document.

Partial payments may be accepted in instances when this has been established by banking rules or when there is special authorization in the encashment commission.

The amounts received (encashed) must be immediately transferred by the performing bank to the disposition of the emitent-bank, which shall be obliged to credit these amounts to the account of the client. The performing bank shall have the right to withhold from the encashed amounts the remuneration due to it and compensation of expenses.

Article 806. Notice of Refusal of Payment

If the payment and/or acceptance was not received, the performing bank shall be obliged to immediately notify the emitent-bank about the reasons for nonpayment or refusal of the acceptance. The emitent-bank shall be obliged immediately to inform the client thereof, having asked for instructions from him relative to further actions.

In the event of the failure to receive instructions concerning further actions within the period established by banking rules, the performing bank shall have the right to return the documents to the bank from which the encashment commission was received.

§ 5. Settlements of Accounts by Cheques

Article 807. General Provisions on Settlements of Accounts by Cheques

A security containing an unconditional instruction of the drawer to the bank to make the payment of the amount specified therein to the payee shall be deemed to be a cheque.

Only the bank where the drawer has means which he has the right to dispose of by means of issuing cheques may be specified as the payer under the cheque when settling accounts by cheque.

The revocation of a cheque before the expiry of the period for the presentation thereof shall not be permitted.

The issuance of a cheque shall not cancel a monetary obligation for the performance of which it is issued.

The procedure and conditions of the use of cheques in payment turnover shall be regulated by the present Code and other legislation.

Article 808. Requisites of Cheque

A cheque must contain:

the name "cheque" incorporated into the text of the document;

the order to the payer to pay the determined monetary amount;

the name of the payer and indication of the account from which the payment must be made;

the indication of the currency of payment;

the indication of the date and place of drawing up the cheque;

the signature of the person who has signed the cheque – the drawer.

The absence in the document of any of the said requisites shall deprive it of the force of a cheque.

A cheque which does not contain an indication of the place of drawing it up shall be considered as signed at the location of the drawer.

The form of the cheque and the procedure for filling it in shall be determined by legislation.

Article 809. Payment of Cheque

A cheque shall be paid at the expense of the means of the drawer.

A cheque shall be subject to payment by the payer on condition of the presentation thereof for payment within the period established by legislation.

The person who has paid the cheque shall have the right to require the transfer to him of the cheque with a notation of payment being received.

Article 810. Transfer of Rights Under Cheque

The transfer of rights under a cheque shall be made in compliance with the rules provided for by the present Article.

An inscribed cheque shall not be subject to transfer.

On a transferable cheque the endorsement to the payer shall have the force of a receipt for receiving payment.

An endorsement performed by the payer shall be invalid.

The person who possesses a transferable cheque received under endorsement shall be considered to be the legal possessor thereof if he bases his right on the uninterrupted (mutually stipulated) sequence of endorsements.

Article 811. Guarantee of Payment (Aval)

Payment under a cheque may be guaranteed in full or partially by means of a guarantee (aval).

An aval may be given by any person except the payer.

An aval shall be filled in on the face side of the cheque or on an additional sheet by means of the inscription "to consider an aval" and an indication by whom and for whom it was given. If not specified for whom it was given, it shall be considered that the aval was given for the drawer.

An aval shall be signed by the avalist with an indication of the place of his residence (or location) and date of performing the inscription.

An avalist shall be liable just as he for whom the aval was given.

His obligation shall be valid even if the obligation which he guaranteed proves to be invalid on any grounds whatever other than the failure to comply with the form.

An avalist who has paid the cheque shall acquire the rights arising from the cheque against he for whom he gave the guarantee and against those who are obliged to the last.

Article 812. Encashment of Cheque

The submission of a cheque to the bank servicing the payee for encashment in order to receive payment shall be considered to be the presentation of the cheque for payment.

The cheque shall be paid in the procedure established by Article 805 of the present Code.

The crediting of means with regard to the encashed cheque to the account of the payee shall be made after receipt of the payment from the payer unless provided otherwise by a contract between the payee and the bank.

Article 813. Duties of Payer

The payer under a cheque shall be obliged to certify by all means accessible to him the genuineness of the cheque, and also that the bearer of the cheque is the person empowered with regard to it.

When paying an encashed cheque, the payer shall be obliged to verify the correctness of the endorsements, but not the signatures of the endorsers.

Losses which arose as a consequence of the payment by the payer of a forged, stolen, or lost cheque shall be placed on the payer or the drawer depending upon by whose fault they were caused.

Article 814. Certification of Refusal to Pay Cheque

The refusal to pay a cheque must be certified by one of the following means:

performance of a protest by a notary in the procedure established by legislation;

notation of the payer on the cheque concerning the refusal to pay it indicating the date of presentation of the cheque for payment;

notation of the encashing bank indicating the date that the cheque was presented in good time and not paid.

The protest or equivalent act must be performed before the expiry of the period for presentation of the cheque for payment.

If the presentation of the cheque occurred on the last day of the period, the protest or equivalent act may be performed on the following work day.

Article 815. Notice of Nonpayment of Cheque

The payee shall be obliged to notify his endorsee and the drawer about the nonpayment within two work days following the day of performance of the protest or equivalent act.

Each endorsee must within two work days following the day of receipt by them of the notice bring to the information of their (preceding) endorsee the notice received by him. Within the same period notice shall be sent to he who gave an aval for this person. A person who has not been sent notice within the said period shall not lose his rights under the cheque. He shall be obliged to compensate losses caused as a consequence of the failure to notify about nonpayment of the cheque within the limits of the amount of the cheque.

Article 816. Consequences of Failure to Pay Cheque

In the event of the refusal of the payer to pay the cheque certified in accordance with Article 814 of the present Code, the payee shall have the right at his choice to bring suit against one, several, or all persons obliged under the cheque (drawer, avalist, endorsee), who shall bear joint and several responsibility to him.

The drawee shall have the right to require from the said persons payment of the amount of the cheque, his costs to receive payment, and also interest in the amount and procedure provided for by Article 327, paragraphs one and two, of the present Code. The same right shall belong to the person obliged under the cheque after he has paid the cheque.

A suit of the payee against the persons specified in paragraph one of the present Article may be presented within six months from the date of the end of the period of presentation of the cheque for payment. Regress demands with regard to suits of the obliged persons against one another shall be cancelled upon the expiry of six months from the date when the respective obliged person satisfied the demand or from the date of bringing suit against him.

Chapter 46. Commission

Article 817. Contract of Commission

Under a contract of commission one party (the attorney) shall be obliged to perform in the name of and at the expense of another person (the principal) determined legal actions. The rights and duties with regard to the transaction concluded by the attorney shall arise directly with the principal.

A commission may affect the performance by the attorney of one or several determined legal actions or the conducting of the affairs of the principal in accordance with his instructions.

Under a contract of commission with exclusive rights of the attorney, one party (the principal) commissions the other party (attorney with exclusive rights) to perform in the name of and at the expense of the principal all actions legally significant for the last within a determined sphere and/or on a determined territory.

The contract of commission shall be concluded in written form.

A contract of commission may be concluded with or without a specification of the period during which the attorney has the right to act in the name of the principal.

Article 818. Remuneration in Contract of Commission

The principal shall be obliged to pay remuneration to the attorney if this is provided for by legislation or the contract of commission.

If a contract of commission is connected with the effectuation of entrepreneurial activity by both parties or one of them, the principal shall be obliged to pay remuneration to the attorney unless provided otherwise by the contract.

In the absence in a contract of commission for compensation of conditions concerning the amount of remuneration or the procedure for the payment thereof, it shall be determined in accordance with Article 356, paragraph four, of the present Code by the usually accepted prices for services of such kind and shall be paid after the fulfillment of the commission.

Remuneration shall be subject to payment also when the attorney properly performed all the required actions but the commission was not fulfilled not through his fault.

The attorney acting as a commercial representative shall have the right in accordance with Article 290 of the present Code to withhold things situated with him which are subject to transfer to the principal as security for his demands under the contract of commission.

Article 819. Performance of Commission in Accordance with Instructions of Principal

An attorney shall be obliged to perform the commission given to him in accordance with the instructions of the principal. The instructions of the principal must be specific, permissible, and possible.

An attorney shall have the right to deviate from instructions of the principal if under the circumstances of the case this is necessary in the interests of the principal and the attorney could not inquire in advance of the principal or did not receive a reply to his enquiry within a reasonable period. In this event an attorney shall be obliged to inform the principal about deviations permitted as soon as notice became possible.

The right to deviate in the interests of the principal from his instructions without a preliminary enquiry about this may be granted to an attorney acting as a commercial representative. In this event the commercial representative shall be obliged within a reasonable period to inform the principal about deviations permitted unless provided otherwise by the contract of commission.

Article 820. Duties of Attorney

An attorney shall be obliged to:

personally perform the commission given to him, except for instances specified in Article 822 of the present Code;

communicate to the principal at his demand all information concerning the course of the performance of the commission;

transfer to the principal without delay everything received under the transactions concluded in performance of the commission;

upon the performance of the commission, return without delay the power of attorney to the attorney, the period of operation of which has not lapsed and submit a report with documents of justification appended, if this is required according to the conditions of the contract or the character of the commission.

Article 821. Duties of Principal

The principal shall be obliged, unless provided otherwise by the contract of commission, to:

provide the attorney with the means necessary for the performance of the commission;

accept without delay that performed by the attorney in accordance with the contract;

compensate the attorney for expenses incurred which were necessary in order to perform the commission;

upon performance of the commission pay the attorney the remuneration if this has been provided for by legislation or by the contract.

Article 822. Transfer of Performance of Commission

An attorney shall have the right to transfer the performance of a commission to another person (deputy) if this has been provided for by the contract of commission or if the attorney was forced to do so by circumstances for the purpose of protecting the interests of the principal.

An attorney who has transferred the performance to another person shall be obliged immediately to notify the principal thereof.

The principal shall have the right to remove the deputy selected by the attorney, except for instances when the deputy was named in the contract of commission.

If a deputy of the attorney is named in the contract, the attorney shall not be liable for the conducting of affairs by the deputy.

If the conducting of affairs by the deputy is provided for in the contract of commission but the deputy is not named therein, the attorney shall not be liable for the guilty actions of the deputy.

If the conducting of affairs by the deputy of the attorney is not provided for in the contract of commission, the attorney shall be liable for any actions of his deputy.

Article 823. Termination of Contract of Commission

A contract of commission shall be terminated as a consequence of:

revocation of the commission by the principal;

refusal of the commission by the attorney;

death of the principal or attorney, deeming either of them to lack dispositive legal capacity, have limited dispositive legal capacity, or to be missing.

The principal shall have the right to revoke a commission, and the attorney to refuse it, at any time. An agreement concerning the waiver of this right shall be null.

If the attorney did not know and should not have known about the termination of the contract of commission, then his actions legally performed according to the instruction of the principal shall oblige the principal (or his legal successor) with respect to third persons and the attorney.

A party who has repudiated a contract of commission with an attorney acting as an entrepreneur must inform the other party about the termination of the contract not later than thirty days in advance unless a longer period has been provided for by the contract. In the event of the reorganization of a juridical person which is a commercial representative, the principal shall have the right to revoke the commission without such prior notice.

Article 824. Consequences of Termination of Contract of Commission

If a contract of commission is terminated before the commission is performed by the attorney in full, the principal shall be obliged to compensate the attorney for the costs incurred by him when performing the commission, and when remuneration was due to the attorney, also to pay remuneration to him commensurate with the work fulfilled by him. This rule shall not apply to the performance by the attorney of the commission after he knew or should have known about the termination of the commission.

Article 825. Legal Succession in Contract of Commission

In the event of the death of an attorney, his heirs or other persons on whom ensuring the preservation of inheritance property has been placed shall be obliged to notify the principal immediately about the termination of the contract of commission and take measures necessary in order to protect the property of the principal, in particular, to preserve things, and also documents of the principal, and then to transfer this property to him. The same duty shall lie on the person who is liquidating a juridical person which is a representative (or attorney).

In the event of the reorganization of a juridical person operating as a representative (or attorney), the principal must be immediately notified thereof. In this instance the rights and duties of such juridical person shall pass to the legal successor thereof unless the principal within a thirty-day period notifies his repudiation of the contract of commission.

Chapter 47. Actions in Another's Interest Without Commission

Article 826. Conditions of Actions in Another's Interest

Actions without a commission, other instruction, or consent of the interested person promised in advance for the purpose of preventing harm to his person or property, performance of his obligation or in his other not unlawful interests (actions in another's interest) must be performed by proceeding from the obvious advantage or benefit and actual or probable intentions of the interested person and with the necessary concern and circumspection under the circumstances of the case.

The rules provided for by the present Chapter shall not apply to actions in the interest of other persons to be performed by State agencies and agencies of self-government of citizens for which such actions are one of the purposes of their activity.

Article 827. Duties of Person Acting in Another's Interest Without Commission

The person acting in another's interest without the commission thereof shall be obliged at the first possibility to notify the interested person thereof. If the interested person approves these actions, then thereafter the rules concerning the contract of commission shall apply to the relations of these parties. In the event of the failure to approve the said actions, responsibility for them shall be placed on the person who acted without a commission.

When it is impossible to inform the interested person, the person who began actions without a commission shall be obliged to bring them to an end, having take all measures within his control with regard to the prevention of negative property consequences for this person. In so doing the person acting without a commission shall be obliged to assume everything that is linked with the conducting of the affair, including the duties with regard to concluded transactions.

If the person who has acted in the interests of another person without his commission does not inform the interested person about this at first possibility, he shall not have the right to demand compensation for expenditures incurred.

The person who has acted in another's interest without commission shall be obliged to continue the activity begun also in the event of the death of the citizen or termination of the activity of the juridical person in whose interests the respective activity is effectuated so long as the heirs (or legal successors) of the interested person could not replace him.

Article 828. Conclusion of Transactions in Another's Interest

Duties with regard to a transaction concluded in another's interest shall pass to the person in whose interest it was concluded from the moment of the approval by him of this transaction and if the other party does not object to such transfer or when concluding the transaction knew or should have known that the transaction was concluded in another's interest. In the event of the transfer of duties under this transaction to the person in whose interests it was concluded, to the last must be transferred also the rights with regard to this transaction.

The person who concluded the transaction may delay the transfer of rights until the moment of compensation to him of expenses incurred by him in connection with the activity in another's interest.

Article 829. Duties of Person in Whose Interests Actions Were Effectuated Without Commission

The person in whose interests actions were effectuated without a commission shall be obliged to compensate he who acted in his interests, necessary expenses, and other real damage. The said duty shall be preserved also in instances when the actions in another's interest were reasonable but the presupposed result was not achieved. However, in the event of the averting of damage to the property of the other person the amount of compensation should not exceed the value of the property.

If the actions of the person directly were not directed towards ensuring the interests of another person, including also when the person performing them erroneously presupposed that he is acting in his own interest and his actions led to unsubstantiated enrichment of the other person, the rules provided for by Chapter 58 of the present Code shall apply. In an event when the actions in another's interest entered into the sphere of his entrepreneurial activity, he shall have the right to demand together with compensation for real damage also the payment of commensurate remuneration.

Expenses and other losses of the person who acted in another's interest incurred in connection with the actions which were undertaken after receipt of approval from the interested person shall be compensated according to the rules concerning the contract of the respective type.

Article 830. Compensation of Harm Caused by Actions in Another's Interest

Relations with regard to compensation of harm caused by actions in another's interest to an interested person or to third persons shall be regulated in accordance with the rules of Chapter 57 of the present Code.

Article 831. Report of Person Who Acted in Another's Interest

The person who acted in another's interest shall be obliged to submit to the person in whose interests the activity was effectuated a report specifying the revenues received and the expenses and losses incurred.

Chapter 48. Commission Agency

Article 832. Contract of Commission Agency

Under a contract of commission agency, one party (commission agent) shall be obliged on behalf of another party (committent) to conclude for remuneration one or several transactions in his own name, but at the expense of the committent. The contract of commission agency must be concluded in written form.

Under a transaction concluded by the commission agent with a third person, the commission agent shall become obliged and acquire rights, even though the committent also was named in the transaction or entered into direct relations with the third person in regard to performance of the transaction.

A contract of commission agency may be concluded for a determined period or without specifying the period of its operation, with or without specifying the territory of the performance thereof, with or without the obligation of the committent not to grant to third persons the right to conclude a transaction in his interests and at his expense, the conclusion of which has been entrusted to the commission agent, and with or without conditions relative to the assortment of goods which are the subject of the commission agency.

The peculiarities of individual types of contract of commission agency may be provided for by legislation.

Article 833. Commission Agency Remuneration

The committent shall be obliged to pay remuneration to the commission agent, and in the instances when the commission agent has assumed the guaranty for performance of the transaction by a third person (del credere), also additional remuneration in the amount and in the procedure established in the contract.

If this amount is not provided for by the contract and can not be determined by proceeding from its conditions, the amount of remuneration shall be established in accordance with Article 356, paragraph four, of the present Code.

If the contract of commission agency was not performed for reasons dependent upon the committent, the commission agent shall retain the right to the commission agency remuneration, and also to compensation for expenses incurred.

Article 834. Performance of Commission Agency Commission

A commission agent must fulfill all obligations and effectuate all rights arising from the transaction concluded by him with a third person.

The commission assumed the commission agent shall be obliged to perform in accordance with the instructions of the committent, and in the absence of such instructions in the contract of commission agency, in accordance with the customs of business turnover or other requirements usually presented, on conditions most advantageous for the committent. If the commission agent has concluded a transaction on conditions more advantageous than those which were specified by the committent, the additional advantage shall be divided between the parties equally unless provided otherwise by the contract.

In instances if the commission agent assumes a guaranty to the committent for the performance of the transaction (del credere), he shall receive the right to additional remuneration in the amount stipulated in the contract of commission agency.

The commission agent shall not be liable to the committent for the failure of a third person to perform the transaction which was concluded with him at the expense of the committent except for instances when the commission agent did not display the necessary circumspection in the choice of this person or assume a guaranty for the performance of the transaction (del credere).

In the event of the failure of the third person to perform the transaction concluded with him by the commission agent, the commission agent shall be obliged immediately to notify the committent thereof, collect and secure the necessary evidence, and also at the demand of the committent transfer rights to him with regard to such transaction in compliance with the rules concerning the assignment of demands (Articles 313-317, 319, and 320 of the present Code).

The assignment of the rights to the committent under a transaction on the basis of paragraph five of the present Article shall be permitted irrespective of the agreement of the commission agent with the third person prohibiting or limiting such assignment. This shall not relieve the commission agent from responsibility to the third person in connection with the assignment of the right in violation of the agreement concerning the prohibition or limitation thereof.

Article 835. Sub-Commission Agency

Unless provided otherwise by the contract, the commission agent shall have the right for the purpose of performance of the contract of commission agency to conclude a contract of sub-commission agency with another person while remaining responsible for the actions of the sub-commission agent to the committent.

Under a contract of sub-commission agency, the commission agent shall acquire the rights and duties of the committent with respect to the sub-commission agent.

In instances when a law permits the conclusion of any transaction only by specially empowered persons, the contract of sub-commission agency may be concluded only with such person.

Until the termination of the contract of commission agency, the committent shall not have the right without the consent of the commission agent to enter into direct relations with the sub-commission agent, unless provided otherwise by the contract of commission agency.

Article 836. Price of Property Being Sold by Commission Agent

The price of the property being sold by a commission agent shall be determined by agreement with the committent unless provided otherwise by legislation or by the contract of commission agency.

Article 837. Deviation from Instructions of Committent

The commission agent shall have the right to deviate from the instructions of the committent in the instances provided for by Article 819 of the present Code.

A commission agent who has sold property at a price lower than agreed with the committent shall be obliged to compensate the last for the difference unless it is proved that he had no possibility to sell the property at the agreed price and the sale for a lower price prevented more losses. In the event when the commission agent was obliged to ask the committent in advance, the commission agent also must prove that he had no possibility to receive the consent of the committent in advance for the deviation from his instructions.

If the commission agent purchased property at a price higher than agreed with the committent, the committent, not wishing to accept such purchase, shall be obliged to declare this to the commission agent within a reasonable period upon receipt of notice thereof concerning the conclusion of a transaction with a third person. Otherwise, the purchase shall be deemed to be accepted by the committent.

If the commission agent communicated that he accepts the difference in price at his own expense, the committent shall not have the right to repudiate the transaction concluded for him.

Article 838. Right to Thing Which Is Subject of Commission Agency

Things received by the commission agent from the committent or acquired by the commission agent at the expense of the committent shall be the ownership of the committent.

The commission agent shall have the right in accordance with Article 290 of the present Code to withhold things which he has and which are subject to transfer to the committent or to the person specified by the committent to secure his demands under the contract of commission agency.

In the event the committent is declared to be insolvent (or bankrupt), the said right of the commission agent shall terminate, and his demands against the committent within the limits of the value of things which he withheld shall be satisfied in accordance with Article 291 of the present Code equally with the demands secured by a pledge.

Article 839. Satisfaction of Demands of Commission Agent from Amounts Due to Committent

A commission agent shall have the right in accordance with Article 343 of the present Code to withhold amounts due to him under the contract of commission agency from all the amounts received by him on the account of the committent. However, the creditors of the committent who enjoy preference with respect to priority of satisfaction of their demands before the pledgeholders shall not be deprived of the right to satisfaction of these demands from the amounts withheld by the commission agent.

Article 840. Responsibility of Commission Agent for Loss, Shortage, or Damage to Property of Committent

A commission agent shall be liable to the committent for loss, shortage, or damage to the property of the committent situated with him.

If the commission agent accepts the property sent by the committent or which comes to the commission agent for the committent, and this property proves to be damaged or deficit, which may be noted from an external inspection, and also damage has been caused by someone to the property of the committent situated with the commission agent, the commission agent shall be obliged to take measures relating to the protection of the rights of the committent, to gather the necessary evidence, and immediately to notify the committent about everything.

A commission agent who has not insured property of the committent situated with him shall be liable for this only in instances when the committent instructed him to insure the property at the expense of the committent or the insuring of this property by the commission agent has been provided for by the contract of commission agency or the customs of business turnover.

Article 841. Acceptance by Committent of That Performed Under the Contract of Commission Agency

The committent shall be obliged to:

accept from the commission agent everything performed under the contract of commission agency;

inspect the property acquired for him by the commission agent and notify the last without delay about the defects discovered in this property;

relieve the commission agent from obligations assumed by him to a third person with regard to the performance of the commission agency commission.

Article 842. Compensation of Expenses for Performance of Commission Agency Commission

The committent shall be obliged, in addition to payment of the commission agency remuneration, and in respective instances also additional remuneration for del credere, to compensate the commission agent for amounts expended by him for performance of the commission agency commission.

The commission agent shall not have the right to compensation of expenses for the keeping of property of the committent situated with him, unless established otherwise in legislation or by the contract of commission agency.

Article 843. Revocation of Commission Agency Commission by Committent

The committent shall have the right at any time to refuse performance of the contract of commission agency, having revoked the commission given to the commission agent. In so doing the losses of the caused by revocation of the commission shall be compensated on the general grounds.

In an event when the contract of commission agency was concluded without an indication of the period of its operation, the committent must inform the commission agent about the termination of the contract not later than thirty days in advance unless a more extended period of notification has been provided for by the contract. In this event the committent shall be obliged to pay remuneration to the commission agent for transactions concluded by him before the termination of the contract, and also to compensate the commission agent for expenses incurred by him before the termination of the contract.

In the event of the revocation of the commission, the committent shall be obliged within the period established by the contract of commission agency, and if such period has not been established, immediately to dispose of his property located within the jurisdiction of the commission agent. If the committent does not fulfill this duty, the commission agent shall have the right to hand over the property for keeping at the expense of the committent or to sell it at the price as advantageous as possible for the committent.

Article 844. Refusal of Commission Agent to Perform Contract of Commission Agency

A commission agent shall not have the right, unless provided otherwise by the contract of commission agency, to refuse the performance thereof, except for instances when the contract was concluded without an indication of the period of its operation. In this event the commission agent must inform the committent about the termination of the contract not later than thirty days in advance, unless a more extended period of notification has been provided for by the contract.

A commission agent shall be obliged to take measures necessary in order to ensure the preservation of the property of the committent.

The committent notified about the refusal of the commission agent to perform the commission shall be obliged to dispose of property situated with the commission agent within fifteen days from the date of receipt of the notification about the refusal of the commission agent to perform the commission, unless another period has been established by the contract. If he does not fulfill this duty, the commission agent shall have the right to hand over the property for keeping or to sell it at the price as advantageous as possible for the committent.

Unless provided otherwise by the contract of commission agency, the commission agent who has refused to perform a commission shall retain the right to commission agency remuneration for the transactions concluded by him before termination of the contract, and also to compensation for expenses incurred by him up to that moment.

Article 845. Termination of Contract of Commission Agency

A contract of commission agency shall terminated as a consequence of:

refusal of the committent to perform the contract;

refusal of the commission agent to perform the contract;

death of the commission agent, deeming him to lack dispositive legal capacity, limited dispositive legal capacity, or to be missing, or to be insolvent.

Article 846. Refusal of Committent of Performance of Contract of Commission Agency Concluded Without Indication of Period

The committent shall have the right at any time to refuse performance of a contract of commission agency concluded without indication of the period, having notified the commission agent about the refusal not later than thirty days in advance unless a longer period of notification has been provided for by the contract.

In this event the committent shall be obliged to pay remuneration to the commission agent for transactions concluded by him before termination of the contract of commission agency, and also to compensate the commission agent for expenses incurred by him before the termination of the contract.

In the event of the refusal of performance of the contract of commission agency, the committent must fulfill the duties provided for by Article 844, paragraph three, of the present Code.

Article 847. Refusal of Commission Agent of Performance of Contract of Commission Agency

A commission agent shall have the right at any time to refuse performance of a contract of commission agency concluded without indication of the period, having notified the committent about the refusal not later than thirty days in advance unless a longer period of notification has been provided for by the contract.

In this event the commission agent shall be obliged to take measures for the preservation of property of the committent situated with him. The committent shall be obliged to dispose of the property situated with the commission agent before the moment of termination of the contract. If he does not fulfill this duty, the commission agent shall have the right either to hand the property over for keeping at the expense of the committent or to sell it at the price as advantageous as possible for the committent.

The commission agent who has refused performance of the contract of commission agency shall have the right to receive commission agency remuneration and compensation of expenses due to him at the moment of termination of the contract.

Article 848. Consequences of Death of Citizen or Liquidation of Juridical Person

In the event of the death of a citizen or the liquidation of a juridical person-commission agent, the contract of commission agency shall terminate.

In the event of the reorganization of a juridical person-commission agent the rights and duties of the commission agent shall pass to the legal successors unless within thirty days from the day of receipt of notice concerning the reorganization the committent communicates concerning the dissolution of the contract.

In the event of the death of the citizen-committent, deeming him to lack dispositive legal capacity or limited dispositive legal capacity, and also in the event of the liquidation of the juridical person-committent, the commission agent shall be obliged to continue performance of the commission given to him so long as the heirs or legal successors (or representatives) of the committent do not issue proper instructions.

Chapter 49. Trust Management of Property

Article 849. Contract of Trust Management of Property

Under a contract of trust management of property one party (founder of management) shall transfer to the other party (trustee manager) property in trust management for a determined period, and the other party shall be obliged for remuneration to effectuate the management of this property in the interests of the founder of the management or person specified by him (beneficiary).

The transfer of property to trust management shall not entail the transfer of the right of ownership to it to the trustee manager.

In effectuating trustee management of property, the trustee manager shall have the right to perform with respect to this property in accordance with the contract of trust management any legal and factual actions in the interests of the beneficiary.

Limitations with respect to individual actions relating to the trust management of property may be provided for by a law or contract.

Transactions with property transferred to trust management the trustee manager shall conclude in his own name, indicating in so doing that he acts as such manager. This condition shall be considered to be complied with if when performing actions not requiring written formalization the other party has been informed about the performance thereof by the trustee manager in this capacity, and in written documents by making the notation "D.U." after the name of the trustee manager.

In the absence of an indication concerning the action of the trustee manager in this capacity, the trustee manager shall be obliged to third persons personally and shall be liable to them only with the property belonging to him.

Article 850. Grounds for Arising (or Founding) of Trust Management of Property

Trust management of property shall arise (or be founded) on the basis of:

a contract of trust management of property concluded by the founder with the trustee manager;

a will in which the executor of the will (or trustee manager) is designated;

the decision of a court;

the decision of an agency of trusteeship and guardianship concerning the establishment of trusteeship over property of the ward;

other legal facts in the instances provided for by a law.

Article 851. Object of Trust Management of Property

Enterprises and other property complexes, individual objects relegated to immoveable property, securities, exclusive rights, and other property may be an object of trust management.

Money, except for instances provided for by a law, may not be an autonomous object of trust management.

Property in economic jurisdiction or operative management may not be transferred to trust management. The transfer to trust management of property in economic jurisdiction or operative management shall be possible only after the liquidation of the juridical person in whose economic jurisdiction or operative management the property is situated, or the termination of the right of economic jurisdiction or operative management of property and the entry thereof into the possession of the owner on other grounds provided for by a law.

Article 852. Subjects of Trust Management of Property

The founder of trust management of property shall be:

the owner of the property;

the person to whom the right of inheritance possession for life of a land plot belongs;

an empowered State agency: with respect to property in State ownership;

an enterprise to which property belongs by right of economic jurisdiction: with the authorization of the owner;

in the instances provided for by a law: a notary, agency of trusteeship and guardianship, court, or other empowered agency.

There may be a trustee manager:

a citizen;

a juridical person.

Property shall not be subject to transfer in trust management to a State agency.

The designation of a trustee manager may be made only with his consent.

Any person, except the trustee manager, may be a beneficiary.

Article 853. Material Conditions of Contract of Trust Management of Property

There must be provided for in the contract of trust management of property:

the list of the property being transferred on trust management under the contract;

the indication of the beneficiary;

the periods for submission of the reports by the trustee manager;

the person who receives the property in the event of the termination of trust management;

the amount and form of remuneration of trustee manager if payment of remuneration has been provided for by the contract.

In the absence of conditions provided for by paragraph one of the present Article, the contract shall be considered to be not concluded.

The contract of trust management of property shall be concluded for a period not exceeding five years. In the absence of the application of one of the parties concerning termination of the contract at the end of the period of operation, it shall be considered to be extended for the same period and on the same conditions which were provided by the contract.

For individual types of property transferred in trust management other maximum periods of operation of the contract may be established by a law.

Article 854. Form of Contract of Trust Management of Property

A contract of trust management of property shall be concluded in written form.

A contract of trust management of immoveable property shall be concluded in the form and in the procedure provided for the contract on the alienation of immoveable property. The transfer of immoveable property in trust management shall be subject to State registration in the same procedure as the transfer of the right of ownership to such property.

The failure to comply with the form of the contract of trust management of property or the requirement concerning registration of the transfer of immoveable property in trust management shall entail the invalidity thereof.

Article 855. Solitary Property in Trust Management

Property transferred in trust management shall be solitary from other property of the founder of the management, and also from property of the trustee manager. This property shall be reflected on a separate balance sheet of the trustee manager and an autonomous account shall be kept with regard to it. A separate bank account shall be opened in order to settle accounts with regard to activity connected with trust management.

Levy of execution for debts of the founder of the management against property transferred by him in trust management shall not be permitted, except for the insolvency (or bankruptcy) of this person. In the event of bankruptcy of the founder of the management, the trust management of this property shall terminate and it shall be included in the bankruptcy mass.

Article 856. Trust Management of Property Encumbered by Rights of Third Persons

The trustee manager must be notified before conclusion of the contract that the property transferred to him in management is encumbered by the rights of third persons. In the event of a violation of this condition the trustee manager shall have the right to require the contract to be deemed invalid with compensation of real damage and the payment of commensurate remuneration.

If the property transferred to trust management was encumbered by the rights of third persons after the conclusion of the contract, and the trustee manager was not informed thereof within a ten-day period, he shall have the right to demand dissolution of the contract of trust management of property with compensation to him of real damage and payment of commensurate remuneration.

Article 857. Rights and Duties of Trustee Manager

The trustee manager shall effectuate within the limits provided for by a law and the contract of trust management of property the powers of the owner with respect to property transferred in trust management.

The rights acquired by the trustee manager as a result of the performance of actions relating to the management of property shall be included in the composition of such property. The duties which arise as a result of the performance of such actions of the trustee manager shall be performed at the expense of this property.

The alienation and pledge of immoveable property transferred in management the trustee manager shall have the right to perform only in instances when this is provided for by the contract of trust management of property.

In order to defend the rights to property in trust management the trustee manager shall have the right to demand any elimination of a violation of his rights (Articles 228, 229, 231, and 232 of the present Code).

The trustee manager shall submit to the founder of the management and beneficiary a report concerning his activity within the periods and in the procedure established by the contract of trust management of property.

Article 858. Transfer of Trust Management of Property

The trustee manager shall effectuate the management of property personally, except for instances provided for by paragraphs two and three of the present Article.

The trustee manager may charge another person to perform actions in the name of the trustee manager which are necessary for the management of the property if he is empowered to do so by the contract of trust management of the property or has received the consent of the founder in written form for this, or is forced to do so by virtue of circumstances in order to ensure the interests of the founder of the management or beneficiary and does not have in so doing the possibility to receive instructions of the founder of the management within a reasonable period.

The trustee manager shall be liable for actions of the entrusted person he selected as though for his own.

Article 859. Responsibility of Trustee Manager

The trustee manager who has not displayed due concern in the trust management of property for the interests of the beneficiary or founder of the management shall compensate the beneficiary for lost advantage for the period of trust management of the property and the founder of the management for losses caused by the loss of or damage to the property, taking into account its natural wear and tear, and also lost advantage.

The trustee manager shall bear responsibility for losses caused unless it is proved that these losses occurred as a consequence of insuperable force or the actions of the beneficiary or the founder of the management.

Obligations relating to a transaction concluded by the trustee manager in excess of the powers granted to him or in violation of the limitations established for him shall be borne by the trustee manager personally. If third persons participating in the transaction did not know and should not have known about the exceeding of powers or the limitations established, the obligations which arose shall be subject to performance in the procedure established by paragraph four of the present Article. The founder of the management may in this event require of the trustee manager compensation for losses caused to him.

Debts relating to obligations which arose in connection with trust management of property shall be paid at the expense of this property. In the event this property is insufficient, recovery may be levied against the property of the trustee manager, and if his property also is insufficient, against the property of the founder of the management not transferred to trust management.

The contract of trust management of property may provide for the granting of a pledge by the trustee manager to secure compensation of losses which may be caused to the founder of the management or to the beneficiary by the improper performance of the contract of trust management.

Article 860. Remuneration of Trustee Manager

The trustee manager shall have the right to remuneration provided for by the contract of trust management of property, and also to compensation of necessary expenses made by him in the trust management of property at the expense of property transferred to management or revenues from the use of this property.

Article 861. Termination of Contract of Trust Management of Property

A contract of trust management of property shall be terminated by:

the application of one of the parties concerning termination of the contract in connection with the expiry of the period of the contract;

the death of a citizen who is a beneficiary or the liquidation of the juridical person-beneficiary unless provided otherwise by the contract;

the death of the citizen who is the trustee manager, his being deemed to lack dispositive legal capacity, to have limited dispositive legal capacity, or to be missing, and also his being deemed as an individual entrepreneur to be insolvent (or bankrupt);

the liquidation of the juridical person-trustee manager or the deeming thereof to be insolvent (or bankrupt);

the refusal of the beneficiary to receive advantages under the contract unless provided otherwise by the contract;

the refusal of the founder of the management of performance of the contract for other reasons than those which have been specified in paragraph six of the present paragraph on condition of the payment to the trustee manager of the remuneration stipulated by the contract;

the dissolution of the contract by decision of a court in the event of the improper effectuation by the trustee manager of his duties;

on other grounds provided for by a law or by the contract.

In the event of the termination of the contract of trust management, the property in trust management shall be transferred to the founder of the management unless provided otherwise by the contract.

In the event of the termination of a contract of trust management of property at the initiative of one of the parties, the other party must be notified not later than three months in advance unless another period has been established by the contract.

Chapter 50. Complex Entrepreneurial License (Franchising)

Article 862. Contract of Complex Entrepreneurial License

Under a contract of complex entrepreneurial license (contract on franchising), one party (complex licensor) shall be obliged to grant to the other party (complex licensee) for remuneration a complex of exclusive rights (licensed complex), including the right to use the firm name of the licensor and protected commercial information, and also other objects of exclusive rights provided for by the contract (trademark, service mark, and inventions and others) provided for by the contract in the entrepreneurial activity of the licensee.

A contract of complex entrepreneurial license shall provide for the use of the licensed complex, business reputation, and commercial experience of the licensor within the determined amount (in particular, the establishment of the minimum and/or maximum amount of use), specifying or not the territory of use applicable to the determined sphere of activity (sale of goods received from the licensor or to be produced by the licensee, rendering of services, fulfillment of work, effectuation of trade activity, and so on).

Only commercial organizations and citizens registered as entrepreneurs may be parties to a contract of complex entrepreneurial license.

The contract of complex entrepreneurial license may be concluded either with or without an indication of the period (contract in perpetuity).

The rules of the present Code concerning intellectual property, unless provided otherwise by the present Chapter or does not arise from the essence of the contract, shall apply to the contract of complex entrepreneurial license respectively.

Article 863. Form of Contract of Complex Entrepreneurial License and Requirements for Registration Thereof

A contract of complex entrepreneurial license must be concluded in written form and shall be subject to registration by the agency which effectuated the registration of the juridical person or individual entrepreneur acting under the contract as the licensor. The failure to comply with this rule shall entail the invalidity of the contract.

Article 864. Complex Entrepreneurial Sublicense

The right of the licensee to authorize other persons to use the licensed complex granted to him or part thereof on conditions agreed by him with the licensor or determined in the contract of complex entrepreneurial license may be provided for by the contract of complex entrepreneurial license. The duty of the licensee to issue within a determined period of time a determined number of sublicenses with or without specifying the territory for the use thereof also may be contained in the contract.

The termination of the contract of complex entrepreneurial license shall terminate the contract of complex entrepreneurial sublicense.

Article 865. Form of Remuneration Under Contract of Complex Entrepreneurial License

The licensee shall pay to the licensor remuneration in the form of fixed lump-sum or periodic payments, deductions from receipts, additions to the wholesale price of goods being delivered by the licensor to him for resale, or in other form provided for by the contract of complex entrepreneurial license.

Article 866. Duties of Licensor

The licensor shall be obliged to:

transfer to the licensee technical and commercial documentation and to grant other information necessary to the licensee in order to effectuate the rights granted to him under the contract of complex entrepreneurial license, and also train the licensee and his workers with regard to questions connected with the effectuation of these rights;

issue to the licensee the licenses provided for by the contract, ensuring the formalization thereof in the established procedure;

render permanent technical and consultation assistance to the licensee, including assistance in training and increasing the qualifications of workers.

Other duties of the licensor also may be provided for by the contract of complex entrepreneurial license.

Article 867. Duties of Licensee

Taking into account the character and peculiarities of the activity being effectuated by the licensee under the contract of complex entrepreneurial license, the licensee shall be obliged to:

use when effectuating the activity provided for by the contract the firm name of the licensor as specified in the contract;

ensure the precise conformity of the quality of the goods produced, services rendered, or work fulfilled on the basis of the contract to the quality of analogous goods, services, or work being produced, rendered, or fulfilled, directly by the licensor;

comply with all instructions and directions of the licensor directed towards achieving the precise conformity of the character, means, and conditions of use of the exclusive rights within the licensed complex, the use by the licensor, including the directions affecting the external and internal formalization of the commercial premises being used by the licensee when effectuating the rights granted to him under the contract;

render to purchasers (or customers) all additional services which they might count upon in acquiring (or ordering) the good (or service, work) directly from the licensor;

refrain from divulging the secrets of production of the licensor and other confidential commercial information received from him;

issue the stipulated quantity of sublicenses if such duty is expressly provided for by the contract;

inform the purchasers (or customers) by the most obvious means for them that he is using the firm name, trademark, service mark, or other means of individualization by virtue of the contract of complex entrepreneurial license.

Article 868. Limiting Conditions of Contract of Complex Entrepreneurial License

Limiting (or exclusive) conditions may be provided for by the contract of complex entrepreneurial license, in particular:

the obligation of the licensor not to issue other analogous complex entrepreneurial licenses for the use thereof on the territory consolidated for the licensee or refrain from direct autonomous activity on this territory;

the obligation of the licensee not to compete with the licensor on the territory of use of the complex entrepreneurial license;

the refusal of the licensee to receive other complex entrepreneurial licenses from competitors (or potential competitors) of the licensor;

the obligation of the licensee to agree with the licensor the location of the commercial premises to be used when effectuating the exclusive rights granted under the contract, as well as the external and internal formalization thereof.

Limiting conditions may be deemed to be invalid upon the suit of the antimonopoly agency or other interested person if they, taking into account the state of the respective market and the economic status of the parties, are contrary to legislation on competition [as amended by Laws of 29 December 2012, No. ЗРУ-345, and of 9 February 2022, No. ЗРУ-752].

Limiting conditions of a contract of complex entrepreneurial license shall be invalid, by virtue of which:

the licensor shall have the right to determine the price of the sale of the good by the licensee or the price of work (or services) being fulfilled (or rendered) by the licensee, or establish the upper or lower limit of the said prices;

the licensee shall have the right to sell goods, fulfill work, or render services exclusively to a determined category of purchasers (or customers) or exclusively to purchasers (or customers) having a location (or place of residence) on the territory determined in the contract.

Article 869. Responsibility of Licensor Relating to Demands Presented to Licensee

The licensor shall bear subsidiary responsibility for demands presented to the licensee concerning the failure of the goods (or work, services) being sold (or fulfilled, rendered) by the licensee under the contract of complex entrepreneurial license to quality.

The licensor shall be liable jointly and severally with the licensee with regard to demands presented to the licensee as the manufacturer of the product (or goods) of the licensor.

Article 870. Change of Contract of Complex Entre-preneurial License

A contract of complex entrepreneurial license may be changed in accordance with the rules of Chapter 28 of the present Code.

The contract shall be considered to be changed from the moment of registration of the respective changes in the procedure established by Article 863 of the present Code.

Article 871. Termination of Contract of Complex Entre-preneurial License

A contract of complex entrepreneurial license concluded with indication of the period may be dissolved in accordance with the rules of Chapter 28 of the present Code.

Each of the parties shall have the right at any time to repudiate a contract of complex entrepreneurial license in perpetuity, having notified the other party thereof six months in advance unless a longer period of notice has been provided for by the contract.

The contract of complex entrepreneurial license shall be terminated in the event of the termination of the right to the firm name which is part of the licensed complex without the replacement thereof by a new firm name.

The dissolution before time of the contract of complex entrepreneurial license concluded with a specification of the period, and also the dissolution of the contract of complex entrepreneurial license in perpetuity, shall be subject to registration in the procedure established by Article 863 of the present Code.

Article 872. Preservation of Contract of Complex Entrepreneurial License in Force in Event of Change of Parties

The transfer to another person of any exclusive right whatever within the licensed complex shall not be grounds for a change or dissolution of the contract of complex entrepreneurial license. The new licensor shall enter this contract in that part of the rights and duties relating to the exclusive right transferred.

In the event of the death of a citizen-licensor, his rights and duties under the contract of complex entrepreneurial license shall pass to the heir on condition that the last was registered or within six months from the date of opening the inheritance is registered as an entrepreneur. Otherwise the contract shall terminate.

The management of the licensed complex in the period before the acceptance by the heir of the rights and duties or before registration of the heir as an entrepreneur shall be effectuated by the manager designated by the notary in the established procedure.

Article 873. Preservation of Contract of Complex Entre-preneurial License in Force in Event of Change of Firm Name

In the event of a change by the licensor of his firm name, the contract of complex entrepreneurial license shall be preserved and operate with respect to the new firm name of the licensor unless the licensee requires the dissolution of the contract. In the event of the preservation of the operation of the contract the licensee shall have the right to require commensurate reduction of the remuneration due to the licensor.

Article 874. Consequences of Termination of Exclusive Right Within Licensed Complex

If in the period of operation of a contract of complex entrepreneurial license the period of operation of the exclusive right has expired which was within the licensed complex, or such right terminated on other grounds, the contract shall be preserved, less the provisions relating to the terminated right, and the licensee, unless provided otherwise by the contract, shall have the right to require commensurate reduction of the remuneration due to the licensor.

Chapter 51. Keeping

§ 1. General Provisions on Keeping

Article 875. Contract of Keeping

Under a contract of keeping one party (keeper) shall be obliged to keep a thing transferred to it by the other party (transferor) and to return this thing intact.

In a contract of keeping in which the keeper is an organization effectuating keeping as one of the purposes of its professional activity (professional keeper) the duty of the keeper to accept a thing for keeping from the transferor within the period provided for by the contract may be provided for.

Article 876. Performance of Duty to Accept Thing for Keeping

A keeper who effectuates keeping as an entrepreneurial or other professional activity may assume under a contract of keeping the obligation to accept a thing of the transferor for keeping and to keep that transferred by the transferor in accordance with the rules provided for by the present Article.

The keeper who has assumed under the contract of keeping the obligation to accept a thing for keeping shall not have the right to demand the transfer of this thing to him for keeping. However, the transferor who has not transferred a thing for keeping within the period provided for by the contract of keeping shall bear responsibility to the keeper for losses caused in connection with the unconstituted keeping unless provided otherwise by a law or the contract.

Unless provided otherwise by the contract of keeping, the keeper shall be relieved from the duty to accept a thing for keeping in instances when the thing is not transferred to him within the period stipulated by the contract, and when this period is not determined, upon the expiry of three months from the day of conclusion of the contract.

Article 877. Form of Contract of Keeping

In instances when a contract of keeping must be concluded in written form (Article 108 of the present Code), the written form of the contract shall be considered to be complied with if the acceptance of the thing for keeping is certified by the keeper by means of the issuance to the transferor of a personal receipt, receipt, certificate, or other document signed by the keeper.

Compliance with the written form shall not be required if the thing is transferred for keeping under extraordinary circumstances (fire, natural calamity, sudden illness, threat of attack, and the like).

The contract of keeping may be concluded by means of the issuance by the keeper to the transferor of a numbered token (or number), or other mark certifying the acceptance of the thing for keeping, if this is permitted by legislation or is customary for the particular type of keeping.

The failure to comply with the simple written form of the contract of keeping shall not deprive the party of the right to refer to witness testimony in the event of a dispute concerning the identity of the thing accepted for keeping with the thing returned by the keeper.

Article 878. Period of Keeping

The keeper shall be obliged to keep a thing during the period stipulated by the contract. If the period of keeping is not provided for by the contract and can not be determined by proceeding from its conditions, the keeping shall be effectuated until the demand of the thing by the transferor.

If the period of keeping is determined by the moment of demand of the thing by the transferor, the keeper shall have the right upon the expiry of the period of keeping of the thing usual under the particular circumstances to require that the transferor take the thing back, having granted him a reasonable period for taking the thing. The failure of the transferor to perform this duty shall entail the consequences provided for by Article 888, paragraphs two and three, of the present Code.

Article 879. Keeping of Things with Pooling

When keeping with pooling, things accepted for keeping may be mixed with things of the same kind and quality of other transferors. The quantity of things of the same kind and quality which is equal or stipulated by the parties shall be returned to the transferor.

Keeping with pooling shall be effectuated only in instances when this is expressly provided for by the contract of keeping.

Article 880. Duty of Keeper to Ensure Preservation of Thing

The keeper shall be obliged to take all measures provided for by the contract of keeping, and also other necessary measures, in order to ensure the preservation of the thing transferred to him for keeping.

The keeper shall be obliged to return to the transferor or other person specified by him as the recipient that thing which was transferred to him for keeping unless keeping with pooling was provided for by the contract. The thing must be returned in that state in which it was accepted for keeping, taking into account the natural deterioration or natural loss thereof.

Simultaneously with the return of the thing the keeper shall be obliged to transfer the fruits and revenues received for the time of its keeping unless established otherwise by the contract of keeping.

Article 881. Use of Thing Transferred for Keeping

The keeper shall not have the right without the consent of the transferor to use a thing transferred for keeping, nor likewise to grant the possibility of use thereof to third persons, except for an instance when the use of the thing being kept is necessary in order to ensure the preservation thereof.

Article 882. Change of Conditions of Keeping

The keeper shall be obliged immediately to inform the transferor about the necessity of changing the conditions of keeping of a thing and shall await his reply.

In the event when a danger of loss or damage of the thing has arisen, the keeper shall be obliged to change the means, place, and other condition of keeping provided for by the contract of keeping without awaiting a reply of the transferor.

If during the keeping a real threat arose of the spoilage of the thing, or the thing already has been subjected to spoilage, or circumstances arose which do not enable the preservation to be ensured, and the timely taking of measures by the transferor can not be expected, the keeper shall have the right autonomously to sell the thing or part thereof at the price which has been formed at the place of keeping. If the said circumstances arose for reasons for which the keeper is not liable, he shall have the right to compensation of his expenses for the sale at the expense of the purchase price.

Article 883. Keeping of Things with Dangerous Properties

If the transferor when handing over for keeping things which are inflammable, explosive, or in general inherently dangerous did not warn the keeper about their properties, they may at any time be rendered harmless or destroyed by the keeper without compensation of losses to the transferor. The transferor shall be liable for losses caused in connection with the keeping of such things to the keeper and to third persons.

In the event of the transfer of things with dangerous properties for keeping to a professional keeper, the rules provided for by paragraph one of the present Article shall apply in the event when such things were handed over for keeping under an incorrect name and the keeper when accepting them could not by means of external inspection certify their dangerous properties.

In the event of keeping for compensation in the instances provided for by paragraphs one and two of the present Article, the remuneration paid for keeping the things shall not be returned, and if it was not paid, the keeper may recover it in full.

If the things specified in paragraph one of the present Article and accepted for keeping with the knowledge and consent of the keeper become, despite compliance with the conditions for their keeping, dangerous for surrounding persons or for the property of the keeper or third persons and circumstances do not permit the keeper to require that they be immediately taken back by the transferor or the transferor does not fulfill this demand, these things may be rendered harmless or destroyed by the keeper without compensation of losses to the transferor. The transferor shall not bear in this event responsibility to the keeper and third persons for losses caused in connection with the keeping of these things.

Article 884. Transfer of Thing for Keeping to Third Person

Unless provided otherwise by legislator or a contract of keeping, the keeper shall not have the right without the consent of the transferor to transfer a thing for keeping to a third person, unless the necessity arose for this in the interests of the transferor and the keeper lacked the possibility to receive his consent. The keeper shall be obliged immediately to inform the transferor about the transfer of the thing to a third person.

The keeper shall be liable for the actions of the third person to whom he transferred the thing for keeping.

Article 885. Remuneration for Keeping

Remuneration for keeping must be paid to the keeper at the end of the keeping, and if the payment for keeping has been provided for by periods, upon the expiry of each period.

If the keeping is terminated before the expiry of the stipulated period for circumstances for which the keeper is not liable, he shall have the right to a commensurate part of the remuneration, and in the event provided for by Article 883, paragraphs one, two, and three, of the present Code, to the entire amount of remuneration.

If the keeping is terminated before time under circumstances for which the keeper is liable, he shall not have the right to demand remuneration for keeping, but must return to the transferor the amounts received on the account of this remuneration.

If upon the expiry of the period provided for by the contract a thing in keeping is not taken back by the transferor, he shall be obliged to pay the keeper commensurate remuneration for the further keeping of the thing.

The rules of the present Article shall apply unless established otherwise by the contract of keeping.

Article 886. Compensation of Expenses for Keeping

Unless provided otherwise by the contract, the expenses for the keeping of a thing shall be included in the amount of remuneration. It shall be presupposed that extraordinary expenses are not included in the amount of remuneration or in the expenses provided for by the contract of keeping.

In the event of keeping without compensation, the transferor shall be obliged to compensate the keeper for necessary actual expenses made, unless provided otherwise by the contract of keeping.

Article 887. Extraordinary Expenses for Keeping

Expenses for the keeping of a thing which exceed ordinary expenses of this nature and which the parties could not foresee in the event of the conclusion of a contract of keeping (extraordinary expenses) shall be compensated to the keeper if the transferor gave consent to these expenses or approved them subsequently, and also in other instances provided for by legislation or by the contract.

When it is necessary to make extraordinary expenses, the keeper shall be obliged to request the transferor for consent to these expenses. If the transferor does not communicate his nonconsent within the period specified by the keeper, or within the time normally necessary for a reply, it shall be considered that he agreed to the extraordinary expenses.

In an event when the keeper has made extraordinary expenses for keeping, not having received the prior consent from the transferor to these expenses, although under the circumstances of the case this was possible, and the transferor subsequently did not approve them, the keeper may demand compensation of extraordinary expenses only within the limits of the damage which might be caused to the thing if these expenses were not made.

Unless provided otherwise by the contract of keeping, extraordinary expenses shall be compensated in addition to the remuneration for keeping.

Article 888. Receipt of Thing Back by Transferor

Upon the expiry of the period of keeping provided for by the contract, the transferor shall be obliged immediately to receive the thing transferred for keeping.

In the event of the evasion by the transferor to receive the thing, the keeper shall have the right, unless provided otherwise by the contract of keeping, to autonomously realize the thing, and in the event when the value thereof exceeds the amount of fifty times the established base calculation amount, in the procedure provided for by Articles 379, 380, and 381 of the present Code [as amended by Law of 3 December 2019, No. ЗРУ-586].

The amount received from the realization of the thing shall be transferred to the transferor, less that due to the keeper.

Article 889. Responsibility of Keeper for Loss, Shortage, or Damage of Thing

The keeper shall be liable for loss, shortage, or damage to a thing accepted for keeping on the grounds provided for by Article 333 of the present Code.

A professional keeper shall be liable for loss, shortage, or damage to a thing being kept unless it is proved that the loss, shortage, or damage occurred:

as a consequence of insuperable force;

because of the latent properties of the thing, of which the keeper did not know and should not have known when accepting it for keeping;

as a result of intent or gross negligence of the transferor.

If the thing being kept is not taken back by the transferor upon the expiry of the period of keeping provided for by the contract, or the period during which the transferor at the demand of the keeper is obliged to take back the thing, then the keeper shall be liable for the loss, shortage, or damage of this thing only when there is intent or gross negligence on his part.

Article 890. Amount of Responsibility of Keeper

Losses caused to the transferor by the loss, shortage, or damaging of a thing shall be compensated by the keeper in accordance with Article 324 of the present Code unless provided otherwise by a law or the contract of keeping.

In the event of keeping without compensation, the losses caused to the transferor by the loss, shortage, or damaging of the thing shall be compensated:

for loss or shortage of the thing: in the amount of the value of the lost or short-delivered things;

for the damaging of things: in the amount by which their value was reduced.

If as a result of the damage for which the keeper is liable the quality of the thing has been so changed that it can not be used for its initial designation, the transferor shall have the right to refuse it and to require compensation from the keeper for the value of this thing, and also of other losses, if this is provided by a law or by the contract of keeping.

Article 891. Compensation of Losses Caused to Keeper

The transferor shall be obliged to compensate the keeper for losses caused by the properties of the thing handed over for keeping if the keeper, in accepting the thing for keeping, did not know and should not have known about these properties.

Article 892. Termination of Obligation of Keeping Upon Demand of Transferor

The keeper shall be obliged at the demand of the transferor to return the thing accepted for keeping even though another period for return was determined by the contract. In this event the transferor shall be obliged to compensate the losses to the keeper caused by the termination before time of the obligation unless provided otherwise by the contract of keeping.

Article 893. Application of General Provisions on Keeping to Individual Types Thereof

The general provisions on keeping shall apply to individual types thereof unless the rules on individual types of keeping provided for by Articles 894-913 of the present Code and in other acts of legislation have established otherwise.

§ 2. Individual Types of Keeping

Article 894. Keeping in Pawnshop

Moveable things designated for personal consumption may be accepted from citizens for keeping in a pawnshop.

The contract of keeping a thing in a pawnshop shall be formalized by the issuance by the pawnshop to the transferor (or client) of an inscribed personal receipt.

A thing handed over for keeping to a pawnshop shall be subject to valuation by agreement of the parties in accordance with the prices for a thing of that type and quality usually established in trade at the moment and at the place of its acceptance for keeping.

A pawnshop shall be obliged to insure to the benefit of the transferor at its expense things accepted for keeping in the full amount of their valuation made in accordance with paragraph three of the present Article.

Article 895. Things Not Demanded from Pawnshop

In the event of the evasion by the transferor of receiving back the thing, the pawnshop shall be obliged to keep it for three months. Upon the expiry of this period, the undemanded thing may be sold by the pawnshop in the procedure established by Article 289, paragraph seven, of the present Code.

From the amount received from the sale of the thing, payment for the keeping thereof shall be paid and other payments due to the pawnshop. The balance of the amount shall be returned by the pawnshop to the possessor of the personal receipt upon the presentation thereof.

Article 896. Keeping of Valuables in Bank

A bank may accept securities, precious metals and stones, other valuables, and also documents, for keeping.

The contract of keeping of valuables in a bank shall be formalized by the issuance by the bank to the transferor of an inscribed deposit document, the presentation of which shall be grounds for the issuance by the bank of the valuables being kept to the transferor.

In instances provided for by the contract of keeping (or deposit) of securities, the bank in addition to ensuring their preservation shall also effectuate legally significant actions with respect to the securities (representation, and so forth).

A contract of keeping of valuables with the use of an individual bank safe (safe box, isolated premise in a bank) may be concluded by means of the performance by the bank of actions relating to the acceptance of valuables for keeping and the issuance to the transferor of a key to the safe, cards identifying the transferor, or other mark or document which certifies the right of the bearer to access to the safe and receipt of the valuables therein.

Unless provided otherwise by the contract, the transferor shall have the right at any time to remove the valuables from the safe, returning them back, and to work with the documents being kept. The bank in so doing shall have the right to record the receipt and return of the valuables by the transferor.

When the transferor received part of the valuables from the safe, the bank shall bear responsibility for the preservation of the remaining part of the valuables.

The rules established by the present Article for keeping valuables in a bank safe shall not extend to an instance when the bank grants its safe to another person for use on conditions of property rental.

Article 897. Keeping in Left Luggage Rooms of Transport Organizations

Left luggage rooms within the jurisdiction of transport organizations shall be obliged to accept for keeping the things of passengers and other citizens irrespective of whether they have travel documents. A contract for keeping in left luggage rooms of transport organizations shall be deemed to be a public [contract].

In confirmation of the acceptance of a thing for keeping in a left luggage room (except for automatic rooms) a receipt or numbered token shall be issued to the transferor.

In the event of the loss of the receipt or token the thing handed over to the left luggage room shall be issued to the transferor upon presentation of evidence of the affiliation of this thing to him.

The amount of the losses incurred by the transferor as a consequence of the loss, shortage, or damaging of things handed over for the left luggage room shall be paid to the transferor within a twenty-four hour period from the moment of presentation of the demand concerning the compensation thereof if when handing over the thing for keeping a valuation was made or if the parties came to an agreement relative to the amount of losses subject to compensation.

A thing may be handed over to the left luggage room for a period within the limits established by special rules or by agreement of the parties. A thing undemanded within the said period the left luggage room shall be obliged to keep for another thirty days. Upon the expiry of this period, an undemanded thing may be sold, and the amount received from the sale distributed in accordance with Article 895 of the present Code.

Article 898. Keeping in Check Rooms of Organizations

Keeping in check rooms of organizations shall be presupposed to be without compensation if remuneration for keeping is not stipulated or by other obvious means is not stipulated when handing over a thing for keeping.

In confirmation of the acceptance of a thing for keeping in the check room the keeper shall issue to the transferor a numbered token or other mark confirming the acceptance of the thing for keeping.

A thing handed over to a check room shall be issued to the bearer of the token. In so doing the keeper shall not be obliged to verify the powers of the bearer of the token to receive the thing. However, the keeper shall have the right to delay the return of the thing to the bearer of the token if doubt has arisen as to the affiliation of the token to the bearer thereof.

The keeper shall have the right to issue a thing from the check room when the transferor has lost the token but the fact of handing over the thing to the check room or affiliation thereof to him does not give rise to doubts by the keeper or is proved by the transferor. The responsibility of the organization for the preservation of things in check rooms, and also the periods for keeping undemanded things, shall be determined according to the rules established by Article 897, paragraphs four and five, of the present Code.

Article 899. Keeping in Hotel

A hotel shall be liable as keeper and without a special agreement concerning this for loss, shortage, or damaging of things deposited at the hotel by the person residing therein, except for instances when the loss, shortage, or damage occurred as a consequence of insuperable force, properties of the thing itself, or through the fault of the person residing himself, persons accompanying him, or his visitors.

A thing entrusted to workers of the hotel, or a thing placed in a place designed for this (hotel room and others) shall be considered to be deposited in the hotel.

A hotel shall be liable for the loss of money, other currency valuables, securities, and other precious things on condition that they were accepted by the hotel for keeping under a separate contract of keeping.

The person residing in the hotel who has discovered a loss, shortage, or damaging of his things shall be obliged without delay to declare this to the administration of the hotel. Otherwise, the hotel shall be relieved from responsibility for the failure to preserve the things.

A hotel shall not be relieved from responsibility for the preservation of things of persons residing therein even though it made an announcement that it does not assume this responsibility.

The periods for keeping and the fate of undemanded things in hotels shall be determined according to the rules established by Article 897, paragraph five, of the present Code.

The rules of the present Article also shall apply with respect to the keeping of things in motels, rest homes, boarding houses, dormitories, sanatoriums, public baths, and also in other organizations having specially allotted places for the keeping of things of citizens visiting the organization.

Article 900. Keeping of Things in Dispute (Sequestration)

Under a contract on sequestration two or several persons between whom a dispute has arisen concerning the right to a thing shall transfer the disputed thing to a third person who is obliged upon the settlement of the dispute to return the thing to that person to whom it was awarded by decision of a court or by agreement of all the disputing persons (contractual sequestration).

A disputed thing may be transferred for keeping by way of sequestration by decision of a court (judicial sequestration).

Either a person assigned by a court or a person determined by mutual consent of the disputing parties may be the keeper under judicial sequestration. In both instances the consent of the keeper shall be required unless provided otherwise by legislation.

Both moveable and immoveable things may be transferred for keeping by way of sequestration.

§ 3. Keeping in Goods Warehouse

Article 901. Goods Warehouse

An organization effectuating the keeping of goods and rendering services connected with keeping as entrepreneurial activity shall be deemed to be a goods warehouse.

Article 902. Goods Warehouse of Common Use

A goods warehouse shall be deemed to be a warehouse of common use if in accordance with legislation it is not relegated to warehouses which might accept goods for keeping from a limited group of persons.

A contract of warehouse keeping concluded by a goods warehouse of common use shall be deemed to be a public contract.

Article 903. Contract of Warehouse Keeping

Under a contract of warehouse keeping, a goods warehouse (keeper) shall be obliged for remuneration to keep the goods transferred to it by the goods-possessor (transferor) and to return these goods intact.

A contract of warehouse keeping shall be concluded in written form. The written form of the contract of warehouse keeping shall be considered to be complied with if the conclusion thereof and the acceptance of the goods at the warehouse are certified by a warehouse document.

Article 904. Keeping of Things With Right of Disposition Thereof

If it follows from legislation or the contract of warehouse keeping that the goods warehouse may dispose of goods handed over to it for keeping, then the rules of Chapter 41 of the present Code shall apply to the relations of the parties; however, the time and place of return of the goods shall be determined by the rules of the present Chapter.

Article 905. Duties of Goods Warehouse

A goods warehouse shall be obliged to comply with the conditions (or regime) of keeping established in standards, technical conditions, technological instructions, instructions for keeping, rules for keeping individual types of goods, and other special normative documents binding upon the warehouse.

A goods warehouse shall be obliged to make an inspection at its expense of goods when accepting for keeping unless provided otherwise by the contract of warehouse keeping.

A goods warehouse shall be obliged to grant to the goods-possessor the possibility to inspect the goods or samples thereof if the keeping is effectuated with depersonalization, take samples, and take measures necessary in order to ensure the intactness of the goods.

In an event when in order to ensure the intactness of the goods it is required to urgently change the conditions of keeping, a goods warehouse shall have the right to take the required urgent measures autonomously. It shall be obliged to inform the goods-possessor about the measures taken.

When discovering damage of the goods during the keeping which exceeds the limits agreed in the contract of warehouse keeping or ordinary norms of natural spoilage, the goods warehouse shall be obliged immediately to draw up an act and on the same day to notify the transferor.

Article 906. Verification of Quantity and State of Good in Event of Return Thereof to Goods-Possessor

The goods possessor and goods warehouse shall have the right each to demand in the event of returning a good to inspect it and verify the quantity thereof. The expenses caused by this shall be borne by he who required inspection of the good or verification of the quantity thereof.

If when returning a good by the warehouse to the goods-possessor the good was not jointly inspected or verified by them, a statement concerning the shortage or damaging of the good as a consequence of the improper keeping thereof must be made to the warehouse in writing when receiving the good, and with respect to shortage or damage which could not be discovered with the ordinary means of accepting the good, within a reasonable period necessary for the discovery thereof.

In the absence of the statement specified in paragraph two of the present Article it shall be considered, unless it is proved otherwise, that the good was returned by the warehouse in accordance with the conditions of the contract of warehouse keeping.

Article 907. Repudiation by Goods Warehouse of Contract of Warehouse Keeping

A goods warehouse shall have the right to refuse performance of contract of keeping in instances when the transferor concealed the dangerous character of a good that threatens the infliction of material damage.

Article 908. Warehouse Documents

Goods warehouses may issue in confirmation of the acceptance of goods for keeping the following warehouse documents:

dual warehouse certificate;

simple warehouse certificate;

warehouse receipt.

A dual warehouse certificate, each part thereof, and a simple warehouse certificate shall be securities.

A dual and a simple warehouse certificate may be the subject of pledge.

Article 909. Dual Warehouse Certificate

A dual warehouse certificate shall consist of the warehouse certificate and the pledge certificate (or warrant), which may be separated one from the other.

On each part of a dual warehouse certificate there must be indicated:

the name and location of the goods warehouse which accepted the good for keeping;

the current number of the warehouse certificate according to the register of the warehouse;

the name of the organization or citizen from which the good was accepted for keeping, and also the location (or place of residence) of the goods-possessor;

the name and quantity of the good accepted for keeping – number of units and/or pieces of the good and/or the measure (weight, volume) of the good;

the period for which the good is accepted for keeping, if such period is established, or an indication that the good is accepted for keeping on demand;

the amount of remuneration for keeping or the tariffs on the basis of which it is calculated, and the procedure of payment for keeping;

the date of issuance of the warehouse certificate.

Both parts of the dual warehouse certificate must have identical signatures of the empowered person and the seal of the goods warehouse (when there are seals) [as amended by Law of 20 August 2015, No. ЗРУ-391. СЗ РУ (2015), no. 33, item 439].

A document which does not correspond to the requirements of the present Article shall not be a dual warehouse certificate.

Article 910. Rights of Holder of Warehouse and Pledge Certificates for Good

The holder of a warehouse and pledge certificates shall have the right to dispose of the good being kept in the warehouse in full.

The holder of the warehouse certificate separated from the pledge certificate shall have the right to dispose of the good, but may not take it from the warehouse until payment of the credit issued under the pledge certificate.

The holder of a pledge certificate shall have the right of pledge to the good in the amount of the credit issued under this certificate and interest thereon. In the event of the pledge of a good, a notation thereof shall be made on the warehouse certificate.

Article 911. Transfer of Warehouse and Pledge Certificates

The warehouse certificate and the pledge certificate may be transferred together or separately under an inscription of endorsement.

Article 912. Simple Warehouse Certificate

A simple warehouse certificate shall be issued to the bearer.

A simple warehouse certificate must contain the information provided by Article 909 of the present Code, and also an indication that it was issued to the bearer.

Article 913. Issuance of Good Under Dual Warehouse Certificate

A goods warehouse shall issue the good to the holder of the warehouse and pledge certificates (dual warehouse certificate) in exchange for both these certificates together.

A good shall be issued by the warehouse to the holder of a warehouse certificate who does not have the pledge certificate but has contributed the amount of the debt with regard to it not other than in exchange for the warehouse certificate and on condition of the presentation together with it of a receipt concerning payment of the entire amount of the debt under the pledge certificate.

The holder of warehouse and pledge certificates shall have the right to demand the issuance of the good in parts. In so doing new certificates for the good remaining in the warehouse shall be issued to him in exchange for the original certificates.

A goods warehouse, notwithstanding the requirements of the present Article, which has issued a good to the holder of a warehouse certificate who does not have the pledge certificate and has not contributed the amount of the debt with regard to it shall bear responsibility to the holder of the pledge certificate for payment of the entire amount secured under it.

Chapter 52. Insurance

Article 914. Voluntary and Obligatory Insurance

Insurance shall be effectuated on the basis of contracts of property or personal insurance concluded by a citizen or juridical person (insurant) with an insurance organization (insurer).

A contract of personal insurance shall be a public contract.

In instances when the duty to insure as insurers of life, health, or property of other persons or his own civil responsibility to other persons at his own expense or at the expense of the interested persons (obligatory insurance) has been placed by a law on the persons specified therein, the insurance shall be effectuated by means of the conclusion of contracts in accordance with the rules of the present Chapter.

Under obligatory insurance the insurant shall be obliged to conclude a contract with the insurer on the conditions provided for by legislation regulating the particular type of insurance.

Instances of the obligatory insurance of life, health, and property of citizens at the expense of assets of the State budget (obligatory State insurance) may be provided for by a law.

Article 915. Contract of Property Insurance

Under a contract of property insurance one party (insurer) shall be obliged for the payment stipulated by the contract (insurance premium) if the event ensues provided for in the contract (insured event) compensate the other party (insurant) or other person to whose benefit the contract was concluded (beneficiary) for losses caused as a consequence of this event to the insured property or losses in connection with other property interests of the insurant (to pay insurance compensation) within the limits of the amount (insured amount) determined by the contract.

Under a contract of property insurance there may be insured:

risk of loss (or perishing), shortage, or damage to determined property;

risk of civil responsibility – risk of responsibility for obligations arising as a consequence of causing harm to life, health, or property of other persons, and in the instances provided for by a law, also responsibility under contracts;

entrepreneurial risk – risk of failing to receive anticipated revenues from entrepreneurial activity because of a violation of their obligations by the contracting parties of the entrepreneur or changes of conditions of this activity under circumstances beyond the control of the entrepreneur.

Article 916. Interests, the Insurance of Which Is Not Permitted

The insurance of unlawful interests shall not be permitted.

The insurance of losses from participation in games, lotteries, and betting shall not be permitted.

The insurance of expenses which a person may be forced to make for the purpose of liberating hostages shall not be permitted.

The conditions of contracts of insurance which are contrary to paragraphs one, two, and three of the present Article shall be null.

Article 917. Insurance of Property

Property may be insured under a contract of insurance to the benefit of the person (insurant or beneficiary) having an interest based on legislation or the contract in the preservation of this property to the benefit of the owner thereof, person having another right to a thing in the property, lessee, independent-work contractor, keeper, commission agent, and the like.

A contract of insurance of property concluded in the absence of an interest of the insurant or beneficiary in the preservation of the insured property shall be invalid.

A contract of insurance of property to the benefit of a beneficiary may be concluded without specifying the name of the beneficiary. In the event of concluding such a contract, a bearer insurance policy shall be issued to the insurant. In the event of the effectuation of the rights under such contract, it shall be necessary to submit this policy to the insurer.

Article 918. Insurance of Responsibility for Causing of Harm

Under a contract of insurance of the risk of responsibility for obligations which arise as a consequence of the causing of harm to the life, health, or property of other persons, the risk of responsibility of the insurant himself, or another person on whom such responsibility may be placed, may be insured.

The person whose risk of responsibility for causing harm has been insured must be named in the contract of insurance. If this person is not named in the contract, the responsibility of the insurant himself shall be considered to be the insured risk.

The contract of insurance of the risk of responsibility for causing harm shall be considered to be concluded to the benefit of the persons to whom harm may be caused (beneficiary) even if the contract was concluded to the benefit of the insurant or other person responsible for causing harm or it is not said in the contract to whose benefit it was concluded.

In the event when responsibility for the causing of harm was insured by virtue of the fact that the insuring thereof is obligatory, and also in other instances provided for by a law or contract of insurance of such responsibility, the person to whose benefit the contract of insurance is considered to be concluded shall have the right to present directly to the insurer a demand concerning compensation of harm within the limits of the insured amount.

Article 919. Insurance of Responsibility under Contract

Insurance of the risk of responsibility for a violation of a contract shall be permitted in the instances provided for by a law.

Under a contract of insurance of the risk of responsibility for a violation of a contract, only the risk of responsibility of the insurant itself may be insured. A contract of insurance not corresponding to this requirement shall be null.

The risk of responsibility for a violation of a contract shall be considered to be insured to the benefit of the party to which under the conditions of this contract the insurant must bear respective responsibility – the beneficiary – even if the contract of insurance is concluded to the benefit of another person or it is not said therein to whose benefit it was concluded.

Article 920. Insurance of Entrepreneurial Risk

Under a contract of insurance of entrepreneurial risk only the entrepreneurial risk of the insurant itself and only to its benefit may be insured.

The contract of insurance of entrepreneurial risk of a person which is not the insurant shall be null.

A contract of insurance of entrepreneurial risk to the benefit of a person which is not the insurant shall be concluded to the benefit of the insurant.

Article 921. Contract of Personal Insurance

Under a contract of personal insurance one party (insurer) shall be obliged for the payment stipulated by the contract (insurance premium) to be paid by the other party (insurant) to pay one time or to pay periodically the amount stipulated by the contract (insured amount) in the event of the causing of harm to the life or health of the insurant himself or other citizen named in the contract (insured person), the reaching by him of a determined age or the ensuing in his life of another event provided for by the contract (insured event).

The right to receive the insured amount shall belong to the person to whose benefit the contract was concluded.

A contract of personal insurance shall be considered to be concluded to the benefit of the insured person if another person is not named in the contract as the beneficiary. In the event of the death of the person insured under the contract in which another beneficiary is not named, the heirs of the insured person shall be deemed to be the beneficiaries.

A contract of personal insurance to the benefit of a person who is not the insured person, including to the benefit of an insurant who is not the insured person, may be concluded only with the written consent of the insured person. In the absence of such consent, the contract may be deemed to be invalid upon the suit of the insured person, and in the event of the death of this person upon the suit of his heirs.

Article 922. Obligatory Insurance

The duty to insure may be established by a law:

the life, health, or property of other persons determined in a law in the event of the causing of harm to their life, health, or property;

the risk of civil responsibility which may ensue as a consequence of the causing of harm to the life, health, or property of other persons or violations of contracts with other persons.

The duty to act as insurant shall be placed by a law on the persons determined therein.

Other types of obligatory insurance may be established by a law.

The duty to insure his own life or health may not be placed on a citizens according to a law.

In the instances provided for by a law or in the procedure established by it, the duty to insure property may be placed on juridical persons having property in economic jurisdiction or operative management which is State ownership.

In instances when the duty of insuring property does not arise from a law, but is based on a contract with the possessor of the property or on the constitutive documents of the juridical person which is the owner of the property, such insurance shall not be obligatory in the sense of the present Article and shall not entail the consequences provided for by Article 924 of the present Code.

Article 923. Effectuation of Obligatory Insurance

Obligatory insurance shall be effectuated by means of the conclusion of a contract of insurance by the person on which the duty of such insurance (as insurant) with the insurer was placed.

Obligatory insurance shall be effectuated at the expense of the insurant, except for obligatory insurance of passengers which in the instances provided for by a law may be effectuated at their expense.

Objects subject to obligatory insurance, the risks from which they must be insured, and the minimum insured amounts shall be determined by legislation.

Article 924. Consequences of Violation of Rules on Obligatory Insurance

The person to whose benefit under a law obligatory insurance must be effectuated shall have the right if it is known to it that the insurance is not effectuated to require in a judicial proceeding the effectuation thereof by the person on whom the duty of insurance has been placed as insurant.

If the person on which the duty of insurance has been placed as insurant does not effectuate it or has concluded a contract of insurance on conditions which worsen the status of the beneficiary in comparison with the conditions determined by a law, it shall, in the event of the ensuing of the insured event, bear responsibility to the beneficiary on the same conditions on which the insurance compensation should have been paid under the proper insurance.

Article 925. Insurer

Juridical persons which are commercial organizations and having a license for the effectuation of insurance of the respective type may conclude contracts of insurance as insurers unless provided otherwise by legislative acts.

The requirements which insurance organizations must meet, the procedure for the licensing thereof, and the effectuation of State supervision over their activity shall be determined by a law.

Article 926. Fulfillment of Duties Under Contract of Insurance by Insurant and Beneficiary

The conclusion of a contract of insurance to the benefit of a beneficiary, including when he is the insured person, shall not relieve the insurant from the fulfillment of the duties under this contract, unless provided otherwise by the contract or the duties of the insurant have been fulfilled by the person to whose benefit the contract was concluded.

The insurer shall have the right to require from the beneficiary, including when the insured person is the beneficiary, the fulfillment of the duties under the contract of insurance, including the duties placed on the insurant but not fulfilled by him, in the event of the presentation by the beneficiary of a demand concerning payment of the insurance compensation under the contract of property insurance or insured amount under a contract of personal insurance. The risk of the consequences of the failure to fulfill or the untimely fulfillment of the duties which should have been fulfilled earlier shall be borne by the beneficiary.

Article 927. Form of Contract of Insurance

The contract of insurance must be concluded in written form.

The failure to comply with this requirement shall entail the invalidity of the contract of insurance.

A contract of insurance may be concluded by means of drawing up one document or handing over by the insurer to the insurant on the basis of his written or oral application the insurance policy (or certificate, receipt) signed by the insurer containing the conditions of the contract of insurance. In this instance the consent of the insurant to conclude a contract on the conditions proposed by the insurer shall be confirmed by the acceptance from the insurer of the said documents and the payment of the insurance premium or – when paying the insurance premium by installment – by the payment of the first contribution.

The insurer when concluding a contract shall have the right to use the standard forms of the contract of insurance (or insurance policy) for individual types of insurance.

Article 928. Insurance Under General Policy

The systematic insuring of various lots of property of the same kind (goods, cargoes, and the like) on the same conditions during a determined period may by agreement of the insurant with the insurer be effectuated on the basis of one contract of insurance: a general policy.

The insurant shall be obliged with respect to each lot of property falling under the operation of the general policy to communicate to the insurer the information stipulated by such policy within the period provided for by it, and if it is not provided for, immediately upon the receipt thereof. The insurant shall not be relieved of this duty even if at the moment of receiving such information the possibility of losses subject to compensation by the insurer already has disappeared.

At the demand of the insurant, the insurer shall be obliged to issue insurance policies for individual lots of insurance falling under the operation of the general policy.

In the event of the failure of the content of the insurance policy to conform to the general policy, preference shall be given to the insurance policy.

Article 929. Material Conditions of Contract of Insurance

When concluding a contract of property insurance, agreement must be reached between the insurant and the insurer concerning:

the determined property or other property interest which is the object of insurance;

the character of the event, in the event of the ensuing of which the insurance is made (insured event);

the amount of the insured amount;

the procedure for determining the amount of insurance compensation if the possibility is provided by the contract of the payment thereof in an amount lesser than the insured amount;

the amount of insurance premium and the period(s) for payment thereof;

the period of operation of the contract.

When concluding a contract of personal insurance, agreement must be reached between the insurant and the insurer concerning:

the insured person;

the character of the event, in the event of the ensuing of which in the life of the insured person the insurance is effectuated (insured event);

the amount of the insured amount;

the amount of insurance premium and the period(s) for the payment thereof;

the period of operation of the contract.

Article 930. Determination of Conditions of Contract of Insurance in Rules of Insurance

The conditions on which a contract of insurance is concluded may be determined in standard rules of insurance of the respective type adopted, approved, or confirmed by the insurer or by an association of insurers (rules of insurance).

The conditions contained in the rules of insurance and not included in the text of the contract of insurance (or policy) shall be obligatory for the insurant (or beneficiary) if the application of these rules is expressly specified in the contract (or policy) and the rules themselves have been set out in a single document with the contract (or policy) or on the reverse side thereof or annexed thereto. In the last event the handing over to the insurant when concluding the contract of the rules of insurance must be certified by an entry on the contract.

When concluding a contract of insurance, the insurant and the insurer may agree concerning changing or excluding individual provisions of the rules of insurance and on including in the contract provisions absent in the rules.

The insurant (or beneficiary) shall have the right to refer in defense of its interests to the rules of insurance of the respective type to which there is a reference in a contract of insurance (or policy) even if these rules by virtue of the present Article are not obligatory for it.

Article 931. Information Granted by Insurant When Concluding Contract of Insurance

When concluding a contract of insurance, the insurant shall be obliged to communicate to the insurer the circumstances known to the insurant having material significance for determining the probability of the ensuing of the insured event and the amount of possible losses from the ensuing thereof (insured risk).

Circumstances specifically stipulated by the insurer in the standard form of a contract of insurance (or policy), the rules of insurance transferred to the insurant, or in his written questionnaire shall be deemed to be material.

If a contract of insurance was concluded in the absence of the answers of the insurant to any questions of the insurer, the insurer may not subsequently demand dissolution of the contract or the deeming thereof to be invalid on the grounds that the respective circumstances were not communicated by the insurant.

If after the conclusion of the contract of insurance it is established that the insurant communicated knowingly false information to the insurer concerning the circumstances specified in paragraph one of the present Article, the insurer shall have the right to require the contract to be deemed invalid and the application of the consequences provided for by Article 123, paragraph two, of the present Code.

The insurer may not demand a contract of insurance to be deemed invalid if the circumstances concerning which the insurant was silent already have disappeared.

Article 932. Right of Insurer to Valuation of Insured Risk

When concluding a contract of insurance of property, the insurer shall have the right to make an inspection of the property to be insured and, when necessary, to organize the conducting of an appraisal for the purpose of establishing its true value [as amended by Law of 17 September 2010, No. ЗРУ-257. СЗ РУ (2010), no. 37, item 315].

When concluding a contract of personal insurance, the insurer shall have the right to investigate the person to be insured in order to evaluate the actual state of his health.

The valuation of insured risk by the insurer on the basis of the present Article shall be not obligatory for the insurant, who shall have the right to prove otherwise.

Article 933. Secrecy of Insurance

An insurer shall not have the right to divulge information concerning the insurant, insured person, and beneficiary, state of their health, and also the property status of these persons received by it as a result of its professional activity. The insurer, for a violation of the secrecy of insurance, depending upon the nature of the violated rights and the character of the violation, shall bear responsibility in accordance with the rules of Articles 985, 1021, and 1022 of the present Code.

Article 934. Insured Amount

The amount within whose limits the insurer is obliged to pay insurance compensation under a contract of property insurance or which it is obliged to pay under a contract of personal insurance (insured amount) shall be determined by agreement of the insurant with the insurer in accordance with the rules of the present Article.

When insuring property or entrepreneurial risk, unless provided otherwise by the contract of insurance, the insured amount must not exceed the true value thereof (insured value), which shall be considered to be:

for property: its true value at the location thereof on the day of concluding the contract of insurance;

for entrepreneurial risk: the losses from entrepreneurial activity which the insurant could anticipate had the ensuing of the insured event not occurred.

In contracts of personal insurance and contract of insurance of civil responsibility, the insured amount shall be determined by the parties at their discretion, except for instances provided by a law [as amended by Law of 21 April 2008, No. ЗРУ-156. СЗ РУ (2008), no. 17, item 129].

Article 935. Insured Value of Property

The value of property with which the insured interest is connected determined by agreement of the parties at the moment of concluding the contract of insurance, unless provided otherwise by legislation, shall be deemed to be the insured value (or insured valuation).

The insured value of property specified in a contract of insurance may not subsequently be contested, except for an instance when the insurer, not taking advantage of his right before concluding the contract to value the insured risk, was intentionally deceived with respect to this value.

Article 936. Partial Property Insurance

If in a contract of insurance of property or entrepreneurial risk the insured amount has been established lower than the insured value, the insurer shall, in the event of the ensuing of the insured event, be obliged to compensate the insurant (or beneficiary) for the losses incurred by the last proportionally to the relation of the insured amount to the insured value.

Article 937. Additional Property Insurance

If property or entrepreneurial risk has been insured only for part of the insured value, the insurant (or beneficiary) shall have the right to effectuate additional insurance, including from a different insurer, but so that the total insured amount under all the contracts of insurance does not exceed the insured value.

The failure to comply with the provisions of paragraph one of the present Article shall entail the consequences provided for by Article 938 of the present Code.

Article 938. Consequences of Insurance in Excess of Insured Value

If the insured amount specified in the contract of insurance of property or entrepreneurial risk exceeds the insured value, the contract shall be null in that part of the insured amount which exceeds the insured value.

The part of the insurance premium paid in excess shall not be subject to return in this event.

If in accordance with the contract of insurance the insurance premium is contributed by installments and at the moment of establishing the circumstances specified in paragraph one of the present Article it was not contributed in full, the balance of the insurance contributions must be paid in the amount reduced proportionally by the reduction of the amount of the insured amount.

If an excess of the insured amount in a contract of insurance was a consequence of fraud on the part of the insurant, the insurer shall have the right to demand the contract be deemed to be invalid and compensation of losses caused to it by this in the amount exceeding the amount of insurance premium received by it from the insurant.

Article 939. Double Insurance

The rules provided for in Article 938 of the present Code respectively shall apply in the event when the insured amount exceeded the insured value as a result of insuring one and the same property or entrepreneurial risk with two or several insurers (double insurance).

In the event of double insurance of property or entrepreneurial risk, each insurer shall bear the duty to pay insurance compensation within the limits of the contract concluded by it; however, the total amount of insurance compensation received from all the insurers may not exceed the real damage.

In so doing the insurant (or beneficiary) shall have the right to receive insurance compensation from any insurer within the limits of the insured amount provided for by the contract concluded with it. If the insurance compensation received does not cover the real damage, the insurant (or beneficiary) shall have the right to receive the deficit amount from another insurer.

An insurer fully or partially relieved from payment of insurance compensation by virtue of the fact that the damage caused was compensated by other insurers shall be obliged to return to the insurant the respective part of the insurance payments, deducting expenses incurred.

The rules of the present Article shall not apply in the event of double personal insurance where each insurer shall fulfill its insurance obligations to the insurant, insured person, and beneficiary autonomously irrespective of the fulfillment of obligations by other insurers.

Article 940. Property Insurance Against Various Insured Risks

Property and entrepreneurial risk may be insured against various insured risks either under one or under individual contracts of insurance, including under contracts with different insurers.

In these instances exceeding the amount of the total insured amount under all contracts over the insured value shall be permitted and the rules of Article 939 of the present Code respectively shall be applied.

Article 941. Co-Insurance

An object of insurance may be insured under one contract of insurance jointly by several insurers (co-insurance). If the rights and duties of each of the insurers have not been determined in such contract, they jointly and severally shall be liable to the insurant (or beneficiary) for payment of the insurance compensation under a contract of property insurance or the insured amount under a contract of personal insurance.

For the joint insuring of large-scale or especially large-scale risks the co-insurers may create simple partnerships (or insurance pools) on the basis of a contract of joint activity.

When there exists a respective agreement between the co-insurers, one of them may represent all of the co-insurers in mutual relations with the insurant (or beneficiary), remaining responsible to the last only in its participatory share.

Article 942. Insurance Premium and Insurance Contributions

By insurance premium is understood payment for insurance which the insurant (or beneficiary) is obliged to pay to the insurer in the procedure and within the periods which have been established by the contract of insurance.

The insurer when determining the amount of insurance premium subject to payment under the contract of insurance shall have the right to apply insurance tariffs worked out by it when determining the premium to be recovered per unit of insured amount, taking into account the object of insurance and the character of the insured risk.

In the instances provided for by a law the amount of insurance premium shall be determined in accordance with insurance tariffs established or regulated by State insurance supervision agencies.

If the contribution of the insurance premium by installments has been provided for by a contract of insurance, the consequences of the failure to pay within the established periods the regular insurance contributions may be determined by the contract.

If the insured event ensued before payment of a regular insurance contribution, the contribution of which has been delayed, the insurer shall have the right to limit the amount of insurance compensation subject to payment under a contract of property insurance or insured amount under a contract of personal insurance in proportion to the part of the insurance premium paid to it, and to set off the amount of delayed insurance contribution.

Article 943. Invalidity of Contract of Insurance

A contract of insurance shall be null in instances when:

the object of insurance did not exist at the moment of concluding the contract;

property was insured under a contract of property insurance which was acquired by criminal means, was the subject of a crime, or is subject to confiscation;

an unlawful interest was insured under the contract;

an event lacking the indicia of probability and chance of the ensuing thereof was provided for in the contract of insurance as an insured event.

A contract of insurance shall be null also in other instances provided for by the present Code and by other laws.

Article 944. Replacement of Insured Person

In the event that under a contract of insurance of the risk of responsibility for causing harm the responsibility of a person other than the insurant has been insured, the last shall have the right, unless provided otherwise by the contract, at any time before the ensuing of the insured event to replace this person by another, having informed the insurer thereof in writing.

The insured person named in the contract of personal insurance may be replaced by the insurant by another person only with the consent of the insured person himself and the insurer.

Article 945. Replacement of Beneficiary

An insurant shall have the right to replace the beneficiary named in the contract of insurance by another person, having informed the insurer thereof in writing. A replacement of a beneficiary under a contract of personal insurance designated with the consent of the insured person shall be permitted with the consent of this person.

The beneficiary may not be replaced by another person after he has fulfilled any of the duties under the contract of insurance or presented a demand against the insurer concerning payment of insurance compensation or the insured amount.

Article 946. Replacement of Insurant

In the event of the death of the insurant which concluded the contract of insurance of property, the rights and duties of the insurant shall pass to the person who accepted this property by way of inheriting. In other instances the passing of the right of ownership the rights and duties of the insurant shall pass to the new owner with the consent of the insurer unless established otherwise by the contract or by legislation.

In the event of the death of the insurant which concluded the contract of personal insurance to the benefit of the insured, the rights and duties determined by this contract shall pass to the insured with his consent. In the event of the impossibility of the fulfillment by the insured of the duties under the contract of insurance, his rights and duties may pass to the persons effectuating in accordance with legislation the duties relating to the protection of his rights and legal interests.

If in the period of operation of the contract of insurance the insurant was deemed by a court to lack dispositive legal capacity or to have limited dispositive legal capacity, the trustee or guardian thereof shall receive the rights and duties of such insurant. The insuring of the responsibility of the insurant to third persons shall end from the moment of the termination or limitation of his dispositive legal capacity.

In the event of the reorganization of the insurant which is a juridical person, the rights and duties in the period of the contract of insurance with regard to this contract shall pass with the consent of the insurer to the respective legal successor in the procedure determined by the present Code.

Article 947. Commencement of Operation of Contract of Insurance

A contract of insurance, unless provided otherwise therein, shall enter into force at the moment of payment of the insurance premium or first payment thereof.

Insurance stipulated by a contract of insurance shall extend to insured events which occurred after the entry of the contract of insurance into force, unless another period for the commencement of the operation of the insurance has been provided for in the contract.

Article 948. Termination Before Time of Contract of Insurance

A contract of insurance shall be terminated before the ensuing of the period for which it was concluded if after its entry into force the possibility of the ensuing of the insured event disappeared and the existence of the insured risk was terminated under circumstances other than the insured event. There shall be relegated to such circumstances, in particular:

the perishing of the insured property for reasons other than the ensuing of the insured event;

termination in the established procedure of entrepreneurial activity by the person who insured the entrepreneurial risk or risk of civil responsibility connected with such activity.

In the event of the termination before time of a contract of insurance under the circumstances specified in paragraph one of the present Article, the insurer shall have the right to part of the insurance premium in proportion to the time during which the insurance operated.

The insurant (or beneficiary) shall have the right to repudiate the contract of insurance at any time if at the moment of repudiation the possibility of the ensuing of the insured event had not disappeared under the circumstances specified in paragraph one of the present Article.

In the event of the repudiation before time by the insurant (or beneficiary) of the contract of insurance, the insurance premium paid to the insurer shall not be subject to return unless provided otherwise by the contract.

Article 949. Consequences of Increase of Insured Risk in Period of Operation of Contract

In the period of operation of a contract of property insurance the insurant (or beneficiary) shall be obliged immediately to communicate to the insurer significant changes in the circumstances communicated to the insurer when concluding the contract which have become known to him, if such changes may materially influence the increase of the insured risk.

Changes shall be deemed to be significant which are stipulated in the contract of insurance (or insurance policy) and in the rules of insurance transferred to the insurant.

An insurer who has been notified about circumstances entailing an increase of the insured risk shall have the right to require a change of the conditions of the contract of insurance or payment of an additional insurance premium commensurate to the increase of risk.

If the insurant (or beneficiary) objects to changes of the conditions of the contract of insurance or additional payment of the insurance premium, the insurer shall have the right to require dissolution of the contract in accordance with the rules provided for by Chapter 28 of the present Code.

In the event of the failure of the insurant or beneficiary to perform the duty provided for in paragraph one of the present Article, the insurer shall have the right to require dissolution of the contract of insurance and compensation of losses caused by dissolution of the contract.

The insurer shall not have the right to require dissolution of the contract of insurance if the circumstances entailing an increase of the insured risk have disappeared.

In the event of personal insurance, the consequences of a change of insured risk in the period of operation of the contract of insurance specified in paragraphs two, three, and four of the present Article may ensue only if they are expressly provided for in the contract.

Article 950. Transfer of Rights to Insured Property to Other Person

In the event of the transfer of rights to insured property from the person in whose interests the contract of insurance was concluded to another person the rights and duties under this contract shall pass to the person to whom the rights to the property passed, except for instances of compulsory seizure of the property of the grounds specified in Articles 197 and 199 of the present Code.

The person to whom the rights to insured property have passed must inform the insurer thereof in writing.

Article 951. Informing Insurer about Ensuing of Insured Event

An insurant under a contract of property insurance shall, after the ensuing of the insured event became known to him, be obliged immediately to inform the insurer or his representative about the ensuing thereof. If a period and/or means of informing has been provided for by the contract, it must be made within the stipulated period and by the means specified in the contract. The same duty shall lie on the beneficiary if he intends to take advantage of the right to insurance compensation under a contract concluded to his benefit.

The failure to perform the duty provided for by paragraph one of the present Article shall give to the insurer the right to refuse to pay the insurance compensation unless it is proved that the insurer knew in good time about the ensuing of the insured event or that the absence of information about this with the insurer could not affect his duty to pay the insurance compensation.

The rules provided for by the present Article respectively shall apply to the contract of personal insurance if the insured event is the death of the insured person or the causing of harm to his health. In so doing the period of notice of the insurer established by the contract may not be less than twenty days.

Article 952. Reduction of Losses from Insured Event

In the event the insured event ensues which is provided for by the contract of property insurance, the insurant shall be obliged to take reasonable and available measures in order to reduce possible losses. In taking such measures, the insurant must follow the instructions of the insurer if they have been communicated to the insurant.

Expenses made for the purpose of reducing losses which are subject to compensation by the insurer, if such expenses were necessary or were made in order to fulfill instructions of the insurer, must be compensated by the insurer even if the respective measures proved to be unsuccessful. Such expenses shall be compensated proportionally in the relation of the insured amount to the insured value, irrespective of whether they may exceed the insured amount together with the compensation of the other losses.

The insurer shall be relieved from compensation of losses which arose as a consequence the fact that the insurant intentionally did not take measures in order to reduce possible losses.

Article 953. Consequences of Ensuing of Insured Event Through Fault of Insurant, Beneficiary, or Insured Person

An insurer shall be relieved from the payment of insurance compensation or insured amount if the insured event ensued as a consequence of the intent of the insurant, beneficiary, or insured person, except for intentional actions which were not committed by him in a state of necessary defense or extreme necessity, and also in instances provided for by paragraphs three and four of the present Article.

Instances of the relief of the insurer from the payment of insurance compensation under contracts of property insurance or a reduction of the amount of compensation in the event of the ensuing of the insured event as a consequence of gross negligence of the insurant or beneficiary may be provided for by a law.

An insurer shall not be relieved from the payment of insurance compensation under a contract of insurance of civil responsibility for causing harm to life or health if the harm was caused through the fault of the person responsible therefor.

An insurer shall not be relieved from the payment of the insured amount which under a contract of personal insurance is subject to payment in the event of the death of the insured person if his death ensued as a consequence of suicide and the contract of insurance has operated at this time for not less than two years.

Article 954. Grounds for Relief of Insurer from Payment of Insurance Compensation and Insured Amount

Unless provided otherwise by a law or contract, the insurer shall be relieved from the payment of insurance compensation and the insured amount when the insured event has ensued as a consequence of:

the influence of a nuclear explosion, radiation, or radioactive poisoning;

military actions, maneuvers or other military measures.

Unless provided otherwise by a contract of property insurance, the insurer shall be relieved from the payment of insurance compensation for losses which arose as a consequence of the seizure, confiscation, requisition, arrest, or destruction of insured property at the order of State agencies.

Article 955. Refusal to Pay Insurance Compensation or Insured Amount

The insurer shall have the right to refuse payment to the insurant (or beneficiary) of insurance compensation under a contract of property insurance or insured amount under a contract of personal insurance in instances when:

the operation of the contract of insurance has terminated before the ensuing of the insured event, including on the grounds specified in Articles 948 and 950 of the present Code;

the contract of insurance is null on the grounds provided for by the present Code or other laws;

the insurer is relieved from payment of insurance compensation or insured amount on the grounds specified in Articles 951-954 of the present Code;

a suit has been brought by the insurer to deem the contract of insurance invalid on the grounds provided for by the present Code or other laws, or dissolution of the contract of insurance as a consequence of the fact that the insurant (or beneficiary) obstructed the investigation of circumstances of the insured event or determination of the amount of losses caused.

The decision of the insurer concerning the refusal to pay insurance compensation or the insured amount must be communicated to the insurant (or beneficiary) not later than within fifteen days after the recourse thereof for payment of the insurance compensation or insured amount and must contain a reasoned substantiation of the reasons for the refusal.

The refusal of the insurer to pay insurance compensation or the insured amount may be contested by means of bringing a suit in court against it.

Article 956. Payment of Insured Amount Under Contract of Personal Insurance

The insured amount under a contract of personal insurance shall be paid to the person to whose benefit the contract was concluded irrespective of the amounts due to the insurant, insured person, or beneficiary under social insurance, social security, other contracts of insurance, or by way of compensation of harm.

The insured amount under a contract of personal insurance shall be paid to heirs of the insured person on the basis of Article 921, paragraph three, of the present Code and shall not be part of the inheritance of the insured person.

Article 957. Transfer to Insurer of Rights of Insurant to Compensation of Damage (Subrogation)

Unless provided otherwise by the contract of property insurance, to the insurer who has paid the insurance compensation shall pass within the limits of the amount paid the right of demand which the insurant (or beneficiary) has against the person responsible for the losses compensated as a result of the insurance. However, a condition of the contract excluding the transfer to the insurer of the right of demand against a person who intentionally caused losses shall be null.

The right of demand which has passed to the insurer shall be effectuated by him in compliance with the rules regulating relations between the insurant (or beneficiary) and the person responsible for the losses.

An insurant (or beneficiary) shall be obliged to transfer to the insurer all documents and evidence and to communicate to him all information necessary for the effectuation by the insurer of the right of demand which has passed to him.

If the insurant (or beneficiary) has waived his right of demand against the person responsible for losses compensated by the insurer, or the effectuation of this right has become impossible through the fault of the insurant (or beneficiary), the insurer shall be relieved from the payment of insurance compensation in full or in respective part and shall have the right to require the return of amount of compensation paid in excess.

Article 958. Transfer to Insurer of Rights to Insured Property

In the event of the insurance of property the insurant (or beneficiary) may after the ensuing of the insured event, with the consent of the insurer, transfer to it the rights to the insured property and receive insurance compensation for the insured amount in full.

Article 959. Reinsurance

The risk of payment of insurance compensation or the insured amount accepted by an insurer under a contract of insurance may be insured by him in full or partially with another insurer(s) under a contract of reinsurance concluded with the last.

The rules of the present Chapter which are subject to application with respect to the insurance of entrepreneurial risk shall apply to the contract of reinsurance unless provided otherwise by the contract of reinsurance. In so doing the insurer under a contract of insurance (principal contract) who has concluded a contract of reinsurance shall be considered to be the insurant in this last contract.

Under reinsurance the insured under this contract shall remain responsible to the insurant under the principal contract of insurance for the payment of insurance compensation or insured amount.

However, in the event of the liquidation of the insurance organization which is the insurer under the principal contract of insurance before the ensuing of the insured event its rights and duties under this contract shall pass in the reinsured part to the insurer under the contract of reinsurance.

The subsequent conclusion of two or several contracts of reinsurance shall be permitted. Each of such contracts shall be considered to be the principal contract of insurance with respect to the subsequent contract of reinsurance.

Article 960. Mutual Insurance

Citizens and juridical persons may insure their property and other property interests specified in Article 915, paragraph two of the present Code on a mutual basis by means of combining in mutual insurance societies the means necessary for this.

The mutual insurance societies shall effectuate the insurance of property and other property interests of their members and shall be noncommercial organizations.

Insurance of property and property interests of their members by mutual insurance societies shall be effectuated directly on the basis of membership unless the constitutive documents of the society provide for the conclusion of contracts of insurance in these instances.

The rules of the present Chapter shall apply to relations relating to insurance between a mutual insurance society and its members unless provided otherwise by a law, constitutive documents of the respective society, or rules of insurance established by it.

The effectuation of obligatory insurance by means of mutual insurance shall be permitted in the instances provided for by a law.

A mutual insurance society may effectuate as insurer the insurance of the interests of persons who are not members of the society if such insurance activity is provided for by its constitutive documents, the society itself is formed in the form of a commercial organization, has a license for the effectuation of insurance of the respective type, and meets the other requirements established by a law.

The insurance of the interests of persons who are not members of a mutual insurance society shall be effectuated by the society under contracts of insurance in accordance with the rules of the present Chapter.

The peculiarities of the legal status of mutual insurance societies and the conditions of their activity shall be determined by legislation.

Article 961. Obligatory State Insurance

For the purpose of ensuring the social interests of citizens and the interests of the State obligatory State insurance of the life, health, and property may be established by a law.

Obligatory State insurance shall be effectuated at the expense of means allotted for these purposes from the State budget.

Obligatory State insurance shall be effectuated directly on the basis of legislation concerning insurance by State insurance and other State organizations specified therein (insurers).

The rules of the present Chapter shall apply to obligatory State insurance unless provided otherwise by legislation concerning insurance and does not arise from the essence of the respective relations relating to insurance.

Chapter 53. Simple Partnership

Article 962. Contract of Simple Partnership

Under the contract of simple partnership (or contract concerning joint activity), two or more persons, called partners (or participants) shall be obliged to combine their contributions and jointly operate without the formation of a juridical person in order to derive profit or achieve another purpose which is not contrary to law.

Only individual entrepreneurs and/or commercial organizations may be the parties to a contract of simple partnership concluded in order to effectuate entrepreneurial activity.

A contract of simple partnership must be concluded in written form.

Article 963. Contributions of Partners

Everything that he contributed to the common cause, including money, other property, professional and other knowledge, skills, and ability, and also business reputation and business reputation, shall be deemed to be the contribution of the partner.

The contributions of partners shall be presupposed to be equal in value unless it follows otherwise from the contract of simple partnership or factual circumstances. The monetary valuation of the contribution of a partner shall be made by agreement between the partners.

Article 964. Common Property of Partners

The property contributed by partners which they possessed by right of ownership, and also the product produced as a result of joint activity and the fruits and revenues received from such activity shall be deemed their common participatory share ownership insofar as not established otherwise by a law or the contract of simple partnership or does not arise from the essence of the obligation.

Property in common participatory share ownership of the partners, and also their common exclusive rights, shall form the common property of the partners. The common property shall be used in the interests of all the partners.

The conducting of bookkeeping records of the common property of the partners may be entrusted by them to one of the juridical persons participating in the contract of simple partnership.

The use of common property by the partners shall be effectuated by their common consent, and in the event of the failure to achieve consent, in the procedure established by a court.

The duties of the partners with regard to the maintenance of common property and the procedure for the compensation of expenses connected with the fulfillment of these duties shall be provided for by the contract of simple partnership.

Article 965. Conducting Common Affairs of Partners

The conducting of common affairs of the participants of contracts of simple partnership shall be effectuated in the procedure provided for by the contract of simple partnership.

When conducting common affairs each partner shall have the right to act in the name of all the partners unless it is established by the contract of simple partnership that the conducting of the affairs shall be effectuated by individual participants or jointly by all of the participants of the contract.

When conducting affairs jointly the consent of all the partners shall be required for the conclusion of each transaction.

In relations with third persons the power of a partner to conclude a transaction in the name of all the partners shall be certified by a power of attorney issued to him by the remaining partners or shall be manifest from the contract of simple partnership.

In relations with third persons the partners may not refer to limitation of the rights of the partner who has concluded the transaction with regard to conducting the common affairs of the partners except for instances when they prove that at the moment of concluding the transaction the third person knew or should have known about the existence of such limitations.

The partner who has concluded a transaction in the name of all the partners with respect to which his right to conduct the common affairs of the partners was limited, or who has concluded in his own name a transaction in the interests of all the partners, shall have the right to compensation for expenses made by him from his own means if there are sufficient grounds to suppose that these transactions were necessary in the interests of all the partners. If losses were caused by such transaction to the other partners, they shall have the right to demand compensation thereof.

Decisions affecting the common affairs shall be adopted by the partners by their common consent unless provided otherwise by the contract of simple partnership.

The participants of a contract empowered to conduct common affairs shall have the right to individual remuneration if this is provided for by the contract of simple partnership.

Article 966. Right of Partner to Information

Each partner shall have the right irrespective of whether he is empowered to conduct the common affairs of the partners, to familiarize himself with all of the documentation relating to the conducting of affairs. The waiver of this right or limitation thereof, including by agreement of the partners, shall be null.

Article 967. Common Expenses, Losses, and Responsibility of Partners

The procedure for covering expenses and losses connected with the joint activity of the partners shall be determined by their agreement. In the absence of such agreement, each partner shall bear expenses and losses in proportion to the value of his contribution to the common cause.

An agreement wholly exempting any of the partners from participation in covering the common expenses or losses shall be null.

Unless the contract of simple partnership is linked with the effectuation of entrepreneurial activity by its participants, then each partner shall be liable for common contractual obligations with all of his property in proportion to the value of his contribution to the common cause.

Partners shall be liable jointly and severally for common obligations which arose not from the contract.

If the contract of simple partnership is linked with the effectuation of entrepreneurial activity by its participants, the partners shall be liable jointly and severally for all common obligations irrespective of the grounds for the arising thereof.

Article 968. Distribution of Profit

The profit received by the partners as a result of their joint activity shall be distributed in proportion to the value of the contributions of the partners to the common cause unless provided otherwise by the contract of simple partnership or other agreement of the partners. An agreement concerning the elimination of any of the partners from participation in the profit shall be null.

Article 969. Partition of Participatory Share of Partner at Demand of His Creditors

The creditor of a participant of the contract of simple partnership shall have the right to present a demand concerning the partition of his participatory share in the common property in accordance with Article 227 of the present Code.

Article 970. Grounds for Termination of Contract of Simple Partnership

A contract of simple partnership shall be terminated as a consequence of:

the declaration of any of the partners to lack dispositive legal capacity, to have limited dispositive legal capacity, or to be missing unless the contract of simple partnership or subsequent agreement provides for the preservation of the contract in relations between the remaining partners;

the declaration of any of the partners to be insolvent (or bankrupt), with the exception specified in paragraph two of the present Article;

the death of a partner or liquidation or reorganization of a juridical person participating in the contract of simple partnership unless the contract or a subsequent agreement provides for the preservation of the contract in relations between the remaining partners or replacement of the deceased partner (or liquidated or reorganized juridical person) by his heirs (or legal successors);

the refusal by any of the partners of further participation in a contract of simple partnership without term, with the exception specified in paragraph two of the present Article;

the dissolution of the contract of simple partnership concluded with a specification of the period, at the demand of one of the partners in relations between them and the remaining partners, with the exception specified in paragraph two of the present Article;

the expiry of the period of the contract of simple partnership;

the partition of the participatory share of the partner at the demand of his creditor, with the exception specified in paragraph two of the present Article;

other grounds provided for by the present Code.

Article 971. Consequences of Termination of Contract of Simple Partnership

In the event of the termination of a contract of simple partnership, the things transferred to the common possession and/or use of the partners shall be returned to the partner who granted them without remuneration insofar as is not provided otherwise by the agreement of the parties.

From the moment of termination of a contract of simple partnership the participants thereof shall bear joint and several responsibility for the failure to perform common obligations with respect to third persons.

The division of property in the common participatory share ownership of the partners and the common rights of demand which have arisen therefrom shall be effectuated in the procedure established by Article 223 of the present Code.

A partner who has contributed an individually specified thing to the common participatory share ownership shall have the right in the event of the termination of the contract of simple partnership to demand the return of this thing to him on condition of compliance with the interests of the remaining partners and creditors.

Article 972. Repudiation of Contract of Simple Partnership Without Period

A statement of repudiation by a person of a contract of simple partnership without period must be made by him not later than three months before the proposed withdrawal from the contract unless another period has been established by the contract.

An agreement concerning limitation of the right to repudiate a contract of simple partnership without period shall be null.

Article 973. Dissolution of Contract of Simple Partnership at Demand of Party

Together with the grounds specified in Article 382, paragraph two, of the present Code, the party of a contract of simple partnership concluded with the specification of a period or with the specification of a purpose as a condition subsequent shall have the right to demand dissolution of the contract in relations between himself and the remaining partners for a justifiable reason with compensation to the remaining partners of the real damage caused by dissolution of the contract.

Article 974. Responsibility of Partner Who Has Renounced Participation in Contract or Required Dissolution Thereof

In the event a contract of simple partnership was not terminated as a result of the statement of one of the participants concerning repudiation of further participation therein or dissolution of the contract at the demand of one of the partners, the person whose participation in the contract has terminated shall be liable to third persons for common obligations which arose in the period of his participation in the contract as if he had remained a participant of the contract of simple partnership.

Article 975. Nontransparent Partnership

It may be provided by a contract of simple partnership that its existence shall not be divulged to third persons (nontransparent partnership). The rules of the present Chapter shall apply to such contract unless provided otherwise by the present Article or does not arise from the essence of the nontransparent partnership.

In relations with third persons each of the participants of a nontransparent partnership shall be liable with all of his property for transactions which he concluded in his name in the common interests of the partners.

In relations between partners, the obligations which arose in the process of their joint activity shall be considered to be common.

Chapter 54. Public Competition

Article 976. Organization of Public Competition

A person who has announced publicly the payment of monetary remuneration or issuance of other reward (or concerning the payment of a reward) for the best fulfillment of work or achievement of other results (public competition) must pay the stipulated reward to whoever in accordance with the conditions for conducting the competition is deemed to be the winner thereof.

A public competition may be open when the proposal of the organizer of the competition to take part in the competition is addressed to all who wish to do so by means of an announcement in the press and other mass media, or be closed when the proposal to take part in the competition is sent to a determined group of persons at the choice of the organizer of the competition.

An open competition may be conditioned by the preliminary qualification of the participants thereof when a preliminary selection of persons who wish to take part therein is conducted by the organizer of the competition.

The announcement concerning a public competition must contain the conditions providing for the essence of the task, the criteria and procedure for evaluating the results of the work or other achievements, the place, period, and procedure for submitting them, the amount and form of the reward, and also the procedure and periods for the announcement of the results.

To a public competition containing an obligation to conclude a contract with the winner of the competition shall apply the rules of the present Chapter insofar as not provided otherwise by Articles 379-381 of the present Code.

Article 977. Change of Conditions and Cancellation of Public Competition

A person who has announced a public competition shall have the right to change its conditions or to cancel a competition only during the first half of the period established for submission of the work.

A notice concerning a change of the conditions or cancellation of the competition must be made by the same means as the competition was announced.

In the event of a change of the conditions of a competition or the cancellation thereof, the person who has announced the competition must compensate the expenses incurred by any person who fulfilled the work provided for in the announcement until it became known or should have become known to him that the conditions of the competition changed or of the cancellation thereof.

If in the event of the change of the conditions of a competition or in the event of the cancellation thereof the requirements specified in paragraphs one or two of the present Article were violated, the person who announced the competition must pay a reward to those who fulfilled the work which satisfies the conditions specified in the announcement.

The person who has announced a competition shall be relieved of the duty to compensate expenses if it is proved that the said work was fulfilled not in connection with the competition, in particular, before the announcement of the competition, or knowingly did not conform to the conditions of the competition.

Article 978. Decision Concerning Payment of Reward

A decision concerning the payment of a reward to the winner of the competition must be rendered and communicated to the participants of a public competition in the procedure and within the periods established in the announcement concerning the competition.

If the results specified in the announcement were achieved in a work fulfilled jointly by two or more persons, the reward shall be distributed between them in accordance with their agreement. If such agreement is not reached, the procedure for the distribution of the reward shall be determined by a court.

Article 979. Use of Works of Science, Literature, and Art of Persons Who Won Public Competition

If the subject of a public competition consists of a work of science, literature, or art, the person who has announced the public competition shall acquire a preferential right to conclude with the author of the work on which the stipulated reward is conferred a contract concerning the use of the work with the payment to him of respective remuneration for this unless provided otherwise by the conditions of the competition.

Article 980. Return to Participants of Public Competition of Works Submitted

The person who has announced a public competition shall be obliged to return to the participants of the competition works not conferred with a reward unless provided otherwise by the announcement concerning the competition and does not arise from the character of the work fulfilled.

Chapter 55. Public Promise of Reward

Article 981. Duty to Pay Reward

The person who has announced publicly the payment of monetary remuneration or the issuance of another reward (concerning the payment of a reward) to whomever performs the action specified in the announcement within the period specified therein shall be obliged to pay the promised reward to anyone who performed the respective action.

The duty to pay the reward shall arise on condition that the promise of the reward enables it to be established to whom it is promised. A person who has responded to the promise shall have the right to require written confirmation of the promise and shall bear the risk of consequences of the failure to present this demand if it turns out in reality that the announcement concerning the reward was not made by the person specified therein.

If the amount was not specified in the public promise of the reward, it shall be determined by agreement with the person who promised the reward, and in the event of a dispute, by a court.

The duty to pay a reward shall arise irrespective of whether the respective action was performed in connection with the announcement made or irrespective thereof.

In instances when an action specified in an announcement was performed by several persons, the right to receive the reward shall be acquired by he who performed the respective action first.

If the action specified in the announcement was performed by two or more persons and it is impossible to determine which of them performed the respective action first, and also if the action was performed by two or more persons simultaneously, the reward shall be divided between them equally or in another amount provided for by an agreement between them.

Unless provided otherwise in the announcement concerning the reward and does not arise from the character of the action specified therein, the conformity of the action fulfilled to the requirements contained in the announcement shall be determined by the person who publicly promised the reward, and in the event of a dispute, by a court.

Article 982. Revocation of Public Promise of Reward

A person who has announced publicly the payment of a reward shall have the right in the same form to renounce this promise except for instances when in the announcement itself the inadmissibility of a renunciation has been provided for or arises therefrom or a determined period has been given for the performance of the action for which the reward is promised, or at the moment of the announcement concerning the renunciation one or several persons who responded already had fulfilled the action specified in the announcement.

The revocation of a public promise of a reward shall not relieve he who announced the reward from compensation of the expenses of persons who responded incurred by them in connection with the performance of the action specified in the announcement. The amount of compensation in all instances may not exceed the reward specified in the announcement.

Chapter 56. Conducting Games and Betting

Article 983. Demands Connected with the Organization of Games and Betting and Participation Therein

The demands of citizens and juridical persons connected with the organization of games or betting based on risk (gambling games and betting) or participation therein shall not be subject to judicial defense, except for the demands of persons who took part in games or betting under the influence of deception, coercion, threat, or ill-intentioned agreement of their representative with the organizer of the games or betting, and demands arising from relations specified in Article 984 of the present Code.

Article 984. Peculiarities of Conducting Lotteries by the State [as amended by Law of 14 September 2007, No. 3РУ-109. СЗ РУ (2007), no. 37-38, item 377]

Relations between the organizers of lotteries – the State, persons who have received an authorization (or license) from an empowered State agency – and the participants of the lotteries are based on a contract. Such contract shall be formalized by the issuance of a lottery ticket and shall be deemed to be concluded from the moment of payment by the participant of the cost of the lottery ticket [as amended by Law of 14 September 2007, No. 3РУ-109. СЗ РУ (2007), no. 37-38, item 377].

The proposal concerning the conclusion of a contract provided for by paragraph one of the present Article must include the conditions concerning the period of conducting the lottery and the procedure for the determination of the winnings and the amount thereof [as amended by Law of 14 September 2007, No. ЗРУ-109. СЗ РУ (2007), no. 37-38, item 377].

In the event of a refusal of the organizer of the lottery to conduct them within the established period, the participants of the lottery shall have the right to demand compensation from the organizer thereof for real damage sustained because of the cancellation of the lottery or postponement of the period thereof [as amended by Law of 14 September 2007, No. ЗРУ-109. СЗ РУ (2007), no. 37-38, item 377].

Persons who in accordance with the conditions of conducting a lottery are deemed to be winners must be paid the winnings by the organizer of the lottery in the amount, form (monetary or in kind), and periods provided for by the conditions of conducting the lottery, and if the period is not specified in these conditions, not later than ten days from the moment of determining the results of the lottery [as amended by Law of 14 September 2007, No. ЗРУ-109. СЗ РУ (2007), no. 37-38, item 377].

In the event of the failure of the organizer of the lottery to perform the duties specified in paragraph three of the present Article, the participant who won the lottery shall have the right to demand the payment of the winnings from the organizer of the lottery, and also the compensation of losses caused by a violation of the contract on the part of the organizer [as amended by Law of 14 September 2007, No. ЗРУ-109. СЗ РУ (2007), no. 37-38, item 377].

Chapter 57. Obligations as Consequence of Causing Harm

§ 1. General Provisions

Article 985. General Grounds of Responsibility for Causing of Harm

Harm caused by the unlawful actions (or failure to act) to the person or property of a citizen, and also harm caused to a juridical person, shall be subject to compensation in full by the person who caused the harm, including lost advantage [as amended 15 December 2000, No. 175-II. Ведомости Олий Мажлиса (2001), no. 1-2, item 23].

The duty of compensation of harm may be placed by a law on a person who is not the causer of the harm.

The duty to pay contributory compensation to a victim above the compensation of harm may be established by a law or by a contract.

A person who has caused harm shall be relieved from compensation of harm if it is proved that the harm was caused not through his fault. Compensation of harm in the absence of the fault of the causer of harm also may be provided for by a law.

Harm caused by lawful actions shall be subject to compensation in the instances provided for by a law.

Compensation of harm may be refused if the harm was caused at the request or with the consent of the victim, and the actions of the causer of the harm do not violate moral principles of society.

Article 986. Warning of Causing of Harm

The danger of causing harm in the future may be grounds for a suit concerning the prohibition of the activity creating such a danger.

If the harm caused is the consequence of the operation of an enterprise, installation, or other production activity which continues to cause harm or threatens new harm, a court shall have the right to oblige the defendant, in addition to compensation of harm, to suspend or terminate the respective activity.

A court may reject a suit concerning the suspension or termination of the respective activity only if the suspension or termination thereof is contrary to social interests. The refusal to suspend or terminate such activity shall not deprive the victim of the right to compensation for the harm caused by this activity.

Article 987. Causing Harm in State of Necessary Defense

Harm caused in a state of necessary defense, unless the limits thereof were exceeded, shall not be subject to compensation.

If when defending against an unlawful attack the defending person caused harm to a third person, he must be compensated by the attacking person.

Harm caused to a person in connection with the suppression of his criminal actions or detention thereof and delivery to the respective agencies shall not be subject to compensation.

Article 988. Causing Harm in State of Extreme Necessity

Harm caused in a state of extreme necessity, that is, in order to eliminate a danger threatening the causer of the harm himself or other persons, if this danger under the given circumstances could not be eliminated by other means, must be compensated by the person who caused the harm, except for instances provided by a law [as amended by Law of 10 August 2015, No. ЗРУ-389. СЗ РУ (2015), no. 32, item 425].

Taking into account the circumstances under which such harm was caused, a court may place the duty of compensating it on a third person in whose interests the causer of the harm acted or relieve both this third person and the causer of the harm fully or partially from compensation of the harm.

Article 989. Responsibility of Juridical Person or Citizen for Harm Caused by Worker Thereof

A juridical person or citizen shall compensate harm caused by a worker thereof when performing labor (or employment, official) duties.

With regard to the provisions of the present Chapter, citizens fulfilling work on the basis of a labor contract, and also on the basis of a civil-law contract, if in so doing they acted or should have acted under a planning task of the respective juridical person or citizen and under the control of the respective juridical person or citizen for the safe conducting of work, shall be deemed to be workers.

Economic partnerships and societies and production cooperatives shall compensate harm caused by their participants (or members) when the last effectuate entrepreneurial, production, or other activity of the partnership and society or cooperative.

Article 990. Responsibility for Harm Caused by State Agencies, Agencies of Self-Government of Citizens, and Also the Officials Thereof

Harm caused to a citizen or juridical person as a result of the illegal decisions of State agencies or agencies of self-government of citizens shall be subject to compensation on the basis of the decision of a court, irrespective of the fault of the officials thereof [as amended by Law of 15 December 2001, No. 175-II. Ведомости Олий Мажлиса (2001), no. 1-2, item 23].

Harm caused to a citizen or juridical person as a result of the illegal actions (or failure to act) of State agencies or agencies of self-government of citizens shall be subject to compensation on the basis of the decision of a court [as amended by Law of 15 December 2001, No. 175-II. Ведомости Олий Мажлиса (2001), no. 1-2, item 23]. The harm shall be compensated in the procedure provided for by Article 15 of the present Code.

Article 991. Responsibility for Harm Caused by Illegal Actions of Agencies Effectuating Pre-Investigative Verification, Agencies of Inquiry or Preliminary Investigation, Procuracy, and Court [as amended by Law of 23 May 2019, No. 3PУ-542]

Harm caused to a citizen as a result of the illegal conviction, illegal bringing to criminal responsibility, illegal application of confinement under guard as a measure of restraint, or written undertaking concerning proper behavior, or the illegal imposition of an administrative sanction in the form of arrest, and also any application of torture and other cruel, inhumane, or humiliating treatment or punishment, shall be compensated by the State in full irrespective of the fault of the officials of the agencies effectuating pre-investigative verification, agencies of inquiry or preliminary investigation, procuracy, and court in the procedure established by a law. By decision of a court compensation of harm may be placed on the officials through whose fault the harm was caused [as amended by Laws of 15 December 2001, No. 175-II, of 23 May 2019, No. 3PУ-542, and of 29 March 2022, No. 3PУ-761].

Harm caused to a citizen or juridical person as a result of other illegal activity of agencies effectuating pre-investigative verification, agencies of inquiry or preliminary investigation, procuracy, and court shall be compensated on the general grounds unless provided otherwise by a law [as amended by Law of 23 May 2019, No. 3PУ-542].

Article 992. Compensation of Harm by Person Who Has Insured His Responsibility

A juridical person or citizen who has insured his responsibility by way of voluntary or obligatory insurance to the benefit of the victim, when insurance compensation is insufficient in order to compensate the harm caused in full, shall compensate the difference between the insured amount and the actual amount of damage.

Article 993. Responsibility for Harm Caused by Minors Up to Fourteen Years of Age

For harm caused by a minor who has not attained fourteen years of age (youth) his parents (or adoptive parents) or trustees shall be liable unless it is proved that the harm arose not through their fault.

If a youth who needs trusteeship is situated in a respective nurturing or medical institution, institution for the social defense of the populace, or other analogous institution which by virtue of a law is his trustee, this institution shall be obliged to compensate the harm caused by the youth unless it is proved that the harm arose not through the fault of the institution.

If a youth has caused harm at the time when he was under the supervision of an educational institution, nurturing, medical, or other institution obliged to effectuate supervision over him, or a person effectuating supervision on the basis of a contract, this institution or person shall be liable for the harm unless it is proved that the harm arose not through their fault in effectuating the supervision.

The duty of the parents (or adoptive parents), trustees, educational institutions, nurturing, medical, and other institutions relating to compensation of harm caused by a youth shall not terminate with the attainment by the youth of majority or receipt by him of property sufficient to compensate the harm.

If the parents (or adoptive parents), trustees, and also other citizens specified in paragraph three of the present Article has died or does not have sufficient means in order to compensate the harm caused, and the causer of the harm himself having full dispositive legal capacity possesses such means, the court shall have the right, taking into account the property status of the parties, and also other circumstances, to adopt a decision concerning compensation of harm fully or partially at the expense of the property of the causer of the harm himself.

Article 994. Responsibility for Harm Caused by Minors in Age from Fourteen to Eighteen Years

A minor from fourteen to eighteen years of age shall bear responsibility on the general grounds autonomously for harm caused.

In the event when a minor from fourteen to eighteen years of age has no property or other sources of revenues sufficient to compensate harm, the harm must be compensated fully or in the insufficient part by his parents (or adoptive parents) or guardian unless they prove that the harm arose not through their fault.

If a minor from fourteen to eighteen years of age who needs guardianship is situated in a respective nurturing or treatment institution, institution for the social defense of the populace, or other analogous institution which by virtue of a law is his guardian, these institutions shall be obliged to compensate the harm fully or in the insufficient part unless it is proved that the harm arose not through its fault.

The duty of parents (or adoptive parents), guardian, and respective institution with regard to the compensation of harm shall terminate upon the attainment of majority by the causer of the harm or when upon attaining majority he has property or other sources of revenue sufficient to compensate the harm, or when he before attaining majority has acquired dispositive legal capacity.

Article 995. Responsibility of Parents Deprived of Parental Rights for Harm Caused by Minors

A court may place on a parent deprived of parental rights responsibility for harm caused by the minor children thereof for three years after the deprivation of the parent of parental rights if the behavior of the child which entailed the causing of the harm was a consequence of the improper effectuation of parental duties relating to nurturing of the child.

Article 996. Responsibility for Harm Caused by Citizen Deemed to Lack Dispositive Legal Capacity

Harm caused by a citizen deemed to lack dispositive legal capacity shall be compensated by his trustee or the organization obliged to effectuate supervision over him unless they prove that the harm arose not through their fault.

The duty of a trustee or the organization with regard to compensation of harm caused by a citizen deemed to lack dispositive legal capacity shall not terminate in the event of the reinstatement of his dispositive legal capacity.

If the trustee is deceased or does not have sufficient means for the compensation of harm, and the causer of harm himself possesses such means, the court shall have the right, taking into account the property status of the victim and the causer, and also other circumstances, to adopt a decision concerning compensation of harm fully or partially at the expense of the property of the causer himself.

Article 997. Responsibility for Harm Caused by Citizen Deemed to Have Limited Dispositive Legal Capacity

Harm caused by a citizen deemed to be limited in dispositive legal capacity as a consequence of the abuse of alcoholic beverages or narcotic means shall be compensated by the causer of the harm himself on general grounds.

Article 998. Responsibility for Harm Caused by Citizen Not Capable of Understanding Significance of His Actions

A citizen who has dispositive legal capacity, and also a minor from fourteen to eighteen years of age, who has caused harm in such a state that he could not understand the significance of his actions or direct them shall not be liable for the harm caused by him.

If harm is caused to the life or health of the victim, the court may, taking into account the property status of the victim and the causer, and also other circumstances, place the duty with regard to compensation of harm fully or partially on the causer of harm.

The causer of harm shall not be relieved from responsibility if he has brought himself into such state by the use of alcoholic beverages, narcotic means, or other means.

If the harm was caused by a person who could not understand the significance of his actions or direct them as a consequence of mental disturbance (mental illness or feeblemindedness), the duty to compensate the harm may be placed by a court on a spouse, parents, or children who have reached majority and who have labor capacity and reside jointly with this person, and who knew about such state of the causer of the harm but did not raise the question of deeming him to lack dispositive legal capacity and instituting a trusteeship over him.

Article 999. Responsibility for Harm Caused by Activity Creating Increased Danger for Surrounding Persons

Juridical persons and citizens whose activity is connected with an increased danger for surrounding persons (means of transport, mechanisms, industrial enterprises, construction sites, possessors of means of transport, and others) shall be obliged to compensate the harm caused by a source of increased danger unless it is proved that the harm arose as a consequence of insuperable force or the intent of the victim.

The duty of compensation of harm shall be placed on that juridical person or citizen who possesses the source of increased danger by right of ownership, right of economic jurisdiction, or right of operative management, or any other legal basis (contract of property rental, power of attorney for the right to drive means of transport, by virtue of the regulation of a respective agency concerning the transfer of the source of increased danger to it, and the like).

The possessors of sources of increased danger shall bear joint and several responsibility for harm caused as a result of the interaction of these sources (collision of means of transport, and so forth) to third persons on the grounds provided for by paragraphs one and two of the present Article.

The harm caused as a result of the interaction of the sources of increased danger to their possessors shall be compensated on the general grounds. In so doing the harm caused through the fault of one party shall be compensated in full by this party, and the harm caused through the fault of both or several parties shall be compensated commensurately with the degree of fault of each of them. When it is impossible to establish the degree of fault of each of the parties, the responsibility shall be distributed among them equally. In the absence of fault of the parties in causing harm, neither of them shall have the right to demand compensation of harm. Each of the parties shall bear in such event the risk of losses incurred by it.

The possessor of a source of increased danger shall not be liable for harm caused by this source if it is proved that the source left the possession of the possessor as a result of unlawful actions (or failure to act) of other persons. Responsibility for harm caused by a source of increased danger shall be borne in such instances by the persons who unlawfully took possession of the source. When there is fault of the possessor in the unlawful seizure of this source from his possession, responsibility may be placed both on the possessor and also on the persons who took possession of the source of increased danger.

Article 1000. Responsibility for Jointly Caused Harm

Persons who have caused harm jointly shall be liable to the victim jointly and severally.

Upon the application of the victim and in his interests a court shall have the right to place on the persons who have jointly caused harm participatory share responsibility.

Article 1001. Right of Regression Against Person Who Caused Harm

The person who has compensated harm caused by another person (or by a worker when performing his labor duties, by a person driving means of transport, and so forth) shall have the right of counter demand (regression) against this person in the amount of the compensation paid unless another amount has been established by a law.

The causer of harm who has compensated harm jointly caused shall have the right to demand from each of the causers a participatory share of the compensation paid to the victim in the amount corresponding to the degree of fault of this causer. If it is impossible to determine the degree of fault, the participatory shares shall be deemed to be equal.

The State which has compensated harm caused by officials of agencies effectuating pre-investigative verification, agencies of inquiry or preliminary investigation, the procuracy, or a court shall have the right of regression against such persons in instances when fault of such persons has been established by the judgment of a court which has entered into legal force [as amended by Law of 23 May 2019, No. 3PY-542].

The State which has compensated harm caused as a result of conducting an anti-terrorist operation shall have the right of regression against the person whose guilty actions caused the conducting of the anti-terrorist operation in the amount of compensation paid [added by Law of 10 August 2015, No. 3PY-389. C3 PY (2015), no. 32, item 425]

The persons who have compensated harm on the grounds specified in Articles 993-996, and 998 of the present Code shall not have the right of counter demand (regression) against the person who caused the harm.

Article 1002. Responsibility for Harm Caused by Domestic Animals

The owner or person in whose possession and use this animal is situated shall bear responsibility on general grounds for harm caused by domestic animals.

Article 1003. Means of Compensation of Harm

In satisfying the demand concerning compensation of harm, the court in accordance with the circumstances of the case shall oblige the person responsible for the harm caused to compensate the harm in kind (to provide a thing of the same kind and quality, to rectify a damaged thing, and so forth) or to compensate the losses caused.

Article 1004. Taking Account of Fault of Victim and Property Status of Person Who Caused Harm

Harm which arose as a consequence of the intent of the victim shall not be subject to compensation.

If the gross negligence of the victim himself furthered the arising or the increasing of the harm, depending on the degree of fault of the victim and the causer of the harm the amount of compensation must be reduced.

In the event of gross negligence of the victim and the absence of fault of the causer of the harm in instances when his responsibility ensues irrespective of fault, the amount of compensation must be reduced or compensation of harm may be refused unless provided otherwise by a law. In the event of causing harm to the life or health of a citizen, refusal of compensation of harm shall not be permitted.

The fault of the victim shall not be taken into account when compensating additional expenses, when compensating harm in connection the death of a breadwinner, and also when compensating expenses for burial.

A court may reduce the amount of compensation of harm caused by a citizen by taking into account his property status, except for instances when the harm was caused by actions (or failure to act) committed intentionally.

§ 2. Compensation of Harm Caused to Life and Health of Citizen

Article 1005. Compensation of Harm Caused to Life or Health of Citizen When Performing Contractual or Other Obligations

Harm caused to the life or health of a citizen when performing contractual obligations, and also when performing duties of military service, service in the internal affairs agencies, and other respective duties shall be compensated according to the rules of the present Chapter unless a higher extent responsibility has been provided by a law or by a contract.

Article 1006. Amount and Character of Compensation of Harm Which Caused Impairment of Health

When mutilation or other impairment of health is caused to a citizen, the earnings (or revenues) lost by the victim which he had or could be determined to have, and also additional expenses incurred caused by the impairment of health, including expenses for treatment, additional nourishment, acquisition of medicines, prosthetics, outside care, sanitorium-resort treatment, the acquisition of special means of transport, and training for another profession shall be subject to compensation if it is established that the victim needs such types of assistance and care and does not have the right to receive them free of charge.

When determining lost earnings (or revenues), the disability pension assigned to the victim in connection with the mutilation or other impairment of health, and likewise other pensions, benefits, and other similar payments assigned both before and after the causing of harm to health shall not be taken into account and shall not entail a reduction of the amount of compensation of harm (or shall not be set-off at the expense of compensation of harm). Earnings (or revenue) received by the victim after the impairment of health also shall not be set-off at the expense of compensation of harm.

The extent and amount of compensation due to the victim in accordance with the present Article may be increased by a law or by a contract.

Article 1007. Determination of Earnings (or Revenue) Lost as Result of Impairment of Health

The amount of earnings (or revenue) lost by the victim which is subject to compensation shall be determined in percentages of his average monthly earnings (or revenue) before the mutilation or other impairment of health or before the ensuing of the loss of his capacity to labor, of the respective degree of loss by the victim of professional capacity to labor, and in the absence thereof, of general capacity to labor.

Within lost earnings (or revenue) of the victim shall be included all types of payment for his labor under labor and civil-law contracts both at the principal place of work and second jobs levied with income tax on natural persons. Payments of an one-off character (monetary contributory compensation for unused leave and severance benefit in the event of termination of labor contract) shall not be taken into account. The benefit paid for the period of temporary lack of labor capacity or pregnancy and birth leave shall be taken into account. Revenues from entrepreneurial activity, and also author's royalty, shall be included in the lost earnings (or revenue), the revenues from entrepreneurial activity being included on the basis of tax inspectorate data [as amended by Law of 31 December 2008, No. 3PУ-197. C3 PУ (2008), no. 52, item 513].

All types of earnings (or revenue) shall be taken into account in the amounts credited before the withholding of taxes.

The average monthly earnings (or revenue) shall be calculated by means of dividing the total amount of his earnings (or revenue) for the twelve months of work which preceded the impairment of health by twelve. In the event when the victim at the time of causing the harm worked less than twelve months, the average monthly earnings (or revenue) shall be calculated by means of dividing the total amount of earnings (or revenue) for the number of months actually worked which preceded the impairment of health by the number of these months.

Months not worked in full by the victim shall at his wish be replaced by the preceding months fully worked or by excluding them from the calculation when it is impossible to substitute them.

In the event when the victim at the moment of causing of the harm was not working, the earnings before termination of the labor contract or the usual amount of remuneration of a work of his qualifications in the particular locality shall, at his wish, be taken into account, but not less than five times the base calculation amount established by legislation[as amended by Law of 3 December 2019, No. 3PУ-586].

If stable changes improving his financial status (increase of earnings in the post held, he was transferred to higher-paid work, took up the job after completing day education), and in other instances when the stability of the change or possibility of change of payment of labor of the victim is proved occurred in the earnings (or revenue) of the victim before the mutilation or other impairment of health was caused to him, when determining his average monthly earnings (or revenue) only the earnings (or revenue) which he received or should have received after the respective changes shall be taken into account.

Article 1008. Compensation of Harm in Event of Impairment of Health of Person Who Has Not Attained Majority

In the event of the mutilation or other impairment of health of a minor who has not attained fourteen years (youth) and does not have earnings (or revenue), the person responsible for the harm caused shall be obliged to compensate the expenses caused by the impairment of health.

Upon the attainment of fourteen years by the victim, and also in the event of the causing of harm to a minor of from fourteen to eighteen years in age who does not have earnings (or revenue), the person responsible for the harm caused shall be obliged to compensate the victim for, in addition to the expenses caused by the impairment of health, also the harm connected with the loss of or reduction of his labor capacity, proceeding from five-times the base calculation amount established by legislation [as amended by Law of 3 December 2019, No. 3PY-586].

If at the time of the impairment to his health a minor had earnings (or revenue), the harm shall be compensated by proceeding from the amount of these earnings (or revenue), but not lower than five-times the base calculation rate established by legislation [as amended by Law of 3 December 2019, No. 3PY-586].

After the commencement of labor activity a minor whose health was previously caused harm shall have the right to demand an increase of the amount of compensation of harm by proceeding from the earnings (or revenue) received, or from the amount of remuneration established for the post occupied by him or the earnings (or revenue) of a worker of the same qualifications at his place of work.

Article 1009. Compensation of Harm to Persons Who Have Incurred Damage as Result of Death of Breadwinner

In the event of the death of the breadwinner, the right to compensation shall be had by:

persons lacking dispositive labor capacity who were dependent on the deceased or had on the day of his death the right to receive maintenance from him;

a child of the deceased born after his death;

one of the parents, spouse, or other member of the family, irrespective of his labor capacity, who did not work and cared for the children, grandchildren, brothers and sisters who had not attained fourteen years who were dependent on him or although they had not attained the said age but in the opinion of medical institutions need outside care by reason of their state of health;

persons who were dependent on the deceased and came to lack labor capacity within five years after his death.

One of the parents, spouse, or other member of the family who does not work and cares for children, grandchildren, brothers, and sisters of the deceased specified in paragraph one of the present Article and came to lack labor capacity during the period of effectuating care shall retain the right to compensation of harm after ending the care of these persons.

The harm shall be compensated to:

a minor: until attaining eighteen years of age;

pupils older than eighteen years: until completion of study in day educational institutions, but not more than up to twenty-three years of age;

women older than fifty-five years and men older than sixty years: for life;

persons with a disability: for the period of disability [as amended by Law of 17 May 2022, No. 3PY-770];

one of the parents, spouse, or other member of the family engaged in caring for children, grandchildren, brothers, and sisters dependent on the deceased: until they attain fourteen years of age.

Article 1010. Amount of Compensation of Harm Incurred in Event of Death of Breadwinner

Harm shall be compensated to persons who have the right to compensation for harm in connection with the death of a breadwinner in the amount of that participatory share of earnings (or revenue) of the deceased determined according to the rules of Article 1007 of the present Code which they have received or had the right to receive for the maintenance while alive. When determining the compensation for harm to these persons within the revenues of the deceased, together with earnings (or revenue) shall be included a pension, maintenance for life, and other analogous payments being received by them while alive.

When determining the amount of compensation for harm, pensions assigned to persons in connection with the death of a breadwinner, and likewise other types of pensions assigned both before and after the death of a breadwinner, and also earnings (or revenue) and stipend received by these persons, shall not be taken into consideration at the expense of the compensation.

The amount of compensation established for each of those having the right to compensation for harm in connection with the death of a breadwinner shall not be subject to further recalculation except for instances of:

the birth of a child after the death of a breadwinner;

the assignment or termination of the payment of compensation to persons caring for children, grandchildren, brothers, and sisters of a deceased breadwinner.

The amount of compensation may be increased by legislation or by a contract.

Article 1011. Compensation of Harm by Heirs of Person Who Caused Harm

The duty with regard to compensation of harm caused by a citizen after his death shall pass to the heirs who accepted the inheritance. The last shall be liable to the victim within the limits of the actual value of the inheritance property which has passed to them. The State or agencies of self-government of citizens to whom escheated property has passed also shall be liable on the same grounds.

Article 1012. Change of Amount of Compensation of Harm

A victim who has partially lost labor capacity shall have the right at any time to require from the person on whom the duty of compensation of harm has been placed a respective increase of the amount of his compensation if the labor capacity thereof has decreased thereafter in connection with the causing of impairment of health in comparison with that which remained at the moment of awarding compensation for harm to him.

A person on whom the duty to compensate harm has been placed which was caused to the health of the victim shall have the right to require a respective reduction of the amount of compensation if the labor capacity of the victim increased in comparison with that which he had at the moment compensation for harm was awarded.

The victim shall have the right to demand an increase of the amount of compensation of harm if the property status of the citizen on whom the duty to compensate harm was placed has improved, and the amount of compensation was reduced in accordance with Article 1004, paragraph five, of the present Code.

A court may at the demand of a citizen who caused harm reduce the amount of compensation for harm if his property status in connection with disability or attainment of pension age was worsened in comparison with that at the moment of awarding compensation for harm, except for instances when the harm was caused by actions committed intentionally.

Article 1013. Increase of Amount of Compensation of Harm in Connection with Increased Cost of Living and Increase of Base Calculation Amount Established by Legislation [as amended by Law of 3 December 2019, No. 3PY-586]

In the event of an increase in the procedure established by legislation of the base calculation amount, the amounts of compensation for lost earnings (or revenue) and other payments awarded in connection with impairment of health or the death of a victim shall be increased proportionately to the increase of the base calculation amount established by legislation [as amended by Law of 3 December 2019, No. 3PY-586].

Article 1014. Payments for Compensation of Harm

Compensation of harm connected with a reduction of labor capacity or the death of a victim shall be made by monthly payments.

When there are justifiable reasons, the court, taking into account the possibilities of the causer of harm, may at the demand of the citizen who has the right to compensation of harm award him the payments due simultaneously, but for not more than three years.

Additional expenses may be recovered for a future period within the limits of the periods determined on the basis of the opinion of medical expert examination, and also, when necessary, preliminary payment of the cost of the respective services and property (acquisition of passes, payment for travel, and payment for special means of transport, and the like).

In instances when the victim in accordance with a law has the right to require the termination or performance before time of the obligation, such demand shall be satisfied by means of the capitalization of the respective time payments.

Article 1015. Compensation of Harm in Event of Termination of Juridical Person

In the event of the reorganization of a juridical person deemed in the established procedure to be responsible for harm caused to life or health, the duty relating to the payment of the respective payments shall be borne by its legal successor. Demands concerning compensation of harm shall also be presented to it.

In the absence or insufficiency of means with the juridical person being reorganized, a producer of agricultural product goods responsible for harm caused to the life and health of a worker in connection with his performance of labor duties, the awarded amounts shall be paid by the State in the procedure provided by legislation. The said amounts also shall be paid by the State in other instances provided by a law [paragraph added by Law of 12 December 2003, No. 568-II. Народное слово, 13 February 2004, no. 30].

In the event of the liquidation of a juridical person deemed in the established procedure to be responsible for harm caused to life or health, the respective payments must be capitalized for the payment thereof to the victim according to the rules established by legislation.

In instances when the capitalization of payments cannot be made in view of the absence or insufficiency of the property at the juridical person being liquidated, the amounts awarded shall be paid to the victim by the State in the procedure provided for by legislation [as amended by Law of 30 August 2001, No. 271-II. Ведомости Олий Мажлиса (2001), no. 9-10, item 182].

Article 1016. Compensation of Expenses for Burial

Persons responsible for harm which caused the death of the victim shall be obliged to compensate necessary expenses for the burial to the person who incurred those expenses.

The benefit for burial received by citizens who incurred these expenses shall not be set-off at the expense of compensation of harm.

§ 3. Compensation of Harm Caused as Consequence of Defects of Goods, Work, or Services

Article 1017. Grounds for Compensation of Harm Caused as Consequence of Defects of Good, Work, or Services

Harm caused to the life, health, or property of a citizen or the property of a juridical person as a consequence of design, prescription, or other defects of a good, work, or service, and also as a consequence of unreliable or insufficient information concerning the good (or work, service), shall be subject to compensation by the seller or the manufacturer (or executor) irrespective of their fault and whether the victim was in contractual relations with them or not.

The rules provided for by the present Article shall be applied only in the instances of the acquisition of the good (or fulfillment of work, rendering of service) for consumption purposes, and not for use in entrepreneurial activity.

Article 1018. Persons Responsible for Harm Caused as Consequence of Defects of Good, Work, or Service

Harm caused as a consequence of the defects of a good shall be subject to compensation at the choice of the victim by the seller or the manufacturer of the good.

Harm caused as a consequence of the defects of work (or service) shall be subject to compensation by the person who fulfilled the work or rendered the service (executor).

Harm caused as a consequence of the failure to grant full or reliable information concerning the good (or work, service) shall be subject to compensation in accordance with the rules of the present Article.

Article 1019. Periods for Compensation of Harm Caused as Result of Defects of Good, Work, or Service

Harm caused as a consequence of defects of a good (or work, service) shall be subject to compensation if it arose during the established periods for the fitness of a good (or work, service), and if the period of fitness is not established, within ten years from the date of manufacture of the good (or acceptance of work, service).

Beyond the limits of the periods specified in paragraph one of the present Article harm shall be subject to compensation if:

in violation of the requirements of a law, the period of fitness is not established;

the person to whom the good was sold, for which the work was fulfilled, or to whom the service was rendered was not warned about necessary actions upon the expiry of the period of fitness and possible consequences in the event of the failure to fulfill the said actions.

Article 1020. Grounds for Relief from Responsibility for Harm Caused as Consequence of Defects of Good, Work, or Service

The seller or manufacturer of a good or executor of work (or service) shall be relieved from responsibility if it is proved that the harm arose as a consequence of insuperable force or a violation by the consumer of the established rules for the keeping or use of the good (or the results of the work, service).

§ 4. Contributory Compensation of Moral Harm

Article 1021. General Provisions

Moral harm shall be compensated contributorily by the causer when fault of the causer is present except for instances provided for by paragraph two of the present Article.

Moral harm shall be compensated contributorily irrespective of the fault of the causer in instances if:

the harm is caused to the life or health of a citizen by a source of increased danger;

the harm is caused to a citizen as a result of his illegal detention, and also any application of torture and other cruel, inhumane, or humiliating types of treatment and punishment, illegal bringing to criminal responsibility, illegal application of confinement under guard or undertaking concerning proper behavior as a measure of restraint, or illegal application of an administrative sanction and illegal arrest [as amended by Law of 29 March 2022, No. ЗРУ-761];

the harm was caused by the dissemination of information defaming honor, dignity, and business reputation;

in other instances provided for by a law.

Article 1022. Means and Amount of Contributory Compensation of Moral Harm

Contributory compensation of moral harm shall be effectuated in monetary form.

The amount of contributory compensation of moral harm shall be determined by a court depending upon the character of physical and moral suffering caused to the victim, and also the degree of fault of the causer in the instances when the fault is the grounds for the contributory compensation. When determining the amount of contributory compensation of harm, the requirements of reasonableness and justness must be taken into account.

The character of physical and moral sufferings shall be valued by the court by taking into account the factual circumstances under which the moral harm was caused and the individual peculiarities of the victim.

Moral harm shall be compensated contributorily irrespective of the property harm subject to compensation.

Chapter 58. Obligations as Consequence of Unfounded Enrichment

Article 1023. Duty to Return Unfounded Enrichment

A person who without grounds established by legislation or transaction acquired or saved property (acquirer) at the expense of another person (victim) shall be obliged to return to the last property unfoundedly acquired or saved (unfounded enrichment), except for instances provided for by Article 1030 of the present Code.

The duty established by paragraph one of the present Article also shall arise if the grounds on which the property was acquired or saved subsequently disappeared.

The rules of the present Chapter shall be applied irrespective of whether the unfounded enrichment is a result of the behavior of the acquirer of the property, the victim himself, third persons, or occurred outside their will.

Article 1024. Correlation of Demands Concerning Return of Unfounded Enrichment with Other Demands in Defense of Civil Rights

Unless established otherwise by legislation and does not arise from the essence of the respective relations, the rules of the present Chapter shall be subject to application also to demands:

concerning the return of that performed under an invalid transactions;

concerning the demanding and obtaining of property by the owner from another's illegal possession;

by one party in an obligation to another concerning the return of that performed in connection with this obligation;

concerning compensation of harm, including that caused by the behavior not in good faith of the person enriched.

Article 1025. Return of Unfounded Enrichment in Kind

Property comprising unfounded enrichment of the acquirer must be returned to the victim in kind.

The acquirer shall be liable to the victim for any, including also for any accidental, shortage or deterioration of the unfoundedly acquired or saved property which occurred after he knew or should have known about the unfoundedness of the enrichment. Before that moment he shall be liable only for intent and gross negligence.

Article 1026. Compensation of Value of Unfounded Enrichment

In the event it is impossible to return in kind property unfoundedly received or saved, the acquirer must compensate the victim for the real value of this property at the moment of its acquisition, and also compensate the losses caused by the subsequent change of the value of this property if the acquirer did not compensate its value immediately after he knew about the unfounded enrichment.

A person who unfoundedly and temporarily used another's property without the intention to acquire it or another's services must compensate the victim for that which he saved as a consequence of such use at the price which existed at the time when the use ended and in that place where it occurred.

Article 1027. Consequences of Unfounded Transfer of Right to Another Person

A person who has transferred by means of assignment of a demand or otherwise a right belonging to him to another person on the basis of a nonexistent or invalid obligation shall have the right to demand the restoration of his previous position, including the return to him of documents certifying the transferred right.

Article 1028. Compensation to Victim of Revenues Not Received

The person who unfoundedly received or saved property shall be obliged to return or to compensate the victim for all revenues which he derived or should have derived from this property from the time when he knew or should have known about the unfounded enrichment.

Interest shall be subject to being calculated on the amount of unfounded monetary enrichment for the use of another's means from the time when the acquirer knew or should have known about the unfoundedness of the receipt or savings of monetary means.

Article 1029. Compensation of Expenditures on Property Subject to Return

In the event of the return of property unfoundedly received or saved or compensation of the value thereof, the acquirer shall have the right to demand compensation from the victim of necessary expenditures incurred for the maintenance and preservation of property from the time from which he is obliged to return revenues, setting off the advantages received by him. The right to compensation of expenditures shall be lost in instances when the acquirer of property intentionally withheld shall be subject to return.

Article 1030. Unfounded Enrichment Not Subject to Return

There shall not be subject to return as unfounded enrichment:

property transferred in performance of an obligation before the ensuing of the period of performance unless provided otherwise by the obligation;

property transferred in performance of an obligation upon the expiry of the period of limitations;

earnings and payments equated thereto, pensions, benefits, stipends, compensation of harm caused to life or health, alimony and other monetary amounts granted to a citizen as means for existence, in the absence of lack of good faith on his part and mathematical error;

monetary amounts and other property granted in performance of a nonexistent obligation if the acquirer proves that the person requiring the return of the property knew about the absence of the obligation or granted the property for the purposes of philanthropy.

Section IV. Intellectual Property

Chapter 59. General Provisions

Article 1031. Objects of Intellectual Property

There shall be relegated to objects of intellectual property:

(1) the results of intellectual activity:

works of science, literature, and art;

performances, phonograms, and transmissions of air and cable broadcasting organizations [as amended by Law of 16 January 2007, ЗРУ-79. СЗ РУ (2007), no. 3, item 21];

computer programs and data bases (hereinafter – computers) [as amended by Law of 16 January 2007, ЗРУ-79. СЗ РУ (2007), no. 3, item 21];

inventions, utility models, industrial designs;

selection achievements;

nondivulged information, including secrets of production (or know-how);

(2) means of individualization of the participants of civil turnover, goods, work, and services:

firm names;

trademarks (or service marks);

names of places of origin of goods;

(3) other results of intellectual activity and means of individualization of participants of civil turnover, goods, work, and services in the instances provided for by the present Code or other laws.

Article 1032. Legal Protection of Objects of Intellectual Property

The legal protection of objects of intellectual property shall arise by virtue of the fact of the creation thereof or as a consequence of the granting of legal protection by an empowered State agency in the instances and in the procedure provided for by the present Code or other laws.

The conditions of granting legal protection to undivulged information shall be determined by a law.

Article 1033. Personal Nonproperty and Property Rights to Objects of Intellectual Property

To the authors of the results of intellectual activity shall belong with respect to these rights the personal nonproperty and property rights.

Personal nonproperty rights shall belong to the author irrespective of his property rights and shall be preserved for him in the event of the transfer of his property rights to the results of intellectual activity to another person.

To the possessors of the right to means of individualization of the participants of civil turnover, goods, work, or services (hereinafter: means of individualization) shall belong the property rights with respect to these means.

The right of authorship (or right to be deemed the author of the result of intellectual activity) shall be a personal nonproperty right and may belong only to the person whose creative labor created the result of the intellectual activity.

The right of authorship shall be inalienable and nontransferable.

If the result was created by the joint creative labor of two or more persons, they shall be deemed to be coauthors. The group of persons who are deemed to be coauthors of a work as a whole may be limited by a law with respect to individual objects of intellectual property.

Article 1034. Exclusive Rights to Objects of Intellectual Property

The exclusive right of the lawful use of this object of intellectual property at his discretion in any form and by any means shall belong to the possessor of property rights to the result of intellectual activity or means of individualization.

The use by other persons of objects of intellectual property with respect to which the exclusive right belongs to right-possessor shall be permitted only with the authorization of the right-possessor [as amended by Law of 16 January 2007, ЗРУ-79. СЗ РУ (2007), no. 3, item 21].

The possessor of an exclusive right to an object of intellectual property shall have the right to transfer this right to another person fully or partially, authorize another person to use the object of intellectual property, and have the right to otherwise dispose of it unless this is contrary to the rules of the present Code and other laws.

Limitations of exclusive rights, including by means of granting the possibility of use of an object of intellectual property to other persons, the deeming of these rights to be invalid, and the termination (or annulment) thereof shall be permitted in the instances, within the limits, and in the procedure established by the present Code and other laws.

Limitations of exclusive rights shall apply on condition that such limitation does not cause unjustified prejudice to the normal use of the object of intellectual property and does not impinge unfoundedly on the legal interests of the right-possessor [as amended by Law of 16 January 2007, ЗРУ-79. СЗ РУ (2007), no. 3, item 21].

Article 1035. Transfer of Exclusive Rights to Another Person

Property rights which belong to the possessor of exclusive rights to an object of intellectual property may, unless provided otherwise by the present Code or other law, be transferred by the right-possessor fully or partially to another person under a contract, and also pass by inheritance and by way of legal succession in the event of the reorganization of a juridical person-right-possessor.

The transfer of property rights under a contract or the transfer thereof by way of universal legal succession shall not entail the transfer or limitation of the right of authorship and other inalienable and nontransferable exclusive rights. The conditions of the contract concerning the transfer or limitation of such rights shall be null.

Exclusive rights which are transferred under a contract must be determined therein. The rights which have not been specified in the contract as alienated shall be presupposed to be not transferred insofar not proved otherwise.

The rules on a license contract shall apply to a contract providing for the granting of an exclusive right in the period of its operation to another person for a limited time.

Article 1036. License Contract

Under a license contract the party possessing an exclusive right to the result of intellectual activity or to a means of individualization (licensor) shall grant to the other party (licensee) an authorization to use the respective object of intellectual property.

The license contract must determine the right being granted and the limits and periods of use.

The license contract shall be presupposed to be for compensation.

The license contract may provide for the grant to the licensee of:

the right of use of an object of intellectual property with preservation for the licensor of the right of the use thereof and the right to issue a license to other persons (simple nonexclusive license);

the right of use of an object of intellectual property with preservation for the licensor of the right of use thereof, but without the right to issue a license to other persons (exclusive license);

other types of license permitted by a law.

Unless provided otherwise in the license contract, the license shall be presupposed to be a simple (nonexclusive) [license].

The contract concerning the granting by the licensor of the right of use of an object of intellectual property to another person shall be deemed to be a contract of sublicense. The licensee shall have the right to conclude a contract of sublicense only in the instances provided for by the license contract.

Responsibility to the licensor for the actions of a sublicensee shall be borne by the licensee unless provided otherwise by the license contract.

Article 1037. Contract on Creation and Use of Results of Intellectual Activity

The author may assume under a contract concerning the creation and use of the results of intellectual activity the obligation to create in future a work, invention, or other results of intellectual activity and to grant to the customer who is not his employer the exclusive rights to the use of this result.

The contract provided for in paragraph one of the present Article must determined the character of the results of intellectual activity subject to creation, and also the purpose or means of the use thereof.

A contract obliging the author to grant to any person the exclusive rights to the use of any results of intellectual activity which this author creates in future shall be null.

The conditions of a contract concerning the creation and use of the results of intellectual activity which limit the author in the creation in future of the results of intellectual activity of a determined nature or in a determined domain shall be null.

Article 1038. Exclusive Right and Right of Ownership

An exclusive right to the result of intellectual activity or means of individualization shall exist irrespective of the right of ownership to the material object in which such result or means of individualization is expressed.

Article 1039. Period of Operation of Exclusive Right to Objects of Intellectual Property

The exclusive right to objects of intellectual property shall operate during the period provided for by the present Code or other laws.

Personal nonproperty rights with respect to objects of intellectual property shall operate in perpetuity.

In the instances provided for by a law, the operation of an exclusive right to objects of intellectual ownership may terminate as a consequence of the nonuse thereof during a determined time.

Article 1040. Means of Defense of Exclusive Rights to Objects of Intellectual Property

The defense of exclusive rights to objects of intellectual property shall be effectuated by the means provided for by Article 11 of the present Code. The defense of exclusive rights also may be effectuated by:

the seizure of material objects with the assistance of which exclusive rights have been violated, and material objects created as a result of such violation;

the obligatory publication concerning a violation permitted, incorporating information therein as to whom the violated right belongs;

the other means provided for by a law.

In the event of a violation of a contract concerning the creation and the use of the results of intellectual activity and means of individualization, the general rules concerning responsibility for the violation of obligations shall apply.

Chapter 60. Author's Right

Article 1041. Object of Author's Right [as amended by Law of 16 January 2007, ЗРУ-79. СЗ РУ (2007), no. 3, item 21]

Author's right shall extend to a work of science, literature, and art which is the result of creative activity, irrespective of designation and merit of the work, and also the means of expression thereof.

Author's right shall extend both to promulgated and to nonpromulgated works in any objective form:

written (manuscript, type-written, musical notation, and so on);

oral (public declamation, public performance, and so on);

sound or video recording (mechanical, tape, digital, optical, and so on);

image (drawing, sketch, painting, map, line drawing, cinema, tele-, video, or photo frame, and so on);

cubic-spatial (sculpture, model, layout, installation, and so on);

other forms.

Author's right shall extend to the form of expression, and not to the ideas, principles, methods, processes, systems, means, or conceptions as such [Article as amended by Law of 16 January 2007, ЗРУ-79. СЗ РУ (2007), no. 3, item 21].

Article 1042. Types of Objects of Author's Right

There shall be relegated to objects of author's right:

literary works (literary-belles lettres, scientific, scholarly, publicist, and the like);

dramatic and scenario works;

musical works with or without text;

musical-dramatic works;

choreographic works and pantomimes;

audiovisual works [as amended by Law of 16 January 2007, ЗРУ-79. СЗ РУ (2007), no. 3, item 21];

works of painting, sculpture, graphics, design, and other works of the decorative arts;

works of applied decorative and stage design;

works of architecture, urban construction, and garden-park art;

photographic works and works obtained by means analogous to photography;

geographic, geological, and other charts, maps, sketches, and works relating to geography, topography, and other sciences;

computer programs of all types, including applied programs and operational systems;

other works meeting the requirements established by Article 1041 of the present Code.

Article 1043. Parts of Work, Derivative and Compiled Works Which Are Objects of Author's Right [as amended by Law of 16 January 2007, ЗРУ-79. СЗ РУ (2007), no. 3, item 21]

There shall be objects of author's right which meet the requirements established by Article 1041 of the present Code:

parts of works (including the name thereof) which may be used autonomously;

derivative works (translations, polishings, annotations, abstracts, summaries, surveys, dramatizations, arrangements, adaptations, and other processing of works of science, literature, and art);

collections (encyclopedias, anthologies, data bases) and other compiled works representing by choice or positioning of the materials a result of creative labor.

Derivative and compiled works shall be protected by author's right irrespective of whether they are works on which they are based or which they include are the objects of author's right [Article as amended by Law of 16 January 2007, ЗРУ-79. СЗ РУ (2007), no. 3, item 21].

Article 1044. Materials Which Are Not Objects of Author's Right [as amended by Law of 16 January 2007, ЗРУ-79. СЗ РУ (2007), no. 3, item 21]

There shall not be objects of author's right:

official documents (laws, decisions and the like), and also official translations thereof;

official symbols and marks (flags, arms, orders, banknotes, land so on);

works of folk creativity;

communications concerning news of the day or communications concerning current events having the character of ordinary press information;

the results received with the assistance of technical means intended for the production of a determined type without the effectuation by a person of creative activity expressly directed towards the creation of an individual work [Article as amended by Law of 16 January 2007, ЗРУ-79. СЗ РУ (2007), no. 3, item 21].

Article 1045. Rights to Draft Official Documents, Symbols, and Marks

The right of authorship to a draft official document, symbol, or mark shall belong to the person who created the draft (draughtsman).

The draughtsmen of draft official documents, symbols, and marks shall have the right to publish drafts also unless this has been prohibited by the agency on whose behalf the draft was worked out. In the event of the publication of a draft, the draughtsmen shall have the right to indicate their names.

When preparing official documents, symbols, and marks on the basis of a draft additions and changes may be made therein at the discretion of the agency effectuating the preparation of the official document, symbol, or mark.

After approval of the draft by the competent agency, it may be used without indicating the name of the draughtsman.

Article 1046. Author of Work. Arising of Authorship. Presumption of Authorship [as amended by Law of 16 January 2007, 3PУ-79. C3 PУ (2007), no. 3, item 21]

The author of a work shall be deemed to be the citizen by whose creative labor it was created.

Author's right on a work of science, literature, land art shall arise by virtue of the fact of the creation thereof. Registration of a work or compliance with any other formalities shall not be required for the arising and effectuation of author's right.

The person designated as the author on the original or example of the work shall be considered to be the author thereof unless proved otherwise.

In the event of the publication of a work anonymously or under a pseudonym (except when the pseudonym of the author leaves no doubt as to his identity), the publisher effectuating publication whose name is designated on the work, in the absence of evidence otherwise, shall be considered the representative of the author and shall have the right to defend the rights of the author and ensure the effectuation thereof. This provision shall operate so long as the author of such work does not disclose his identity and does not declare his authorship [Article as amended by Law of 16 January 2007, 3PУ-79. C3 PУ (2007), no. 3, item 21].

Article 1047. Coauthorship

The author's right to a work created by the joint creative labor of two or more citizens shall belong to the coauthors jointly, irrespective of whether this work forms one integral whole or consists of parts, each of which also has autonomous significance.

Part of the work shall be deemed to have autonomous significance if it may be used irrespective of the other parts of this work.

Each of the coauthors shall have the right to use the part of the work created by him having autonomous significance unless provided otherwise by agreement between them.

Relations between the coauthors shall be determined, as a rule, on the basis of an agreement. In the absence of such agreement the author's right to a work shall be effectuated by all of the authors jointly, and the remuneration shall be distributed among them equally.

If the work of coauthors forms one integral whole, then none of the authors shall have the right without sufficient grounds to prohibit the use of the work.

Article 1048. Author's Right to Derivative Work [as amended by Law of 16 January 2007, 3PY-79. C3 PY (2007), no. 3, item 21]

To the author of a derivative work shall belong author's right to the processing of the work of science, literature, and art effectuated by him.

The author of a derivative work shall enjoy the author's right to the work created by him on condition of compliance by him with the rights of the author of the work subjected to processing.

The author's right of the author of a derivative work shall not obstruct other persons from effectuating their own processing of a work which has become the basis for processing [Article as amended by Law of 16 January 2007, 3PY-79. C3 PY (2007), no. 3, item 21].

Article 1049. Rights of Persons Organizing Creation of Works

Persons organizing the creation of works (manufacturers of audiovisual works, publishers of encyclopedias, producers, and the like) shall not be deemed to be the authors of respective works. However, in the instances provided for by the present Code or other laws, such persons shall acquire the exclusive rights to the use of these works [as amended by Law of 16 January 2007, 3PY-79. C3 PY (2007), no. 3, item 21].

The manufacturer of a film shall have the right in the event of any use of this work to indicate his name or to require such indication.

The exclusive rights to the use of such publications shall belong to the publisher of encyclopedias, encyclopedic dictionaries, periodical and continuing collections of scholarly works, newspapers, journals, and other periodical publications. The publisher shall have the right in the event of any use of such publications to indicate their name or require such indication. The authors of works included in such publications shall retain the exclusive rights to the use of their works irrespective of publication as a whole unless provided otherwise by the author's contract [as amended by Law of 16 January 2007, ЗРУ-79. СЗ РУ (2007), no. 3, item 21].

Article 1050. Marks of Protection of Author's Right

The possessor of an exclusive author's right may in order to notify his rights use a mark of protection of author's right which is placed on each example of the work and consists of three elements:

the Latin letter «C» in a circle;

the name of the possessor of the exclusive author's rights;

the year of first publication of the work.

Unless it is proved otherwise, the right-possessor shall be considered to be the person designated on the mark of protection of the author's right.

Article 1051. Personal Nonproperty Rights of Author

The following personal nonproperty rights shall belong to the author of a work:

right to be recognized as the author of a work (right of authorship) [as amended by Law of 16 January 2007, ЗРУ-79. СЗ РУ (2007), no. 3, item 21];

right to use or authorize to use a work under the genuine name of the author, pseudonym, or without designation of the name, that is, anonymously (right to author's name) [as amended by Law of 16 January 2007, ЗРУ-79. СЗ РУ (2007), no. 3, item 21];

right to promulgate or authorize to promulgate a work in any form (right to promulgation), including right to recall [as amended by Law of 16 January 2007, ЗРУ-79. СЗ РУ (2007), no. 3, item 21];

right to defend a work, including the name thereof, against any distortion or any other infringement capable of causing damage to the honor or dignity of the author (right to defend reputation of author) [as amended by Law of 16 January 2007, ЗРУ-79. СЗ РУ (2007), no. 3, item 21].

An author shall have the right to retract a previously taken decision concerning promulgation of a work (right of recall) on condition of compensation to the persons who have received the right to use the work of losses caused by such decision, including lost advantage. If a work already has been promulgated, the author shall be obliged publicly to notify the recall thereof. In so doing he shall have the right to withdraw at his own expense previously manufactured examples of the work. These provisions shall not apply to employment works unless provided otherwise in the contract with the author [paragraph added by Law of 16 January 2007, ЗРУ-79. СЗ РУ (2007), no. 3, item 21].

In the event of the publication, public performance, or other use of a work the making of any changes whatsoever in the work itself, name thereof, and designation of the name of the author shall be permitted only with the consent of the author [paragraph added by Law of 16 January 2007, ЗРУ-79. СЗ РУ (2007), no. 3, item 21].

It shall be prohibited without the consent of the author to supply the work thereof in the event of publication with illustrations, preface, afterword, commentaries, or any explanations whatsoever [paragraph added by Law of 16 January 2007, ЗРУ-79. СЗ РУ (2007), no. 3, item 21].

Personal nonproperty rights shall belong to the author irrespective of the property rights thereof and shall be retained form him in the event of the transfer of exclusive rights to use of the work [paragraph added by Law of 16 January 2007, ЗРУ-79. СЗ РУ (2007), no. 3, item 21].

An agreement of the author with anyone and the statement of the author refusing to effectuate personal nonproperty rights shall be null.

Article 1052. Right of Authorship [repealed by Law of 16 January 2007, ЗРУ-79. СЗ РУ (2007), no. 3, item 21]

Article 1053. Right to Author's Name [repealed by Law of 16 January 2007, ЗРУ-79. СЗ РУ (2007), no. 3, item 21]

Article 1054. Right to Inviolability of Work [repealed by Law of 16 January 2007, ЗРУ-79. СЗ РУ (2007), no. 3, item 21]

Article 1055. Right to Publication of Work [repealed by Law of 16 January 2007, ЗРУ-79. СЗ РУ (2007), no. 3, item 21]

Article 1056. Property Rights of Author [as amended by Law of 16 January 2007, ЗРУ-79. СЗ РУ (2007), no. 3, item 21]

To the author shall belong the exclusive rights to the use of a work in any form and by any means.

Juridical and natural persons, except for instances provided for by the present Code and other laws, may use a work only by contract with the right-possessor or other empowered person, including under a contract with the organizations managing property rights on a collective basis or, in the absence thereof, under a contract with an organization performing the functions and duties of these organizations [paragraph added by Law of 16 January 2007, ЗРУ-79. СЗ РУ (2007), no. 3, item 21].

Exclusive rights of the author to the use of a work shall mean the right to effectuate or authorize the following actions:

to reproduce the work (right to reproduction);

to disseminate the original or examples of the work by means of the sale or other transfer of the right of ownership (right to dissemination);

to bring a work to general information (right to bring to general information);

to hire out the original or examples of the work (right to hire out);

to import examples of the work for the purpose of dissemination, including examples manufactured with the authorization of the possessor of exclusive author's rights (right to import);

to communicate a work for general information by means of transfer by wires (or cable) or with the assistance of other analogous means (right to communicate by cable);

to rework, arrange, or otherwise process a work (right to process);

to publicly show the work (right to public show);

to publicly perform the work (right to public performance);

to communicate a work for general information by means of transfer with the assistance of wireless means (right to broadcast);

to translate the work (right to translation);

to repeatedly communicate a work for general information if such communication is effectuated by another organization and not by the organization initially effectuating the communication (right to repeated communication for general information) [as amended by Law of 16 January 2007, ЗРУ-79. СЗ РУ (2007), no. 3, item 21].

The author shall have the right to receive remuneration for each type of use of his work (right to remuneration) [paragraph by Law of 16 January 2007, ЗРУ-79. СЗ РУ (2007), no. 3, item 21].

If examples of a public work have been lawfully introduced into civil turnover by means of the sale thereof or other transfer of the right of ownership, their further dissemination shall be permitted without the consent of the author and without payment thereto of remuneration, except for instances provided for by a law [as amended by Law of 16 January 2007, ЗРУ-79. СЗ РУ (2007), no. 3, item 21].

A work shall be considered to be used irrespective of it being used for the purpose of deriving revenue or the use thereof not directed towards this [as amended by Law of 16 January 2007, ЗРУ-79. СЗ РУ (2007), no. 3, item 21].

The practical application of the provisions comprising the content of the work (inventions, other technical, economic, organizational, and similar solutions) shall not be considered the use of the work in the sense of author's right [as amended by Law of 16 January 2007, ЗРУ-79. СЗ РУ (2007), no. 3, item 21].

Article 1057. Disposition of Right to Use of Work [repealed by Law of 16 January 2007, ЗРУ-79. СЗ РУ (2007), no. 3, item 21]

Article 1058. Limitations of Author's Rights

The limitation of exclusive rights of the author and other persons to use a work shall be permitted only in the instances provided for by Articles 1059-1062 of the present Code or other laws.

The said limitations shall be applied on condition that this does not inflict unjustified damage on the normal use of the work and does not impinge unjustifiably the legal interests of the author [Article as amended by Law of 16 January 2007, ЗРУ-79. СЗ РУ (2007), no. 3, item 21].

Article 1059. Reproduction of Works for Personal Purposes Without Consent of Author and Without Payment of Remuneration [as amended by Law of 16 January 2007, ЗРУ-79. СЗ РУ (2007), no. 3, item 21]

The reproduction of a promulgated work for personal purposes which has been issued shall be permitted without the consent of the author or other right-possessor and without the payment of remuneration except for instances provided for by a law [as amended by Law of 16 January 2007, ЗРУ-79. СЗ РУ (2007), no. 3, item 21].

The rules of paragraph one of the present Article shall not apply with respect to:

use of the works of architecture in the form of buildings and installations [as amended by Law of 16 January 2007, ЗРУ-79. СЗ РУ (2007), no. 3, item 21];

use of data bases or material parts thereof;

use of computer programs, except for instances provided for by a law [as amended by Law of 16 January 2007, ЗРУ-79. СЗ РУ (2007), no. 3, item 21];

reprographic reproduction of books (as a whole) and music texts [as amended by Law of 16 January 2007, ЗРУ-79. СЗ РУ (2007), no. 3, item 21].

Article 1060. Free Public Performance of Works

The public performance of published musical works during official, religious, and burial ceremonies to the extent justified by the character of such ceremonies shall be permitted without the consent of the author or other right-possessor and without the payment of remuneration [as amended by Law of 16 January 2007, ЗРУ-79. СЗ РУ (2007), no. 3, item 21].

Article 1061. Use of Works for Purposes of Performance of Pre-Investigative Verification, Inquiry, Preliminary Investigation, Administrative or Judicial Proceeding [as amended by Laws of 16 January 2007, ЗРУ-79, and of 23 May 2019, No. ЗРУ-542]

The use of works for the purposes of the performance of a pre-investigative verification, inquiry, preliminary investigation, administrative and judicial proceeding to the extent justified by the purpose of the use shall be permitted without the consent of the author or other right-possessor and without the payment of remuneration [as amended by Laws of 16 January 2007, and of 23 May 2019, No. ЗРУ-542].

Article 1062. Author's Right to Employment Work [as amended by Law of 16 January 2007, ЗРУ-79. СЗ РУ (2007), no. 3, item 21]

The personal nonproperty rights of an author to a work created by way of fulfilling an employment duties or an employment planning task (employment work) shall be retained for the author of the work [as amended by Law of 16 January 2007, ЗРУ-79. СЗ РУ (2007), no. 3, item 21].

The exclusive rights of use of an employment work shall belong to the employer unless provided otherwise in the contract between him and the author [as amended by Law of 16 January 2007, ЗРУ-79. СЗ РУ (2007), no. 3, item 21].

The amount of remuneration for each type of use of an employment work and the procedure for the payment thereof shall be established by the contract between the author and employer. Upon the expiry of ten years from the moment of promulgation of the work, and with the consent of the employer – also earlier, the author shall acquire in full the right to use of the work and receipt of remuneration irrespective of the contract concluded with the employer [as amended by Law of 16 January 2007, ЗРУ-79. СЗ РУ (2007), no. 3, item 21].

The right of the author to use an employment work by a means not conditioned by the purpose of the planning task shall not be limited.

The employer shall have the right in the event of any use of an employment work to specify its name or to require such indication [as amended by Law of 16 January 2007, ЗРУ-79. СЗ РУ (2007), no. 3, item 21].

The provisions of the present Article shall not extend to the creation by way of fulfillment of employment duties or employment planning task of the employer of encyclopedias, encyclopedic dictionaries, periodical and continuing collections of scholarly works, newspapers, journals, and other periodical publications provided for by Article 1049, paragraph three, of the present Code [paragraph added by Law of 16 January 2007, ЗРУ-79. СЗ РУ (2007), no. 3, item 21].

Article 1063. Sphere of Operation of Author's Right [as amended by Law of 16 January 2007, ЗРУ-79. СЗ РУ (2007), no. 3, item 21]

In accordance with the present Code the author's right shall extend to:

works of authors and other initial possessors of author's right who are citizens of the Republic Uzbekistan or have a permanent whereabouts on the territory of the Republic Uzbekistan;

works published for the first time in the Republic Uzbekistan irrespective of citizenship and permanent whereabouts of the authors thereof;

works protected in the Republic Uzbekistan in accordance with international treaties of the Republic Uzbekistan.

Works shall also be considered to be published for the first time in the Republic Uzbekistan if within thirty days after the date of first publication beyond the limits of the Republic Uzbekistan it was published on the territory of the Republic Uzbekistan.

When granting protection on the territory of the Republic Uzbekistan to a work in accordance with international treaties of the Republic Uzbekistan the author of a work shall be determined according to the law of the State on whose territory the legal fact occurred which served as grounds for possession of the author's right [Article as amended by Law of 16 January 2007, ЗРУ-79. СЗ РУ (2007), no. 3, item 21].

Article 1064. Commencement of Operation of Author's Right [repealed by Law of 16 January 2007, ЗРУ-79. СЗ РУ (2007), no. 3, item 21]

Article 1065. Period of Operation of Author's Right

An author's right shall operate throughout the life of the author and fifty years after his death, except for instances provided for by the present Article and other laws [as amended by Law of 16 January 2007, ЗРУ-79. СЗ РУ (2007), no. 3, item 21].

An author's right to a work created in coauthorship shall operate throughout the lives of the coauthors and fifty years after the death of the last of the authors who has survived the other coauthors.

An author's right to a work lawfully promulgated under a pseudonym or anonymously shall operate for fifty years after the promulgation thereof. If within the said period the pseudonym or anonym divulges his identity or his identity no longer leaves doubts, the periods specified in paragraph one of the present Article shall be applied [as amended by Law of 16 January 2007, ЗРУ-79. СЗ РУ (2007), no. 3, item 21].

The author's right to a work first issued after the death of the author shall operate for fifty years after the issuance thereof [as amended by Law of 16 January 2007, ЗРУ-79. СЗ РУ (2007), no. 3, item 21].

The right of authorship, the right to author's name, and the right to defense of the reputation of the author shall be protected in perpetuity [as amended by Law of 16 January 2007, ЗРУ-79. СЗ РУ (2007), no. 3, item 21].

When granting protection to a work in accordance with international treaties of the Republic Uzbekistan the period of operation of author's right on the territory of the Republic Uzbekistan shall be determined in accordance with the present Article. But this period may not exceed the period of operation of author's right established in the country of origin of the work [paragraph added by Law of 16 January 2007, ЗРУ-79. СЗ РУ (2007), no. 3, item 21].

Calculation of the periods provided for in the present Article shall commence from the first of January following the year in which the legal fact occurred which is grounds for commencement of the running of the period [as amended by Law of 16 January 2007, ЗРУ-79. СЗ РУ (2007), no. 3, item 21].

Article 1066. Transfer of Work to Public Weal

The expiry of the period of operation of an author's right to a work shall means the transfer thereof to the public weal [as amended by Law of 16 January 2007, 3PУ-79. C3 PУ (2007), no. 3, item 21].

[paragraph two repealed by Law of 7 October 2013, 3PУ-355. C3 PУ (2013), no. 41, item 543].

Works which are public weal may freely be used by any person without the payment of remuneration. In so doing the personal nonproperty rights of the author must be complied with [as amended by Law of 16 January 2007, 3PУ-79. C3 PУ (2007), no. 3, item 21].

Article 1067. Author's Contract

The property rights provided for by Article 1056, paragraph three, of the present Code may be transferred by the right-possessor to another person only by the conclusion of an author's contract, except for instances established by the present Code and other laws [as amended by Law of 16 January 2007, 3PУ-79. C3 PУ (2007), no. 3, item 21].

The transfer of property rights of an author may be effectuated on the basis of an author's contract concerning the transfer of exclusive rights or on the basis of an author's contract concerning the transfer of nonexclusive rights [paragraph added by Law of 16 January 2007, 3PУ-79. C3 PУ (2007), no. 3, item 21].

An author's contract concerning the transfer of exclusive rights shall authorize the use of a work by a determined means and within the limits established by a contract only to the person to whom these rights are transferred [paragraph added by Law of 16 January 2007, 3PУ-79. C3 PУ (2007), no. 3, item 21].

An author's contract concerning the transfer of nonexclusive rights shall authorize the use to the user of the work equally with the possessor of exclusive rights who transferred such rights and/or to other persons who received authorization for use of this work by the same means [paragraph added by Law of 16 January 2007, 3PУ-79. C3 PУ (2007), no. 3, item 21].

The rights to be transferred under an author's contract shall be considered to be nonexclusive unless expressly provided otherwise in the contract [paragraph added by Law of 16 January 2007, 3PУ-79. C3 PУ (2007), no. 3, item 21].

Author's right to a work shall not be connected with the right of ownership to a material object in which the work is expressed [paragraph added by Law of 16 January 2007, ЗРУ-79. СЗ РУ (2007), no. 3, item 21].

Transfer of the right of ownership to a material object or rights of possession to a material object shall not entail in and other itself the transfer of any author's rights to the work expressed in this object [paragraph added by Law of 16 January 2007, ЗРУ-79. СЗ РУ (2007), no. 3, item 21].

Article 1068. Conditions of Author's Contract

An author's contract must provide:

means for the use of the work (specific rights to be transferred under the particular contract);

amount of remuneration and/or the procedure for determining the amount of remuneration for each means of use of the work and the procedure and periods for payment thereof.

An author's contract may provide other conditions also which the parties consider to be necessary [paragraph added by Law of 16 January 2007, ЗРУ-79. СЗ РУ (2007), no. 3, item 21].

In the absence in the author's contract of a condition concerning the period for which the right of use of the work is transferred, the contract may be dissolved by the author upon the expiry of five years from the date of conclusion thereof if the user was informed in writing about this six months before dissolution of the contract.

In the absence in the author's contract of a condition concerning the territory within whose limits the right of use of the work operates, the operation of the right transferred under the contract shall be limited to the territory of the Republic Uzbekistan.

The right to use a work not expressly provided for transfer by an author's contract shall be considered to be not transferred [paragraph added by Law of 16 January 2007, ЗРУ-79. СЗ РУ (2007), no. 3, item 21].

The rights to the use of a work unknown at the moment of concluding the contract may not be the subject of an author's contract.

Remuneration shall be determined in an author's contract in the form of a percentage of the revenue for the respective means of use of the work or if this is impossible to effectuate in connection with the character of the work or peculiarities of the use thereof, in the form of an amount fixed in the contract or otherwise [as amended by Law of 16 January 2007, ЗРУ-79. СЗ РУ (2007), no. 3, item 21].

If in an author's contract concerning publication or other use of a work the remuneration is determined in the form of a fixed amount, the maximum print-run of the work must be established in the contract.

The rights transferred under an author's contract may be transferred wholly or partially to other persons only in an event when this is expressly provided for by such contract [as amended by Law of 16 January 2007, ЗРУ-79. СЗ РУ (2007), no. 3, item 21].

A condition of an author's contract limiting the author in the creation in the future of works on the particular theme or in a particular domain shall be void [paragraph added by Law of 16 January 2007, ЗРУ-79. СЗ РУ (2007), no. 3, item 21].

Conditions of an author's contract which are contrary to the requirements of the present Code or other laws shall be invalid [paragraph added by Law of 16 January 2007, ЗРУ-79. СЗ РУ (2007), no. 3, item 21].

Article 1069. Form of Author's Contract

An author's contract must be concluded in written form, except for instances provided for by a law.

Article 1070. Responsibility Under Author's Contract

A party who has not performed or improperly performed obligations under the author's contract shall be obliged to compensate losses caused to the other party, including lost advantage.

Article 1071. Period of Operation of Author's License Contract [repealed by Law of 16 January 2007, ЗРУ-79. СЗ РУ (2007), no. 3, item 21]

Article 1072. Responsibility for Unlawful Use of Work Without Contract [repealed by Law of 16 January 2007, ЗРУ-79. СЗ РУ (2007), no. 3, item 21]

Article 1073. Legal Regulation of Authors' Relations

Authors' relations shall be regulated by the present Code and other legislation.

Chapter 61. Neighboring Rights

Article 1074. Objects of Neighboring Rights [as amended by Law of 16 January 2007, ЗРУ-79. СЗ РУ (2007), no. 3, item 21]

To objects of neighboring rights shall be relegated performances, phonograms, and transmissions of broadcasting and cable organizations [as amended by Law of 16 January 2007, ЗРУ-79. СЗ РУ (2007), no. 3, item 21].

Article 1075. Subjects of Neighboring Rights

Performers, manufacturers of phonograms, and broadcasting and cable organizations shall be subjects of neighboring rights [as amended by Law of 16 January 2007, ЗРУ-79. СЗ РУ (2007), no. 3, item 21].

The registration of an object of neighboring rights or compliance with any other formalities shall not be required for the arising and effectuation of neighboring rights [paragraph added by Law of 16 January 2007, ЗРУ-79. СЗ РУ (2007), no. 3, item 21].

Juridical and natural persons, including those effectuating the broadcasting by air and communication by cable (including re-transmission), except for instances provided by the present Code and other laws, may use a work, performance, phonogram, or transmission by a broadcasting or cable organization only under a contract with the right-possessor or other empowered person. Re-transmission must be effectuated in compliance with the rights of authors, performers, manufacturers of phonograms, and other right-possessors for broadcasting by air, communication by cable, and bringing to general information [paragraph added by Law of 16 January 2007, ЗРУ-79. СЗ РУ (2007), no. 3, item 21].

Article 1076. Marks of Protection of Neighboring Rights

The possessors of exclusive rights to a phonogram and/or performance recorded on such phonogram may for notification of their rights use a mark of protection of neighboring rights, which shall be placed on each example of the phonogram and/or on each container containing it and shall consist of three elements [as amended by Law of 16 January 2007, ЗРУ-79. СЗ РУ (2007), no. 3, item 21]:

the Latin letter «P» in a circle;

the name of the possessor of the exclusive neighboring rights;

the year of first publication of the recording.

Unless proved otherwise, the manufacturer of a phonogram shall be deemed to be the juridical or natural person whose name is designated on this phonogram and/or on the container containing it by a usual means [paragraph added by Law of 16 January 2007, ЗРУ-79. СЗ РУ (2007), no. 3, item 21].

Article 1077. Rights of Performer

The following rights shall belong to a performer:

right to name;

right to defense of performance against any distortion or any other infringement capable of causing damage to the honor and dignity of the performer;

exclusive rights to use of the performance in any form, including the right to receipt of remuneration for each type of use of the performance thereof [as amended by Law of 16 January 2007, ЗРУ-79. СЗ РУ (2007), no. 3, item 21].

Exclusive rights of a performer to use a performance shall mean the right to effectuate or authorize the following actions:

to reproduce a recording of a performance (right to reproduction);

to disseminate the original or examples of the recording of a performance by means of the sale or other transfer of the right of ownership (right to dissemination);

to bring a recording of a performance to general information (right to bring to general information);

to hire out original or example of recording of performance, even after the dissemination thereof with the consent of the performer and irrespective of the right of ownership to the original and examples (right to hire out);

to transmit a performance on the air or communicate by cable if the performance used for such transmission was not previously transmitted on the air or not effectuated with the use of a recording (right to transmit in air or communicate by cable an unrecorded performance);

to transmit on the air or communicate by cable a recording of a performance, if initially this recording was manufactured not for commercial purposes (right to transmit on the air or communicate by cable the recording of a performance) [as amended by Law of 16 January 2007, ЗРУ-79. СЗ РУ (2007), no. 3, item 21].

If the examples of a recording of a performance have been lawfully introduced into civil turnover by means of the sale thereof or other transfer of the right of ownership, their further dissemination shall be permitted without the consent of the performer and without the payment of remuneration thereto [paragraph added by Law of 16 January 2007, ЗРУ-79. СЗ РУ (2007), no. 3, item 21].

To performances effectuated by way of the fulfillment of employment duties or employment planning task of an employer the provisions of Article 1062 of the present Code shall apply respectively [paragraph added by Law of 16 January 2007, ЗРУ-79. СЗ РУ (2007), no. 3, item 21].

Performers must effectuate their rights in compliance with the rights of the authors of the works being performed [as amended by Law of 16 January 2007, ЗРУ-79. СЗ РУ (2007), no. 3, item 21].

Limitations of the right to use a performance shall be established by a law.

The recording of a performance shall be considered to be used irrespective of whether it was used for the purpose of deriving revenue or the use thereof was not directed towards this [paragraph added by Law of 16 January 2007, ЗРУ-79. СЗ РУ (2007), no. 3, item 21].

Article 1078. Rights of Manufacturer of Phonogram [as amended by Law of 16 January 2007, ЗРУ-79. СЗ РУ (2007), no. 3, item 21]

To the manufacturer of a phonogram shall belong the exclusive rights to the use of this phonogram in accordance with the present Code and other laws [as amended by Law of 16 January 2007, ЗРУ-79. СЗ РУ (2007), no. 3, item 21].

The exclusive rights of a manufacturer of a phonogram to use of the phonogram shall mean the right to effectuate or to authorize the following actions:

to reproduce a phonogram (right to reproduction);

to disseminate the original or examples of the phonogram by means of sale or other transfer of the right of ownership (right to dissemination);

to bring a phonogram to general information (right to bring to general information);

to hire out the original or examples of a phonogram even after the dissemination thereof effectuated by the manufacturer of the phonogram or with the consent thereof, and irrespective of the right of ownership to the original and examples (right to hire out);

to import the original or examples of the phonogram for the purposes of dissemination, including examples manufactured with the authorization of the possessor of the exclusive rights to the phonogram (right to import);

to transmit a phonogram on the air or communicate by cable (right to transmit on the air or communicate by cable);

to rework or by other means to process a phonogram (right to rework) [as amended by Law of 16 January 2007, ЗРУ-79. СЗ РУ (2007), no. 3, item 21].

The manufacturer of a phonogram shall have the right to receive remuneration for each type of use of its phonogram [paragraph added by Law of 16 January 2007, ЗРУ-79. СЗ РУ (2007), no. 3, item 21].

If examples of a published phonogram have lawfully been introduced into civil turnover by means of the sale thereof or other transfer of the right of ownership, their further dissemination thereof shall be permitted without the consent of the manufacturer of the phonogram and without payment of remuneration thereto [paragraph added by Law of 16 January 2007, ЗРУ-79. СЗ РУ (2007), no. 3, item 21].

Exclusive rights of a manufacturer of a phonogram provided for by paragraph two of the present Article may be transferred under a contract to other persons. The provisions of Articles 1067, 1068, and 1069 of the present Code shall apply respectively to such contract [paragraph added by Law of 16 January 2007, ЗРУ-79. СЗ РУ (2007), no. 3, item 21].

The manufacturers of phonograms must effectuate their rights in compliance with the rights of authors and performers of works and performances used [as amended by Law of 16 January 2007, ЗРУ-79. СЗ РУ (2007), no. 3, item 21].

A phonogram shall be considered to be used irrespective of whether it was used for the purpose of deriving revenue or the used thereof was not directed to this [paragraph added by Law of 16 January 2007, ЗРУ-79. СЗ РУ (2007), no. 3, item 21].

Article 1079. Rights of Broadcasting or Cable Organization [as amended by Law of 16 January 2007, ЗРУ-79. СЗ РУ (2007), no. 3, item 21]

The exclusive rights to use its transmission in accordance with the present Code and other laws shall belong to a broadcasting or cable organization [as amended by Law of 16 January 2007, ЗРУ-79. СЗ РУ (2007), no. 3, item 21].

The exclusive rights of a broadcasting or cable organization to use its transmission shall mean the right to effectuate or authorize the following actions:

to reproduce a recording of the transmission (right to reproduction);

to disseminate the original or examples of a recording of the transmission by means of sale or other transfer of the right of ownership (right to dissemination);

to bring a recording of the transmission to general information (right to bring to general information);

to record the transmission (right to recording);

to communicate a transmission for general information in places with paid entry (right to communicate for general information in places with paid entry);

to re-transmit a transmission (right of re-transmission);

to communicate a transmission for general information by cable or to transmit a transmission on the air (right to communication by cable or broadcast on the air) [paragraph added by Law of 16 January 2007, ЗРУ-79. СЗ РУ (2007), no. 3, item 21].

A broadcasting or cable organization shall have the right to receive remuneration for each type of use of its transmission [paragraph added by Law of 16 January 2007, ЗРУ-79. СЗ РУ (2007), no. 3, item 21].

Exclusive rights of a broadcasting or cable organization provided for by paragraph two of the present Article may be transferred under a contract to other persons. The provisions of Articles 1067, 1068, and 1069 of the present Code shall apply respectively to such contract [paragraph added by Law of 16 January 2007, ЗРУ-79. СЗ РУ (2007), no. 3, item 21].

A broadcasting or cable organization must effectuate its rights in compliance with the rights of the authors and performers of works and performances used, and in appropriate instances, the rights of the manufacturers of phonograms and broadcasting and cable organizations [as amended by Law of 16 January 2007, ЗРУ-79. СЗ РУ (2007), no. 3, item 21].

The transmission of a broadcasting or cable organization shall be considered to be used irrespective of whether it was used for the purpose of deriving revenue or the use thereof was not directed towards this [paragraph added by Law of 16 January 2007, ЗРУ-79. СЗ РУ (2007), no. 3, item 21].

Article 1080. Rights of Cable Broadcasting Organization [repealed by Law of 16 January 2007, ЗРУ-79. СЗ РУ (2007), no. 3, item 21]

Article 1081. Responsibility for Failure to Perform or Improper Performance of Contract on Use of Neighboring Rights and for Unlawful Use of Work Without Contract [repealed by Law of 16 January 2007, ЗРУ-79. СЗ РУ (2007), no. 3, item 21]

Chapter 62. Right to Industrial Property (Right to Invention, Utility Model, Industrial Design)

Article 1082. Legal Protection of Invention, Utility Model, and Industrial Design

The right to an invention, utility model, and industrial design shall be protected on condition of the issuance of a patent.

The requirements for an invention, utility model, or industrial design under which the right arises to receive a patent and the procedure for the issuance thereof by the empowered State agency, shall be established by a law [as amended by Laws of 26 December 2011, ЗРУ-312, and of 5 October 2020, No. ЗРУ-640].

Article 1083. Right of Use of Invention, Utility Model, and Industrial Design

To the patent possessor shall belong the exclusive right of use of the invention, utility model, or industrial design defended by a parent at his discretion, including the right to produce the product with the application of defended solutions, apply the technological processes in own production defended by the patent, or propose for sale the manufactures containing the defended solutions, and import respective manufactures.

Other persons besides the patent possessor shall not have the right to use an invention, utility model, or industrial design without his authorization, except for instances when such use in accordance with the present Code or other law is not a violation of the rights of the patent possessor.

The unsanctioned manufacture, application, import, proposal for sale, sale, other introduction into civil turnover, or keeping of a manufacture for this purpose manufactured with the application of a patented invention, utility model, or industrial design, and also the application of a means protected by a patent to an invention, or the introduction into civil turnover or keeping for this purpose of a manufacture manufactured directly by the means protected by the patent for the invention shall be deemed to be a violation of the exclusive right of the patent possessor.

A manufacture shall be considered to be manufactured by the patented means insofar as not proved otherwise.

Article 1084. Disposition of Right to Patent

The right to receive a patent, the rights arising from the registration of an application, the right to possession of a patent, and the rights arising from the patent may be transferred wholly or partially to another person.

Article 1085. Right of Authorship

To the author of an invention, utility model, or industrial design shall belong the right of authorship and the right to confer a special name on the invention, utility model, or industrial design.

The right of authorship and other personal rights to an invention, utility model, or industrial design shall arise from the moment of origin of the rights based on the patent.

Special rights, privileges, and preferences of a social character may be consolidated for the author of an invention, utility model, or industrial design.

The person specified in an application as an author shall be considered to be the author insofar as not proved otherwise. Only facts and circumstances which existed before the right arose may be involved as evidence.

Article 1086. Coauthors of Invention, Utility Model, and Industrial Design

The mutual relations of coauthors of an invention, utility model, or industrial design shall be determined by agreement between them.

Noncreative assistance in the creation of an invention, utility model, or industrial design (technical, organizational, or mathematical assistance, assisting the formalization of rights, and the like) shall not entail in and of itself coauthorship.

Article 1087. Employment Inventions, Utility Models, or Industrial Designs

The right to receive a patent to an invention, utility model, or industrial design created by a worker when fulfilling their employment duties or a specific planning task of the employer (employment invention) shall belong to the employer if this has been provided in the contract between them.

The amount, conditions, and procedure for payment of remuneration to the author for an employment invention, utility model, or industrial design shall be determined by an agreement between him and the employer. In the event of the failure to reach agreement, the decision shall be adopted by a court. If it is impossible to measure the contribution of the author and the employer to the creation of the invention, utility model, or industrial design, the right to half of the advantage received or which the employer should have received shall be recognized for the author.

Article 1088. Form of Contract on Transfer of Right to Patent

The contract on the transfer of the right to a patent (or the assignment of the patent) must be concluded in written form and shall be subject to registration in the empowered State agency. The failure to comply with the written form or requirements concerning registration shall entail the invalidity of the contract [as amended by Laws of 26 December 2011, 3PY-312, and of 5 October 2020, No. 3PY-640].

Article 1089. Form of Authorization (or License) for Use of Invention, Utility Model, and Industrial Design

The license contract and sublicense contract shall be concluded in written form and subject to registration in the empowered State agency. The failure to comply with the written form or requirement concerning registration shall entail the invalidity of the contract [as amended by Laws of 26 December 2011, 3PY-312, and of 5 October 2020, No. 3PY-640].

Article 1090. Responsibility for Violation of Patent

At the demand of the patent possessor the violation of a patent must be terminated, and the offender shall be obliged to compensate the patent possessor for losses incurred by him. Together with losses the patent possessor shall have the right to recover from the offender revenues received by him as a consequence of the violation.

Chapter 63. Rights to New Varieties of Flora and New Strains of Fauna

Article 1091. Protection of Rights to New Varieties of Flora and New Strains of Fauna

The rights to new varieties of flora and new strains of fauna (selection achievements) shall be protected on condition of the issuance of a patent.

The requirements under which the right arises to receive a patent and the procedure for the issuance of the patent for selection achievements shall be established by a law.

To relations connected with the right to selection achievements and protection of these rights respectively shall apply the rules of Article 1084-1090 of the present Code unless provided otherwise by the rules of the present Chapter and by a law.

Article 1092. Rights of Author of Selection Achievement to Remuneration

The author of a selection achievement who is not the patent possessor shall have during the period of operation of the patent the right to receive remuneration from the patent possessor for use of the selection achievement.

The amount and conditions of payment of remuneration to the author of a selection achievement shall be determined by the contract concluded between him and the patent possessor.

Article 1093. Rights of Patent Possessor

To the possessor of a patent to a selection achievement shall belong the exclusive right to the use of this achievement within the limits established by a law.

Article 1094. Duties of Patent Possessor

The possessor of a patent to a selection achievement shall be obliged to maintain the respective variety of flora or respective strain of fauna within the period of the operation of the patent so that the indicia specified in the description of the variety or strain drawn up when registering them is preserved.

Chapter 64. Defense of Undivulged Information Against Illegal Use

Article 1095. Right to Defense of Undivulged Information

The person who lawfully possesses technical, organizational, or commercial information, including secrets of production (know-how) unknown to third persons (undivulged information), shall have the right to defense of his information against illegal use if the conditions established by Article 98 of the present Code are complied with.

The right to defense of undivulged information against illegal use shall arise irrespective of the fulfillment with respect to such information of any formalities whatever (the registration thereof, receiving a certificate, and so forth).

The rules concerning the defense of undivulged information shall not apply with respect to information which in accordance with a law may not comprise an employment or commercial secret (information concerning juridical persons, rights to property and transactions with such which is subject to State registration, information subject to submission as a State statistical report, and others).

The right to defense of undivulged information shall operate so long as the conditions provided for by Article 98 of the present Code are preserved.

Article 1096. Responsibility for Illegal Use of Undivulged Information

A person who without legal grounds has received or disseminated undivulged information or used it shall be obliged to compensate he who lawfully possesses such information for the losses caused by the illegal use thereof.

If the person who illegally used undivulged information received it from a person who did not have the right to disseminate it, of which the acquirer of the information did not know and should not have known (good-faith acquirer), the lawful possessor of the undivulged information shall have the right to require of him compensation of losses caused by the use of the undivulged information after the good-faith acquirer knew or should have known that the use thereof is illegal.

A person who lawfully possesses undivulged information shall have the right to require from he who illegally uses it the immediate termination of the use thereof. However, a court, taking into account the means expended by a good-faith acquirer of undivulged information for the use thereof, may authorize the further use thereof on conditions of a compensated exclusive license.

A person who autonomously and lawfully has received information comprising the content of undivulged information shall have the right to use this information irrespective of the rights of the possessor of the respective undivulged information and shall not be liable to him for such use.

Article 1097. Transfer of Right to Defend Undivulged Information Against Illegal Use

The person who possesses undivulged information may transfer all or part of the information comprising the content of this information to another person under a license contract.

The licensee shall be obliged to take proper measures to protect the confidentiality of the information received under a contract and shall have the same rights for the defense thereof against illegal use by third persons as does the licensor. Insofar as not provided otherwise in the contract, the duty to preserve the confidentiality of information shall lie on the licensee also after termination of the license contract if the respective information continues to remain undivulged information.

Chapter 65. Means of Individualization of Participants of Civil Turnover, Goods, Work, and Services

§ 1. Firm Name

Article 1098. Right to Firm Name

A juridical person shall have the exclusive right to use a firm name on goods, the packaging thereof, in an advertisement, signboards, prospectuses, accounts, printed publications, official letterheads, and other documentation connected with its activity, and also when showing goods at exhibitions and fairs which are conducted on the territory of the Republic Uzbekistan.

The firm name of a juridical person shall be specified in its constitutive documents. The right to a firm name shall arise from the moment of State registration of a juridical person [as amended by Law of 18 September 2006, No. ЗРУ-52. СЗ РУ (2006), no. 37-38, item 371].

The firm name of a juridical person which is similar to one already registered such that this may lead to the identity of the respective juridical persons may not be registered.

Article 1099. Use of Firm Name of Juridical Person in Trademark

The firm name of a juridical person may be used in the trademark belonging to it.

Article 1100. Operation of Right to Firm Name

The exclusive right to the name registered in the Republic Uzbekistan as the designation of a juridical person shall operate on the territory of the Republic Uzbekistan.

The exclusive right to a name registered or generally-recognized in a foreign State shall operate on the territory of the Republic Uzbekistan in the instances provided for by a law.

The operation of the right to a firm name shall terminate with the liquidation of the juridical person or with a change of the firm name thereof.

Article 1101. Alienation of Right to Firm Name

The alienation and transfer of the right to a firm name of a juridical person shall be permitted only in instances of the reorganization of the juridical person and alienation of the enterprise as a whole.

The possessor of the right to a firm name may authorize another person to use his name (or issue a license). However, in so doing the measures excluding the deception of a consumer must be stipulated in the license contract.

§ 2. Trademark (or Service Mark)

Article 1102. Legal Protection of Trademark

The legal protection of a trademark (or service mark) shall be granted on the basis of the registration thereof.

The right to a trademark shall be certified by a certificate concerning the registration of the trademark (or service mark) [as amended by Law of 15 December 2000, No. 175-II. Ведомости Олий Мажлиса (2001), no. 1-2, item 23].

Article 1103. Right of Use and Inviolability of Trademark [as amended by Law of 15 December 2000, No. 175-II]

The possessor of the right to a trademark shall have the exclusive right to use and dispose of the mark belonging to him. The exclusive right to make changes in and additions to the trademark also shall belong to the possessor of the right to a trademark [as amended by Law of 15 December 2000, No. 175-II]

Any introduction of it into turnover in the procedure established by a law shall be considered to be use of the trademark.

In the event of the publication, public performance, or other use of a trademark, the making of any changes in the trademark itself or in the designation thereof shall be permitted only with the consent of the possessor of the right to the trademark [added by Law of 15 December 2000, No. 175-II].

The right to inviolability of a trademark shall belong to the possessor of the right to a trademark [added by Law of 15 December 2000, No. 175-II].

Article 1104. Consequences of Failure to Use Trademark

In the event of the failure to use a trademark on the territory of the Republic Uzbekistan without justifiable reasons continuously during the last three years, the registration thereof may be annulled on the basis of the decision of a court at the demand of any interested person [as amended by Laws of 18 April 2017, No. 3PY-429, and of 5 October 2020, No. 3PY-640].

The issuance of a license for the use of a trademark shall be considered to be the use thereof.

Article 1105. Transfer of Right to Trademark

The right to a trademark with respect to all the classes of goods, work, and services specified in the certificate or part thereof may be transferred by the right-possessor to another person under a contract.

The transfer of the right to a trademark shall not be permitted if it may be a cause of delusion with respect to the good or the manufacturer thereof.

The transfer of the right to a trademark, including the transfer thereof under a contract or by way of legal succession, must be registered in the empowered State agency [as amended by Laws of 26 December 2011, No. 3PY-312, and of 5 October 2020, No. 3PY-640].

Article 1106. Form of Contract on Transfer of Right to Trademark

A contract on the transfer of the right to a trademark or the granting of a license must be concluded in written form and registered at the empowered State agency [as amended by Laws of 26 December 2011, No. 3PY-312, and of 5 October 2020, No. 3PY-640].

The failure to comply with the written form and the requirement concerning registration shall entail the invalidity of the contract.

Article 1107. Responsibility for Violation of Right to Trademark

A person unlawfully using a trademark shall be obliged to terminate the violation and compensate the possessor of the trade mark for the losses incurred by him.

A person unlawfully using a trademark shall be obliged to destroy manufactured depictions of the trade mark and remove from the good or packaging thereof the trademark being used illegally or designation similar to it to the extent of confusion.

In the event it is impossible to fulfill the requirements established by paragraph two of the present Article, the respective good shall be subject to destruction.

Article 1107[1]. Exhaustion of Exclusive Right to Trade Mark [added by Law of 18 April 2017, No. ЗРУ-429. СЗ РУ (2017), no. 16, item 265]

The use of this trademark by other persons with respect to goods which were lawfully introduced into civil turnover directly by the possessor of the trademark or with his consent shall not be a violation of the exclusive right to a trademark.

§ 3. Name of Place of Origin of Good

Article 1108. Legal Protection of Name of Place of Origin of Good

The legal protection of the name of a place of origin of a good shall be granted on the basis of the registration thereof.

The name of a place of origin (or indication of origin) of a good shall be deemed to be the name of the country, population centre, locality, or other geographic object used for designation of the good, the special properties of which are determined exclusively or primarily by the natural conditions or other factors or combining of natural conditions and these factors characteristic for this geographic object.

The historical name of a geographic object may be the name of the place of origin of a good.

A designation, although it represents or contains the name of the geographic object but has entered into the Republic Uzbekistan into general use as the designation of a good of a determined type not connected with the place of its manufacture, shall not be deemed to be the name of a place of origin of a good and shall not be subject to registration for the purposes of the legal protection thereof in accordance with the rules of the present paragraph. This, however, does not deprive the person whose rights have been violated by the use not in good faith of such name of the possibility of the defense thereof by other means provided for by a law.

The registration of a name of origin of a good shall be effectuated by the empowered State agency [as amended by Laws of 26 December 2011, No. 3PY-312, and of 5 October 2020, No. 3PY-640].

A certificate on the right of use of a name of origin of a good shall be issued on the basis of registration.

The procedure and conditions of registration, the issuance of certificates, and the deeming them to be invalid and the termination of an action of registration and certificates shall be determined by a law.

Article 1109. Right of Use of Name of Place of Origin of Good

A person possessing the right of use of the name of place of origin shall have the right to place this name on a good, packaging, advertisement, prospectuses, accounts, and to use it otherwise in connection with the introduction of the particular good into civil turnover.

The name of a place of origin of a good may be registered by several persons either jointly or independently of one another in order to designate a good meeting the requirements specified in Article 1108, paragraphs one, two, and three of the present Code. The right of use of the name of a place of origin of a good shall belong to each of such persons.

The alienation and other transactions concerning the assignment of a right of use of the name of a place of origin of a good and the granting of use by it on the basis of a license shall not be permitted.

Article 1110. Sphere of Operation of Legal Protection of Name of Place of Origin of Good

The legal protection of the names of places of origin of goods situated on the territory of the Republic Uzbekistan shall be granted in the Republic Uzbekistan.

The legal protection of a name of place of origin of a good situated in another State shall be granted in the Republic Uzbekistan if this name has been registered in the country of origin of the good, and also in the empowered State agency in accordance with the present Code [as amended by Law of 26 December 2011, No. 3PY-312, and of 5 October 2020, No. 3PY-640].

Article 1111. Responsibility for Unlawful Use of Name of Place of Origin of Good

A person having the right of use of a name of place of origin of a good, and also organizations for the defense of the rights of consumers, may require of anyone who illegally uses this name the termination of the use thereof, removal of the good, the packaging thereof, letterheads, and similar documentation illegally using the name of designation similar thereto to the degree of confusion, destruction of manufactured depictions of the name or designation similar thereto to the degree of confusion, and if this is impossible, seizure and destruction of the good and/or packaging.

The person possessing the right of use of the name of place of origin of a good shall have the right to require compensation of losses incurred from the violator of this right.

Section V. Inheritance Law

Chapter 66. General Provisions on Inheriting

Article 1112. Grounds of Inheriting

Inheriting shall be effectuated by will and by operation of law.

Inheriting by operation of law shall occur when a will is lacking or does not determine the fate of all of the inheritance, and also in other instances established by the present Code.

Article 1113. Composition of Inheritance

All rights and duties belonging to the decedent at the moment of opening of the inheritance whose existence does not terminate with his death shall be part of the inheritance.

Rights and duties inextricably connected with the person of the decedent shall not be part of the inheritance:

the rights of membership or participation in commercial and other organizations which are juridical persons unless established otherwise by a law or by the contract;

the right to compensation of harm caused to life or health;

the rights and duties which arose in alimony obligations;

the rights to a pension, benefit, and other payments on the basis of legislation on labor and social security;

personal nonproperty rights not connected with property [rights].

Personal nonproperty rights and other nonmaterial benefits which belong to the decedent may be effectuated and defended by the heirs.

Article 1114. Inheriting of Property Which is Common Joint Ownership

The death of a participant of common joint ownership shall be grounds for determining his participatory share in the right to common property and the separation of common property or the partition therefrom of the participatory share of the deceased participant in the procedure established by Article 226 of the present Code. In this event the inheritance shall be opened with respect to common property coming to the participatory share of the deceased participant, and when separation of the property in kind is impossible, with respect to the value of such participatory share.

The participant of common joint ownership shall have the right to bequeath his participatory share in the right to common property which will be determined after this death in accordance with paragraph one of the present Article.

Article 1115. Inheriting of Right to Land Plot [as amended by Law of 6 June 2022, No. 3PY-775]

The inheriting of a right to a land plot shall be regulated by the rules of the present Code unless established otherwise by a law [as amended by Law of 6 June 2022, No. 3PY-775].

Article 1116. Opening of Inheritance

An inheritance shall be opened as a consequence of the death of a citizen or the declaration of him to be deceased by a court.

The day (or when necessary, the moment) of death of the decedent shall be deemed to be the time of opening of the inheritance, and when he is declared to be deceased, the day of entry into force of the judicial decision concerning the declaration of a citizen to be deceased unless another day has been specified in the decision of the court.

If within one calendar day (twenty-four hours) persons died who had the right to inherit one after the other, they shall be deemed to be deceased simultaneously, the inheritance shall be opened after each of them, and the heirs of each of them shall be called to inherit.

Article 1117. Place of Opening of Inheritance

The place of opening an inheritance shall be the last permanent place of residence of the decedent. If the last place of residence of the decedent is unknown, the place of opening the inheritance shall be deemed to be the location of immoveable property belonging to the decedent or the principal part thereof, and in the absence of immoveable property, the location of the principal part of the moveable property.

Article 1118. Heirs

Citizens who are alive at the moment of the opening of an inheritance, and also children conceived during the life of the decedent and born alive after the opening of the inheritance, may be heirs by will and by operation of law.

Juridical persons which were created at the moment of the opening of the inheritance, the State, and agencies of local self-government of citizens also may be heirs by operation of law.

Article 1119. Elimination of Unworthy Heirs from Inheritance

Persons who intentionally deprived the decedent of life or any of the possible heirs or who committed an attempt on their life shall not have the right to inherit either by will or by operation of law. Persons with respect to whom the testator drew up a will after the commission of the attempt on his life shall constitute an exception.

Persons who intentionally obstructed the effectuation by the decedent of his last will and by doing so facilitated the calling of these persons themselves or persons near to them to inherit or increased the participatory share of the inheritance due to them shall not have the right to inherit either by will or by operation of law.

Parents after children with respect to whom they were deprived of parental rights and were not restored in these rights at the moment of opening of the inheritance, and also parents (or adoptive parents) and children who have reached majority (or adopted children) who have evaded the fulfillment of duties placed on them by virtue of a law with regard to the maintenance of the decedent shall not have the right to inherit by operation of law.

Circumstances serving as the grounds for eliminating unworthy heirs from inheriting shall be established by a court upon the suit of the person for whom such elimination gives rise to property consequences connected with the inheriting.

The rules of the present Article also shall apply to a testamentary refusal.

The rules of the present Article shall extend to any heirs, including those having the right to an obligatory participatory share.

Chapter 67. Inheriting by Will

Article 1120. General Provisions

The expression of will of a citizen with regard to the disposition of the property belonging to him or the right thereto in the event of death shall be deemed to be a will.

A will must be drawn up personally. The conclusion of a will through a representative shall not be permitted.

A citizen may bequeath all of his property or part thereof to one or several persons both within and not within the group of heirs by operation of law, and also to juridical persons, the State, or agencies of self-government of citizens.

The testator shall have the right without explanation to deprive owner, several, or all heirs by operation of law of the inheritance. The deprivation of an heir by operation of law of the inheritance shall not extend to his descendants who inherit by right of representation if it does not arise otherwise from the will.

The decedent shall have the right to conclude a will containing a disposition concerning any property.

The decedent shall have the right to conclude a will containing a disposition concerning the property which at the moment of concluding the will does not belong to him. If at the moment of opening the inheritance such property will belong to him, the respective disposition shall be valid.

The decedent shall be free to revoke or to change a will concluded at any moment after the conclusion thereof and shall not be obliged in so doing to specify the reasons for the revocation or change.

The decedent shall not have the right to place on persons designated as heirs by him in the will the duty in turn to dispose of determined property bequeathed to them in the event of their death.

Article 1121. Will with Condition

The testator shall have the right to condition the receipt of an inheritance by a determined lawful condition relative to the character of behavior of the heir.

Unlawful conditions included in the disposition concerning the designation of an heir or deprivation of the right of inheriting shall be invalid.

A condition included in a will which is not fulfilled by the heir by reason of his state of health or by virtue of other objective reasons may be deemed invalid upon the suit of the heir.

Article 1122. Subdesignation of Heirs

The testator may, if an heir specified in the will dies before the opening of the inheritance, does not accept it, or refused it or is eliminated from inheriting as an unworthy heir by way of Article 1119 of the present Code, and also in the event of the failure to fulfill by an heir under a will of law conditions of the decedent, designate another heir (subdesignation of heir).

Article 1123. Inheriting Part of Property Remaining Unbequeathed

The part of property remaining unbequeathed shall be distributed among the heirs by operation of law who are called to inherit by way of Articles 1134-1143 of the present Code.

Among these heirs shall be those heirs by operation of law to whom another part of the property was left by will.

Article 1124. General Rules on Form of Will

A will must be concluded in written form, specifying the place and time of drawing it up.

There shall be deemed to be wills concluded in written form:

notarially certified wills;

wills equated to notarially certified.

A will in written form must be signed in the own hand of the testator.

If the testator by virtue of physical defects, illness, or illiteracy can not sign the will in his own hand, at his request it may be signed in the presence of a notary or other person certifying a will in accordance with a law, or another person, specifying the reasons by virtue of which the testator could not sign the will in his own hand.

There may not sign a will in place of the testator:

notary or other person certifying the will;

person to whose benefit the will was drawn up or testamentary refusal was made, the spouse of such person, his children, parents, grandchildren and great-grandchildren, and also heirs of the testator by operation of law;

citizens not possessing dispositive legal capacity in full;

illiterate and other persons not capable of reading the will;

persons previously convicted for false evidence.

Article 1125. Notarially Certified Will

A notarially certified will must be written by the testator or copied from his words by the notary. When the notary copies the will from the words of the testator, generally-accepted technical means (typewriter, personal computer, and so forth) may be used.

A will copied by a notary from the words of the testator must be fully read by the testator in the presence of the notary before signature of the will.

If the testator by virtue of physical defects, illness, or illiteracy is not in a state personally to read the will, the text thereof shall be read aloud for him by the notary, of which a respective entry shall be made on the will specifying the reasons for which the testator could not personally read the will.

At the wish of the testator, the will shall be certified by a notary without familiarization with the contents thereof (secret will).

A secret will at risk of the invalidity thereof must be written and signed by the testator in his own hand. The will in the presence of two witnesses and a notary must be sealed in an envelope on which the witnesses place their signatures, specifying their surname, forename, and patronymic and permanent place of residence. The envelope signed by witnesses shall have a seal placed on it in the presence of the witnesses and the notary into another envelope on which the notary makes an inscription of certification.

Article 1126. Will Equated to Notarially Certified

There shall be equated to notarially certified wills:

wills of citizens situated for treatment in hospitals, military hospitals, other inpatient treatment institutions or residing in homes for the aged and persons with a disability which are certified by the chief doctors, deputies thereof for the medical part or duty doctors of these hospitals, military hospitals, and other treatment institutions, and also the heads of military hospitals and the directors or head doctors of homes for the aged and persons with a disability [as amended by Law of 17 May 2022, No. 3PY-770];

wills of citizens situated during a voyage on vessels proceeding under the flag of the Republic Uzbekistan which are certified by the masters of these vessels;

wills of citizens situated on exploration or other similar expeditions which are certified by the heads of these expeditions;

wills of military servicemen, and at stationing points of military units where there are no notaries, also the wills of civilian persons working in such units, members of their families, and members of the families of military servicemen which are certified by the commanders of the military units;

wills of persons situated in places of deprivation of freedom or confined under guard which are certified by the heads of the respective institutions;

wills of persons residing in population centers where there is no notary which are certified by officials having the right to perform notarial actions in accordance with a law.

The rules of Article 1125 of the present Code shall apply to wills provided for in paragraph one of the present Article, except for the requirements concerning the notarial certification of the will.

Article 1127. Revocation and Change of Will

The testator shall have the right at any time to revoke a will made by him as a whole or to change by means of revocation, change, or addition individual testamentary dispositions contained therein, having made a new will.

The will may be revoked by means of the destruction of all the examples thereof by the testator or notary or by other officials upon the written disposition of the testator.

A will drawn up earlier shall be revoked by a subsequent will in full or in that part in which it is contradictory.

A will previously made which is revoked fully or partially by a subsequent will shall not be restored if the last was in turn revoked or changed by the testator.

Article 1128. Secrecy of Will

A notary, other official certifying a will, and also a citizen who signed a will in place of the testator shall not have the right before the opening of the inheritance to divulge information affecting the content of the will, nor the drawing up, revocation or change thereof.

Article 1129. Interpretation of Will

In the event of the interpretation of a will by a notary, executor of the will, or a court, the literal significance of the words and expressions contained therein shall be taken into account. In the event of the ambiguity of the literal meaning of any provision of the will it shall be established by means of a comparison of this provision with other provisions and the meaning of the will as a whole.

Article 1130. Invalidity of Will

A will concluded in the improper form shall be invalid. The invalidity of a will shall also be based on the rules of the present Code concerning the invalidity of transactions.

A will may be deemed to be invalid as a consequence of a violation of the procedure for drawing up, signature, and certification of the will established by the present Code upon the suit of the person for whom the deeming of the will to be invalid has property consequences.

The invalidity of individual dispositions contained in the will shall not affect the validity of the remaining part of the will.

In the event of deeming the will to be invalid, the heir who under this will is deprived of the inheritance shall receive the right to inherit on general grounds.

Article 1131. Performance of Will

The testator may commission the performance of the will to a person specified by him in the will who is not an heir (executor of will). The consent of this person to be executor of the will must be expressed by him either in an inscription in his own hand on the will itself or in a statement appended to the will.

By agreement between them the heir shall have the right to commission the execution of the will to one of the heirs or to another person. In the event such agreement is not achieved, the executor of the will may be designated by a court upon the demand of one or several heirs.

The executor of the will shall have the right at any time to refuse performance of the duties placed on him by the testator, having notified beforehand the heirs under the will. Relieving the executor of the will from his duties also is possible by decision of the court according to the application of the heirs.

The executor of a will must:

effectuate the protection of the inheritance and management thereof;

take all possible measures so as to notify all heirs and recipients of a legacy about the opening of the inheritance and legacies to their benefit;

receive the amounts due to the decedent;

issue to the heirs the property due to them in accordance with the will of the decedent and with a law;

ensure the performance by the heirs of the legacies placed on them;

perform testamentary placements or require from the heirs under the will the performance of a testamentary placement.

The executor of a will shall have the right to act in his own name in judicial and other cases connected with the management of the inheritance and performance of the will, and also may be involved in such cases.

The executor of a will shall effectuate his functions within the period reasonably necessary to relieve the inheritance of debts, recover amounts due to the decedent, and for the entry of all the heirs into possession of the inheritance. In any event the said period may not be more than one year from the day of opening of the inheritance.

The executor of a will shall have the right to compensation of necessary expenses relating to management of the inheritance and performance of the will at the expense of the inheritance. The payment of remuneration to the executor at the expense of the inheritance may be provided for in the will.

Upon the performance of a will, the executor of a will shall be obliged to grant a report to the heirs at their request.

Article 1132. Testamentary Legacy

The testator shall have the right to place on the heir by will the performance at the expense of the inheritance of any obligation whatever (testamentary legacy) to the benefit of another or several persons (recipient of legacy) who shall acquire the right to demand performance of the testamentary legacy.

The recipient of the legacy may be persons either within or not within the group of heirs by operation of law.

The subject of a testamentary legacy may be the transfer to the recipient of the legacy in ownership or in another right to a thing within the inheritance, the acquisition and transfer to him of property not within the inheritance, the fulfillment for him of determined work, rendering to him of a determined service, and the like.

An heir on whom the performance of a testamentary legacy has been placed by the testator must perform it only within the limits of the true cost of the inheritance which has passed to him, deducting the debts of the decedent falling on his part.

If the heir on whom the testamentary legacy is placed has the right to an obligatory participatory share in the inheritance, his duty to perform the legacy shall be limited by the limits of the value of the inheritance which has passed to him which exceeds the amount of his obligatory participatory share.

In instances when the testamentary legacy is placed on all or several heirs, the legacy shall encumber each of them commensurately with his participatory share in the inheritance unless provided otherwise by the will.

On the heir to whom the dwelling house, apartment, or other dwelling premise passed the testator shall have the right to place the obligation to grant to another person the use for life of this premise or a determined part thereof. In the event of the subsequent transfer of the right of ownership to the dwelling premise the right of use for life shall retain force.

The right of use for life of a dwelling premise shall be inalienable, nontransferable, and shall not pass to the heirs of the recipient of the legacy.

The right of use of a dwelling premise for life granted to the recipient of the legacy shall not be grounds for residence of members of the family thereof unless specified otherwise in the will.

In the event of the death of the heir on whom the testamentary legacy was placed or in the event of his failure to accept the inheritance, the performance of the testamentary legacy shall pass to the other heirs who received his participatory share, or to the State or agency of self-government of citizens if the property has become escheat.

A testamentary legacy shall not be performed in the event of the death of the recipient of the legacy before the opening of the inheritance or after the opening of the inheritance but before the moment when the heir under the will succeeded in accepting it.

The recipient of a legacy shall not be liable for debts of the decedent.

Article 1133. Placement of Duties

The testator may place the duty on an heir by will to perform any action or to refrain from such, not granting to anyone the right to demand as a creditor the performance of this duty. In order to effectuate a generally-useful purpose, such duty may be placed on the executor of the will, the decedent allotting part of the property for the performance of the placement.

To a placement the subject of which is actions having a property character the rules contained in Article 1132 of the present Code shall apply.

The duty to perform the placement shall terminate if in accordance with the present Code the participatory share of the inheritance due or belonging to the heir on whom the duty has been laid to perform the placement shall pass to other heirs.

Chapter 68. Inheriting by Operation of Law

Article 1134. General Provisions

Heirs by operation of law shall be called to inherit by way of the priority provided for by Articles 1135-1141 of the present Code.

In the event of inheritance by operation of law an adopted person and his descendants, on one side, and the adoptive person and his relatives on the other, shall be equated to blood relatives.

Adopted persons and their descendants shall not inherit by operation of law after the death of the parents of the adopted person and others of his blood relatives in the ascending line.

The parents of an adopted person and others of his blood relatives in the ascending line shall not inherit by operation of law after the death of the adopted person and his descendants.

Each subsequent priority of heirs by operation of law shall receive the right to inherit in the event of the absence of heirs of the preceding priority, the elimination thereof from the inheritance, or their failure to accept the inheritance or the refusal thereof.

Article 1135. First Priority of Heirs by Operation of Law

In the first priority the children of the decedent (including adopted), spouse and parents (or adoptive) of the decedent shall receive the right to inherit by operation of law. To the heirs of the first priority shall be relegated also the children of the decedent who were born after his death.

Article 1136. Second Priority of Heirs by Operation of Law

In the second priority the own full and half brothers and sisters of the decedent, and also his grandfather and grandmother on the side of the father and on the side of the mother shall receive the right to inherit by operation of law in equal participatory shares.

Article 1137. Third Priority of Heirs by Operation of Law

In the third priority own uncles and aunts of the decedent shall receive the right to inherit in equal participatory shares.

Article 1138. Fourth Priority of Heirs by Operation of Law

In the fourth priority other relatives of the decedent up to the sixth degree of kinship inclusive, the relatives closer in degree of kinship having a preferential right to the inheritance in relation to relatives of a remoter degree of kinship, shall receive the right to inherit by operation of law.

Heirs of the fourth priority called to inherit shall inherit in equal participatory shares.

Article 1139. Fifth Priority of Heirs by Operation of Law

In the fifth priority dependents of the decedent who lack labor capacity shall receive the right to inherit by operation of law if they do not inherit on the basis of Article 1141 of the present Code.

Article 1140. Inheriting by Right of Representation

Inheriting by right of representation shall presuppose the passing of the participatory share of an heir by operation of law to the descendants thereof in the event of his death before the opening of the inheritance, the participatory share being divided equally among the descendants who are in an identical degree of kinship with the heir by operation of law being represented.

In the event of inheriting by the direct line of descendance the right of representation shall operate without limitation of the degree of kinship, and in the event of inheriting by a collateral line, the right of representation shall be received respectively by the nephews (or nieces) of the decedent representing his own brothers (or sisters), or the first cousins of the decedent representing his own uncle or aunt.

Article 1140[1]. Transfer of Right to Acceptance of Inheritance (Inheritance Transmission) [added by Law of 14 September 2010, No. ЗРУ-255. СЗ РУ (2010), no. 37, item 313]

If an heir called to inherit by will or by operation of law died after the opening of the inheritance without having succeeded in accepting it, the right to accept the inheritance due to him shall pass to his heirs by operation of law, and if all the inheritance property was bequeathed – to his heirs by will (inheritance transmission). The right to accept an inheritance by operation of inheritance transmission shall not enter into the composition of the inheritance which opened after the death of such heir.

The right to accept an inheritance which belong to a deceased heir may be effectuated by his heirs on the general grounds.

The right of an heir to accept part of the inheritance as an obligatory participatory share provided by Article 1142 of the present Code shall not pass to his heirs.

Article 1141. Dependents Lacking Labor Capacity of Decedent

To the heirs by operation of law shall be relegated persons lacking labor capacity who for not less than one year before the death of the decedent were dependent on him and resided jointly with him. When there exist other heirs by operation of law, they shall inherit together with the heirs of that priority which is called to inherit.

Persons lacking labor capacity relegated to the heirs by operation of law specified in Articles 1136-1138 of the present Code but not within the group of heirs of that priority which is called to inherit shall inherit together with the heirs of that priority if not less than a year before the death of the decedent they were dependent on him irrespective whether they resided together with the dependent.

Persons called to inherit on the basis of the present Article shall when there are other heirs by operation of law inherit together not more than a one-fourth part of the inheritance.

Article 1142. Right to Obligatory Participatory Share in Inheritance

Minors or children lacking labor capacity of the decedent, including adopted, and also his spouse and parents lacking labor capacity, including adoptive, shall inherit, irrespective of the content of the will, not less than half of the participatory share which would be due to each of them in the event of inheriting by operation of law (obligatory participatory share).

To the obligatory participatory share shall be credited all that the heir having the right to such participatory share receives from the inheritance under any grounds, including the value of the property consisting of ordinary domestic household articles and the value of the testamentary refusal established to the benefit of such heir.

Any limitations and encumberments established in the will for an heir having the right to an obligatory participatory share in an inheritance shall be valid only with respect to that part of the inheritance passing to him which exceeds the obligatory participatory share.

Article 1143. Rights of Spouse in Event of Inheriting

The right of inheriting belonging to a spouse by virtue of a will or law shall not affect the other property rights thereof connected with being married with the decedent, including the right of ownership to part of the property jointly acquired in the marriage.

[paragraph two repealed by Law of 27 August 2004, No. 672-II. C3 PY (2004), no. 37, item 408].

Article 1144. Protection of Inheritance in Management Thereof in Event of Inheriting by Operation of Law

In an event if part of the property is inherited by will the executor of the will designated by the decedent shall effectuate the protection of the entire inheritance and manage it, including that part of the inheritance which passes by way of inheriting by operation of law.

The executor of a will designated in accordance with Article 1131 of the present Code by heirs under the will or by a court shall effectuate the functions relating to the protection of the entire property as a whole and the management thereof unless the heirs by operation of law require the designation of a manager of the inheritance in order to perform the said functions with respect to that part of the inheritance passing by way of inheriting by operation of law.

The manager of an inheritance shall be designated by the notary at the place of opening the inheritance at the request of one or several heirs by operation of law. An heir by operation of law who does not agree with the designation of the manager of the inheritance or the choice thereof shall have the right to contest the appointment of the manager of the inheritance in a court.

If heirs by operation of law are absent or unknown, the agency of State power in the localities or agency of self-government of citizens must apply to the notary with a request concerning the designation of the manager of the inheritance. In the event of the appearance of the heirs by operation of law, the manager of the inheritance may be recalled at their demand with compensation to him of necessary expenses and payment of reasonable remuneration at the expense of the inheritance.

The manager of an inheritance shall effectuate the powers provided for by Article 1131 of the present Code with respect to the executor of the will insofar as does not arise otherwise from the peculiarities of the inheriting by operation of law.

The manager of an inheritance shall have the right to compensation at the expense of inheritance of necessary expenses relating to the protection of the inheritance and management thereof, and unless provided otherwise by an agreement with the heirs, also to remuneration.

Chapter 69. Acquisition of Inheritance

Article 1145. General Provisions

An heir shall acquire the right to the inheritance due to him or part thereof (participatory share) from the time of opening of the inheritance unless he subsequently refuses the inheritance, is not deprived of the right to inherit, and does not lose the right to inherit as a consequence of the testamentary disposition being deemed invalid concerning the designation of him as an heir.

Article 1146. Issuance of Certificate Concerning Right to Inheritance

The notary and the place of opening an inheritance shall be obliged at the request of the heir to issue him a certificate concerning the right to inheritance.

The certificate concerning the right to inheritance shall be issued upon the expiry of six months from the day of opening the inheritance.

In the event of inheriting by operation of law and also by will, the certificate may be issued before the expiry of the said period if the notary has data concerning the fact that in addition to the persons who have applied for the issuance of the certificate there are no other heirs with respect to the respective property or the entire inheritance.

Article 1147. Right to Refuse Inheritance

An heir shall have the right to refuse an inheritance at any time from the day of opening the inheritance [as amended by Law of 14 September 2010, No. ЗРУ-255. СЗ РУ (2010), no. 37, item 313].

The refusal of an inheritance shall be performed by the filing of a statement by the heir at the notary at the place of opening the inheritance.

The refusal of an inheritance through a representative shall be possible if the power for such refusal has been specially provided for in a power of attorney.

The refusal of an inheritance may not subsequently be revoked or taken back.

[paragraph five repealed by Law of 14 September 2010, No. ЗРУ-255. СЗ РУ (2010), no. 37, item 313].

Article 1148. Limitations of Right to Refuse Inheritance

If an heir is called to inherit either by will or by operation of law, he shall have the right to refuse the inheritance due to him on one of these grounds or on both grounds.

An heir shall have the right to refuse an inheritance due to him by right of augmentation irrespective of inheriting the remaining portion of the inheritance.

In the event of the refusal of an inheritance the heir shall have the right to specify that he refuses it in favor of other persons from among the heirs by will or by operation of law.

Except for the instances provided for in the present Article, the refusal of part of an inheritance, the refusal of an inheritance with reservations, or under condition shall not be permitted.

Article 1149. Right to Refuse Receipt of Testamentary Legacy

The recipient of a legacy shall have the right to refuse a testamentary legacy. A partial refusal, refusal with reservations, under a condition, or to the benefit of another person shall not be permitted.

The right provided for by the present Article shall not depend on the right of the recipient of a legacy who is simultaneously an heir to refuse the inheritance.

If the recipient of a legacy takes advantage of the right provided for by the present Article, the heir encumbered by a testamentary legacy shall be relieved of the duty to perform it.

Article 1150. Separation of Inheritance

Any of the heirs by operation of law who have accepted the inheritance shall have the right to require separation of the inheritance.

The inheritance shall be separated by agreement of the heirs in accordance with the participatory shares due to them, and when agreement is not achieved, in a judicial proceeding.

The rules of the present Article shall apply to the separation of an inheritance among the heirs by will in instances when the entire inheritance or part thereof has been bequeathed to the heirs in participatory shares without specifying specific property.

Article 1151. Rights of Absent Heirs

If among the heirs there are persons whose whereabouts is unknown, the remaining heirs, the executor of the will (or manager of the inheritance) and the notary shall be obliged to take necessary measures to establish their whereabouts and call them to inherit.

If an absent heir called to inherit whose whereabouts has been established has not refused the inheritance, the remaining heirs shall be obliged to notify him about their intention to separate the inheritance. If within three months from the moment of such notice the absent heir does not inform the other heirs about his wish to participate in the agreement concerning the separation of the inheritance, the remaining heirs shall have the right to make the separation by agreement among themselves, having partitioned a participatory share due to the absent heir [as amended by Law of 14 September 2010, No. ЗРУ-255. СЗ РУ (2010), no. 37, item 313].

If within one year from the day of opening the inheritance the whereabouts of the absent heir has not been established and there is no information concerning his refusal of the inheritance, the remaining heirs shall have the right to make the separation according to the rules of paragraph two of the present Article.

When there exists a conceived but unborn heir, the separation of the property may be made only after the birth of such heir.

If a conceived but unborn heir is born alive, the remaining heirs shall have the right to make the separation of the inheritance only with the partition of an inheritance participatory share due to him. In order to protect the interests of the newly-born, a representative of a trusteeship and guardianship agency must be invited to participate in the separation.

Article 1152. Inheriting of Enterprise

Unless established otherwise by agreement of all the heirs who have accepted the inheritance, an enterprise which is part of an inheritance shall not be subject to separation in kind and shall enter into the common participatory share ownership of the heirs in accordance with the participatory shares due to them.

Article 1153. Preferential Right of Individual Heirs to Property Within Inheritance

In the event of the separation of an inheritance the heirs within three years from the opening of an inheritance who were living jointly with the decedent shall have a preferential right to receive from the composition of the inheritance the dwelling house, apartment, or other dwelling premise, and also household utensils and household articles.

In the event of the separation of an inheritance, the heirs who possessed together with the decedent the right of common ownership to property shall have the preferential right to receive in kind from the composition of the inheritance the property in common ownership.

When effectuating preferential rights specified in paragraphs one and two of the present Article the property interests of the other heirs participating in the separation must be complied with. If as a result of the effectuation of these rights the property forming the inheritance is insufficient to grant to the other heirs the participatory shares due to them, the heir who effectuates the preferential right must grant them respective monetary or property contributory compensation.

Article 1154. Augmentation of Inheritance Participatory Shares

In instances of the refusal of the heir of an inheritance or his falling away under circumstances specified in Article 1119 of the present Code, the part of the inheritance which would have been due to such heir shall go to the heirs by operation of law called to inherit and shall be distributed among them in proportion to their inheritance participatory shares.

If the decedent bequeathed all of the property to heirs designated by him, the part of the inheritance due to the heir who has refused the inheritance or who has fallen away shall go to the remaining heirs by will and shall be distributed among them in proportion to their testamentary participatory shares insofar as not provided otherwise by the will.

The rules contained in paragraph one of the present Article shall not apply:

if an heir has been subdesignated for the heir who has refused or fallen away;

in the event of the refusal of the heir of the inheritance in favor of a determined person;

in instances when under inheriting by operation of law the refusal or falling away of an heir entails the calling of heirs of the next priority of heirs to inherit.

Article 1155. Expenses Subject to Payment at Expense of Inheritance

Demands concerning compensation of necessary expenses caused by the pre-death illness of the decedent, expenses for burial of the decedent, expenses connected with the acquisition of the inheritance, the protection and management thereof, and the performance of the will, and also payment of remuneration to the executor of the will or manager of the inheritance, shall be subject to satisfaction at the expense of the inheritance before distribution thereof among the heirs. These demands shall be subject to satisfaction from the value of the inheritance preferentially before all other demands, including those secured by mortgage or other pledge.

Article 1156. Recovery of Debts of Testator by Creditors

The creditors of the testator shall have the right to present their demands arising from obligations of the decedent to the executor of the will (or manager of the inheritance) or to the heirs. In this event the heirs shall be liable as joint and several debtors within the limits of the value of the property which has passed to each heir.

Article 1157. Escheat

If there are no heirs either by operation of law or by will or none of the heirs has the right to inherit or they all refuse the inheritance, the inheritance property shall be deemed to be escheated.

Inheritance property shall be deemed to be escheated on the basis of the decision of a court upon the application of an agency of State power in the localities or agency of self-government of citizens at the place of opening the inheritance upon the expiry of three years from the day of opening the inheritance. The inheritance property may be deemed to be escheated before the expiry of the said period if the expenses connected with protection of the inheritance and management thereof have exceeded the value thereof [as amended by Law of 14 September 2010, No. 3PУ-255. C3 PУ (2010), no. 37, item 313].

Escheated property shall pass to the ownership of the agency of self-government of citizens at the location of the respective property, and in the event of the refusal of the property, to the ownership of the State.

The protection of escheated property and the management thereof shall be effectuated in accordance with Article 1144 of the present Code.

Section VI. Application of Norms of Private International Law to Civil Law Relations

Chapter 70. General Provisions

Article 1158. Determination of Law Subject to Application to Civil Law Relations Complicated by Foreign Element

The law subject to application to civil law relations with the participation of foreign citizens or foreign juridical persons or complicated by another foreign element shall be determined on the basis of the present Code, other laws, international treaties, and recognized international customs, and also on the basis of agreement of the parties.

Agreement of the parties concerning choice of law must be clearly expressed or directly arise from the conditions of the contract and circumstances of the case considered in their aggregate.

If in accordance with paragraph one of the present Article it is impossible to determine the law subject to application, the law most closely connected with the civil law relations complicated by a foreign element shall be applied.

The application of a norm of foreign law may not be limited only on the basis that the particular norm has a public-law character.

Article 1159. Legal Qualification

Legal qualification of legal concepts by a court or other State agency shall be based on the interpretation thereof in accordance with the law of the Republic Uzbekistan as the country of the place of consideration of the dispute unless provided otherwise by a law.

If legal concepts are not known to the law of the Republic Uzbekistan as the country of the place of consideration or the dispute or are known under another name or with other content and can not be determined by means of interpretation according to the law of the Republic Uzbekistan, then the law of a foreign State also may be applied in the event of the legal qualification thereof.

Article 1160. Establishment of Content of Norms of Foreign Law

When applying foreign law, a court or other State agency shall establish the content of the norms thereof in accordance with their official interpretation, practice of application, and doctrine in the respective foreign State.

For the purpose of establishing the content of the norms of foreign law a court or other State agency may apply in the established procedure for assistance and explanation to the Ministry of Justice and other competent national agencies and institutions, including those situated abroad, or enlist experts.

Persons participating in a case shall have the right to present documents confirming the content of norms of foreign law to which they refer in substantiation of their demands or objections and otherwise assist the court or other State agency in establishing the content of these norms.

If the content of norms of foreign law, notwithstanding the measures undertaken in accordance with the present Article, is not established within reasonable periods, the law of the Republic Uzbekistan shall be applied.

Article 1161. Reverse Renvoi and Renvoi to Law of Third Country

Any renvoi to foreign law in accordance with the rules of the present Section, except for instances provided for by the present Article, must be considered as a renvoi to material and not to the conflicts law of the respective country.

Reverse renvoi to the law of the Republic Uzbekistan and renvoi to the law of a third country shall apply in instances of the application of foreign law according to Article 1168, Article 1169, paragraphs one, three, and five, and Articles 1171 and 1174 of the present Code.

Article 1162. Consequences of Circumvention of Law

Agreements and other actions of participants of relations regulated by the present Code directed towards circumvention of the rules of the present Section concerning the law subject to application to subordinate the respective relations to another law shall be invalid. In this event the law of the respective State subject to application in accordance with the present Section shall be applied.

Article 1163. Reciprocity

A court or other State agency shall apply foreign law irrespective of whether the law of the Republic Uzbekistan is applied in the respective foreign State to analogous relations, except for instances when the application of foreign law on the principle of reciprocity is provided for by a law of the Republic Uzbekistan.

If the application of foreign law depends upon reciprocity, it shall be supposed that it exists insofar as not proved otherwise.

Article 1164. Reservation Concerning Public Policy

Foreign law shall not be applied in instances when the application thereof would be contrary to the fundamental principles of the legal order (public policy) of the Republic Uzbekistan. In these instances the law of the Republic Uzbekistan shall apply.

A refusal to apply foreign law may not be based merely on distinctions of a legal, political, or economic system of the respective foreign State from the legal, political, or economic system of the Republic Uzbekistan.

Article 1165. Application of Imperative Norms

The rules of the present Section shall not affect the operation of imperative norms of law of the Republic Uzbekistan regulating the respective relations irrespective of the law subject to application.

When applying the law of any country according to the rules of the present Section the court may apply imperative norms of the law of the other country having a close connection with the relations if according to the law of this country such norms must regulate the respective relations irrespective of the law subject to application. In so doing the court must take into account the designation and character of such norms, and also the consequences of the application thereof.

Article 1166. Application of Law of Country with Multiplicity of Legal Systems

In instances when the law of the country in which several territorial or other legal systems operate is subject to application, the legal system shall be applied in accordance with the law of this country.

Article 1167. Retorsion

Retaliatory limitations (retorsion) may be established by the Government of the Republic Uzbekistan with respect to the rights of citizens and juridical persons of those States in which there are special limitations of the rights of citizens and juridical persons of the Republic Uzbekistan.

Chapter 71. Conflicts Norms

§ 1. Persons

Article 1168. Personal Law of Natural Person

The personal law of a natural person shall be considered to be the law of the country whose citizenship this person has. When a person has two or more citizenships, the personal law shall be considered to be the law of the country with which the person is most closely connected.

The personal law of a stateless person shall be considered to be the law of the country in which this person permanently resides.

The personal law of a refugee shall be considered to be the law of the country which granted asylum.

Article 1169. Legal Capacity and Dispositive Legal Capacity of Natural Person

The legal capacity and dispositive legal capacity of a natural person shall be determined by his personal law.

Foreign citizens and stateless persons shall enjoy in the Republic Uzbekistan civil legal capacity equally with citizens of the Republic Uzbekistan except for instances established by laws or international treaties of the Republic Uzbekistan.

Civil dispositive legal capacity of a natural person with respect to transactions and obligations arising as a consequence of the causing of harm shall be determined according to the law of the country of the place of concluding the transactions or the arising of the obligations for the causing of harm.

The legal capacity of a natural person to be an individual entrepreneur and to have the rights and duties connected therewith shall be determined according to the law of the country where the natural person is registered as an individual entrepreneur. In the absence of a country of registration, the law of the country of the principal place of effectuating individual entrepreneurial activity shall be applied.

The deeming of a natural person to lack dispositive legal capacity or to have limited dispositive legal capacity shall be subordinate to the law of the country of the court.

Article 1170. Deeming Natural Person to be Missing and Declaring Him to be Deceased

The deeming of a natural person to be missing and declaring him to be deceased shall be subordinate to the law of the country of the court.

Article 1171. Name of Natural Person

The rights of a natural person to a name and to the use and defense thereof shall be determined by his personal law insofar as does not arise otherwise from the rules provided for by Article 19, paragraphs four and seven, and by Articles 1179 and 1180 of the present Code.

Article 1172. Registration of Acts of Civil Status of Citizens of the Republic Uzbekistan Outside Limits of Republic Uzbekistan

The registration of acts of civil status of citizens of the Republic Uzbekistan residing outside the limits of the Republic Uzbekistan shall be effectuated in consular institutions of the Republic Uzbekistan. Legislation of the Republic Uzbekistan shall be applied in so doing.

Article 1173. Recognition of Documents Issued by Agencies of Foreign State in Certification of Acts of Civil Status

Documents issued by competent agencies of foreign States in certification of acts of civil status performed outside the limits of the Republic Uzbekistan according to the laws of the respective States shall be deemed valid in the Republic Uzbekistan with respect to citizens of the Republic Uzbekistan, foreign citizens, and stateless persons when legalization or apostille is present [as amended by Law of 10 April 2012, No. ЗРУ-322. СЗ РУ (2012), no. 15, item 164].

Article 1174. Trusteeship and Guardianship

Trusteeship or guardianship over minors, persons lacking dispositive legal capacity, or persons who have reached majority and are limited in dispositive legal capacity shall be established and removed according to the law of the country of the court.

The duty of the trustee (or guardian) to accept a trusteeship (or guardianship) shall be determined according to the personal law of the person appointed as trustee (or guardian).

The legal relations between the trustee (or guardian) and the person under trusteeship (or guardianship) shall be determined according to the law of the country whose institution appointed the trustee (or guardian).

However, if the person under trusteeship (or guardianship) resides in the Republic Uzbekistan, the law of the Republic Uzbekistan shall apply if it is more favorable for this person.

A trusteeship (or guardianship) established over citizens of the Republic Uzbekistan residing outside the limits of the Republic Uzbekistan shall be deemed to be valid in the Republic Uzbekistan if there are no objections of the respective consular institution of the Republic Uzbekistan based on a law against the establishment of the trusteeship (or guardianship) or against the recognition thereof.

Article 1175. Law of Juridical Person

The law of a juridical person shall be considered to be the law of the country where this juridical person is founded.

Article 1176. Legal Capacity of Juridical Person

Civil legal capacity of a juridical person shall be determined by the law of the juridical person.

A foreign juridical person may not refer to the limitation of powers of an organ or representative thereof to conclude a transaction not known to the law of the country in which the organ or representative of the foreign juridical person concluded the transaction.

Article 1177. National Regime of Activity of Foreign Juridical Persons in Republic Uzbekistan

Foreign juridical persons shall effectuate in the Republic Uzbekistan entrepreneurial and other activity regulated by civil legislation unless provided otherwise by a law of the Republic Uzbekistan for foreign juridical persons.

Article 1178. Participation of State in Civil-Law Relations with Foreign Element

The rules of the present Section shall apply on general grounds to civil-law relations with a foreign element with the participation of the State unless provided otherwise by a law.

§ 2. Personal Nonproperty Rights. Intellectual Property

Article 1179. Defense of Personal Nonproperty Rights

The law of the country where an action or other circumstance occurred which served as the grounds for a demand concerning the defense of such rights shall apply to personal nonproperty rights.

Article 1180. Rights to Intellectual Property

The law of the country where the defense of such rights is requested shall apply to rights to intellectual property.

Contracts having as their subject rights to intellectual property shall be regulated by the law determined according to the provisions of the present Section on contractual obligations.

§ 3. Transactions. Representation. Periods of Limitation

Article 1181. Form of Transaction

The form of a transaction shall be subordinate to the law of the place of the conclusion thereof. However, a transaction concluded abroad may not be deemed to be invalid as a consequence of the failure to comply with the form if the requirements of the law of the Republic Uzbekistan have been complied with.

A foreign economic transaction, if even one of the participants is a juridical person of the Republic Uzbekistan or a citizen of the Republic Uzbekistan, shall be concluded, irrespective of the place of concluding the transaction, in written form.

The form of a transaction with respect to immoveable property shall be subordinate to the law of the country where this property is situated, and with respect to immoveable property which is entered in a State register in the Republic Uzbekistan, to the law of the Republic Uzbekistan.

Article 1182. Power of Attorney

The form and period of a power of attorney shall be determined according to the law of the country where the power of attorney is issued. However, a power of attorney may not be deemed to be invalid as a consequence of the failure to comply with the form if the requirements of the law of the Republic Uzbekistan have been complied with.

Article 1183. Period of Limitation

The period of limitation shall be determined according to the law of the country applicable to regulate the respective relation.

Demands to which the period of limitation does not extend shall be determined according to the law of the Republic Uzbekistan if even one of the participants of the respective relation is a citizen of the Republic Uzbekistan or a juridical person of the Republic Uzbekistan.

§ 4. Rights to Thing

Article 1184. General Provisions on Law Applicable to Rights to Thing

The right of ownership and other rights to a thing to immoveable and moveable property shall be determined according to the law of the country where this property is situated unless provided otherwise by a law.

The affiliation of property to immoveable or moveable things, and also another legal qualification of property, shall be determined according to the law of the country where this property is situated.

Article 1185. Origin and Termination of Rights to Thing

The origin and termination of rights to a thing to property shall be determined according to the law of the country where this property was situated at the moment when the action or other circumstance occurred which served as the grounds for the origin or termination of rights to a thing unless provided otherwise by laws of the Republic Uzbekistan.

The origin and termination of rights to a thing to property which is the subject of a transaction shall be determined according to the law of the country to which the particular transaction is subordinate, unless established otherwise by agreement of the parties.

The origin of the right of ownership to property as a consequence of acquisitive prescription shall be determined by the law of the country where the property was situated at the moment of the ending of the period of acquisitive prescription.

Article 1186. Rights to Thing to Means of Transport and Other Property Subject to Entry in State Register

Rights to a thing to means of transport and other property subject to entry in State registers shall be determined according to the law of the country where these means of transport or property have been registered.

Article 1187. Rights to Thing to Moveable Property En Route

The right of ownership and other rights to a thing to moveable property en route with regard to a transaction shall be determined according to the law of the country from which this property was sent unless established otherwise by agreement of the parties.

Article 1188. Defense of Rights to Thing

The law of the country where the property is situated or the law of the country of the court shall apply at the choice of the applicant to the defense of the right of ownership and other rights to a thing.

The law of the country in which this property is situated shall apply to the defense of the right of ownership and other rights to a thing to immoveable property. The law of the Republic Uzbekistan shall apply with respect to property which is entered in a State register of the Republic Uzbekistan.

§ 5. Contractual Obligations

Article 1189. Choice of Law by Agreement of Parties of Contract

A contract shall be regulated by the law of the country chosen by agreement of the parties unless provided otherwise by a law.

The parties to a contract may select the applicable law either for the contract as a whole or for individual parts thereof.

The choice of applicable law may be made by the parties to a contract at any time, either when concluding the contract and subsequently. The parties also may at any time agree concerning a change of the law applicable to the contract.

Article 1190. Law Applicable to Contract in Absence of Agreement of Parties

In the absence of agreement of the parties to a contract concerning the law subject to application to this contract, the law of the country shall be applied where the party is founded, has a place of residence, or principal place of activity and is:

the seller: in a contract of purchase sale;

the donor: in a contract of gift;

the lessor or hirer: in a contract of lease (or property hire);

the lender: in a contract of uncompensated use;

the independent-work contractor: in a contract of independent-work;

the carrier: in a contract of carriage;

the expeditor: in a contract of transport expediting;

the creditor: in a contract of loan or other credit contract;

the attorney: in a contract of commission;

the commission agent: in a contract of commission agency;

the keeper: in a contract of keeping;

the insurer: in a contract of insurance;

the surety: in a contract of suretyship;

the pledgor: in a contract of pledge;

the licensor: in a contract of license concerning the use of exclusive rights.

In the absence of agreement of the parties to a contract concerning the law subject to application, there shall apply irrespective of the provisions of paragraph one of the present Article:

to a contract concerning immoveable property: the law of the country where this property is situated;

to a contract concerning joint activity and a contract of construction independent-work: the law of the country where such activity is effectuated or the results provided for by the contract are created;

to a contract concluded at auction, with regard to a competition, or on the stock exchange: the law of the country where the auction or competition is conducted or the stock exchange is situated.

To contracts not enumerated in paragraphs one and two of the present Article, in the absence of agreement of the parties concerning the law subject to application, the law of the country where the party is founded, has a place of residence, or principal place of activity which effectuates the performance having decisive significance for the content of such contract shall be applied. In the event it is impossible to determine the performance having decisive significance for the content of the contract, the law of the country with which the contract is most closely connected shall be applied.

Article 1191. Law Applicable to Contract on Creation of Juridical Person with Foreign Participation

The law of the country where a juridical person is founded shall apply to the contract on the creation of a juridical person with foreign participation.

Article 1192. Sphere of Operation of Applicable Law

The law applicable to a contract by virtue of the provisions of the present paragraph shall encompass, in particular:

interpretation of the contract;

rights and duties of the parties;

performance of the contract;

consequences of the failure to perform or improper performance of the contract;

termination of the contract;

consequences of the nullity or invalidity of the contract;

assignment of the demands and transfer of debt in connection with the contract.

With respect to the means and procedure for performance, and also the measures which must be adopted in the event of the improper performance, besides the applicable law the law of the country in which performance occurs also shall be taken into account.

§ 6. Extracontractual Obligations

Article 1193. Obligations from Unilateral Actions

The rules of paragraph 4 of the present Section shall apply to obligations from unilateral actions (public promise of reward, activity in another's interest without commission, and others).

Article 1194. Obligations as Consequence of Causing Harm

The rights and duties with regard to obligations arising as a consequence of causing harm shall be determined according to the law of the country where the action or other circumstance occurred which served as grounds for the demand concerning compensation of harm.

The rights and duties with regard to obligations arising as a consequence of the causing of harm abroad, if the parties are citizens or juridical persons of the same State, shall be determined according to the law of this State.

Foreign law shall not apply if the action or other circumstance serving as the grounds for the demand concerning compensation of harm is not unlawful according to legislation of the Republic Uzbekistan.

Article 1195. Responsibility for Damage Caused to Consumer

To a demand concerning compensation of damage which arose for a consumer in connection with the purchase of a good, the fulfillment of work, or the rendering of a service there shall apply at the choice of the consumer:

the law of the country where the residence of the consumer is situated;

the law of the country where the residence or the location of the producer or the person fulfilling the work or rendering the service is situated;

the law of the country where the consumer acquired the good, accepted the result of the work, or the service was rendered to him.

Article 1196. Unfounded Enrichment

The law of the country where the enrichment occurred shall apply to the obligations arising as a consequence of the unfounded enrichment.

If the unfounded enrichment arises as a consequence of the grounds disappearing for which property is acquired or saved, the applicable law shall be determined according to the law of the country to which this grounds was subordinated. The concept of unfounded enrichment shall be determined according to the law of the Republic Uzbekistan.

§ 7. Inheritance Law

Article 1197. Relations Relating to Inheriting

Relations relating to inheriting shall be determined according to the law of the country where the testator had the last permanent place of residence insofar as not provided otherwise by Articles 1198 and 1199 of the present Code unless the testator has chosen in the will the law of the country of which he is a citizen.

Article 1198. Legal Capacity of Persons to Draw Up and Revoke Will, Form of Will, and Act of Revocation Thereof

The legal capacity of a person to draw up and revoke a will, and also the form of the will and act of revocation thereof, shall be determined according to the law of the country where the testator had a permanent place of residence at the moment of drawing up the act unless the law of the country of which he is a citizen is chosen by the testator. However, the will or revocation thereof may not be deemed to be invalid as a consequence of the failure to comply with the form if the last satisfies the requirements of the law of the place of drawing up the act or of the Republic Uzbekistan.

Article 1199. Inheriting of Immoveable Property and Property Subject to Inclusion in State Register

The inheriting of immoveable property shall be determined according to the law of the country where this property is situated, and property which is entered in a State register of the Republic Uzbekistan, according to the law of the Republic Uzbekistan.

www.ingramcontent.com/pod-product-compliance
Lightning Source LLC
LaVergne TN
LVHW092116300926
849161LV00002B/147
* 9 7 8 1 6 1 6 1 9 6 8 3 7 *